Source Book of Self-Discipline
A Synthesis of *Moralia in Job*
by Gregory the Great

American University Studies

Series VII
Theology and Religion
Vol. 117

PETER LANG
New York · San Francisco · Bern
Frankfurt am Main · Paris · London

Source Book of Self-Discipline

A Synthesis of *Moralia in Job*
by Gregory the Great

A Translation of Peter of Waltham's
Remediarium Conversorum

by
Joseph Gildea, O.S.A.

PETER LANG
New York · San Francisco · Bern
Frankfurt am Main · Paris · London

Library of Congress Cataloging-in-Publication Data

Peter, of Waltham, fl. 1190-1196.
   [Remediarium conversorum. English]
   Source book of self-discipline : a synthesis of
Moralia in Job by Gregory the Great : a translation
of Peter of Waltham's Remediarium conversorum /
by Joseph Gildea.
     p. cm. – (American university studies. Series
VII, Theology and religion ; vol. 117)
   Includes bibliographical references.
   1. Gregory I, Pope, ca. 540-604. Moralia in Job.
2. Bible. O.T. Job–Commentaries. I. Gildea, Joseph.
II. Gregory I, Pope, ca. 540-604. Moralia in Job.
III. Title. IV. Series.
BS1415.P44513   1991   241'.0414–dc20   91-17221
ISBN 0-8204-1650-9   CIP
ISSN 0740-0446

Die Deutsche Bibliothek-CIP-Einheitsaufnahme

Gildea, Joseph:
Source Book of self-discipline : a synthesis of
Moralia in Job by Gregory the Great ; a translation
of Peter of Waltham's Remediarium conversorum /
Joseph Gildea.–New York; Berlin; Bern;
Frankfurt/M.; Paris; Wien: Lang, 1991
  (American university studies : Ser. 7, Theology
and religion ; Vol. 117)
  ISBN 0-8204-1650-9
NE: American university studies / 07

The paper in this book meets the guidelines for permanence and
durability of the Committee on Production Guidelines for Book
Longevity of the Council on Library Resources.

© Peter Lang Publishing, Inc., New York 1991

Printed in the United States of America.

CONTENTS

FOREWORD

The publication in 1985 of the third and final volume of *Moralia in Job* (Corpus Christianorum, Series Latina, 143b: Turnholti, ed. Marcus Adriaen), made it possible to determine that the *Moralia* synthesis, *Remediarium Conversorum*, comprises approximately one-fourth of Gregory's monumental work on the biblical Book of Job.

This succinct account of Gregory's career appeared in *Dawn of the Middle Ages* by Michael Grant (New York, 1981; 1986 ed., p. 15):

> St. Gregory I the Great (ca. 540–604) rose to the imperial rank of prefect of the city of Rome and then became a monk; he was subsequently elected to the papacy in 590 at a critical time in the history of Italy and of the Church. His moral efforts to rally the Italian populace, and stem the tide of Lombard and other invasions, also enabled him to establish the secular basis of the papacy, which, largely through his efforts, became the prestigious institution it would remain throughout the Middle Ages and beyond. A critical development under his pontificate was the encouragement and establishment of monastic life, on the Benedictine model, as a major ally and instrument of the papal Church. Gregory also began the revival of Christianity in the British Isles by sending Augustine as a missionary to Kent in 597. His diverse and prolific writings, dealing with many points of faith and morals, earned him the title of Fourth Doctor of the Church.

It is noteworthy that Augustine, first archbishop of Canterbury, also died in 604, the year in which Mellitus was appointed first bishop of London. In the corresponding year of this twentieth century, Thomas J. Shahan in *The Middle Ages: Sketches and Fragments*, published at New York and elsewhere, wrote of Gregory (p. 30): "No pope has ever exercised so much influence by his writings, on which the Middle Ages were largely formed as far as practical ethics and the discipline of life were concerned." The *Moralia*, originally delivered as talks to Gregory's monastic community at Constantinople where he was papal envoy, were copied down by the monks and revised by him over a period of decades (ca. 579–602).

For somewhat sparse information about Peter of Waltham and its sources, the reader is referred to the Preface (in English) and to the Appendix of the Latin edition of *Remediarium Conversorum* [Associated University Presses: Cranbury, New Jersey, 1984]. Not indicated in the pages that follow are the loci in the *Moralia* of *Remediarium* passages: these references are given in the Latin edition. To the bibliographical data supplied in the footnotes of the Preface are now to be added: *Grégoire le Grand*, ed. Jacques Fontaine, Robert Gillet, and Stan Pellestrandi [CNRS 1982 Conference], Paris, 1986; G. R. Evans, *The Thought of Gregory the Great*, Cambridge, 1986; Carol Ellen Straw, *Gregory the Great, Perfection in Imperfection* [cf. Bibliographical Essay, pp. 261–266], Berkeley, 1988; Philippe Delhaye, *Enseignement et morale au XIIᵉ siècle*, Fribourg, 1988; Robert Markus, *The End of Ancient Christianity*, Cambridge, 1990. Attention is also directed to the availability [Brepols Publishers] of *Thesaurus sancti Gregorii Magni: Series A — Formae* (1986). In preparation is Series B, which will be a thematic concordance.

It remains to be said that in *Revised Medieval Latin Word–List* (London, 1965), the entry "***Remediarium [Conversorum], title of a book c1396,***" is from the medieval catalogue of the library of Meaux, Rolls Series xliii (London, 1866–68), III, p. xc; the editor, E. A. Bond, notes: "another title of the *Pantheologus* of Peter, archdeacon of London." The foregoing data were supplied by Richard Sharpe, Assistant Editor, *Dictionary of Medieval Latin from British Sources*, together with the following comments: "The confusion between three London Peters has been pretty thorough over the years—P. of Waltham, archdeacon in the 1190s; P. of Blois, archdeacon 1200–1212; and P. of Cornwall, prior of Holy Trinity. The last is the author of *Pantheologus* . . . and has nothing to do with the *Remediarium*." However, it is not surprising that on the Continent, in the course of the thirteenth century, a Benedictine monk made a compilation of the specifically moral passages in Gregory's work. The redactor was Simon of Affligem, mentioned in 1575 by Joannes Trithemius in *De viris illustribus Ordinis S. Benedicti*, lib. II, cap. cxxv, p. 462; cf. N. Häring, "Der Literaturkatalog von Affligem," *Revue bénédictine*, LXXX (1970), 64–91; cap. 56. V. Fèvre treats of this and other compendiums in his 1858 Sorbonne dissertation, *Etude sur Morales de Saint Grégoire le Grand sur Job*, pp. 85–86.

Observe finally that Robert E. Rodes, Jr. in *Ecclesiastical Administration in Medieval England: The Anglo–Saxons to the Reformation* (Notre Dame / London, 1977), p. 102, clarifies the role of an archdeacon: "This ancient office originally involved serving the bishop as a kind of executive officer and head of the clerical *familia*. By the end of the twelfth century, it had come to involve the exercise of definite judicial functions over a specific portion of a diocese. In England, there was generally one archdeacon to a county."

PROLOGUE

To the Reverend Father, Bishop Richard III of the church of London, from Peter, his Archdeacon of the same church: So run among things temporal that you may obtain the eternal prize![1] Your exhortation has frequently reminded me of the blessedness of mental solitude and of evangelical poverty. And in order that you might win over the soul of a spoiled son and might more easily bend his spirit to the desire of a holy change of heart, you have communicated to me the devout mode of life you have in mind and the secret of the conversion on my part that you seek.

However, since my mind, held captive by the pleasure of temporal things, reeled on hearing holy promptings, I devoted myself with particular impetuosity to the reading of Holy Scripture, lest the seed sown by such a kind father—carried away by the birds, or choked by thorns, or otherwise ruined—should fail to flower and bear fruit.[2] Looking through the writings of the Fathers in search of a remedy for my malady, at last I fastened on the Book of Morals by Gregory as an anchor. I did so because in reading it the chafed mind would stir with warmth and alongside the flowing, saving waters would grow strong and become fruitful.[3] Drawing from this source those who are abandoned check the unrestrained torrent of their passions; the just derive strength for virtuously persevering in holy discipline; sinners perceiving therein their defilement, discern how obviously lacking they are in achievement; there too the penitent considering their past sins, humbly take note of their progress; those who are turned the wrong way and deserve to be condemned to the place of torment after the barren fulfillment of their desires, are filled with dread; those who are headed aright and are ready for eternal laurels after the happy outcome of their struggle, find refreshment in these pages.

But insofar as the historical import is stated by Gregory, the allegorical depth is developed, and the distinctiveness of various habits is described, such difficult matters, spread throughout so many volumes, cannot be easily grasped by one whose mind is narrowed and agitated by temporal concerns; and if at times by great application they should be understood, only by sincere and disengaged recollection can they be kept in mind. After diligently considering this fact in the light of my limited capacity, I made use of my stylus to extract only the moral passages, grouping from many volumes in cohesive and shortened form those which, alike in their construction or related in their content, shared an affinity. This I did so that I might always have at hand a reserve whence my spirit could allay its pangs of hunger, and so that to any traveler unwilling or not free to have recourse to the river, I might offer a ladle from which to sip at least the boundless waters of the river, and also so that anyone not presuming to swim along with the elephant in the depths of the river might not fear to wade with the lamb into the shallows.[4]

I have divided this little work into two parts, each of which consists of six books. In the first part there is a discussion of the motives and iniquities of the wicked and of the misfortunes resulting from these iniquities. In the second part the beginnings of the justification of the saints, their state of being and blessed destiny are considered.

Accordingly, the six books of the first part are entitled: On the Suggestions of the Devil, On Sin, On the Vices, On the Rich, On the Reprobate, On the Punishment of the Reprobate. For when the suggestions of the devil through consent are admitted to the innermost part of the heart, they engender the snares of sin. When pleasure is derived from sin, it leads to special vices, to which the rich of this world and the wicked being prone, are after their short–lived sensual pleasures borne off to the eternal prison of death.

The second part likewise comprises six books, entitled: On God's Grace, On Penitence, On the Virtues, On Prelates, On the Just, On the Glory of the Just. For the grace of God bringing the sinner to penitence, gives increase to the virtues, adorned with which the hierarchy and the rest of the faithful, after the completion of their labors, are raised to the eternal reward of life.

Consequently, the present treatise is called *Source Book of Self–Discipline* because the six sections of the second part undoubtedly bring together the correctives for the failings that are discussed in the six sections of the first part. The suggestions of the devil incite us indeed to sin, but the grace of God, the most potent remedy against these suggestions, anteceding anything good in us, stirs us to penitence, a cleansing agent which effectively abolishes sin. And just as sin is committed by thought, word and deed, so penitence by compunction of heart, by oral confession and by giving of alms is perfected. Through love of sin, however, we fall into special vices. But through the practice of penitence we are lifted up to the virtues which, inimical to the vices, proffer appropriate remedies for them. But the rich for the most part, in order that they may satisfy their ambition, wickedly immerse themselves in vices and having spurned heavenly things, devoting themselves to earthly things only, they covet the increase of transitory possessions and the amassing of wealth. On the other hand, those among the just who are placed in charge of others because of the merit of their virtues, rejecting what is passing and meditating on heavenly matters, diligently attend to increasing their master's money, so that faithful in a few things, they may be put in charge of many.[5] The aspirations, therefore, of the prelates of the church, thoroughly contrary to the desires of the rich, bestow remedies suited to the avoidance of these latter cravings. Similarly, to the carnal passions of all the reprobate are opposed the spiritual predilections of the just, since the former with the bridle of holy temperance removed, give in to the ignoble enticements of the flesh; but the latter, restraining by temperate control illicit emotions, with a spiritual rod chastise carnal desires and to avoid the perversity of the reprobate, administer adequate antidotes. Further, eternal punishment results from the carnal pleasures of the reprobate; on the other hand, the labors of the just have as effect the ineffable glory which in contrast to the penalties of the reprobate, brings to the just the desired restorative.

And now I should like each reader of this book, if it should by chance find at least one reader, to be prevailed upon to say with charitable affection and pious consideration: May Peter's soul rest in peace!

In addition, it should be noted that alongside each section of this treatise there is found [in the manuscript] mention of the book in the *Moralia* from which the section is derived. Similarly, if a given passage is composed of selections from different books, this too is indicated in the margin, so that should the reader wish to drink from the fountain whence the rivulet emanates, he may without difficulty find what he is seeking.

For your part, my esteemed Father Richard, by your prayers frequently supply moisture to what you have planted, so much so that God giving the increase, both of us may happily merit the flower of humble conversion and the fruit of holy renewal.

PART ONE

BOOK 1

THE SUGGESTIONS OF THE DEVIL

1

The most noble condition of man, so created that he was able not to die, who of his own accord was made debtor to death

The very mode of man's condition shows how far he surpasses all other things. For the power to reason which was conferred on man proclaims how much rational nature excels all things which lack either life or sense or reason.

Man was placed in paradise so that if he attached himself by the chains of love to an obedient following of his Creator, he might one day make a transition to the heavenly country of the angels without bodily death. He was made immortal, in such wise however that if he sinned, he would be capable of dying, and was made in such wise mortal that if he did not sin, he would be capable of never dying: through free will he would earn the blessedness of that realm in which he would be capable neither of sinning nor of dying. That state to which since the time of the Redemption the elect pass with death of the body intervening, our first parents—if they had remained steadfast in the state of their creation—would certainly have attained without bodily death.

Hence, the first man was so created that by the accessions of time his life could only be extended not spun to an end; but since of his own accord he fell into sin when he did what was forbidden, he was made subject to a transitory career, which man now, oppressed by fondness for the present life, both undergoes and longs for without ceasing. For in order that he may not come to an end, he longs to live on, yet by the accessions of life he is daily advancing to his end. Nor does he well perceive how insignificant the added portions of time are, except when those things which seemed to be long in coming are in a moment brought to an end. And so the land of man was paradise, which could have harbored him unshaken if by force of innocence he had chosen to stand fast, but because by sin he fell into the waves of a changeable state, after the land he came into the seas of the present life.

Thus, as we have said, the first man was so fashioned that whereas he remained, time passed on and he did not journey on together with it. For he stood still as the moments ran on since he did not approach the end of his life through the increase of his days. He stood more firm the closer he clung to him who is ever stationary. But after he did what was forbidden, having offended his Creator, he began at once to pass onward together with time.[1] In other words, having lost the stability of an immortal condition, the stream of mortal being engulfed him.[2] And while borne along through youth to old age and through old age to death, he learned, as he journeyed on, what he was when he remained stationary. And because we are sprung from his stock, we retain like shoots the bitterness of our root. Since we derive our origin from him, we inherit his course of life at our birth, so that every moment of every day that we live, we are constantly drawing away from life, its length decreasing through the very means by which it is believed to increase.

Accordingly, the devil by overthrowing us in that root of our first parent rightfully, as one might say, held man captive who, created with free will, yielded consent to him when he prompted what was unjust. In fact, he who was endowed with life in the freedom of his own will was of his own accord made debtor to death.

2
Through envy the devil uses lawful power willfully and constantly to suggest evil to man

The devil through envy inflicted on unharmed man in paradise the wound of pride because having lost angelic bliss, he knew himself to be inferior to man's immortality; this wounding was done in order that man who had not been subject to death when created, might deserve it when he became prideful.

However, although he always aims at afflicting the just, that same enemy of ours knows that without receiving the power from our Creator he is not able to tempt us in the least degree. Hence all the devil's will is unjust, and yet as long as God permits it, all his power is just. For of himself he unjustly seeks to try all men, but those that are to be tempted God does not permit to be tried otherwise than justly. Whence also in the Book of Kings it is written of the devil: *The evil spirit from the Lord came upon Saul.* [3] Whereupon the question justly arises: If it was the Spirit from the Lord, why should it be called an evil spirit; and if an evil spirit, why from the Lord? But by the two expressions are comprehended both the just power and the unjust will in the devil. For he himself is called an evil spirit with respect to a most evil will, and the same spirit is said to be from the Lord with respect to the most just power bestowed on him.

For it is well written of him: *Out of his nostrils goeth smoke, like that of a pot heated and boiling.*[4] By the word nostrils the wiles and suggestion of the devil are signified. But by smoke the cloud of most wicked thought is to be understood. Now smoke goes forth from the nostrils of the devil when by his crafty inspirations he heaps up in the heart of the reprobate the heat of many thoughts from love of this temporal life; and he multiplies, as it were, clouds of smoke when he crowds together in the mind of earthly men the most trifling anxieties of this present life. This smoke coming forth from his nostrils sometimes affects for a while the eyes even of the elect. For the prophet was enduring this smoke within when he said: *My heart is disturbed because of anger.*[5] He was oppressed by its pouring in upon him, saying: *My heart is troubled within me and the light of my eyes is not with me.*[6] This smoke deadens indeed the keenness of the heart because with the cloud of its darkness it disturbs the serenity of inward peace. But God cannot be recognized except by a tranquil heart. Whence it is again said by the same prophet: *Be still and know that I am God.*[7] But that mind cannot be at ease which is oppressed with inundations of this smoke because massive earthly thoughts are crowded into the mind from love of the present life. The light of eternal rest is therefore lost through this smoke because the eye of the heart is darkened when it is confused by the irritation of cares.

But this smoke annoys the minds of the elect in one way, and blinds the eyes of the reprobate in another. For it is dispersed from the eyes of the good by the breath of spiritual desires, so as not to become dense through the prevalence of wretched thoughts. But in the minds of the reprobate the more freely it masses itself by means of foul thoughts, the more entirely does it remove from them the light of truth. This smoke pours into the hearts of the reprobate so many unlawful desires that it swells out, so to speak, into as many clouds before them. And we certainly are acquainted with clouds of smoke: as some of them are dissipated above, others rise up from below; so too with carnal thoughts: although some evil desires pass away, others take their place.

The smoke therefore rises in as many clouds from the nostrils of Leviathan as there are certainly plagues by which he consumes the fruit of the reprobate heart with his secret inspiration. But the Lord carefully explains still further the power of this smoke when he immediately adds: *Like that of a pot heated and boiling.*[8] For the pot is heated when the mind of man is stirred up by the persuasion of the malignant enemy. But the pot boils when by consent it is presently inflamed with the desires of evil persuasions; and it gives rise in boiling to about as many waves as there are corruptions by which it extends itself into outward action. For the prophet had beheld this heat of carnal concupiscence, that is, the heat of the pot arising from the smoke of Leviathan, when he said: *I see a boiling cauldron, and the face thereof from the face of the north*.[9] For the pot of the human heart is heated from the face of the north when it is inflamed with unlawful desires by the instigation of the adversary spirit. For he who says: *I will sit in the mountain of the covenant, in the sides of the north,* [10] *I will exalt my throne above the stars of God, I will be like the most High,* [11] inflames with the malignant blasts of his persuasion, as with fires placed beneath it, the mind of which he has once gained possession in order that being discontented with what is before it, it may be so unceasingly agitated by desires as to seek some things presently to be condemned and to condemn other things which it has obtained; at one time to be eager for its own profit, at another to oppose another's advantages even to its own loss; at one time to satisfy the allurements of the flesh, and at another to be as if carried away on high by pride of thought, all concern for the flesh having been put aside, and to raise itself up wholly unto the haughtiness of exaltation. Therefore because a heart which is inflamed by the instigations of this Leviathan is led astray by various desires, its smoke is rightly said to be like a heated and boiling pot, because its self–consciousness, fired by his temptations, is aroused by as many seethings as there are thoughts by which it is puffed up within.

3

Types of the devil's schemes

His troops have come together and have made themselves a way by me. [12] His (God's) troops are evil spirits, who are engaged in seeking the death of men. They make their way in the hearts of the afflicted when amid the adversities that are sustained externally, they do not cease to instill evil thoughts as well. Concerning them it is further declared: *And they have besieged my tabernacle round about.* [13] For they besiege a tabernacle round about when they encircle the mind on every side with their temptings; by most wicked promptings they persuade that mind at one time to mourn for things temporal, at another to despair of things eternal, yet again to go headlong into impatience and to cast words of blasphemy against God.

Yet it is very bewildering that when troops are mentioned *his* is added to show, of course, that these same troops belong to God. In this regard, if we make a distinction between the power and the will of the evil spirits, it becomes evident why they are called God's troops. For evil spirits incessantly aspire to do us harm; but while they have an evil will derived from themselves, they do not have the power of doing harm unless the supreme will gives them permission. And while they indeed long to hurt us unjustly, they are unable to hurt anyone unless they are justly permitted by the Lord. So whereas the will is unjust in them and the power just, they are at one and the same time called troops and God's troops to show it is by themselves that they aim to inflict evil things unjustly and it is owing to God that things so desired they accomplish justly.

Therefore we should understand that our enemy proceeds against our good actions in three ways in order, it is clear, that everything which is done aright before the eyes of men may be spoiled in the sight of the one who judges the heart. For sometimes in a good work he defiles the intention so that all that follows in action may issue forth the more impure and unclean the more he makes everything turbid from its source. But sometimes he has no power to spoil the intention of a good deed but in the very act sets himself up as it were along the path so that when the person goes forth more secure in the purpose of his heart, since evil is lying in wait he may be waylaid and come to grief. And sometimes he neither corrupts the intention nor overthrows it along the way, but he ensnares the good deed in the conclusion of the act. And to the extent that he pretends to have gone further off, either from the abode of the heart or from the path of the deed, with greater craftiness he awaits the termination of the good action; and the more he has put a man off his guard by seeming to retire, so much the more suddenly does he at times pierce him with a more severe and incurable wound.

To be sure, he defiles the intention in a good work because when he sees men's hearts ready to be deceived, he presents to their ambition the glitter of passing favor so that in the proper things they do they may be inclined by distortion in their intention to make the lowest things their aim. Hence rightly under the image of Judaea is it said by the prophet of every soul that is caught in the snare of improper intention: *Her adversaries are become her lords*.[14] That is to say: When a good work is undertaken without good intent, the opposing spirits have dominion over the soul from the commencement of the undertaking and the more completely possess it insofar as they hold their power from the very beginning.

But when they are unable to corrupt the intention, they conceal snares which they set in the way in order that the heart in doing what is good may be turned aside toward evil, so that what at the outset it had proposed to do in a certain way, it may in fact bring to completion far otherwise than it had planned. For often as long as human praise is bestowed on a good deed, it alters the mind of the doer, and although not sought after, yet when offered it is pleasing. And whereas by this pleasure the mind that is well–disposed is weakened, it is shaken from all resoluteness of innermost intention. Often anger finds its way into our equitable action and while by zealousness for what is right it immoderately unsettles the mind, it impairs the healthiness of our inward tranquility. Often sadness slips alongside seriousness of mind and overcasts with a veil of sadness every deed which the mind commences with a good intention. And this characteristic is sometimes more slowly divested the more belated it is in becoming associated with the mind that strains forward. Often immoderate joy attaches itself to a good deed, and while it calls upon the mind for more mirth than is fitting, it discards all the import of seriousness from our good action. Because the Psalmist, then, had seen that even those who set out well are met by snares on the way, filled with the prophetic spirit he rightly said: *In this way wherein I walked they have hidden a snare for me.*[15] This observation is well and subtly intimated by Jeremias, who while intent on telling of outward events, indicated happenings within ourselves: *There came some from Sichem and from Silo and from Samaria, fourscore men, with their beards shaven and their clothes rent, and mourning, and they had offerings and incense in their hand, to offer in the house of the Lord. And Ismael the son of Nathanias went forth from Maspath to meet them, weeping all along as he went; and when he had met them, he said to them: Come to Godolias the son of Ahicam. And when they were come to the midst of the city, Ismael the son of Nathanias slew them.*[16] For they shave their beards who disown confidence in their own powers. They rend their clothes who are unsparing in disregard for external glory. They come to offer up in the house of the Lord incense and gifts who set out to couple prayer with works in sacrifice to God. But if in the very path of holy devotion they fail to keep a wary eye on every side, Ismael the son of Nathanias goes forth to meet them since assuredly every evil spirit, following the first Satan and thus engendered by the sin of pride, presents itself as a snare to deceive. Of such a spirit it is well said: *Weeping all along as he went*, because in order that he may waylay devout souls and strike at them, he hides himself under the cloak of virtue, and whereas he pretends to side with those who really mourn and is thereby more securely admitted to the interior of the heart, he destroys whatever virtue is hidden there. For the most part he pledges guidance to higher things. Hence he is asserted to have said: *Come to Godolias the son of Ahicam*; and while he promises greater things, he robs us even of the little that we have. Hence again it is rightly said: *When they were come to the midst of the city, he slew them.* So then, he slays in the midst of the city the men coming to offer gifts to God because those souls who are devoted to godly works, unless they watch over themselves with great circumspection, lose their life as they advance, the enemy intercepting them unaware as they go bearing the sacrifice of devotion. From the hands of this enemy there is no escape unless they speedily have recourse to penitence. Hence it is fitly added at this point: *But ten men were found among them that said to Ismael: Kill us not; for we have stores in the field, of wheat and barley and oil and honey. And he slew them not.*[17] For the treasure in the field is hope in penitence, a treasure which, because it is not visible, is kept buried in the earth of the heart. They then who had treasures in the field were saved because they who after the fault of their unwariness are again sorrowful do not perish when taken captive.

But when the old adversary neither strikes while the intention is formed nor intrudes on the path of actualization, he sets the more troublesome snares at the end. He so much the more harasses the termination as he sees that it is all that is left for him to prey upon. Now the prophet had seen these snares set at the end of his course when he said: *They will watch my heel.*[18] For because the end of the body is in the heel, what is signified by it but the end of the action? Whether then they are evil spirits or all wicked men who are their followers, they watch the heel of the man when they seek to spoil the end of a good action. Hence it is said to that serpent: *She shall watch thy head, and thou shalt watch her heel.*[19] For to watch the serpent's head is to keep an eye upon the beginnings of his suggestions. Yet when he is caught at the start, he endeavors to strike the heel because although he does not strike the intention with his first suggestion, he strives to ensnare at the end. Now if the head is once and for all corrupted in the intention, the middle and end of the action that follows is held securely by the cunning adversary since he sees that the whole tree, which he spoiled at the root with his poisonous tooth, bears fruit for him.

4

The suggestion of the devil, gentle at first, is easily withstood; but if it grows strong, it is difficult to overcome

He setteth up his tail like a cedar.[20] The first suggestion of the serpent is gentle and delicate and is easily crushed by the foot of virtue. But if it is carelessly allowed to gain strength and if access to the heart is freely offered, it acquires such power as to weigh down the enslaved mind and to increase to intolerable strength. He is said therefore to set up his tail like a cedar because once his tempting is admitted into the heart, he rules as if by right in all subsequent attacks. The head of this malignant enemy therefore is grass, his tail a cedar, because by way of enticement he effaces himself at his first suggestion, but gaining greater power by repetition, he is strengthened as the culmination of temptation draws close. For everything which he suggests at first can be overcome, but afterwards follows that which can scarcely be surmounted. For he first directs pleasant words to the mind as if giving counsel, but when he has once implanted the taste for pleasure, he is thereafter bound to it almost abidingly by unbridled habit. Here again is reason for saying that he sets up his tail. For he wounds with his fang, binds with his tail, because he strikes with the first suggestion but binds the mind when it is stricken so that it cannot escape as the heightening of temptation reaches its final stage. For since sin gains entry in three ways, being committed by suggestion of the serpent, by pleasure of the flesh, by consent of the will, the devil first puts forth his tongue, suggesting; afterwards he inserts his venom, leading on to delight; but lastly he clenches his tail, taking possession by consent. Hence it is that some persons condemn in themselves sins which have been committed through long habit and avoid them in intent, but despite their opposition cannot avoid committing them. This is the outcome because when they do not crush the head of Behemoth, they are frequently, even against their will, bound by his tail. And the latter has become hard as a cedar against them because it has evolved from the alluring pleasure of its initial encirclement even to the violence of constraint. Let it therefore be said: *He setteth up his tail like a cedar*,[21] in order that everyone should the more avoid the beginnings of temptation, the more he understands that its completion cannot be easily eluded.

It should also be taken into account that to those whom he has seized he generally suggests more grievous sins when he knows that they are approaching the end of this present life, and the more he considers himself at the point of bringing temptation to completion, the more heavy burdens of iniquities he loads upon them. Behemoth therefore clenches his tail like a cedar because those whom he has seized by evil beginnings he makes worse at the end in order that the sooner his temptings are to cease, the more vigorously they may be completed. For since he is intent on making their suffering equal to his own punishment, the more ardently does he strive before their death to augment every sin. But frequently Behemoth possesses the heart of someone already miserably subject to him, but yet divine grace repels him, and the hand of mercy ejects him whom the captive will brought into itself. And when he is expelled from a heart he endeavors to inflict sharper jabs of sin in order that the mind assaulted by him may feel those waves of temptations which it did not experience even when possessed by him. This is all expressed in the Gospel when the unclean spirit is said at the Lord's command to go forth from a young person. For when the boy possessed by the devil was presented to him, it is written: *Jesus threatened the unclean spirit, saying: Deaf and dumb spirit, I command thee, go out of him and enter not anymore into him. And crying out and greatly tearing him he went out of him.*[22] Observe that he had not torn him when he possessed him; he tore him when he came out, because he certainly besets the thoughts of the mind with greater affliction at the time when compelled by divine power, he faces expulsion. And the one whom he had possessed as a dumb spirit, he left with cries because frequently, when in possession, he inflicts smaller temptations; but when he is being expelled from the heart, he confuses it with fiercer disruption.

5

The suggestion of the devil first creeps gently and later violently drags away

He shall suck the head of asps, and the viper's tongue shall kill him.[23] The asp is a small serpent, whereas the viper is more sizable. Asps produce eggs and their young are hatched from the eggs. But when vipers have conceived, their young move about in the womb and bursting the parental loins or entrails issue live from the womb. Hence it is thought to be named viper because it is a parent by violence [*vi parit*]. Indeed the viper is born in such a way that it comes forth by violence and is brought into the world by the killing of the mother. What then is represented by the small asps if not the concealed suggestions of impure spirits, who steal upon the hearts of men by slight promptings at first? And what is represented by the viper's tongue if not the violent temptation of the devil? For at first he steals upon them gently; afterwards he drags them even by force. And so a person is said to apply his mouth to the head of asps because the little beginning of secret suggestion is first engendered in the heart, but the viper's tongue kills him because afterwards the captive soul is deadened by the poison of violent temptation. First with sly recommendations unclean spirits speak to the heart of man, and while these spirits persuade with gentleness, they instill what is tantamount to the venom of asps. Hence it is written: *They have broken the eggs of asps and have woven the webs of spiders. He that shall eat of their eggs shall die; and that which is brought out shall be hatched into a basilisk.*[24] Breaking the eggs of asps on the part of wicked men is to manifest by evil deeds the recommendations of evil spirits which lurk in their hearts. Likewise, weaving the web of spiders is, on account of the lust of this world, to be absorbed in any temporal employments. Whereas these pursuits are set up without fixedness, the gusting wind of earthly life relentlessly carries them off. And it is fittingly added: *He that shall eat of their eggs shall die*, because he who is heedful of the recommendations of impure spirits kills in himself the life of the soul. *And that which is brought out shall be hatched into a basilisk*, because the suggestion of the evil spirit that is concealed in the heart is nurtured to full iniquity. For basilisk means the king of serpents. But who is king of the reprobate if not the devil? Therefore that which is brought out shall be hatched into a basilisk because he who entertains in his mind the suggestions of the asp to be nurtured, having been made part of the wicked head, becomes part and parcel of the devil.

The text at the beginning of this section is, however, subject to another interpretation. For because the asp kills quickly by its venom but the viper more slowly, by the asp a violent and sudden temptation is indicated but by the viper a gradual and prolonged one. And hence in the case of the asp, death is attributed to sucking the head but in the case of the viper, to the tongue because often a sudden temptation, as soon as the victim figuratively applies his mouth, kills the soul caught off guard, whereas a long temptation, because its recommending evil things consists of protracted suggestion, kills with its tongue as does a viper.

6

The complexity of sins arising from the suggestion of the devil

The sinews of his flanks are closely knit.[25] These sinews are the deadly implications of his artifices. For by them he stirs up the strength of his artfulness and corrupts the inconstant hearts of men. His flanks are wicked suggestions with which he rages in the corrupting of the mind and begets in the defiled soul the offspring of wicked works. But the sinews of these flanks are closely knit because the indications of his suggestions are bound together by complicated devices in order to make many sin in such a way that if they perhaps desire to forsake a sin, they cannot escape it without being entangled in another sin, so that in forsaking a fault they may commit a fault, and may be unable to release themselves from one unless they consent to be bound by another. This point we make clearer by setting forth from the usual activity of men some instances of this involvement. But because the Church includes people in three classifications, namely, the married, the celibate, and the rectors—whence both Ezechiel saw three men set apart, that is, Noe, Daniel, and Job,[26] and the Lord in the Gospel, by referring to some persons in the field, some in bed, and some in the mill,[27] undoubtedly typifies three groups in the Church—it clearly suffices for us to choose one instance from each group.

Thus one man as he seeks the friendships of this world, binds himself by an oath made to another leading a similar life that he will conceal the latter's secrets with complete silence; but he to whom the oath has been sworn is discovered to be guilty of adultery to such an extent that he even seeks to kill the husband of the adulteress. But he who has taken the oath has second thoughts and is beset by contrary considerations: he is afraid of remaining silent about the matter lest thereby he should be an accomplice both in adultery and homicide; he is afraid to disclose it lest he should be guilty of perjury. He is therefore constrained by the closely knit sinews of the devil's flanks because to whichever side he leans, he is afraid of not being free from the infection of wrongdoing.

Another man forsakes all worldly things and seeking in everything to subjugate his own will, wishes to subject himself to the authority of another, but he examines with insufficient care the one who is to rule over him in the Lord. And when, as it may turn out, he who is unwisely chosen has begun to rule over him, acts that are godly are forbidden and those that are worldly are commanded. The one who has subjected himself, therefore, considering either what the fault of disobedience is or what the corruption of life in the world is, both trembles to obey and fears to disobey, lest by obeying he should forsake God in his commands or again by disobeying should despise God in the superior he has chosen; and lest by obeying unlawful commands he should exercise against God that subjection which he seeks for the sake of God, or again by disobeying he should make subject to his own judgment the one whom he had sought as his own judge. Clearly therefore through the defect of his indiscretion is he fettered by the closely knit flank sinews who either by obeying or certainly by disobeying is bound by the fault of his transgression. He was trying to subjugate his own will, and he takes steps even to strengthen it by spurning his superior. He decided to forsake the world entirely, and he is actually compelled to return to the cares of the world by the will of the superior. The sinews therefore are closely knit when the tactics of the enemy constrict us in such a way that the knots of sin hold the firmer the more we seek to loosen them.

Someone else, failing to consider the burden of ecclesiastical distinction, is elevated by bribes to an eminent position. But because every such post is accompanied by more tribulations than honors, when his heart is weighed down by grief, his fault is recalled. He laments that he has attained a laborious role in a blameworthy manner, and overwhelmed by its difficulty, he learns how reprehensible is what he permitted. Acknowledging therefore that he is guilty because of the bribes he paid, he wishes to abandon the lofty position he has gained, but he fears that it would be a more serious sin to have resigned the charge of the flock he had assumed. He wishes to take care of the flock entrusted to him, but he fears it would be a worse fault to hold the authority of pastoral influence that he purchased. He sees therefore that through unlawful striving for distinction he is encumbered by sin on every side. For he sees that in any event he is guilty of crime whether the flock he has once taken charge of is abandoned, or on the other hand a sacred office is retained when purchased in a worldly manner. He is afraid whichever way he turns, suspicious and fearful on every side, lest remaining in his purchased office he

should not properly grieve that he has not corrected his fault by simply abandoning it, or in truth while endeavoring to atone for one fault by resigning his
authority, he should in turn commit another by this very forsaking of his flock.
Therefore because Behemoth binds with such intricate knots that a mind
when brought into doubt, binds itself firmer in sin by the very means whereby it
attempts to free itself from sin, it is rightly said: *The sinews of his flanks are closely knit*. For the more the signs of his artifices are relaxed, as if about to release
us, the more they are entwined to hold us fast.

There is however a useful way whereby his craftiness may be overcome:
when the mind is constricted between lesser and greater sins, if no avenue of
escape from sin is open, the lesser evils are always to be preferred. Because
even he who is shut in by a round of walls lest he escape, takes flight where the
wall is found lowest. And Paul when he observed certain incontinent persons
in the Church, made concessions for the smallest faults in order that they
might avoid greater ones, saying: *For fear of fornication, let every man have his
own wife*.[28] And because those who are married are then only without sin in
the marriage act when they come together not for the gratification of lust but
for the begetting of children, in order to show that what he had conceded was
not without sin, though of least degree, he immediately added: *But I speak this
by indulgence, not by commandment*.[29] For that which is pardoned, and not
commanded, is not without fault. There was surely perception of sin; he made
provision for that which could be pardoned. But when we are subjected to a
dilemma, it is to our advantage to yield to the least transgressions so that we
may not sin in grave matters and go unpardoned. The close–knit sinews of Behemoth are frequently parted when we pass to the greatest virtue through the
commission of smaller faults.

7

The counsels of the devil and the difference between counsels and suggestions

The bones of Leviathan are like pipes of brass.[30] By bones are meant his
counsels, for as the posture and strength of the body reside in the bones, so
does all his malice stand in crafty designs. For he does not oppress anyone by
force, but he slays him by the artfulness of his deadly persuasion. And again, as
the marrow strengthens the bones which it moistens, so his counsels, infused
with the power of a spiritual nature, the subtlety of his mind strengthens. But
his testicles differ from his bones, that is, his suggestions from his designs, inasmuch as by the former he openly implants what is noxious, but by the latter,
when counseling as if for good purposes, he leads into sin; by the former he

overcomes in fighting, by the latter he trips up as if he were advising. Whence also his bones, that is, these same designs, are properly compared to pipes of brass. For pipes of brass are usually adapted to sonorous melodies, which on reaching the ears, while they offer a soothing strain attract the inner workings of the mind to outward delights, and when the sound is sweet that they utter to the ears, they weaken the resistance of the heart to the flow of pleasure. And when the hearing is drawn on to delight, the understanding is relaxed from the firmness of its strength. So also when his crafty designs supposedly give counsel but do so with gentle persuasion, they withdraw the heart from its resolute intention, and in uttering sweet sounds they foster a disposition to harmful things. They are like pipes of brass then, which when heard with pleasure plunge the mind from its inward resolution into the enjoyment of external activity. For this it is that Behemoth especially strives for in prosecuting his deception: to be able to utter sweetly what he says when he advances his scheme of wickedness as if for our good in order that he may beguile the mind by showing its purported usefulness and corrupt the mind by concealing its iniquity.

We reveal these matters more clearly and fully by briefly setting forth a few of the claims of his counsels. Consider that a person content with his own possessions has resolved not to be entangled with any of the world's occupations, being greatly afraid of losing the advantages of his peace and utterly disdaining to accumulate wealth by sin. The crafty enemy in approaching him, in order to undermine his intention of sincere devotion, secretly offers a suggestion as if for his benefit, saying: Those things that you have are sufficient at present, but what do you intend to do when these fail? For if nothing is provided after these, you have what must now be expended for your children, but goods must yet be acquired to be laid away. Even what you have can soon fail if prudent foresight ceases to provide what is lacking. Can not worldly business be discharged and yet sin be avoided in doing so in order that it may both furnish outward means and yet not sway inward righteousness? He insinuates these thoughts, flattering as he does so, and is already secretly concealing the snares of sin in the worldly business that he has in mind. His bones therefore are like pipes of brass because his pernicious suggestions flatter the listener with the sweetness of the voice that is giving him counsel.

Someone else has resolved not merely not to seek worldly advantages but also to renounce all that he possesses. His purpose is to exercise himself the more freely in the discipleship of heavenly magisterium, the more he has disburdened himself, abandoning and trampling under foot the things which could weigh down their possessor. The lurking enemy addresses his heart with secret suggestion, saying: Whence has arisen the boldness of such great temerity that you believe you can stand firm in renouncing everything? Your Redeemer has formed you in one way, and you set yourself up in another; he would make you more strong and robust if he had wished you to follow his footsteps with the neediness of want. Do not most men never give up their earthly patrimonies and yet purchase by these, through works of compassion, the eternal good of a heavenly inheritance? He suggests these things with flattery, but secretly in his deceit joins deadly pleasures to the very things he advises him to retain before the eyes of him who retains them so that he may attract the deluded heart to outward pleasures and may nullify its most profound longings for perfection. His bones therefore are like pipes of brass because when his crafty designs utter outwardly a soothing sound, they press for the forfeiture of interior riches.

Another having given up all his outward possessions in order that he may grasp the sequence of higher learning prepares also to repress his inmost wishes so that by submitting himself to the stricter behests of another he may renounce not merely his evil desires, but—to add to his perfection—deny himself also even in good resolves and may carry out all he ought to do at the will of another. This man the crafty enemy the more gently addresses the more ardently he strives to cast him down from his more lofty position, and soon—beguiling him with deadly suggestions—he says: O what great marvels you will be able to perform by yourself if you do not submit yourself in any way to the judgment of another! Why do you reduce your progress from a desire for improvement? Why do you infringe on the goodness of your intention when you endeavor to extend it further than is necessary? For what did you do wickedly when exercising your own will? Why then do you require the control of another over you since you will be by yourself fully competent for living well? He suggests these things flatteringly, but he secretly prepares in the carrying out of one's own will occasions for the exercise of pride, and while he praises the heart for its inward rectitude, he cunningly probes in which area to subvert it with sin. His bones therefore are like pipes of brass because his hidden designs in the very act of flattering and pleasing the mind ruinously divert it from its right intention.

Another, having fully subdued his will, has already eliminated many sins of the old man both by reform of life and by the grief of penitence, and is inflamed with greater zeal against the sins of others the more—entirely dead to himself—he is freed from his own iniquities. The crafty enemy, because he knows that by his zeal for righteousness he is benefiting others besides himself, attacks him with words advising him as if for his advantage, saying: Why do you extend yourself to attend to the concerns of others? O that you may have strength to consider your own! Do you not consider that when you are stretched forth to the concerns of others, you are found unequal to attend to your own? And of what use is it to wipe off the blood of another's wound and by neglect to extend the corruption of your own? While he speaks thus, as if giving advice, he takes away the zeal of charity and destroys with the sword of secretly instilled sloth all the good which could result from charity. For if we are commanded to love our neighbors as ourselves, it is right for us to be vehement against sin with zeal for them as for ourselves. Because, then, he estranges the mind from its own resolution while he pleasingly offers advice, it is rightly said: *His bones are like pipes of brass.* For when by his deceptive designs he utters a sound pleasing to the mind of the hearer, he charms as with a pipe of brass so as to deceive by means of his allurements.

8

The devil tempts us in matters to which he knows the mind is more easily inclined

A snare lies hidden in the ground for him and a trap in the path.[31] A snare is hidden in the ground when sin is hidden under earthly interests. For the enemy in carrying out his plots shows to the human mind something to desire in earthly gain and hides the snare of sin that it may impede the soul so that his prey may see what he longs for and yet never see in what snare of sin he is placing his foot. A trap, implying deceit, is put upon the path by our willful enemy when in the course of worldly activity, which the mind is inclined to follow, the snare of sin is prepared. This would not so easily entrap if it were visible, for a trap is so set that while the bait is displayed, the trap is not itself seen by the one who is following the path. Similar to bait in a trap is advantage gained by sin or worldly prosperity attained by wickedness. So when profit is sought with covetousness, it is as if the invisible trap brings the mind to a halt. Thus there are often set before the mind—along with sin—honors, riches, health, and temporal life; while the impaired mind sees these things as sustenance and does not see the trap, by the sight of the food that it desires it is caught fast in the sin that is not seen. There are in fact types of dispositions that are not far removed from established evil characteristics. Thus austere temperaments are usually found to be united either to cruelty or to pride; likewise, temperaments that are easygoing and lighthearted beyond what is fitting are sometimes allied to lust and lax conduct. Therefore our enemy looks upon the temperaments of individuals and the defects to which they are prone, and he confronts them with those objects to which he sees that the mind is most readily inclined, so that to the blithe and lighthearted temperaments he often suggests dissoluteness and sometimes vainglory, but to austere minds he proposes anger, pride, or cruelty. So he sets a trap where he sees the path of the mind is, for he introduces a peril of deception where he has found the way of a likely frame of mind.

9

**The devil conceals vices under the cloak of virtues
in order to deceive**

And crying out they wept.[32] Sometimes the scheming enemy assumes a semblance of pity that may end in cruelty; such is the case when he prevents a fault being corrected by self–discipline so that what is not restrained in this life may be punished with the fire of hell. Sometimes he offers to the eye the image of discretion and leads us on to snares of indiscretion; this happens when at his instigation we supposedly from prudence allow ourselves more nourishment on account of our weakness but are imprudently stirring up against ourselves assaults of the flesh. Sometimes he counterfeits affection for good works but thereby imposes upon us restlessness in our efforts; this occurs when someone cannot remain quiet and ostensibly fears to be charged with idleness. Sometimes the enemy exhibits the image of humility so that he may remove the effect of our being helpful. Such is the case when he declares to some that they are weaker and more useless than they are so that whereas they consider themselves too unworthy, they may fear to perform actions whereby they could benefit their neighbors.

But these vices that the old enemy conceals under the cloak of virtues are very minutely probed by the hand of compunction. For the one who really grieves within, resolutely determines beforehand what things are to be done outwardly and what are not.

Concerning the aforesaid dissembling by the devil it is written: *His cartilage is like plates of iron.*[33] What is to be understood by cartilage but simulation? For cartilage has the appearance of bone but has not its strength. And there are some vices that have the appearance of rectitude but proceed from the weakness of sin. For our enemy cloaks himself with such malicious artifice that he frequently makes faults appear as virtues before the eyes of the deluded mind, so that a person expects rewards of some kind for the very conduct that deserves to meet with eternal punishments. For cruelty is frequently exercised in punishing sins and is considered justice, and immoderate anger is believed to be the stamp of righteous zeal; and when sinners ought to be carefully dissuaded from their wayward habits, they are lost by being violently called to task. Frequently negligent remissness is regarded as gentleness and forbearance, and while delinquents are spared temporally more than is proper, they are cruelly destined to eternal punishments. Liberality is sometimes believed to be compassion, and while miserly holding of possessions is a fault, there is no fear of what has been given being more extravagantly dissipated. Possessiveness is sometimes considered frugality, and although it is a grievous fault not to give, selfishness is considered a virtue. The stubbornness of the wicked is often called constancy, and when a mind does not permit itself to be swerved from its wickedness, it revels as if defending what is right. Inconstancy is often regarded as tractability, and because a person does not keep full faith with anyone, he considers himself on that account a friend of everyone. Sometimes helpless fear is believed to be humility, and although someone oppressed by temporal fear refrains from the defense of truth, he thinks that according to the precedence established by God he yields humbly to those more important than he. Sometimes boldness in speech is thought to be a privilege accorded by truth, and when through pride the truth is impugned, pretentiousness in speaking is equated with defense of the truth. Indolence is commonly looked upon as a way of maintaining peace and although not to be zealous in doing right betokens a grave fault, it is believed to be a mark of great virtue merely to abstain from evil conduct. A spirit of restlessness is often called watchful solicitude and when a person cannot bear inactivity, by doing what he likes he thinks that he is duly performing an exercise of virtue. Heedless impetuosity in taking action is often credited as zeal for a worthy pursuit, and although the benefit one seeks is diminished by untimely action, it is considered that the quicker a thing is done, the better. Delay in pursuing a good purpose is seen as deliberation, and when gain is sought in consultation, the advantage is offset by insidious tardiness. When a fault therefore is viewed as a virtue, we are compelled to reflect that the more slowly the mind abandons its fault, the more it fails to be ashamed of what it does; and the more the same result is assured, the more the mind, deceived by the appearance of virtue, seeks on that account the recompense of rewards. But a fault that gives rise to shame is easily corrected because it is felt to be a fault. Since therefore error is corrected with greater difficulty when it is believed to be a virtue, it is rightly said: *His cartilage is like plates of iron.* For the more craftily the evil spirit exhibits his cunning under the cloak of virtue, the more firmly does he hold the mind captive in sin.

Hence it is that sometimes those who are directed toward the way of holiness are only gradually improved when they have fallen into error. For they consider what they do to be right and devote their perseverance to vice as if it

were the cultivation of virtue. They believe what they do to be right and therefore cater the more earnestly to their own judgment.

10

**The way in which sin begets sin when a fault, beginning in the
likeness of reason, leads to sin**

The paths trodden by the reprobate are entangled.[34] It should be understood
that commonly one sin is committed by the occurrence of another sin. Thus to
theft there is often joined the deceit of denial, and often the sin of deceit is
increased by the guilt of perjury. Often an offense is committed with shameless presumptuousness, and often—a sequel worse than any fault in
itself—there is even boasting about the commission of the misdeed. For although self-exaltation is likely to develop from virtue, yet sometimes the
foolish mind exalts itself because of the wickedness it has done. But when
transgression is joined to transgression, what else is this but the steps of the
wicked becoming bound in entangled paths and entwined chains? Hence it is
rightly said by Isaias against the perverse mind under the likeness of Judaea:
*And it shall be the lair of dragons and the pasture of ostriches, and demons and
onocentaurs shall meet, and the hairy ones shall cry out one to another.*[35] For what
is denoted by the dragons except malice, and what by the name of ostriches
except hypocrisy? An ostrich indeed has the outward appearance of being able
to fly but has not the capability of flight; hypocrisy too impresses upon all be-
holders an image of sanctity on its part but fails to maintain the life of sanctity.
Therefore in the perverse mind the dragon lies down and the ostrich feeds
since underlying malice is cunningly covered and the guise of goodness is set
before the eyes of spectators. But what is represented by the name onocentaurs if not those who are both lustful and haughty? For in the Greek language
onos signifies an ass, and by the designation ass lust is denoted, according to the
testimony of the prophet who says: *Whose flesh is as the flesh of asses.*[36] But by
the designation bull the neck of pride is denoted, as is said by the Psalmist in
the Lord's word concerning the Jews in their pride: *Fat bulls have besieged me.*[37]
Thus onocentaurs are they who, being subject to vicious habits of lust, lift up
their neck for the very same reason for which they ought to have been abased.
Such persons in serving their fleshly gratifications, all sense of shame being
put far from them, not only do not grieve that they have lost uprightness but
further even rejoice in the work of confusion. Now the demons meet with the
onocentaurs since the evil spirits readily obey the wishes of all those whom
they see rejoicing in the things which they ought to bewail. Hence it is properly
added: *And the hairy ones shall cry out one to another.*[38] Now who are repre-

sented by the hairy ones if not those whom the Greeks call pans and the Latins incubuses? Their form begins in the likeness of a man but terminates in the extremity of a beast. Therefore by the designation hairy one is denoted the coarseness of every sin, which even if it begins under the pretext of reason, yet always tends toward irrational emotions. And like a man ending in a beast, sin—while beginning in the likeness of reason—passes on to an end devoid of reason. Thus often the pleasure of eating is enslaved by gluttony, and it pretends to satisfy the requirement of nature, and while it distends the belly by gluttony, stirs up the body to lust. Now one hairy one cries to another when one wickedness perpetrated leads to the the perpetration of another, and as if by a kind of voice of thought, a sin already committed invites another sin which yet remains to be committed. For often, as it has been said, gluttony declares: If you do not support the body with plentiful sustenance, you can not continue in useful labors. And when it has inflamed the mind by the desires of the flesh, lust also soon forms words of its own suggestion, saying: If God did not wish human creatures to be united corporally, he would never have made bodies suited to such union. And when it suggests these things as reasonable, it leads the mind to unrestrained indulgence of the passions. Often when the mind is called to task, at once it looks for the support of deceit and denial, not considering itself guilty if by telling lies it may defend its activities. Thus the hairy ones shall cry out one to another when under some semblance of reasoning, a sin following out of the occasion of a preceding sin ensnares the corrupt soul. And when weighty and harsh sins sink it low, it is as if the hairy ones ruled it, gathered together in it in concord; and thus it comes to pass that the ways of their paths are always entangling themselves worse and worse, when sin taking occasion of sin binds the lost soul.

11

By tempting suggestions unlawful pleasures are injected under pretense of necessity

Disfigured with calamity and misery.[39] If unhealthy flesh is through neglect not diligently cared for, it deteriorates further in disease by a scaly deposit, and while to the misfortune of sickness the wretchedness of neglect is added, heavier inconvenience is borne by the disfigurement that appears.

Therefore human nature having been created unhurt but having sunk into disease by defection of its own will, it fell into deep distress because weighed down by countless necessities, it encountered in this life only that which would bring affliction. But since we attend unduly to those same necessities of our nature and overlook the care of the soul, by the wretchedness of neglect we add to our infirmity the foulness of sin. For natural necessities usually have about them this very dangerous characteristic: attendant in large part upon ministering to them is obscurity as to what is carried out with usefulness in view and what is to be attributed to self-gratification. Frequently—indeed when the chance of being led astray is present—while we render necessity its due we cater to the fault of self-gratification, and under cover of infirmity we justify ourselves in facing up to self-examination and hide under the pretense of doing what is useful. But to let loose the frailty of our nature by neglect is nothing else than to add misery to affliction, and by that misery to redouble the foulness of vices. Whence holy men, in everything they do, discriminate with the most earnest intention lest the frailty of their nature exact from them more than is due and lest under the cloak of necessity the evil of gratification spring up in them. For they suffer in one way from infirmity and in another way from the prompting of temptation, and having been assigned the role of most impartial arbiters between necessity and pleasure, they alleviate the latter by taking countermeasures and control the former by exercising restraint. This is the reason why even if they are exposed to the affliction of their infirmity, yet they never are abased to the foulness of misery by neglectfulness. For simply to be in affliction is to endure the necessities of nature from the frailty of flesh still liable to corruption. These same necessities he longed to avoid who said: *Deliver me from my necessities.*[40] For he knew that for the most part sins of sensual pleasures that emerge are occasioned by necessities, and lest he might of his own will commit anything unlawful, he sought to have eradicated the very trait he innately bore within himself.

But on the other hand, the evil-minded take delight in those necessities of their corrupt state, because they twist these needs to sensual purposes. For while they minister to nature by restoring their bodies with food, through the gratification of the palate they are stuffed by pleasurable overindulgence. When they seek clothing for covering the limbs, they look not only for apparel that may cover but also adorn, and against the numbness of cold not only what may protect by thickness but likewise delight by softness; not only what may soothe the touch by smoothness, but also beguile the eye by color. So then, to turn occasion of necessity to the use of pleasure, what else is it but to join the foulness of misery to one's own affliction?

12

The devil makes light of divine threats so that he may wantonly practice deception

And he will render to man his justice.[41] It is called our justice, not as being of ourselves, but as made ours by divine bounty, as we say in the Lord's prayer: *Give us this day our daily bread.*[42] Note that we both call it ours and yet pray for it to be given to us. For it becomes ours when we receive it, but yet it is God's because it is given by him. And it is therefore God's as of his giving, and it becomes truly ours by our accepting it. It is in this way then that God in this text renders to man his justice, not that which he had of himself but that which he received, having been created in such a state as to have it and in which, having fallen, he declined to continue. God therefore will render to man that justice for which he was created so that he may take delight in clinging to God, may dread his threatening sentence, may no longer trust the alluring promises of the crafty serpent.

For our ancient enemy ceases not daily to do what he did in paradise; he endeavors to root out the words of God from the hearts of men and to plant there the false blandishments of his own promising. Day by day he belittles the threatenings of God and invites belief in his own false promises. For he falsely promises temporal things to minimize in the minds of men those eternal punishments God threatens. For when the enemy promises the glory of this life, what else does he say but: *Taste and you shall be as gods?*[43] As if he said plainly: Lay hold on worldly desires and appear lofty in this world. And when he endeavors to remove the fear of the divine sentence, what else does he utter but the question he addressed to our first parents: *Why has God commanded you that you should not eat of every tree of paradise?*[44] But because man, having been redeemed, has received as a divine gift that righteousness lost soon after his creation, he exerts himself more vigorously against the allurements of crafty persuasion, because he has learned by experience how obedient he ought to be to the divine command. And he whom sin then led to punishment, by his punishment is now restrained from sin, so that he may be the more fearful of offending, the more through the fear of punishment he declares the evil he has done.

13

Oftentimes in dreams the devil soothes the wicked and assails the righteous

Thou wilt frighten me with dreams and terrify me with visions.[45] It is important to examine in how many ways images from dreams affect the mind. For sometimes dreams are engendered by fullness or emptiness of the stomach, sometimes by illusion, sometimes by illusion and thought combined, sometimes by revelation, sometimes however by thought and revelation combined. Now the two causes mentioned first we all know by experience, while the four others we find in the pages of sacred Scripture. For unless dreams were frequently caused through illusion by our secret enemy, the wise man would never have pointed this out by saying: *For dreams and vain illusions have deceived many.*[46] Or for that matter: *You shall not divine nor observe dreams.*[47] By these words surely it is shown how great an abomination are things connected with auguries. Again, unless they sometimes came from thought and illusion together, Solomon would not have said: *Dreams follow many cares.*[48] And unless dreams sometimes had their origin in the mystery of revelation, Joseph would not in a dream have seen himself chosen rather than his brothers, [49] nor would the spouse of Mary have been warned in a dream by an angel to take the Child and to flee into Egypt.[50] Again, unless dreams sometimes proceeded from thought and revelation together, the prophet Daniel in discussing the vision of Nabuchodonosor would not have begun speaking on the basis of thought, saying: *Thou, O king, didst begin to think in thy bed what should come to pass hereafter: and he that revealeth mysteries showed thee what shall come to pass.*[51] And soon afterwards: *Thou sawest, and behold there was as it were a great statue. This statue, which was great and high, tall of stature, stood before thee,* and so on.[52] Thus while Daniel speaks awesomely of the dream about to be fulfilled and shows in what thoughts it had its rise, it is made plain that the occurrence may frequently proceed from thought and revelation combined.

But without doubt, since dreams differ in so many respects, credence ought to be given to them the less easily in proportion as it less easily appears from what influencing cause they spring. For often to those whom the evil spirit hinders when they are awake through love of the present life, he promises favorable conditions even when they sleep. And those whom he sees to be in dread of misfortunes, he threatens more cruelly by the representations of dreams that he may influence the incautious mind in a different way, and either by elevating it with hope or depressing it with dread, may unsettle it. Often too he strives to influence the hearts of the saints themselves by dreams so that at least for a passing moment they may be swayed from the aim of sound thought, though they at once rid the mind of the delusive fantasy. But our treacherous foe, insofar as he is unable to get the better of them when awake, assails them all the more when they sleep. Yet heavenly dispensation justly allows him in his malevolence to do so lest in the hearts of the elect sleep alone should go without the benefit of suffering. Therefore it is well said to him who rules over all: *If I say: My bed shall comfort me, and I shall be relieved speaking with my self on my couch: Thou wilt frighten me with dreams and terrify me with visions,*[53] because surely God orders all things wonderfully and does himself what the evil spirit seeks to do unjustly, but he allows it to be done only justly. Now because the life of the righteous is both troubled by temptation while on watch and also harassed by illusion while dreaming, it undergoes externally the trials of its corruption and bears painfully within itself unlawful thoughts. So the question arises: What is to be done in order to rescue the "foot of the heart" from the snares of so many stumbling blocks?

14

God mercifully grants us virtues and the devil guilefully suggests vices

By what way is the light spread, and heat divided upon the earth?[54] By the word light is designated righteousness, as it is written: *The people that walked in darkness have seen a great light.*[55] But everything which is spread is cast, not continuously, but with a kind of spacing. And light is therefore said to be spread because, though we already behold some things as they really are, yet we do not see other things as they should be seen. For spread light had possessed the heart of Peter, who had shone forth with such great brightness of faith and of miracles, and yet while he was imposing the weight of circumcision on the converted Gentiles, he did not know the right thing to say.[56] Light therefore is spread in this life, for constant understanding with respect to all things is not bestowed. For while we comprehend one thing as it is and do not know another, we both see as it were partially in spread light and remain partially in darkness. But our light will no longer be spread when our mind lifted up entirely to God will shine forth.

Because it is not known in what ways this same light is infused into the heart of man here below, it is rightly said in the form of a question: *By what way is the light spread?* As if it were openly said by the Lord: Tell me in what order I pour my righteousness into the secret recesses of the heart when I am not seen even in my approach, and yet I invisibly alter the visible works of men; when I illumine one and the same mind, now with one virtue and again with another, and yet to some degree I permit it through spread light still to remain in the darkness of temptation. Let ignorant man be asked by what way the light is spread, as if it were openly said:: While I soften the hard hearts, bend the rigid, smooth the rough, warm the cold, strengthen the weak, recall the wandering, confirm the wavering, behold if you can by what paths I come incorporeally and shed light on them. For all these things we behold when they are done, but we do not know how they are inwardly brought about. The Truth shows us in the Gospel that this way of light is invisible to us, saying: *The spirit breatheth where he will and thou hearest his voice; but thou knowest not whence he cometh and whither he goeth.*[57]

But because when the light is spread, temptations by the hidden adversary presently spring up against the enlightened mind, it is rightly added: *Heat is divided upon the earth.* For the crafty foe strives to inflame with unlawful desires the minds of those whom he sees shining forth with the light of righteousness, so that they frequently feel themselves more beset with temptations than at the time when they did not gaze upon the rays of inward light. Whence also the Israelites, after they had been called, complain against Moses and Aaron about their increasing labor, saying: *(Let) the Lord see and judge, because you have made our savor to stink before Pharaoh and his servants; and have given him a sword to kill us.*[58] For when they wished to depart from Egypt, Pharaoh had taken away the straw (to make brick), and yet required tasks of the same amount. The mind therefore secretly murmurs, as it were, against the law, after the knowledge of which it endures sharper stings of temptations, and when it beholds its labors increasing because it is displeasing to its adversary, it grieves that it is offensive, so to speak, in the eyes of Pharaoh. Heat therefore follows after light because after the illumination by heavenly gift, the struggle of temptation is increased.

But the heat is rightly said also to be divided, because individuals are not assailed by all vices but by certain ones which are at hand and placed close to them. For the ancient enemy observes the distinguishing trait of each person and then sets the snares of temptations. For one person is of a cheerful, another of a moody, another of a timid, another of a proud disposition. In order to catch us more easily, our secret adversary prepares deceptions closely related to our varied characters. For because pleasure borders on mirth, he holds out lust to cheerful dispositions. And because melancholy easily slips into anger, he offers the cup of discord for the moody. Because the timid dread punishments, he threatens the fearful with terrors. And because he beholds the proud elated with praises, by flattering applause he entices them to whatever he pleases. He lays snares therefore against people one by one, by vices adapted to them. For he would not easily lead them captive, if he were either to offer bribes to the lustful, or bodily pleasures to the covetous, or if he were to assail the greedy by the pride of abstinence, or the abstinent by the folly of gluttony, or if he were to seek to capture the gentle by eagerness for the contest, or the angry by the dread of fear. Since therefore in the intensity of temptation he slyly lurks in ambush against each one by himself and secretly lays the snares suited to his habits, it is rightly said: *Heat is divided over the earth*.

But when there first comes the question: *By what way is the light spread*, there follows immediately: *And heat divided over the earth?* This no doubt shows that heat is also divided by the same way in which light is spread. For when the lofty and incomprehensible grace of the Holy Spirit illumines our minds with its light, it also so disposes and modifies the temptations of the adversary that they do not come upon us in unison or that those only that can be endured assail the mind already illuminated by God, so that they do not burn us with the fire of their full strength when they torture us with the heat of their touch. This Paul affirms when he says: *God is faithful, who will not suffer you to be tempted above that which you are able; but will make also with temptation issue, that you may be able to bear it*.[59] This heat then our crafty adversary divides in one way, and our merciful Creator in another. The former divides in order to make the heat more destructive; the latter, to make it more tolerable.

15

The multiplicity of the devil's suggestions, coming as it were from a supposed giver of pleasing potions

He hath been acceptable to the gravel of Cocytus.[60] *Cocytus* in the Greek language is the term for lamentation, usually of women or the timorous. Now the wise of this world, barred from the light of truth, tried to search out and retain some traces of truth. Hence they thought that the river Cocytus flowed in the lower regions, implying that they who commit deeds deserving of punishment come to grief in the nether world. But it is up to us who now have the light of truth to look askance at the faintness of carnal wisdom and to see that in the utterance of Job *Cocytus* means the lamentation of the weak. For it is written: *Do ye manfully, and let your heart be strengthened*.[61] For those who refuse to be strengthened in God have recourse to lamentation through weakness of spirit. Now we are accustomed to calling gravel the little stones of rivers which the flowing water carries along with it. What then is denoted by the gravel of Cocytus but the lost, who, surrendering to their gratifications, are in the state of ever being dragged by the river to the lowest depths? For they who refuse to take a strong stand against the pleasures of this life become gravel of Cocytus since by their daily laxness they are going the way of lamentation, to mourn forever in the hereafter for weakly acceding now to their pleasures. And whereas our old enemy, having often entered into the hearts of the reprobate—while he bestows gifts on them, while he exalts them with worldly honors, while he displays delights to their eyes, while he has all drifting souls admiring and following him—it is well said of him: *He hath been acceptable to the gravel of Cocytus*. For since the elect despise him, since they mentally trample on him with disdain, those who love and follow him are those who are as it were carried along by the water of pleasure to everlasting lamentation, who through earthly concupiscence each day tumble by degrees to the lowest depth like gravel. For to some he proffers the taste of his sweetness through pride, to others in turn through avarice, envy, deceitfulness, lust; and for as many kinds of evil to which he offers enticement he presents just as many drafts of his sweetness. For when he presses upon the mind anything proud, what he says becomes sweet because the unrighteous person longs to appear superior to others. While he strives to pour avarice into the mind, what he speaks in secret becomes sweet because by abundance need is avoided. While he suggests anything envious, what he says becomes sweet because when the perverse mind sees another brought low, it exults in not seeming at all inferior to him. When he prompts any deceitfulness, what he says is made sweet since by the very fact that it deceives others, it appears to itself to be clever. When he advocates lust to the impressionable soul, what he recommends is rendered sweet because it weakens the will opposing pleasure. Therefore, for all the evil tendencies that he instills in the hearts of carnal persons, he holds out to them, as it were, that many drafts of his sweetness. However, that sweetness, as I have already said, has attraction only for those intent on present gratifications who are inveigled into everlasting lamentation.

16

When the devil cannot by himself deceive us, he tries to do so through those who are close to us

And his wife said to him: Dost thou still continue in thy simplicity? Bless God, and die.[62] The old adversary is accustomed to tempt mankind in two ways, so that through him the hearts of the steadfast are either crushed by tribulation or softened by persuasion.

Now from the words of Job's wife, euphemistically urging him to *curse* God, we ought to observe attentively that the old enemy attempts to influence our state of mind not only by himself but also by means of those who are close to us. For when he cannot subvert our hearts by his own persuading, then he seeks on the sly to do so by the tongues of those around us. For hence it is written: *Beware of thy own children: and take heed of them of thy household.*[63] Hence it is said by the prophet: *Let every man take heed of his neighbor, and let him not trust in any brother of his.*[64] Hence it is again written: *And a man's enemies shall be they of his own household.*[65] For when the crafty adversary sees that he is rejected by the hearts of the upright, he seeks out those whom they love very much and he speaks coaxingly by the words of those who are most dear to them so that while the force of love penetrates the heart, the sword of his persuasion may easily force its way through the defenses of inward uprightness. Thus after Job's loss of his possessions, after the death of his children, after the wounds and deformation of his body, the old enemy sets into motion the tongue of his wife. And worthy of note is the time when she strove to corrupt the mind of her husband with poisoned talk. For it was after the wounds that words were brought into play, doubtlessly so that as the power of pain grew greater, the untoward stress of persuasion might easily prevail.

But we should take into account that in the Church persons, when unspiritual, exert themselves to support what is wrong, at one time out of fear, and at another out of audacity, and when they themselves go wrong either from timidity or pride, they endeavor to instill these qualities, as if out of love, in the hearts of the righteous. So Peter before the death and resurrection of our Lord, maintained an unspiritual outlook; with a similar disposition the son of Sarvia, a follower of David, remained loyal to him. Yet the one sinned by fear, the other by pride. For Peter, when he heard of his master's impending death, said: *Lord, be it far from thee; this shall not be unto thee.*[66] But Abisai, not enduring the wrongs offered to his leader, says: *Shall Semei for these words not be put to death, because he cursed the Lord's anointed?*[67] But to Peter it is immediately said: *Go behind me, Satan.*[68] And Abisai together with his brother at once heard the words: *What have I to do with you, ye sons of Sarvia? Why are you a satan this day to me?*[69] Those therefore who suggest evil are by the mode of address accounted apostate angels who by their enticing words urge unlawful deeds as if out of love. But they are much the worse who give into this sin not from fear but from pride, of whom the wife of blessed Job served as a special example since she sought to suggest proud speech to her husband, saying: *Dost thou still continue in thy simplicity? Bless God, and die.* She blames the simplicity in her husband because despising all transitory things, with a pure heart he longs only for eternal things. As though she said: Why dost thou in thy simplicity seek after the things of eternity, and in resignation groan under the weight of present ills? Going beyond bounds, scorn eternity and even by dying escape from present afflictions.

17

The devil's suggestions cannot harm us unless of our own free will we consent to them

He hath compassed me round about with his lances; he hath wounded my loins.[70] Holy Church is besieged with lances by her enemy whenever she is in her members attacked by the cunning opponent with spears of temptation. We are indeed rightly said to be compassed round with lances since our old enemy assails us on every side with the thrust of his temptation. For often while the appetite is restrained so that lust may be subdued, he strikes the mind with the goads of vainglory. But if the body should not be worn down by the infliction of abstinence, the flame of lust kindles itself against the mind. Often, while we strive to observe thriftiness, we fall into parsimony. Often, even while we give liberally the things we possess, we are led into avarice because we seek to amass again what we may distribute. Whereas then the spears of the old enemy assail us on all sides, it is under these circumstances rightly said: *He hath compassed me round about with his lances.* And because the crafty enemy indeed recommends every sin but we by consenting to his recommendations commit it, there is this further observation: *He hath wounded my loins,* for lust lies in the loins. Hence also he who desired to abolish the pleasure of lust from the heart preached the words: *(Have) the loins of your mind girt up.*[71] When therefore the old enemy lures faithful people into lust, surely he attacks them in the loins. Here, it should also be noted, Job does not say he has *wounded* but *wounded together.* For just as to talk is sometimes an act of one person but to talk together involves two or perhaps many persons, so our old enemy, because he does not lead us astray without our own will, is by no means said to wound our loins but to wound our loins together: the reason is that what he wickedly suggests we fulfill, giving way by our own will; and we, as it were, together with him wound ourselves, because we are led to do what is evil of our own free will.

18

The devil tempts religious persons in one way, the worldly–minded in another

Who can discover the face of his garment?[72] Leviathan tempts in one way the minds of men which are religious and in another those which are devoted to this world, for he offers openly to the wicked the evil things they desire, but secretly lying in wait for the godly, he practices deception under a show of sanctity. To the former as friends he presents himself more manifestly as wicked, but with regard to the latter as strangers he covers himself, so to speak, with a cloak of respectability in order to introduce secretly, hidden under cover of doing good, the evils which he cannot openly extend to them. Whence also his cohorts, when they are unable to do harm by open wickedness, often assume the guise of a good action and show themselves as wicked indeed in conduct but yet falsely portray themselves as virtuous by their appearance. For if the wicked were openly evil, they would not be accepted at all by the good, but they take on something of the likeness of the good in order that, while good persons welcome in them the appearance which they esteem, they may absorb also the poison they avoid since both are mingled. Whence the apostle Paul, beholding some men passing themselves off as apostles while fastidiously indulging themselves, declares: *For Satan himself transformeth himself into an angel of light. Therefore it is no great thing if his ministers be transformed as the ministers of justice.*[73] Joshuà feared this transformation when on seeing an angel he asked him on whose side he was, saying: *Art thou one of ours, or of our adversaries?*[74] His purpose surely was that if the angel were of the opposing side, he might from knowing that he was suspected, desist from practicing deception. Because therefore Leviathan in attempting a work of iniquity frequently clothes himself with a semblance of sanctity, and because the raiment of his simulation cannot be detected except by divine grace, it is well said: *Who will discover the face of his garment?* In answer, you must supply: If not I, the Lord, who endow the minds of my servants with the grace of most subtle discernment, so that, his malice being revealed, they may see his face exposed, which he keeps covered under the vesture of sanctity.

19

The devil plots more against those who spurning earthly things, desire celestial things

He will drink up a river, and not wonder: and he trusteth that the Jordan may run into his mouth.[75] By the word river is designated the downward course of the human race, which rises at its birth as if from the source of its fountain, proceeding down as if flowing to its lowest level at its death. But by the expression Jordan are signified those who have already been imbued with the sacrament of baptism. For since our Redeemer chose to be baptized in this river, all who have been baptized must be denoted by the name of that stream with which this same sacrament came to be associated. Because therefore the devil drew to himself like a river the human race flowing downward from the beginning of the world even to the time of redemption, scarcely a few of the elect escaping him, it is now well said: *He will drink up a river, and not wonder.*

But since even after the coming of the mediator he seizes some of the faithful who fail to live righteously, it is rightly added: *And he trusteth that the Jordan may run into his mouth.* As if it were plainly said: Before the time of the Redeemer of the world he drank up the world without wondering, but what is far worse, even after the coming of the Redeemer he trusts that he is able to swallow up some who have been sealed with the sacrament of baptism. For he consumes some called Christians because he unsettles them by causing error in their faith itself. But others he does not turn aside from the integrity of faith but leads them to the practice of evildoing. Others he is unable to bend as much as he wishes toward deeds of impurity, but he inwardly diverts them from the zeal of their intention so that when they separate their minds from charity, whatever they do outwardly may not be righteous. And they retain the faith, but they do not hold fast to the life of faith because they either openly do those things which are unlawful or else from their perverted heart their actions are wicked even though they seem to be holy. For since some persons are faithful in what they profess but not in their lives, hence it is said by the voice of Truth: *Not every one that saith to me, Lord, Lord, shall enter the kingdom of heaven.*[76] Hence he says again: *And why call you me, Lord, Lord; and do not the things which I say?*[77] Hence Paul says: *They profess that they know God; but in their works they deny him.*[78] Hence John says: *He who saith that he knoweth him, and keepeth not his commandments, is a liar.*[79] Hence it is that the Lord complains of his people of old: *This people honoreth me with their lips, but their heart is far from me.*[80] Hence also the Psalmist says: *They loved him with their mouth, and with their tongue they lied unto him.*[81] But it was no wonder that the devil before the water of the cleansing, before the heavenly sacraments, before the bodily presence of the Redeemer, drank up, with the yawning gulf of his deep persuasion, the river of the human race. But it is very remarkable, very terrible, that even after knowledge of the Redeemer he grasps many with his open mouth, that he pollutes them after the water of the cleansing, that after heavenly sacraments he bears them away to the depths of hell. Let it be said then, let it be said fearfully by the voice of Truth: *He will drink up a river, and not wonder: and he trusteth that Jordan may run into his mouth.* For the devil accounted it no great thing that he seized unbelievers, but he now bestirs himself with all his might to bring death to those whom he repines at seeing regenerated against him. Let no one then trust that faith without works can be sufficient for him when we know that it is written: *Faith without works is neutral.*[82] Let no one think that he has fully escaped the malicious attack of Behemoth by a mere profession of faith, because he has already taken in a river but still thirsts after Jordan; and Jordan flows into his mouth as often as any Christian lapses into iniquity. We have now escaped his mouth by the aid of faith, but we must take earnest care not to relapse by hazardous behavior. If attention in walking is neglected, it is futile to attempt keeping to the straight way by believing, because the way of faith leads indeed to the heavenly country but does not bring to a happy end those who wander off.

We have another point to consider more closely in this matter. For those represented as we said by Jordan can also be designated by "river." For they who have already acknowledged their belief in the truth but fail to live accordingly can properly be called a river because they move from a higher to a lower condition. But the Hebrew word for Jordan means "their descent." And there are some who in seeking the ways of truth abandon their own selves and come down from the pride of their old life; and when they desire eternal things, they entirely set themselves apart from this world by not only refraining from seeking the goods of others but even abandoning their own; and not only do they not seek worldly glory but they turn it down even when it is offered. This accords with what is said by the voice of Truth: *If any man will come after me, let him deny himself.*[83] For a man denies himself if, having repressed the arrogance of pride, he shows before the eyes of God that he has forsaken self. Hence the Psalmist says: *I will remember thee from the land of Jordan and Hermoniim.*[84] For Jordan, as I said, is interpreted Descent, but Hermoniim, Anathema, that is, Alienation. He therefore remembers God from the land of Jordan and of Hermoniim who by the fact that he humbles himself and becomes weaned from self is induced to remember his Creator. But the ancient enemy considers it no great happening since he holds under the rule of his tyranny those who seek after earthly things. For we know, as the prophet attests, that *his meat is dainty.*[85] Nor does he consider it astonishing if he swallows up those whom pride exalts, greed demoralizes, pleasure slackens, wickedness straitens, anger inflames, discord separates, envy embitters, lust defiles and kills. He will therefore swallow up a river and will not wonder because he judges it no great event when he devours those who, by the very pursuits of their life, run downwards. But he earnestly endeavors to lay hold of those whom he sees already united to heavenly things, having scorned the things of earth. And hence, when the river has been swallowed up, it is rightly added: *And he trusteth that Jordan may run into his mouth*, because he is intent on lurking in ambush and seizing those whom he sees casting themselves down from the glory of the present life out of love for their heavenly country. Some indeed forsake the world, abandon the vanities of transient honors, and seeking the lowliness of humility, transcend by good living the fashion of human ways and rise to such eminence of accomplishment that they indeed effectuate distinguished achievements. But because they fail to act under cover of circumspection, afflicted by the thrust of vainglory, they fall to greater ruin from on high. For hence it is that the eternal judge, who probes the secrets of the heart, foretelling the occurrence of this ruin, gives warning when he says: *Many will say to me in that day: Lord, Lord, have we not prophesied in thy name and cast out devils in thy name and done many miracles in thy name? And then will I profess unto them: I never knew you; depart from me, you that work iniquity, I know not who you are.*[86] Hence also it is said by the prophet: *The Lord called for judgment unto fire, and it will devour the great deep and will eat up a part of the house.*[87] For judgment is called for unto fire, when the sentence of justice for the punishment of eternal burning is already divulged. And it devours the great abyss because it burns up the wicked and incomprehensible minds of men which now conceal themselves from men even under the miracles of signs. But a part of the house is eaten up because gehenna devours those also who now boast, as it were, by their holy deeds of being in the number of the elect. They therefore who are here called Jordan are there called a part of the house. The ancient enemy therefore trusts that even Jordan may run into his mouth because he sometimes destroys by the deceits of his cunning even those who are thought to be chosen.

20

The devil assails more vigorously those whom he views as offering resistance

Who are ready to raise up Leviathan.[88] All they who treat with indifference worldly things and with thoughtful application seek the things that are above, raise up Leviathan against themselves because they incite his malice by their manner of life. For those who are subject to his will are in effect peacefully possessed by him and their proud ruler enjoys a kind of security while he lords it over their hearts with unshaken power. But it is no longer so when the soul of each individual is again stirred to longing for his Creator; when he forsakes the sluggishness of negligence and dispels the coldness of previous inactivity with the fire of holy love; when he recalls his inborn freedom and is ashamed to be held in bondage by his enemy. That enemy then considers himself scorned and sees that the ways of God are embraced; he repines that his captive struggles against him; he is at once fired with jealousy, at once urged on to conflict, at once stirs up countless temptations against the soul that opposes him and he spurs himself to affliction in all sorts of ways so that launching the thrusts of temptation, he may pierce the heart which he long held without disturbance. For he slept, as it were, while he remained at rest in the corrupt heart. But he is raised up by the challenge of encounter when he is bereft of his unholy despotism.

For as long as we live, our enemy is the more eager to conquer us the more he perceives that we are rebelling against him. He abstains from striking those whom he imagines that he can quietly possess. But he is stirred up more vehemently against us inasmuch as he is expelled from our hearts, supposedly his own rightful dwelling place. This tendency was, according to divine plan, foreshadowed in the person of our Lord, who did not permit the devil to tempt him until after his baptism in order to intimate what his followers' way of life was to involve: they would have to endure more acute deceits of temptation after they were making progress in the supernatural life.

Often also when we apply ourselves to the sacred writings, we more grievously endure the artifices of the evil spirits because they bestrew upon our minds the dust of earthly thoughts so that they may darken our searching eyes as they face the light of inner vision. The Psalmist had undergone this when he said: *Depart from me, ye malignant: and I will search the commandments of my God*,[89] thus clearly indicating that he could not search into the commandments of God since he was suffering in mind the snares of the evil spirits. In the history of Isaac we find such a similitude concerning the evildoing of the Philistines who filled up with earth the wells which Isaac had dug.[90] For these very same wells we ourselves dig when we penetrate the depths in the hidden meanings of holy Scripture. These wells however the Philistines secretly fill up when unclean spirits bring earthly thoughts to us as we strive toward deep truths: in effect they cut off the water of divine knowledge which has been discovered.

Therefore because complacency frequently begets negligence, to keep it from generating carelessness it is written: *Son, when thou comest to the service of God, stand in justice and in fear: and prepare thy soul for temptation*.[91] Take the case of someone who is quick to gird himself for the service of God. What else does he do but prepare for encounter with the old adversary so that set free he may take blows in the strife who, when serving in captivity under despotic power, was submissive? But in the very fact that the mind is braced to meet the enemy, that it has overcome some vices and is striving against others, at a given time it happens that something remiss is allowed to remain, nevertheless not so as to cause great injury.

And often the mind that surmounts many forcible adversities is unable to master an inner failing however slight although it may be intently on guard. This is undoubtedly the effect of divine dispensation, lest being resplendent with virtue on every count, it be lifted up with pride, so that while it sees in itself some blameworthy trifle and yet has not the power to subdue it, may never attribute the victory to itself, but to the Creator only, in those instances in which it was able to prevail.

21

Against those who resist him the devil augments his snares and means of attack

After the earth has been dug up, *he goeth forward to meet armed men.*[92] Armed enemies are unclean spirits, equipped with countless deceits against us. When they cannot foist evil works on us, they present them to our gaze under the appearance of virtues and hide themselves under varied armor lest they be seen by us in their naked wickedness. We go forward to meet these armed enemies when we catch sight of their disguises at a distance. We thus go forward after the earth has been dug up when after worldly pride has been repressed, we search out in a state of wonder the guileful tactics of unclean spirits. We go forward as cited when after fleshly wickedness has been overcome, we contend with spiritual vices. For he who as yet struggles only feebly against himself, vainly enters into conflict waged against him externally. For how does he who is subjugated by sins of the flesh refrain from those of the spirit? Or how does he seek triumph from the exertion of strife outside himself who still succumbs in the war against lust?

Again, we certainly go forward to meet armed enemies when by zealous exhortation we prevent their scheming even as it concerns the heart of someone else. For we virtually go from the place where we were to another place to meet our enemies when we put aside regular concern for ourselves and fend off evil spirits from the mind of our neighbor. Whence it is frequently the case that crafty enemies tempt the more terribly in his own regard the soldier of God who is presently the victor in his personal struggle, the more forcefully he is seen to prevail against them in another's heart as well. Their purpose in again challenging him to defend himself is that they may more freely force their way into hearts defended by his exhortation. And since they cannot overcome him, they try at least to keep him occupied so that while shaken concerning himself, not this soldier of God but he whom he had been accustomed to defend may perish. But the mind that is immovably fixed on God disdains the thrusts of temptation and does not fear unduly the spears of terror. For relying on the help of grace from above, he sees to the ills of his own weakness in such a way as not to neglect those of others.

At the same time, when the devil perceives the zeal of a holy mind opposing him and helping others, he labors to confound it with augmented temptation. Hence it frequently happens that those in authority with others subject to them endure more severe struggles with temptation so that, just as in physical warfare, when the leader himself is put to flight, the mutual support of the resisting forces may be easily sundered. Therefore the crafty enemy, seeking various injuries from his blows against the heavenly warrior, wounds him at one time by trickery with an arrow from the quiver, at another shakes a spear before his face because in fact he both conceals some vices and other defects under the guise of virtues and visibly presents others as they are. For when he sees the soldier of God in a weakened condition, then he requires no veils of deceit. But when he notices that he is firmly opposed, he then unmistakably sets up stratagems against hostile strength.

22

Ways of resisting the devil's temptations

Often our old enemy, after he has inflicted temptations, retires for a while not to put an end to the wickedness he has brought to bear but to throw people off guard and returning suddenly, to force his way in more easily. Hence it is that he returns once more to test Job, whom God—while keeping fast in his mercy—gives over to Satan, saying: *Behold, he is in thy hand; but yet save his life.*[93] God so forsakes us that he guards us, and so guards us that in our temptation he shows us our weakness.

Satan immediately went forth from the presence of God and wounded Job from the sole of his foot even to the top of his head, because when he is given leave, beginning with the least and reaching even to the nobler extremities, he distresses and penetrates almost the whole scope of the mind with temptation. But he does not infringe upon the soul because the design of our spiritual purpose resists temptations so that although enjoyment may take hold of the mind, it does not move to consent the resolve of holy uprightness. Yet, the wounds of delight are to be cleansed by the abrasiveness of penitence, and the vagaries of thought are to be made clean by the chastening of austerity.

Hence is added: *With a potsherd he scraped the corrupt matter.*[94] By potsherd is understood forcibleness of severity, and by corrupt matter, the laxness of unlawful imagination. When stricken therefore we scrape corrupt matter with a sherd when we become clean by judging ourselves harshly. Or by sherd is understood the frailness of mortality through which we clean away corrupt matter when by thinking about our mortality we wipe away the decay of vile self-gratification, but which is soon washed away if the frailty of our nature is borne in mind like a sherd in the hand.

For thoughts are not to be deemed insignificant when they do not lead to action, yet are turned over in the mind in an unlawful way. Hence our Redeemer said: *Whosoever shall look on a woman to lust after her hath already committed adultery with her in his heart.*[95] The decay therefore is wiped away when sin is not only excised from action but also from thought. Hence it is that Jerobaal when he was winnowing grain from the chaff saw the angel at whose bidding he boiled a kid and laid it upon a rock and poured out the broth thereon, which the angel touched with a rod and there arose a fire from the rock and consumed it.[96] Therefore to beat corn with a winnow is to separate the grains of virtues from the chaff of vices with accurate judgment. But to those so engaged the angel presents himself since the Lord is more ready to communicate interior truths when men free themselves from external things. And he orders a kid to be killed, that is, every appetite of the flesh to be sacrificed, and the flesh to be laid upon a rock, that is, Christ. This we do when in imitation of Christ we crucify our body. Thereon we pour the broth when in union with him we empty ourselves of carnal thoughts. These the angel touches with a rod since God's help is never wanting to our goodwill. Fire arising from the rock consumes the broth and the flesh because the broth of compunction coming from Christ sets fire to the heart so that it consumes everything in it that is unlawful in action and in thought.

23

The devil's suggestions are to be repressed with staunch disapprobation

We should be aware that it is in prosperity that the mind is generally affected by pressing temptation; yet on occasion we at the same time experience external trials and are burdened by the pressure of temptation so that scourges torture the flesh and carnal suggestion floods the mind. Appropriately then to so many physical ills of blessed Job there are still added the words of his refractory wife, who says: *Dost thou still continue in thy simplicity? Bless God and die.*[97] The refractory wife represents carnal thought provoking the mind since it often happens, as has been said above, that we are both harassed externally by affliction and wearied within by carnal suggestion. It is on this account that Jeremias laments, saying: *Abroad the sword destroyeth and at home there is death alike.*[98] The sword destroys abroad when vengeance outwardly strikes and pierces us, and at home there is the likeness of death since conscience is not free of the baseness of temptation. Hence David says: *Let them become as dust before the wind: and let the angel of the Lord straiten them.*[99] For he that is driven by the gusts of temptation in the heart is lifted up like dust in the wind; and when in the midst of these attacks the severity of God is felt, what else is it but the angel of the Lord that brings affliction?

But these adverse happenings take place differently with respect to the reprobate and the elect. The former are so tempted that they consent. The latter undergo temptations, to be sure, but they resist. The mind of the former is won over with a sense of delight although what is wrongfully suggested displeases them for a while, yet later meets with deliberate acceptance. But the latter so receive the attacks of temptation that they are vexed at having to resist unceasingly, and if at any time the mind being tempted is drawn to entertain pleasure, yet they are ashamed at delight overtaking them and reprove with strict censure everything carnal found emerging within them.

Hence it is at once rightly added: *Thou hast spoken like one of the foolish women. If we have received good things at the hand of God, why should we not receive evil?*[100] For it is proper that the holy mind should silence in itself by spiritual correction anything worldly that murmurs captiously, lest the flesh either by speaking harshly lead to impatience or by speaking enticingly reduce it to the laxity of lust. Therefore let strong censure, reproving the dictates of unlawful thinking, solidify the dissolute softness of what is base by saying: *Thou hast spoken like one of the foolish women.* And, on the other hand, let the consideration of benefits repress the discontent of bitter thought, saying: *If we have received good things at the hand of God, why should we not receive evil?*

24

Prayers and tears extinguish the flame of the devil's suggestions

His breath kindleth coals.[101] What are called coals but the minds of reprobate men, afire with earthly desires? For they are on fire when they seek after things temporal, undoubtedly because their longings, which do not permit the mind to be peaceful and sound, inflame them. The breath of Leviathan therefore kindles coals as often as his secret suggestion lures the minds of men to unlawful pleasures. For it ignites diverse minds with firebrands of pride, of envy, of lust, of avarice. For he applied the torch of pride to the mind of Eve when he prevailed upon her to spurn the words of the Lord's command. [102] He kindled the mind of Cain with the flame of envy when he was grieved at the acceptance of his brother's sacrifice and fell into the extreme crime of fratricide.[103] He inflamed the heart of Solomon with the torches of lust and overcame him with such love for women that having been led even to the worship of idols, he forgot the reverence due to his maker when he was pursuing the pleasures of the flesh.[104] He also burnt up the mind of Achab with the fire of avarice when he urged him with impatient desires to seek the vineyard of another and thus led him even to the guilt of homicide.[105] Leviathan therefore blows on the coals with a breath as great as the effort of secret suggestion with which he heatedly inclines the minds of men to what is forbidden.

Whence also it is at once added: *And a flame cometh forth out of his mouth*.[106] The flame from his mouth is indeed the very instigation of secret suggestion. For he directs words of evil persuasion to the mind of each person, but what issues from his mouth is a flame because the mind burns with desires when it is incited by his suggestions. Whatever the devil suggests is a fire by which unfruitful timber is burnt up. The fire of earthly concupiscence reaches the mind of those who have no desire to become like precious metals. Whoever therefore does not wish to suffer from the flame of his mouth should take care, according to the declaration of the teacher of truth,[107] to be found not wood, hay, stubble, but gold, silver, precious stones, because the fire of his persuasion burns the more fiercely, the more liable each one has rendered himself to yielding consent. But because a mind, placed in this corruptible flesh, is by no means allowed to be spared the heat of his persuasion, it remains for it, when singed by its malignant blasts, to have recourse unceasingly to the help of prayer. For a swell of tears quickly extinguishes the flame of his suggestions.

Accordingly, let each one of us subject himself more fully to the Lord, the more realistically he weighs the adversary's power arrayed against him. For what are we but dust? And what is he but one of the heavenly spirits, and moreover their leader? Who then can be eager for battle on his own when he, although dust, contends with the leading angel? Yet it is fitting for him who believed that he was strong when he had forsaken his Creator, to be conquered by dust, in order to learn in defeat that he failed through pride. But he roars fiercely in his rage because the depths are torturesome, because man ascends to the heights, because humanity thus lifted up abides in that loftiness from which he, great spirit that he is, lies castaway forever. But the degree of their merits altered the standing of their intellects. Thus indeed did pride deserve to be abased, humility to be exalted, to such a degree that a heavenly spirit endures hell by exalting himself and he who was of the earth through humility reigns forever above the heavens.

25

We must always be on watch against the devil's snares

All the elect so long as they are in this life do not promise themselves assurance of security. Apprehensive of temptations at all times, they fear the plottings of the hidden enemy; even if temptations cease, they are greatly disturbed by suspicion. For often rash reassurance has been for many a serious danger so that they came to know the plots of the crafty enemy not when they were tempted but when they had already been felled. So we have to be always on guard in order that the mind, constantly solicitous, may never be curbed in its heavenly intentness, abandoning watchful efforts, giving way to idle thoughts as if lying comfortably at ease, but may not be taken by surprise and exposed to dishonor when the satanic corrupter comes. Instead, the soul must always be alert for encounter with the adversary, precaution must always be taken against secret snares. For hence the prophet Habacuc says: *I will stand upon my watch.*[108] Hence again it is written: *Set thee up a watch–tower, make to thee bitterness, thou that bringest good tidings to Sion.*[109] Hence it is said by Solomon: *Blessed is the man that is always fearful: but he that is hardened in mind shall fall into evil.*[110] Hence he says again: *Every man's sword upon his thigh, because of fears in the night.*[111] The fears in the night are the hidden snares of temptation. But the sword upon the thigh is vigilant watching, repressing the enticement of the flesh. In order then that the fear by night, that is, secret and sudden temptation, may not steal upon us, it is always necessary that the sword of watching should be girded on and press our thigh. For holy men are in such a way assured concerning hope that nevertheless they are ever distrustful concerning temptation since to them it is said: *Serve the Lord with fear: and rejoice unto him with trembling,*[112] so that from hope should spring rejoicing and from distrust, trembling. In their stead the Psalmist says again: *Let my heart rejoice that it may fear thy name.*[113] Here it is to be noted that he does not say: Let it rejoice that it may be secure, but: Let it rejoice that it may fear. For they remember that although an action of theirs may be brought to a favorable issue, they are still in this life, concerning which it is said by Job himself: *The life of man upon earth is trial [a warfare].*[114] They remember again that it is written: *For the corruptible body is a load upon the soul: and the earthly habitation presseth down the mind (that museth upon many things).*[115] They remember and they fear, and they do not presume to promise themselves faultlessness in themselves, but placed between the joy of hope and the fear of temptation, they trust and they fear, they are encouraged and they waver, they are assured and they are diffident.

26

The various names of the devil according to his different evil qualities

Leviathan is interpreted their addition, referring to men and rightly so, since the devil does not refrain from adding to man's first sin which he instigated. Perhaps in reproach for that act he is called Leviathan. For by promising divinity to those in paradise he pledged himself to give something additional; while he made this promise he cleverly took away what they had. Hence the prophet uses these words: *Leviathan, the bar serpent; Leviathan, the crooked serpent.*[116] With tortuous windings he crept close to men since while he promised the impossible, he snatched away the possible. In order to indicate he is both hard and soft, the prophet calls him a bar and a serpent. For by malice he is hard, by his blandishments, soft; so he is called a bar because he strikes dead, a serpent because he softly lets deceits stream in.

For Satan is also called a lion for his cruelty, and a tiger because he is marked by stripes of disguise and by diversity of wiliness. He is likewise called ant lion, a very little creature and a foe to ants, which hides itself under the dust, kills the ants and devours them. Thus the devil, being cast out of heaven upon the earth, lying in wait for the souls of the righteous along the path of their search for sustenance in the performance of good works, kills them like ants carrying their crumbs. He is rightly called ant lion, for he is strong as a lion for those who yield to him, weak as an ant to those who resist him.

By the title North is also indicated he who constricts the hearts of sinners with the iciness of insensibility.[117]

He is also called a serpent,[118] slippery and crooked, because for the deceiving of man, he spoke through the mouth of a serpent. He is called crooked because he stood not in the uprightness of truth; slippery, because if to his first suggestion, there is no resistance, suddenly while not perceived he slips into the interior of the heart.

Evil spirits are also called foxes and birds. Foxes are very cunning animals that hide themselves in ditches and caves, and when they show themselves, they do not run in straight lines, but by twisting, circuitous ways.

As we know, birds lift themselves in the air with lofty flight. Therefore by the name foxes are denoted sly and cunning demons; by the name birds, these selfsame proud demons. Hence it is written: *The foxes have holes and the birds of the air nests; but the Son of man hath not where to lay his head.*[119] This is equivalent to saying: The deceitful and haughty demons find their dwelling in your heart, that is, the imagination of your lofty spirit, but the Son of man has not where to lay his head, that is: My humility finds no rest in your proud mind.

Denoted by the title of destruction and death are the evil spirits, who were seen to be the authors of destruction and of death, as for instance of their leader himself under the image of his emissary it is said by John: *And his name was Death,*[120] to whom all spirits of pride are subject.

By the name beast is understood the ancient enemy who cruelly sought the deception of the first man and by evilly persuading him tore the integrity of his life to pieces. Because he could not reach so far in his temptation as to injure the mind of our Redeemer, he strove for his death in the flesh. This beast undoubtedly possessed the hearts of many of the elect, but the Lamb has by his death driven him out of them. Whence also the Lord says in the Gospel: *Now shall the prince of this world be cast out.*[121] For while the Lord has, by a wonderful and righteous judgment, enlightened and accepted the confessions of the humble, he has forsaken and closed the eyes of the proud. Whence it is said to him by the Psalmist: *Thou hast appointed darkness and it is night; in it shall all the beasts of the woods go about: the young of lions roaring after their prey. and seeking their meat from God.*[122] For God in truth appoints darkness when, in passing judgment in satisfaction for sins, he withdraws the light of his wisdom. And it becomes night because the mind of wicked men is blinded with the errors of their own ignorance. In the night all the beasts of the field go about when malignant spirits, lying concealed in the darkness of deceit, enter into the hearts of the reprobate by fulfilling their evil purposes. In the night also the young of lions roar because spirits rise up with importunate temptations as the ministers of most wicked but still lofty powers. But yet they seek their food from God because doubtlessly they are unable to seize souls unless by a just judgment they are permitted by God to prevail. Here it is also fittingly added: *The sun ariseth, and they are gathered together: and they shall lie down in their dens,*[123] because, when expelled from the minds of the faithful by the light of truth at the Incarnation, they returned, as it were, to their dens when they possessed the hearts of unbelievers only.

As we have said, the devil is also called Leviathan, that is, their addition, or by another interpretation, serpent in the waters. He is called as well Behemoth, which is interpreted as monster. So too is he called a beast, a dragon, a bird. We learn more readily the meaning of his names if we accurately examine the craft of his cunning. For he comes from heaven to earth, and no longer raises himself up by any aspiring to the hope of heavenly things. He is an irrational quadruped by the inanity of his foul action, a dragon by his malice in doing harm, a bird by the levity of his subtle nature. For because he knows not what he is doing against himself, he is a monster with brute sense; because he maliciously seeks to hurt us, he is a dragon; but because he is haughtily exalted by the subtlety of his nature, he is clothed with feathers. Again, because he is in his wicked activity employed by divine power for our benefit, he is a beast; because he secretly stings, he is a serpent; but because he sometimes through his indomitable pride fancies himself to be an angel of light, he is a feathered creature. For although he harasses mankind with his baffling skill in wickedness, yet he intensely tempts by way of three vices, so that he may bring some under his power by lust, some by malice, and some by pride.

He is therefore rightly designated in what he attempts to do by the name associated with his actions when he is called a beast, a dragon or a bird. For in those whom he incites to the folly of lust, he is a beast; in those whom he inflames to do malicious injury, he is a dragon; but in those whom he exalts to the haughtiness of pride as though they knew lofty things, he is a bird. But in those whom he defiles equally with lust, malice and pride, he exists as a beast, dragon and bird at the same time. For he has worked his way into the hearts of those deluded by him in as many forms as the evils in which he entangled them. He is therefore called by the name of many things because he is changed into various kinds of forms before the eyes of those who are deceived by him. For when he tempts someone by the lust of the flesh, and yet does not overcome him, by change of suggestion the heart is fired with malice. Because therefore he could not make his approach as a monster, he draws near as a dragon. Unable to corrupt with the poison of malice, still by placing in view the person's good qualities the heart is exalted to pride. He could not therefore steal up to this man as a dragon, but yet by bringing before him the phantom of vainglory, he flew before the gaze of his thought as a bird. This winged creature is doubtlessly raised up the more cruelly against us, the less it is fettered by any weakness of its own nature.

Therefore, in order that we may be able to resist vigorously Satan's suggestions, counsels and deceptions, we must give heed to the command of the Psalmist when he enjoins us: *Take a psalm and bring hither the timbrel.*[124] In a timbrel there is dried leather so that it may resound. To take a psalm and bring a timbrel is to receive the heart's spiritual song and give back the temporal emaciating of the body. By these two things, prayer and fasting, devils are cast out,[125] with the help of the mediator of God and men, Christ Jesus, who with the Father and the Holy Spirit lives and reigns, God, for ever and ever. Amen.

BOOK 2

SIN

Prologue

In the second book of Part 1, the subject is sin, the frequent consequence of the devil's suggestions. There are actually three ways of committing sin: by thought, word and deed. Hence a suitable development of our subject matter is based on examination of these three forms of sin.

Whoever seeks a remedy for sin should have recourse to the second book of Part 2, whose subject is penitence. There he will find the remedy for the sin of thought, of word, and of deed; he will be instructed in detail concerning compunction of heart, oral confession and giving of alms.

1

The nature of sin

Sin has no underlying principle because it has no subsistence in its own proper nature. For evil has no substance. But having some sort of existence, it is syncretized with the nature of good. And although the apostle John tells us that there is no difference between iniquity and sin when he says: *Iniquity is sin*,[1] yet in the ordinary usage of speech, iniquity means something more than sin; everyone frankly acknowledges that he is a sinner, yet he is sometimes loath to call himself iniquitous. But between crime and offense there is this difference, that crime involves an even greater burden than sin, but an offense does not, because when a sacrifice is commanded to be offered under the Law, what is enjoined for a sin is the same as for an offense. And crime occurs only in deed, whereas offense commonly exists in thought. Hence it is said by the Psalmist: *Who can understand sins?*[2] Thus, works of sin are more easily identified in proportion to their visibility, but sins of thought are difficult to apprehend, in that they are committed without being seen.

There is this difference between sin and crime that all crime is sin, but not all sin is crime. And in this life there are many without crime, but no one can be without sin. And hence the holy preacher, when he was describing a man worthy of the grace of the priesthood, did not say: If any be without sin, but: *If any be without crime.*[3] Who indeed can be without sin, since John says: *If we say that we have no sin, we deceive ourselves and the truth is not in us*?[4] In this differentiation between sins and crimes, we should reflect that a number of sins defile the soul, but crimes render it lifeless. Whence blessed Job, in characterizing the crime of lust, says: *It is a fire that devoureth even to destruction,*[5] because in fact the guilt of this heinous misdeed does not simply stain to the point of defilement, but consumes to the point of destruction.

Therefore, everyone made heedful by longing for eternity who is desirous of appearing unspotted before the judge who is to come, examines himself the more thoroughly now, the more he gives thought to how he may then present himself to this terrible judge free from care; he begs to be shown wherein he offends so that he may punish that failing in himself by penance and by judging himself here may not be held accountable on judgment day.

But meanwhile we must observe what great chastisement of our pilgrimage afflicts us, who have reached such a state of blindness that we do not know our own selves. We commit evil and yet do not promptly realize it, even after it is committed. For the mind, banished from the light of truth, finds in itself nothing but darkness, and frequently sets foot in the snare of sin and does not know it.

2
Sin is committed in three ways

We must understand that sin is committed in three ways. For it is brought about either through ignorance or weakness or of set purpose. And we sin more grievously from weakness than through ignorance, but much more grievously of set purpose than from weakness. Paul had sinned from ignorance, as he said of himself: *Who before was a blasphemer and a persecutor and contumelious. But I obtained the mercy of God because I did it ignorantly in unbelief.*[6] But Peter sinned through weakness because a single statement of a servant maid impaired in him all that strength of faith which he had professed to the Lord, and with his voice he thoroughly denied the Lord to whom he remained true in his heart.[7] But because a fault of weakness or ignorance is wiped away the more easily, the less willfully it was committed, Paul amended by knowledge his deficiencies in certain matters, and Peter strengthened the root of faith, dislodged and, as it were, already withering, by watering it with his tears. But those persons sinned purposely of whom the master himself said: *If I had not come and spoken to them, they would not have sin; but now they have no excuse for their sin.*[8] And shortly thereafter: *They have both seen and hated both me and my Father.*[9] For not to do good is one thing; to hate a teacher of goodness, another. As it is one thing to sin from lack of reflection and another to sin deliberately. For a sin is often committed without reflection, which is, however, condemned after consideration and deliberation. For it frequently happens that a man through weakness loves what is right but cannot live up to it. But to sin deliberately is neither to love nor to do what is good. As it is therefore sometimes a more serious offense to love sin than to commit it, likewise it is more sinful to have hated righteousness than not to have performed it. There are some then in the Church who not only refrain from doing good but even persecute it, and who even detest in others what they themselves neglect to do. The sin of these persons is in truth committed not from weakness or ignorance, but purposely because if they indeed wished to perform good deeds and still were not able to do so, they would at least love in others what they themselves neglect. For if they were to do no more than desire these deeds themselves, they would not hate them when performed by others; but because they despise in their lives and persecute censoriously these same good deeds which they know of by report, it is rightly said: *Who on purpose have revolted from him.*[10]

Whence also it is rightly added: *And would not understand all his ways,*[11] because often they reject even knowledge of those things whose practice they disdain. For since it is written: *That servant who knew not the will of his lord and did things worthy of stripes shall be beaten with few stripes, and that servant who knew the will of his lord and did not according to his will, shall be beaten with many stripes,*[12] they consider that ignorance assures them of impunity for sinning. But they are deprived of sight by the night of pride alone and therefore do not discern that it is one thing to be ignorant, another to have refused to learn. For not to know is ignorance; to have refused to learn, pride. And they are so much the more without excuse for not knowing, the more what they should know is presented to them even against their will.

3

Sin is committed in the heart in four ways, by action in four ways

Sin is committed in the heart in four ways, and in four ways it is carried out by action. For in the heart it is committed by suggestion, pleasure, consent, and boldness of self–defense. Now suggestion comes to pass through the enemy; pleasure, through the flesh; consent, through the spirit; boldness of self–defense, through pride. For the cause of fault, which ought to terrify the mind, exalts it, and in throwing down uplifts, but by uplifting casts down more grievously. And hence that uprightness of the first man our old enemy dashed down by these four blows. For the serpent tempted, Eve was pleased, Adam yielded consent and even when interrogated refused through boldness to confess his sin. In the human race this process is daily carried on because what was set in motion by the first parent of our race has become familiar. The serpent tempted because the hidden enemy secretly suggests evil to man's heart. Eve was pleased because worldly inclination, in response to the serpent, soon gives itself up to pleasure. But in fact Adam, set above the woman, agreed with her because while the flesh is attracted to enjoyment, the spirit also being under pressure bends down from its uprightness. And Adam, when interrogated, would not confess his sin since to the extent that the spirit is by committing sin cut off from truth, it becomes the more perversely obdurate in the temerity of its downfall. In these four ways sin is also carried out in action. For first the fault occurs in secret, but afterwards it is displayed before men's eyes without the shame of guilt; next it even develops into a habit and finally, either by the delusions of false hope or the stubbornness of despair, it gains full strength.

The secret fault in the mind is therefore born of suggestion; but when pleasure is present, it is not ashamed to appear openly. Hence the prophet says: *And they have proclaimed abroad their sin as Sodom, and they have not hid it.*[13] For when the sinner is not disturbed by his wickedness, he is even strengthened in it by the supports of most pernicious habit. But while the sin has begun to turn into habit, he surely feeds himself either with the false hope of divine mercy or with the open wretchedness of despair, so that he is the less likely ever to be brought to amendment, the more he either inordinately conjures up his merciful Creator or is inordinately fearful over what he has done. A deterioration of this state of mind takes place since the tongue of many like him adds support: those who extol with their praise even evil deeds are numerous; whence it comes about that the fault grows continually, nourished by approbation. Moreover, the injury that is perceived as praiseworthy goes unattended. Hence it is well said by Solomon: *My son, if sinners shall entice thee, consent not to them.*[14] For sinners entice when they either offer by their allurements wicked acts to be done or extol them by marks of favor when they are done. Is he not enticed of whom the Psalmist says: *For the sinner is praised in the desires of his soul: and the unjust man is blessed?*[15]

It should be known that the first three ways of being sinners as they are listed are more easily corrected, but the fourth is amended with greater difficulty. And hence our Savior brings back to life a girl in her home, a young man outside the gate, Lazarus in addition from the grave. For the one who sins in secret is as yet lying dead in the house. He is already being carried outside the gate whose iniquity is done openly, even to the shame of commission in public. But he is weighed down by the burial mound who in the commission of sin is burdened with the sufferance of habit. But all these in mercy the Lord restores to life since frequently divine grace illumines with the light of its favor those who are dead not only in secret sins but likewise in open evildoings and those who are burdened with the heavy mass of evil habit. But from a disciple's report our Savior knows indeed of a fourth dead person and he does not raise him to life since it is extremely difficult for a person, whom after continuance in a bad habit the tongues of flatterers also enthrall, to be released from the death of the soul. Of such a person it is justly said: *Let the dead bury their dead.*[16] For the dead bury the dead as often as sinners heap approval on sinners. For what else is it to sin but to lie down in death? But they who honor the sinner with their approbation bury the deceased under the funeral pile of their words. Now Lazarus too was dead, yet he was not buried by the dead. For believing women had laid him under the ground, and they also made his death known to the giver of life. Hence he at once came back to the light, for when the soul is dead in sin, it is sooner brought back to life if kept in prayerful remembrance by the living. But sometimes, as has been said above, false hope does not carry off the soul but a more destructive despair pierces it; while this cuts off all hope of pardon, it feeds the soul with the enticement of error to a greater degree.

4

Unless every sin is quickly wiped away, it either begets another sin or is the punishment of another sin

Every sin which is not soon wiped out by penitence is either a sin and a cause of sin, or a sin and the punishment of sin. For a sin that penitence does not before long remove leads on by its own gravity to another.

This virtual seed of error Paul had clearly detected in the unbelieving and vacillating when he said: *When they knew God they have not glorified him as God or given thanks, but became vain in their thoughts.*[17] But he immediately sets down what sprang up from this seed of error, saying: *Wherefore God gave them up to the desires of their heart unto uncleanness; to dishonor their own bodies among themselves.*[18]

The subsequent pit of sins is covered over by the fault of former sin so that he who knowingly commits sin may afterwards justly lapse, even unexpectedly, into other sins. For since almighty God grants time for penitence, which human malice nevertheless misuses for the practice of its iniquity, our guilt is doubtlessly permitted to increase by the just judgment of God in order that it may be accumulated to be struck eventually a greater blow. For hence Paul says again of certain persons: *To fill up their sins always.*[19] Hence it is said to John by the voice of an angel: *He that hurteth, let him hurt still; and he that is filthy, let him be filthy still.*[20] Hence David says: *Add thou iniquity upon their iniquity: and let them not come into thy justice.*[21] Hence again it is said of the Lord by the same psalmist: *... through visitations by evil angels, he made a way for a path to his anger.*[22] For the Lord justly permits the heart that has been weighed down by former demerits to be deceived also by the subsequent persuasions of evil spirits, for when it is deservedly led into sin, its guilt is augmented in its punishment. For a way is broader than a path. But to make out of a path a way to his anger is by strictly judging to extend the causes of his anger so that they who refused when enlightened to act rightly, may when justly blinded still so act as to deserve to be punished in a higher degree. Hence it is said by Moses: *For as yet the iniquities of the Amorrhites are not at the full.*[23]

But frequently one and the same sin is also a sin that is both a punishment and a cause of sin. We shall make this more clear by citing examples. For instance, unrestrained gluttony excites the fullness of flesh to the heat of lust. But lust, when committed, is often concealed by perjury or murder lest it should be punished by the intervention of human laws. Let us suppose that a man has given free rein to his gluttony, that overcome by his gluttony he has committed the sin of adultery, that being detected in adultery he has secretly murdered the husband of the adulteress lest he should be brought to judgment. This adultery, then, placed between gluttony and murder, springing from the one and giving rise to the other, is a sin and both the punishment of the preceding sin and the cause of the following sin.

Concerning this matter it is also written: *He hath torn me with wound upon wound.*[24] In her weak members holy Church is torn with wound upon wound when sin is added to sin so that transgression piles up beyond measure. Thus for him whom avarice forces to robbery and robbery leads into deceit so that the sin committed is further defended by falsehood, what else has happened to this man but that he is torn with wound upon wound? Whence also it is well said by the prophet: *Cursing and lying and killing and theft and adultery have over-flowed; and blood hath touched blood.*[25] For by the word blood sin is usually denoted. Hence one who longs to be set free from sin cries out in penitence: *Deliver me from blood.*[26] So blood has touched blood when sin is piled upon sin.

5

Sins of thought

His eyes are upon the ways of men: and he considereth all their steps.[27] The mind approaches in a way by so many steps nearer to God as it profits from that many holy inspirations. And, on the other hand, it departs so many steps farther from him as it deteriorates by that many evil thoughts. Whence it happens that while thought does not show itself, yet the sin is already performed by reason of the very guilt of the thought, as it is written: *Hand in hand, the wicked shall not be innocent.*[28] This is as much as to say: When the hand rests from sinful deeds, yet the evil man, by reason of his thoughts, is not innocent. Because, then, we know that not merely our actions, but even our thoughts are strictly weighed, what shall we incur from proceeding to wicked action, if God judges so exactly the progression of the heart? Mark that no man witnesses the secret vagaries of our mind, and yet in the sight of God we are taking so many steps as we actuate that many desires. We are delinquent in his eyes as often as we waver from the straight path by the instrumentality of unstable thought. For unless this constant flow of our minds swelled in his sight, he would not indeed exclaim through the prophet: *Take away the evil of your devices from my eyes.*[29] But speaking thus he attests that he cannot endure, as it were, the force of our secret wickedness. This cannot be hidden from him because surely everything unlawful which is conceived in secret by us is thrust offensively before his sight. But it is written: *All things are naked and open to his eyes.*[30]

6

Sins of thought may be grave although no deed is involved

If I have sinned and thou hast spared me for an hour: why dost thou not suffer me to be clean from my iniquity?[31] The Lord spares the sinner for an hour when he does away with the guilt of sin as soon as tears have been granted. But he does not suffer us to be clean from our iniquity since we indeed freely committed sin, but sometimes against our will we sustain the remembrance of it with a sense of pleasure. For often what has been dismissed from the sight of the judge when tears occur, returns to mind and the conquered fault tries to insinuate itself again for the pleasure it affords and is engaged again in the former contest with revived attack so that what it once did in the body, it may afterwards activate in the mind by persistent thought. Whence the prophet says: *My sores are putrified and corrupted because of my foolishness.*[32] For sores to grow corrupt is for healed wounds of sin again to involve themselves in temptation and at their suggestions, after the skin of penitence has grown over, to experience the fetidness and pain of sin again. In this process nothing is done outwardly; sin is committed inwardly by thought alone, and the soul is placed under a tight binding of guilt if it is not removed by concerned lamentation.

Whence it is well said by Moses: *If there be among you any man that is defiled in a dream by night, he shall go forth out of the camp, and shall not return before he be washed with water in the evening; and after sunset he shall return into the camp.*[33] For the dream by night is the secret temptation through which by dark thought something shameful is conceived in the heart that is not fulfilled in bodily deed. But he who is defiled through a dream by night is commanded

to go forth out of the camp because it is proper that he who is defiled with impure thought should look upon himself as unworthy of association with any of
the faithful. In the evening he is washed with water when, seeing his offense,
he is changed over to tears of penitence. Then after being washed he returns
at sunset who after tears of penitence, the flame of unlawful thought dying
down, is restored to expectation of friendly regard by the faithful.

7

Idle thoughts destroy peacefulness

What is more troublesome in this life than to seethe with earthly desires?
Or what is here and now more full of repose than not to long for anything in
this world? Hence it is that the Israelite people received the keeping of the
Sabbath as a gift; it is hence on the contrary that Egypt was afflicted with a
multitude of flies. For the people that follows God receives the Sabbath, that
is, rest of the spirit so that it would not be worn out in this life by any craving of
carnal desires. But Egypt, which is likened to this world, is afflicted with flies.
For the fly is an exceedingly intrusive and restless creature. By it what else is
represented but relentless troubles of carnal desires? Whence it is said elsewhere: *Dying flies spoil the sweetness of the ointment*,[34] because superfluous
thoughts, which in the mind oppressed by things carnal are constantly both
springing into life and dying away, destroy that sweetness with which each individual has been inwardly anointed by the Spirit because they do not permit him
to enjoy it to the full. Egypt therefore is afflicted with flies because the hearts
of those who love earthly life are stricken with the disquietudes of their desires
and are overwhelmed by the hordes of carnal thoughts, so that they cannot be
lifted up to the desire of interior rest. Hence when truth comes to the heart
with the singular help of its fidelity, it first banishes the seething of carnal
thoughts and afterwards bestows virtuous gifts. This is clearly suggested by the
sacred Gospel story of the ruler's daughter: asked to revive her, the Lord
came, and then it is written: *And when the multitude was put forth, he went in and
took her by the hand. And the maid arose.*[35] So the crowd is put forth in order
that the maid may be raised up, because if the importunate multitude of worldly cares is not first expelled from the inner recesses of the heart, the soul that
lies dead within cannot arise. For while it is distraught with countless imaginings of earthly desires, it does not focus attention on matters that concern its
own well–being.

8

Through the eyes we are drawn to unlawful thoughts and through consent are bound by sinful pleasure

And if my eye hath followed my heart.[36] By keeping inward strength an effort must be made to train the external faculties so that if the heart should happen to covet something forbidden, the eye being restrained by the control of discipline may refuse to look at it. For as temptation is often brought on through the eyes, so sometimes being conceived inwardly it forces the eyes to support it outwardly. Thus frequently an object is considered with an innocent mind but by physical view the mind is pierced by the sword of concupiscence. For David did not look purposely at the wife of Urias because he had entertained desire for her, but rather he lusted after her because he beheld her incautiously.[37] But it happens by the test of fitting retribution that he who uses the external eye carelessly is not unjustly made blind in the interior eye. But often concupiscence is domineering within, and the mind being seduced, after the manner of a despot requires the bodily senses to serve its wants and obliges the eye to serve its pleasures, and so to speak, opens the window of light to the dark of blindness. Hence holy men, when they feel themselves besieged by sinister enjoyment, with the control of discipline restrict the eyes themselves by which a likeness of any kind enters the mind, lest the enticing sight should minister to perverse thought. If this tactful custody of the eyes is ever neglected, uncleanness of thought is soon transformed into action.

Thus care should be taken by us because we must not look at what is not to be coveted lest we give thought to lasciviousness. For indeed the image once fixed in the heart by means of the eye is with difficulty dispelled by the power of great effort. So our eyes provide a kind of ravishment unto sin. Eve would not have touched the forbidden tree if she had not first looked incautiously at it. Hence with the voice of Judaea the prophet says: *My eye hath wasted my soul.*[38] For by coveting things visible, through the bodily eye invisible virtues were lost.

On the other hand, blessed Job restrained his eyes by the strength of wisdom. For he says: *I made a covenant with my eyes, that I would not so much as think upon a virgin.*[39] For he knew that lust has to be checked in the heart, he knew by the gift of the Holy Spirit that our Redeemer at his coming would go beyond the precepts of the Law and take away from his elect not only lust of the flesh but also of the heart, saying: *It is written: Thou shalt not commit adultery. But I say to you that whosoever shall look on a woman to lust after her, hath already committed adultery with her in his heart.*[40] For by Moses is condemned

lust committed, but by the author of purity, lust visualized. For hence it is that
Peter says to the disciples: *Wherefore, having girt up the loins of your mind, being
sober, trust perfectly in the grace which is offered to you.*[41] For to gird up the loins
of the flesh is to prevent lust from taking place, but to gird up the loins of the
mind is to shut it out from thought. Hence it is that the angel who addresses
John is described as being girt above the breasts with a golden girdle.[42] For
because the purity of the New Testament curbs lust of the heart as well, the
angel who appeared in it came girt at the breast. A golden girdle rightly binds
him because whoever is a citizen of the heavenly country does not now forsake
impurity from fear of punishment but from longing for charity.

But at this point it should be noted that it is one thing which the mind
encounters from temptation of the flesh, and another when through consent it
is fettered by gratifications. For very often it is beset by wrong thinking and
resists, but frequently when it conceives anything wrong, it turns this over
within itself to the point of desire. And certainly impure thought does not at
all defile the mind when it strikes but when the mind is subdued by way of the
inducement of pleasure. Hence Paul says: *Let no temptation take hold on you,
but such as is human.*[43] For that is human temptation by which we are very
often affected in thought even against our will, because in order that even
things forbidden sometimes come to mind, it is indeed enough to be susceptible to this occurrence from the burden of human nature, subject to corruption.
But beyond that it is devilish and not human temptation, when to that which
the corruptibility of the flesh suggests, the mind attaches itself by consent.
Hence again Paul says: *Let not sin reign in your mortal body.*[44] For he forbade
not that sin should be, but that it should reign, in our mortal body, because in
flesh as subject to corruption it may not reign, but cannot help but be. For the
mortal body simply to be tempted with regard to sin is sin, because so long as
we live, we are not perfectly and in every way without sin; since sacred teaching
could not wholly eliminate sin, reign over the dwelling-place of our heart was
denied it so that unlawful longing, though it very often enters as a thief into our
good thoughts, should not even if it gains entrance, exercise dominion.

<h2 style="text-align:center">9</h2>

We are afflicted with unlawful thoughts when we are freely engaged in worldly pursuits

Noteworthy is the fact that the reason we are sometimes distressed by the
onslaught of unlawful thoughts is that we freely engage in certain worldly pursuits. And hence the priest of the Law is enjoined to consume with fire the
limbs of the victim cut into pieces, the heart and the parts about the liver, but

the entrails and the feet are first to be washed with water.[45] We also offer our own selves as a sacrifice to God when we dedicate our lives to his service. We set the parts of the sacrifice cut into pieces upon the fire when we offer up the deeds of our lives differentiated according to the virtues. The head and the parts contained about the liver we burn when in our faculty of sense, whereby all the body is controlled, and in our hidden desires we are kindled with the flame of divine love. And yet it is ordered that the feet and the entrails of the victim be washed with water. For with the feet the earth is touched, and in the entrails excrements are carried, since frequently even now we are afire with the desire for eternity, already with a full sense of devotion we are eager in longing for our death; but whereas by reason of our frailty there is still something worldly about our work, even some of the forbidden things which we have already subdued, we foster in our hearts. And while unclean temptation defiles our thoughts, what else is this but the carrying of excrement by the entrails of the victim? But that they may be fit to be burned, let them be washed since it is necessary that tears of fear wash unclean thoughts which love from on high consumes in receiving the sacrifice. And whatever burdens the mind, proceeding either from ineffective resistance or from the remembrance of former practice, is to be washed so that it may burn so much the more pleasingly in the sight of its examiner, the less—when it shall begin to enter his presence—it sets upon the altar of its prayer along with itself anything earthly, anything impure.

10

Those who do not know how to control their thoughts are in a way subservient to the devil as their controller

Let his strength be wasted with famine: and let hunger invade his ribs.[46] It is the practice of the just to express a wish for what is to happen not in a spirit of cursing but of foreseeing. Thus every man, because he consists of soul and body, is as it were made up of strength and weakness. So man's weakness is understood to be his frail body; his strength, his rational soul that resists by reason the attacks of vice. This strength is wasted by famine because the soul of the unrighteous is not refreshed by interior food. Of this hunger it is said through the prophet: *I will send forth a famine into the land; not a famine of bread, or a thirst of water, but of hearing the word of the Lord.*[47] The senses of the mind, however, are designated by the ribs, for as the ribs encase the inmost parts of the body, so do the senses of the mind protect hidden thoughts. Therefore hunger invades the ribs when all spiritual refreshment being removed, the senses of the mind fail and cannot either rule or guard its thoughts. Hence it happens that when thoughts are dispersed, the mind being deceived strives after exterior glory and is pleased with nothing except the external beauty it has seen.

However, a rich man might have wealth and glory without guilt if he had been willing to possess them with humility. But he is made lofty by possessions, puffed up by honors, disdains the rest of the world and places his life's whole hope and trust in the mere abundance of possessions. Hence a certain rich man said: *Soul, thou hast much goods laid up for many years; take thy rest, eat, drink, make good cheer.*[48] When God beholds these thoughts, he strips him of this trust. Hence it is added: *Let his confidence be rooted out of his tabernacle: and let destruction tread upon him as a king.*[49] The tabernacle of the wicked is this world; death designates the devil, who brought in death, or for that matter, sin, by which the reprobate are drawn along to death. Thus his confidence is rooted out of the earth when each perverse person, who in this life had provided for himself many goods according to his desire, is overthrown by sudden death, and destruction treads upon him like a king because he is either degraded here by evil habits, or at the time of his death, when he is carried by the devil to punishment, he is brought under the power of the demon.

11

Evil thoughts through which the devil dwells in the heart of the unrighteous beget evil deeds

When the opportunity of committing sin is not available to the unrighteous, thoughts of desire are not absent from their hearts. And since they always follow the devil in what they do, they strongly pledge themselves to him in thought as well. And so there is first sin in thought and afterwards in action. Whence it is said to the daughter of Babylon: *Come down, sit in the dust, O virgin daughter of Babylon, sit on the ground.*[50] For whereas dust is always earth, earth is not always dust. What then are we to understand by dust but thoughts which, while they persistently and silently fly up in the mind, blind its eyes? And what is denoted by the earth but an earthly action? And because the mind of the reprobate is first cast down to evil by thought and afterwards by action, to the daughter of Babylon who was lowered by the judgment of inner uprightness, it is rightly said in a denouncing sentence that first she should sit in the dust and afterwards on the ground because unless she had bowed down to evil in thought, she would never have remained attached to it in practice.

Next the text reads: *Let the companions of him that is not dwell in his tabernacle.*[51] This is to say that in his mind apostate angels shall have their dwelling place along with most wicked thoughts, which are in fact the companions of him who for this reason no longer is because he has renounced the supreme essence and on that account is by a decadence spreading day after day actually tending not to be, in that he once fell away from him who truly is. He is moreover rightly said not to be since he has lost well–being, though he has not lost the essence of his nature.

Still, further educing the thoughts of the unrighteous in greater detail, the text declares: *Let brimstone be sprinkled in his tent.*[52] Brimstone or sulfur so feeds the fire that it emits the most fetid odor. By brimstone we understand carnal sin. While it fills the mind with wicked thoughts that are like foul vapors, it is preparing everlasting fires for the soul. Hence the Lord is said to have rained down fire and brimstone upon Sodom,[53] to mark out the stain of her guilt by the very character of her punishment. And so this sulfur is sprinkled upon the habitation of the wicked man as often as the corrupt pleasure of the flesh rules his soul.

Whereas evil thoughts unceasingly occupy him and prevent his bringing forth the fruit of good works, it is rightly added: *Let his roots be dried up beneath: and his harvest destroyed above.*[54] By roots which lie out of sight and bring forth a sprout into open view are designated thoughts: while they are not seen in the heart, they produce visible works. Therefore when the unrighteous man sets his thoughts on things below and neglects to seek the delights of everlasting verdure, he lets his roots be dried up beneath. The harvest is work in the open field, which indeed is destroyed above since all activity by the wicked is of no account in God's judgment although it may seem good to men.

12

Vigilant care of thoughts is to be taken so that they may be without reproach before God, to whose eyes all things are exposed and manifest

No one can judge how many evils we commit every moment by the irregular processes of our thought. For it is easy to avoid deeds of wickedness but very difficult to free the heart from unlawful thoughts. And yet it is written: *Woe to you that devise that which is unprofitable.*[55] And again: *In the day when God shall judge the secrets of men,*[56] after prefacing: *Their thoughts between themselves accusing or also defending one another.*[57] And again: *With deceitful lips and a double heart have they spoken.*[58] And again: *For in your heart you work iniquity in the earth.*[59] Consequently, since against our will it works its way into our mind, we must carefully consider how much guilt attaches to an evil thought in the eyes of God.

Indeed, our more profound and simplest thoughts are open to the eyes of God. *For*, as it is written, *all things are naked and open to his eyes*.[60] And often there is fear of appearing irregular before the eyes of men in what we do, and in the realm of thought we are not afraid of the regard of the one who sees all things without being seen. For we are much more visible inwardly to the eye of God than we are outwardly to men. And hence all holy persons practice outward and inward circumspection and fear to seem either outwardly reprehensible or inwardly and secretly blameworthy. Hence it is that the living creatures which are seen by the prophet are recorded to be full of eyes round about and within.[61] For he who regulates his outward aspects respectably but disregards the inward, has eyes round about but not within. But all who are holy, because they at once view their exterior ways on all sides that they may provide good examples in themselves to their brethren, and watchfully give attention to their interior ways because they are preparing themselves to be irreproachable before the probing eye of the internal judge, are described as having eyes both round about and within. And to please God, even more do they set in order their internal affairs, as is said by the Psalmist of holy Church: *All the glory of the king's daughter is within*.[62] But because she keeps her outward features also irreproachable, he justly added concerning her: *In golden borders, clothed round about with varieties*,[63] so that she should be at once beautiful to herself within and to others exteriorly, both enhancing herself by interior glory and instructing others by the exterior example of deeds.

13
Evil deeds cannot be curtailed if guilt abides in thought

If thou wilt put away from thee the iniquity that is in thy hand, and let not injustice remain in thy tabernacle: then mayst thou lift up thy face without spot; and thou shall be steadfast, and shall not fear.[64] Every sin is either committed in thought alone, or it is done in thought and deed together. Therefore iniquity in the hand is guilt in deed, but injustice in the tabernacle is iniquity in the mind. For our mind is not unfittingly called a tabernacle, in which we are hidden within ourselves when we are not seen in outward demeanor. For first the text urges that iniquity be removed from the hand, and afterwards that injustice be cut off from the tabernacle; for whoever has already cut away from himself external wicked deeds surely must in recovering his senses examine himself shrewdly in the purpose of his heart lest sin of which he rid himself in act still endure in thought. Hence too it is well said by Solomon: *Prepare thy work without, and diligently till thy ground, that afterward thou mayst build thy house*.[65] For what is it when the work is prepared, to till the ground with care exteriorly, if not—the briars of iniquity having been removed—to cultivate our enterprise unto bearing of fruit? And after the tilling of the ground, what else does returning to build our house show than that we very often learn from good deeds how much purity of life we should build up in our thoughts? For almost all good deeds come from thought, but there are some fine points of thought which proceed from action; for as the deed is derived from the mind, so on the other hand the mind is instructed by the deed. For the soul that is instilled with the beginnings of divine love prescribes things which should be done, but after the deeds so prescribed have started to be accomplished, the soul—being instructed by its own actions—learns how little it saw when it began to prescribe good deeds. Thus the ground is tilled externally so that the house may afterwards be built. For very often we learn from outward activity how much refinement of righteousness we should maintain in our hearts. For the mind can never be fully raised aloft in thought when it still goes astray in deed.

If we thoroughly cleanse these two (*iniquity in the hand, injustice in the tabernacle*), we then at once lift our face without spot to God. For the soul is the inner face of man by which we are recognized so that we may be regarded with love by our Creator. Now to lift up this face is to raise the soul to God by prayerful observances. But there is a spot that mars the uplifted face when consciousness of its own guilt accuses the aspiring mind, for it is at once severed from all hopeful confidence if when absorbed in prayer it be wracked by recollection of sin not yet overcome. For it loses hope in being able to obtain what it longs for, truly aware of its still refusing to do what it has been told from above. Hence it is said by John: *If our heart does not reprehend us, we have confidence towards God. And whatsoever we shall ask, we shall receive of him.*[66] Hence Solomon says: *He that turneth away his ears from hearing the law, his prayer shall be an abomination.*[67] For our heart blames us in prayer when it recalls that it resists the precepts of the one whom it implores, and the prayer becomes an abomination when there is a turning away from the instruction of the law, since it is surely fitting that anyone should be excluded from the favors of the one to whose commands he will not be subject.

14

Sins of speech

Shall not he that speaketh much hear also? Or shall a man full of talk be justified?[68] The impudent are accustomed to contradict routinely what others have correctly stated, lest—if they assent to the statements—they should seem of less importance. By such persons the words of the righteous, however few have been voiced, are judged great in amount since to the extent that the hearers' evil habits are impugned, they are oppressive to their ears. Whence that is even considered a crime which by proper assertion is uttered against crimes. Job indeed had expressed firm and truthful opinions; Sophar reproving him in the text given above calls him verbose, because whereas wisdom reprimands faults by the mouth of the righteous, it sounds like excessive volubility to the ears of the foolish. For wrongheaded men deem nothing right but what they themselves think, and they consider the words of the righteous worthless in the degree that they find them at variance with their own notions. And yet Sophar did not put forth a deceptive pronouncement that a man full of talk shall not be justified, because while anyone overflows with words, forfeiting the gravity of silence, he lessens watchfulness of mind. For hence it is written: *And the service of justice (shall be) quietness.*[69] Hence Solomon says: *As a city that lieth open and is not compassed with walls, so is a man that cannot refrain his own spirit in speaking.*[70] Hence he says again: *In the multitude of words there shall not want sin.*[71] Hence the Psalmist bears witness, saying: *A man full of tongue shall not be established in the earth.*[72] But the power of a true statement is diminished when it is not delivered under the safeguard of discretion. Thus it is that a man full of talk shall not be justified. But a good thing is not well said should no attention be given to the person being addressed. For a true declaration against the wicked, if it is aimed at the virtue of the good, loses its own virtue and rebounds with blunted force in proportion to the firmness of what it strikes.

But the wicked cannot hear good words with patience, and when they neglect the amending of their life, they ready themselves with words of refutation. The uninstructed mind therefore is severely irritated by statements of truth and considers silence to be a punishment; it judges all that is said aright to be disparagement and mockery of itself, for when the voice of truth is directed to the ears of evil men, guilt impinges on the mind. By the rebuking of vices, in proportion as the mind is affected by consciousness within, it is stirred up to the desire of open denial. It cannot bear the voice, because being nettled in the wound of its guilt, it suffers pain, and by what is said against the wicked in general, it suspects that it is itself attacked in a special manner. For what it inwardly remembers having done, it is ashamed to hear publicly mentioned. Thereupon it prepares itself for defense so that it may cover the shame of its guilt by words of pernicious denial. For as the righteous, concerning certain things which have been done unrighteously by them, consider the voice of correction to be the ministry of charity, so the recalcitrant think of it as the affront of mockery. The former immediately prostrate themselves in obedience, the latter are lifted up to the madness of self–defense. Hence Truth says by Solomon in praise of the righteous man: *Teach a just man, and he shall make haste to receive it.*[73] Hence he looks down upon the obstinacy of the wicked, saying: *He that teacheth a scorner doth an injury to himself.*[74] For it usually happens that when they cannot defend the evils that are reproved in them, they become worse from a feeling of shame, and are so haughty in their defense of themselves that they seek out faults disparaging the life of the reprover, and so they do not regard themselves as guilty, but they even charge others with guilty deeds. When they are unable to find real ones, they pretend that they themselves also share what they may seem to rebuke with even-handed justice.

15
Four ways of speaking / Those who curse

Everything that is said can according to its character be placed in one of four categories: bad things said badly; good things, well; bad things, well; good things, badly. A bad thing is badly said when wrong advice is given, as it is written: *Bless (= Curse) God, and die.*[75] A good thing is well said when realities are properly stated, as John says: *Do penance; for the kingdom of heaven is at hand.*[76] A bad thing is well said when a fault is mentioned by the speaker simply to be reproved, as Paul says: *Their women have changed the natural use into that use which is against nature.*[77] In the same passage he mentioned also detestable bad deeds of men,[78] but he related these unseemly things in a seemly way so that by telling of unbecoming things, he might recall many to behavior that is becoming. But a good thing is badly said when what is proper is mentioned with an improper purpose, as the Pharisees are reported to have said to the blind man who had received his sight: *Be thou his disciple.*[79] For they certainly said this for the purpose of reviling him, not as advocating what they said. Or as Caiphas says: *It is expedient that one man should die for the people and that the whole nation perish not.*[80] It was a good thing that he said, but not with a good purpose, for while he sought the cruelty of Christ's death, he prophesied the grace of redemption.

However, it is to be noted that he sins gravely who asks for that to be done by God which he himself either could not do at all or if he could, it would by no means be proper. For when individuals beset an enemy with curses, what else do they wish God to do in his regard but that which they are either unable or ashamed to do themselves? In fact, for that enemy they wish death, which even if they can, they are afraid to bring upon him lest they should either be convicted of murder or appear wicked even when they are. What then is it to say to God: *Kill the man whom I hate*, if not to cry out to him in plain words: Do that to my enemy which it is not proper for me to do to him, sinner though he be? We must therefore keep in mind that it is written: *Bless, and curse not*;[81] and again: *Not rendering evil for evil, nor railing for railing.*[82]

But it is the merit of complete eminence to endure adversities bravely externally, and mercifully internally. In addition there are some shortcomings in the life of communities that cannot be corrected faultlessly by the reprover, and as a result when they either taint the one who corrects them or do not thoroughly hinder the one who is responsible for them, with great acuity of judgment they should be disregarded, and by thus going unnoticed, be tolerated. When we are affected by these defects, they are more quickly dismissed from our hearts if we discern our own misdemeanors against our neighbors. Whence it is said by Solomon: *Do not apply thy heart to all words that are spoken: lest perhaps thou hear thy servant reviling thee. For thy conscience knoweth that thou also hast often spoken evil of others.*[83] For insofar as we reflect on what we have been toward others, we are the less aggrieved that others are the same toward us, because the injustice of another punishes in us what our conscience itself justly reproves.

16

Two ways of cursing

Holy Scripture makes mention of cursing in two ways, namely one which it approves, another which it condemns. For a curse is pronounced one way by the judgment of justice, in another way by the malice of revenge. Thus a curse was pronounced by the decision of justice upon the first man himself when he committed sin and heard the words: *Cursed is the earth in thy work.*[84] A curse is pronounced by the decision of justice when it is said to Abraham: *I will curse them that curse thee.*[85] Again, because a curse may be uttered not by decision of justice but by the malice of revenge, we are admonished by the voice of the apostle Paul in his preaching when he says: *Bless, and curse not*;[86] and again; *Nor shall railers possess the kingdom of God.*[87] God therefore is said to curse, and yet man is forbidden to curse because what man does from the malice of revenge, God does only in the exercise and power of justice. But when holy men pronounce a sentence of cursing, they do not burst forth therein from the wish of revenge but from the exactness of justice. For they consider God's accurate judgment within, and they realize that they must strike evils which spring forth openly with a curse; and they are guilty of no sin in cursing inasmuch as they do not diverge from interior judgment. It is hence that Peter cast the sentence of a curse upon Simon who offered him money, saying: *May thy money perish with thee.*[88] For he who said *may* showed that he spoke this not in the indicative but in the optative mood. Hence Elias said to the two captains of fifty that came to him: *If I be a man of God, let fire come down from heaven, and consume thee.*[89] And upon how reasonable a base of truth the sentence of each one was grounded, the outcome of the case demonstrated. For both Simon perished in eternal ruin and the two captains of fifty were consumed by fire descending from above. Thus the ensuing decisiveness discloses with what mind the sentence of a curse is pronounced. For when both the innocence of the one who curses remains, and he that is cursed is thereby dispatched to utter destruction, from the termination of each case we infer that the sentence is taken up and ratified by the sole judge of what is within.

It should be noted, however, that David, who to those that rendered him evil, did not render it in turn, when Saul and Jonathan fell in war, curses the mountains of Gelboe in the following words: *Ye mountains of Gelboe, let neither dew, nor rain come upon you,* and so on.[90] For the mountains of Gelboe for this reason are cursed that while no fruit is produced from the parched land, the possessors of the land might be stricken with the damage of that barrenness, so that they might themselves receive the sentence of the curse who had deserved as the just retribution of their iniquity to have the death of the king visited upon them.

Similarly, Jeremias the prophet, since he saw his preaching obstructed by the obstinacy of his hearers, issued a curse, saying: *Cursed be the man that brought the tidings to my father, saying: A man child is born to thee.*[91] Therefore, because these words are to all outward appearances at variance with reason, as are the words of David given above, the literal sense already shows that in these words the holy man is not speaking literally; devoid of human reason outwardly, it is full of greater mystery within. The mutability of man, which came as deserved punishment, is signified by the person of the changeable prophet, but by his father, this earth from which we spring. That man who brings the tidings of our birth to our father is the old enemy who, when he sees us agitated in our thoughts, prompts the minds of evil persons, having preeminence according to the pattern of this world, to influence us deceitfully. And when he has seen us perform acts of weakness, commends these with applause as brave, and tells as it were of male children when he rejoices that we have been corrupters of the truth by lying. He gives tidings to the father that a man child is born when he shows the world the one whom he has influenced, turned into a corrupter of innocence. For when it is said to anyone committing a sin or acting proudly: You have acted like a man, what else is this but reporting that a man child is born in the world? Justly then is the man cursed who brings tidings of the birth of a man child, because by his tidings the depraved joy of our corrupter is indicated.

17
Two kinds of expressions that are very harmful to human beings

There are two types of speech which are very troublesome and harmful to mankind, the one which seeks to praise even improper things, the other which strives always to chide even virtuous ones. The former is carried downward with the stream, the latter tries to close off the channels and riverbed of truth. Fear represses the one, pride upraises the other. The one endeavors to obtain favor by applause; anger, tò be displayed in rivalry, disquiets the other. The one cowers openly, the other is in constant ferment from opposition. Therefore, blessed Job reproaches his friends for being of this second type when he says: *You dress up speeches only to rebuke*.[92] But he at once indicated how the temerity of unjust censure is adopted, when he added: *And you utter words to the wind*.[93] For to utter words to the wind is to talk idly. For often when the tongue is not restrained from idle words, free rein is also given to the rashness of foolish reproof. For it is by certain steps in its decline that the indolent soul is thrown into the pitfall. Thus while we neglect guarding against idle words, we are brought to harmful ones, so that it first affords pleasure to speak of the affairs of others, and afterwards the tongue by detraction berates the life of those it talks about and sometimes even breaks out into open insults. Hence provocations are sown, quarrels arise, flames of hatred are kindled, peace of heart is totally destroyed. Hence it is well said by Solomon: *The beginning of quarrels is as when one letteth out water*.[94] For to let out water is to let loose the tongue in a flood of words. On the other hand, Solomon speaks in a positive way, saying: *Words from the mouth of a man are as deep waters*.[95] The beginning of quarrels is as when one lets out water, for he who fails to hold his tongue disrupts harmony. Hence it is conversely written: *He that putteth a fool to silence appeaseth anger*.[96]

But that everyone subject to much talking cannot maintain uprightness of justice the prophet testifies, who says: *A man full of tongue shall not be established in the earth*.[97] Hence again Solomon says: *In the multitude of words there shall not want sin*.[98] Hence Isaias says: *The service of justice (shall be) quietness*,[99] thus pointing out that justice of mind is devastated when we do not refrain from immoderate talking. Hence James says: *If any man think himself to be religious, not bridling his tongue but deceiving his own heart, this man's religion is vain*.[100] Hence he says again: *Let every man be swift to hear, but slow to speak*.[101] Hence he again adds: *The tongue (is) an unquiet evil, full of deadly poison*.[102]

Hence Truth warns us in his own words, saying: *Every idle word that men shall speak, they shall render an account for it in the day of judgment.*[103] For an idle word is that which lacks either cause of just necessity or intention of dutiful usefulness. If then an account is to be rendered for idle speech, it is very earnestly to be considered what punishment follows after that loquaciousness wherein we sin even by words of pride.

18

Idle speech is offset by holy men through good deeds

I will lay my hand upon my mouth.[104] In the usage of Holy Scripture, it is customary for work to be understood by hand, speech by the mouth. Therefore to lay the hand upon the mouth is by the virtue of a good deed to cover over the faults of unguarded speech. But can anyone, however unexcelled, be found who does not sin by idle words? Witness the words of James: *Be ye not many masters, for in many things we all offend.*[105] And again: *The tongue no man can tame.*[106] And Truth himself, reproving faults of the tongue: *But I say unto you that every idle word that men shall speak, they shall render an account for it in the day of judgment.*[107] But holy men take care to offset before the eyes of God the faults of the tongue by the merits of their life; they strive to bury their lack of moderation in words by the weight of good works. Whence in holy Church the hand is laid upon the mouth when in her elect the fault of idle speech is daily covered by the virtue of good actions. For it is written: *Blessed are they whose iniquities are forgiven: and whose sins are covered.*[108] But since it is again written: *All things are naked and open to his eyes,*[109] how can things be covered that can never be hidden from the eyes of him to whom all things are naked? But since what we conceal we place lower, and in order to cover that which is placed beneath surely superimpose that with which we cover it, we are said to cover our sins, which in effect we place beneath when we renounce them; and we draw something else over them when we choose afterwards for this purpose to manifest the work of good deeds. He therefore who abandons his former evil deeds and afterwards does good works, by this increment covers his past iniquity, over which he spreads the merits of good deeds.

19

Lying

All falsehood is iniquity, and all iniquity falsehood, because whatever is at variance with the truth surely conflicts with uprightness. But sometimes it is worse to ponder falsehood than to speak it. For speaking frequently results

from hastiness, but pondering from intentional sin. And who could be unaware by what great difference the sin is marked whether a man lies hastily or
deliberately? But Job in order to adhere completely to the truth, declares that
he would neither contrive lying nor let it escape his lips.[110] For all lying is with
great care to be guarded against, although sometimes there may be a manner
of lying which is of less gravity if a man should lie to be of service to another.
But because it is written: *The mouth that belieth killeth the soul*,[111] and: *Thou
wilt destroy all that speak a lie*,[112] this kind of lying those who are disciplined
also avoid with the greatest care so that not even the life of anyone should by
their falsehood be protected, lest they harm their own soul while they strive to
benefit another's earthly life, although this particular kind of sin we believe to
be very easily remitted. For if any sin is to be pardoned by subsequent good
works, how much more easily is that cleared away which is accompanied by
compassion, the mother of good works?

But there are some who from the deceit of the midwives try to maintain
that this species of lying is not sin, chiefly because, when those women lied, it is
written: *That the Lord built them houses*.[113] By this way of recompensing it is
more truly known what the offense of lying merits. For the reward of their
kindness which could have been paid them in eternal life, on account of the
associated sin of lying is reduced to an earthly recompense so that in their own
life, which they wished to protect by lying, they should receive in turn the good
which they did, and not have any reward of their service to which they might
look forward thereafter. For although the matter is being carefully weighed
with subtle distinctions, it was from love of the present life they lied, not with a
view to the reward. For by the act of sparing, they tried to protect the life of the
infants; by the act of lying, their own life.

And although in the Old Testament a few such cases may be found, the
careful reader will never find there this or a similar kind of lying practiced by
those who were disciplined, although the lie might seem to have the likeness of
truth; and perhaps it might be a slighter offense under the Old Testament
wherein with victims of bulls and goats the sacrifice was not truth itself but a
shadowing of the truth. For in the New Testament, after incarnate Truth has
been manifested, we advance to higher precepts; and it is proper that certain
actions which among the chosen race were of service to a shadow of the truth,
we should abandon. But if anyone wishes to defend his lying by the Old Testament, because there for certain persons it was less harmful, he must say that
the theft of another's property and the retaliation for an injury, which were
there allowed to the weak, cannot be injurious to himself. It is clear to every-

one with what great censure Truth reproaches all these actions; having become incarnate, his foreshadowing left in the past, he instructs us in these matters.

20

How much those who tell lies must labor

Tribulation shall terrify him, and distress shall surround him, as a king that is prepared for battle.[114] In all that the wicked man does, he is surrounded with tribulation and distress because his soul is confused with disturbance and mistrust. A man secretly desires to seize another's goods by force and he works things out in his mind so that he may not be found out. Another man, abandoning truth, decides to tell a lie so that he may deceive the mind of those who hear him. But what great labor it is to watch carefully that his falsehood may not be found out! For he pictures to himself what answer may be made to him by those who know the truth, and with great deliberation he considers how by the speciousness of falsehood he may surmount the proofs of truth. He covers himself on all sides, and against that wherein he might have been detected, he casts about for an answer resembling truth, whereas if he were willing to tell the truth, he surely could have done so without trouble. For the way of truth is smooth, and the road of falsehood toilsome. And hence it is said by the prophet: *For they have taught their tongue to speak lies, they have labored to commit iniquity.*[115] Therefore it is well said: *Tribulation shalt terrify him and distress shalt surround him, as a king that is prepared for battle*, because within himself he is wearied by fretfulness of mind who forsakes truth, the companion of security. And he is rightfully compared to a king prepared for battle, because in the very evil he does he is terrified and hurries on, he trembles from remorse and pants from desire, he is apprehensive and is prideful, he quakes with misgivings and lifts up his spirit through boldness; he is surrounded with distress as a king that is prepared for battle because false in what he does, false in what he says, he is afraid lest he lose his own soldiers, that is, the pretensions of falsehood, and be exposed to the shafts of truth if he happens to lack a counterstroke of falsehood.

21

Flattery

God forbid that I should judge you to be just: till I die I will not depart from my innocence.[116] He departs from his innocence who thinks highly of the unrighteous, as Solomon attests in saying: *He that justifieth the wicked, and he that condemneth the just, even both are abominable before God.*[117] For there are some who, while they extol with praise men's evil deeds, aid the growth of what they ought to have reproved. For hence it is said by the prophet: *Woe to those that sew cushions under every elbow, and make pillows for the heads of persons of every age.*[118] For a cushion is put in place to provide comfortable rest. Therefore whoever flatters those acting wrongfully places a pillow under the head or the elbow of a reclining person, so that the one that should have been reproached on account of sin, being supported in it by commendation, may rest comfortably. Hence again it is written: *And the people built up a wall: and they daubed it.*[119] For by the term wall the rigidity of sin is denoted. And so to build up a wall is for someone to raise against himself obstacles of sin. But they daub the wall who flatter those who commit sins so that what the latter build by acting wickedly, the former by flattery embellish.

Those who engage in flattery are designated by the name locusts, as it is written: *Wilt thou lift him up like the locusts?*[120] Locusts at various times signified the Jewish people, the converted gentiles, by way of a parable the resurrection of the Lord, holy preachers, the tongue of those who flatter.

By locusts are designated the Jews, as it is written of John: *He ate locusts and wild honey.*[121] John indeed points out Christ, who assimilates into his own body wild honey, that is the gentiles, and locusts, that is, in part, the Jews. The latter, however, as locusts, took leaps when they promised they would fulfill God's commands. But quickly departing from these, they fell to earth. By locusts paganism is also signified, as is attested by Solomon, who says: *The almond tree shall flourish, the locust shall be made fat, the caper tree shall be destroyed.*[122] By the almond, which flowers before all other trees, are indicated the beginnings of the Church at whose preaching the locust, that is, barren paganism, is made fat and imbued by the dew of heavenly grace. The caper tree is destroyed because Judaea, remaining in its barrenness, lost the due order of proper living. By the locust is also designated Christ in his resurrection. Whence it is also said by the prophet: *I am shaken off as locusts.*[123] Beset by his persecutors even unto death, wrested from their hands by the upsurging of a sudden resurrection, he escaped. Holy preachers are likewise called locusts: they take their stance in the active life and by their wings they raise themselves aloft to the contemplative life.

By the word locust the tongue of the flatterer is expressed, a fact which the plagues of Egypt, dispatched from heaven, attest; they were evils once inflicted corporally as required by the offenses of the Egyptians, but they signified spiritually the evils which afflict on a daily basis the souls of the wicked. For it is written: *The burning wind raised the locusts: and they came up over the whole land of Egypt: and they covered the whole face of the earth, wasting all things. And the grass of the earth was devoured, and what fruits soever were on the trees.*[124] For Egypt was affected by these plagues so that shaken by them and grieving over the external affliction, it might consider what devastating losses it was enduring by inward neglect, and while it perceived insignificant yet highly cherished things externally perishing, it might also understand through their guise the more severe punishments it had suffered within. But what are indicated by the symbol of locusts—which damage men's agricultural products more than any other insects—but the tongues of flatterers, who corrupt the mind of earthly men whenever they observe them performing any good works by praising them excessively? For the fruit of the Egyptians is the activity of the vainglorious that locusts destroy when flattering tongues incline the heart of the one who does good works to seek transitory commendations. But the locusts devour the grass when flatterers extol as well the words of speakers. They devour also the fruits of trees when by empty praise they weaken even the actions of those already viewed as strong.

22

Those who delight in praise and flattery

His bread in his belly shall be turned into the gall of asps within him.[125] That bread in the belly signifies the fullness of earthly gratification in the mind. So, if the unrighteous is filled now with the praise given him, if he takes delight in honors, his bread in his belly shall be turned into the gall of asps within him because the fullness of transitory enjoyment will in the final retribution be turned into bitterness: what was here believed to be the praise of glory is known to have been the gall of asps, that is, the seduction of evil spirits. For the wicked then see that they are poisoned with the venom of the old serpent when, being delivered over to avenging flames, they are tormented along with their seducer. And so this bread has one taste in the mouth but another in the belly because the joy of transitory pleasure is sweet while it is savored here in a way by chewing, but it turns bitter in the belly because when the joy is passed, it is swallowed with punishing effect.

Or at least because bread is not unsuitably interpreted as the understanding of holy Scripture, which refreshes the soul and supplies it with resources for proper action, the hypocrite generally endeavors to be well instructed in the mysteries of the sacred writings—not that he may live by them, but that it may appear to the rest of the world how learned he is—his bread in his belly is turned into the gall of asps within him because while he boasts of knowledge of the sacred law, he changes the beverage of life into a cup of poison for himself and dies reprobate from the same source whence he seemed to draw instruction unto life. Nor is what follows unfittingly taken to be the meaning of the words of our text: sometimes the hypocrite, while he applies himself to the word of doctrine for vain display, being blinded by divine judgment, understands in a wrong sense that very word he examines with a wrong motive. But when he falls into heretical error, it is his lot that as by the gall of asps, so does this unfortunate person perish by bread; and in his learning he finds death because in the words of life he does not seek life.

23

Detraction

Why do you persecute me as God, and glut yourselves with my flesh?[126] God is a just persecutor, as it is written of him: *The one that in private detracted his neighbor, him did I persecute.*[127] But the evil persecutor is he who is inflamed not with the ardor of purifying but with the torches of envy. When men therefore assail the weakness of others in the spirit of discipline, let them be mindful of their own frailty and thus exercise forbearance toward others, knowing that they themselves stand in need of discipline. Otherwise they punish in the way only God can, as if they were without failings.

But it is well added: *And glut yourselves with my flesh?* It must be remembered that those who feed on detraction of a neighbor surely glut themselves with the flesh of another. Whence it is said by Solomon: *Be not in the feasts of great drinkers, nor in their revelings, who contribute flesh to eat.*[128] For to contribute flesh to eat is in the language of detractors to tell in turn the shortcomings of neighbors. Concerning the punishment of detractors there is added this text: *Because they that give themselves to drinking and that club together shall be consumed: and drowsiness shall be clothed with rags.*[129] They are given to drinking who become intoxicated with reproach of another's life. But to club together is—in the same way that each individual is accustomed to contribute food to be eaten as his share—in the conversation of detraction to contribute words. But they that are given to drinking and that club together shall be consumed because, as it is written: *Every detractor shall be rooted out.*[130] But drowsiness shall be clothed with rags because death finds despised and wanting in good works the one whom the sluggishness of his detraction took hold of here for seeking out the misdemeanors of another's life.

Yet there are some who, though they from inner hunger restore themselves by the word of God, though they already sustain themselves against the temptations of the body by the virtue of continency, yet still fear to be struck by human aspersions, and often while they dread the thrusts of the tongue, they choke themselves with the noose of sin.

And hence it is added: *Thou shalt be hidden from the scourge of the tongue.*[131] The scourge of the tongue is the reproach of affront that is rendered. They strike the righteous with the scourge of the tongue who persecute their words by jeering. For often the tongue, while it taunts, diverts someone from a good deed, and thrusts itself out like a scourge to lacerate the person of the fainthearted. The scourge of the tongue the prophet had seen lying in wait for the upright soul when, promising heavenly aid, he said: *He hath delivered me from the snare of the hunters: and from the sharp word.*[132] For hunters seek nothing other than flesh. But we are delivered from the snare of the hunters and from the sharp word, when we overcome by disdaining them the snare of carnal persons and the insults of those who scoff. For their words are sharp that are directed against our righteous ways. And to escape the sharpness of words is to trample underfoot the mockings of detractors by disregarding them. The holy soul then is hidden from the scourge of the tongue because while in this world it does not seek the honor of applause, neither does it feel the insults of detraction.

24

Mockery and evil suasion

Would that the unrighteous, while scorning to be changed for the better, did unworthy things in such a way as not to proffer them for others to do! Would that their own death alone were enough for them and that by their poisonous influence they did not destroy another's life as well! For they are resentful that others are what they are not, they are distressed that others attain what they lose. For if by chance they see any good originating in the acts of others, they quickly root them out with the force of destructive reproachfulness. Whence it is written: *And they ate grass and barks of trees.*[133]

For what is denoted by grass but the delicate emerging life of those who are starting out well, and what by the barks of trees, but the external works of those who already seek the sublime? For evil men, when they see those beginning aright, either by deriding or as if counseling them, act in opposition to them. But when they consider that certain persons are already progressing to the highest things, they draw those persons away from some of their works because they cannot fully offset their advancements. Thus for them to eat grass and the bark of trees is by poisonous influence as by a malicious ravening to nullify the aims of those beginning aright or the progress of those reaching for the heights after the manner of trees. The reprobate eat grass when by scoffing they consume the beginnings of the weak. They also eat the bark of trees when with the force of evil counsel they tear away from the life of those growing rightly the protection of good deeds. Now the latter they strip like trees in certain areas, but the former, which like grass they uproot while despising them, they consume as what they tread upon. The strength of some already rising on high they demolish in part, but the tender growth of some still lowly placed they utterly destroy.

But at times some are treated with derision for their good works and repulsed by insults, withdraw inwardly and establish themselves the more firmly in God as they find no place of rest elsewhere. All hope is fixed in God and amid mocking abuse only inner esteem is sought. And the soul becomes a neighbor to God in proportion to its being alien to human esteem; at once it pours itself out in prayer and pressed down by external force, it is refined with greater purity to penetrate all that is within. But there are some who are both weighed down by human expressions of mockery and yet may not be heard by God. For when derision directed to sin springs up, no virtuous merit accrues to the subject of such mockery. For the priests of Baal calling out to him with loud voices were mocked by Elias when he said: *Cry with a louder voice; for he is a god, and perhaps he is talking, or is in an inn.*[134] But this mocking was not the occasion of virtue because it came about by the just deserts of sin.

25

Deceitful lips

For when evil shall be sweet in his mouth, he will hide it under his tongue.[135] Evil is sweet in the mouth of the wicked because iniquity is sweet in his thought. For the mouth of the heart is thought, of which it is written: *With deceitful lips and with a double heart have they spoken.*[136] But this evil that is sweet in the mouth of the wicked is hidden under his tongue because the harshness of malice, which lies concealed in the mind, is covered by the veil of inoffensive speech. For the evil would be on the tongue and not under it if the wicked person in speaking disclosed the ill will of his perversity. On the other hand, when most of the righteous see persons acting badly who should be dealt harsh rebukes, they put harshness on the tongue, but under the tongue hide their beneficence of mind. Whence it is said to holy Church by the voice of the spouse: *Honey and milk are under thy tongue.*[137] For they that are unwilling to reveal the mildness of their attitude toward the weak, but in speaking censure them with a degree of harshness—and yet among their harsh words intersperse a trace of suavity—these persons clearly have sweetness not on the tongue but under it, because along with harsh words which they utter, they voice some that are gentle and softened, whereby the afflicted mind may be cheered by kindness. In like manner, some of the wicked, because they have evil not upon the tongue but under it, in their words put forth mild things and in their thoughts are forming adverse manifestations. For it is hence that Joab held the chin of Amasa with his right hand, but secretly putting his left hand to his sword, he shed out his bowels.[138] For to hold the chin with the right hand is to caress as if benevolently. But he puts his left hand to his sword who in secret strikes malevolently. Hence again it is written concerning their leader himself: *Under his tongue are labor and sorrow.*[139] For he that does not openly display the harm that he has in mind does not put forth with the tongue the labor and sorrow of those whose destruction he seeks, but keeps them under the tongue.

26

Deceitful speech and evil deeds

They gnawed in solitude.[140] Sometimes interior solitude is taken to be the virtue of contemplation. But in this text, where solitude is denounced, the reference is to the absence of goodness. And hence under the figure of Judaea, Jeremias mourns over the soul of the sinner, saying: *How doth the city sit solitary that was full of people!*[141] But when it said by blessed Job concerning evildoers: *They gnawed in solitude*, it is instructive to look at what is said by the Psalmist: *His enemies shall lick the ground.*[142]

For there are two kinds of men who gratify their own ambition, namely, one that always makes use of blandishments of the tongue to serve avarice, another that turns to robbery by open force. For we gnaw when we wear away anything outwardly by great exertion. But the tongue is passed over what cannot easily be eaten: it is tasted by the softness of the tongue being pressed upon it. All persons then who—even under pretense of faith, living wickedly, seek another's possessions but are not able to seize what they long for—try by flattering words and, as it were, by charming sweetness to appropriate the things coveted, what else is this but to lick the ground? Because the earthly things that they cannot take by force, they strive to make their own by the softness of the tongue. As for those who are supported in this world by power of any kind—and coveting the holdings of others, disdain indeed to gain them by deceit because they are still able by unjust strength to fulfill their wishes—what they long for, these persons do not lick but gnaw: they undermine the life of their neighbors by the forcibleness of power as by the crunch of teeth.

27

God does not pass over random thoughts nor trifling words

Doth not he consider my ways, and number all my steps?[143] By the term ways Job designates ways of acting. Thus it is said by Jeremias: *Make your ways and your doings good.*[144] But by the word steps we understand either the motions of minds or the advancements of merit. By these steps indeed Truth calls us to himself, saying: *Come to me, all you that labor and are burdened.*[145] For the Lord tells us to come to him not surely by the steps of the body, but by the advances of the heart. For he himself says: *The hour cometh, when you shall neither on this mountain, nor in Jerusalem, adore the Father.*[146] And a little later: *The true adorers shall adore the Father in spirit and in truth. For the Father also seeketh such to adore him.*[147] He implies therefore that the steps are in the heart when he both calls us that we should come and yet declares that it is not by motion of the body that we pass to other things. But the Lord so considers the ways of each one and so numbers all his steps that by his judgment not even the most minute thoughts or the slightest words, which have become trifling for us by frequent use, remain unexamined. For hence he says: *Whosoever is angry with his brother shall be in danger of the judgment. And whosoever shall say to his brother, Raca, shall be in danger of the council. And whosoever shall say, Thou fool, shall be in danger of hell fire.*[148] Raca in Hebrew speech is an interjection, which indeed shows the mind of one who is angry, but does not constitute a precise word of anger. Thus anger without utterance is first reproved, then anger with utterance but not yet formed by an exact word; and finally anger is also reproved which is filled out together with vocal emission by verbal completeness. And it is to be noted the Lord asserts that by anger one is in danger of judgment; by an expression of anger, Raca, in danger of the council; by a full declaration, Thou fool, in danger of hell fire. For by the degrees of offense, the character of the sentence increased, because in the judgment the case is still under examination, in the council however the sentence of the case is now defined, but in the fire of hell the sentence that emanates from the council is decreed. And therefore because the Lord numbers all the steps of human actions with exact consideration, unexpressed anger is assigned to the judgment; anger that is expressed, to the council; anger made explicit in speech, to hell fire. This exactness of God's consideration the prophet had beheld when he said: *O most mighty, great, and powerful: the Lord of hosts is thy name. Great in counsel and incomprehensible in thought: whose eyes are open upon all the ways of the children of Adam to render unto every one according to his ways and according to the fruit of his devices.*[149]

Thus the Lord considers those ways with careful analysis so that in each one of us he should neither overlook those good qualities he should reward, nor leave without rebuke the evil ones that obviously displease him. For hence it is that the angel of the church of Pergamus he at the same time praises in some matters and in others rebukes, saying: *I know where thou dwellest, where the seat of Satan is. And thou holdest fast my name and hast not denied my faith.*[150] And shortly thereafter: *But I have against thee a few things; because thou hast there them that hold the doctrine of Balaam.*[151] Hence it is said to the angel of the church of Thyatira: *I know thy works and thy faith and thy charity and thy ministry and thy patience and thy last works, which are more than the former. But I have against thee a few things; because thou sufferest the woman Jezabel, who calleth herself a prophetess, to teach and to seduce my servants, to commit fornication, and to eat of things sacrificed to idols.*[152] Notice that he mentions good things and yet does not let go without penance evil things that need to be corrected because indeed he so considers the ways of each one and so takes account of his steps, numbering them, that by exact judgment he thoroughly determines both how far each one is advancing to what is good, or how far, by turning aside to evil, he may impede his advances. For the increase of merits which is heightened by the aims of a good life, is very often held back by the intermingling of evil, and the good that the mind builds up by some things it accomplishes, it tears down by other destructive means. Whence holy men put greater restraint upon their thoughts the greater awareness they have of being more strictly examined by the heavenly judge. For they examine their thinking, they seek to discover if they have fallen short in any way so that they may become the less blameworthy to that judge the more they blame themselves day by day without ceasing. And yet on this account they do not already take for granted the joys of security because they realize they are observed by him who sees in them things which they are not themselves able to see.

28

The reticence of the good and the verboseness of the proud

But who can withhold the words he hath conceived?[153] There are three kinds of men, differing from one another in qualities exercised in varying degrees. For there are some who conceive evil things to say and do not restrain themselves in speech by any calm intervals of silence. And there are others who, whereas they conceive evil things, restrict themselves by strong control of silence. And there are some, made strong by the exercise of virtue, who have advanced to such an eminent degree that, in the matter of speech, they do not even conceive any evil thoughts in the heart that they need to restrain by keeping silent. But good men in general check hastiness of speech with the rein of counsel, and they take careful thought lest, in giving way to looseness of the tongue, they should by heedless speech offend their hearer's sensitivities. Hence it is well said by Solomon: *The beginnings of quarrels is as when one letteth out water.*[154] For water is let out when the flowing of the tongue is set free. And he that lets out water gives rise to the beginnings of quarrels because through an unrestrained tongue the commencement of discord is initiated. Thus, as the wicked are capricious in mind, so they are impetuous in speech and fail to keep silent, carefully weighing what they should say. And what a fitful mind conceives, a more fitful tongue straightway articulates.

For the proud man, the more influential he is in this life relinquishes the more rashly control of his tongue, making thoughtless remarks of every sort, sparing no one his words, directing insults to some, casting greater abuse upon others. But sometimes he gets carried away in blasphemy against his Creator, as it is said by the Psalmist of such persons: *They have set their mouth against heaven: and their tongue hath passed through the earth.*[155] And hence the rich man, being buried in hell, begs to have drops of water placed on his tongue by the finger of Lazarus.[156] From this narration we learn that the faculties with which a man has sinned most are those that burn more vehemently.

29

Silence and when silence should be ended

All proud men seek not to possess knowledge but to display it. Against this tendency Moses well says: *The vessel that hath no cover, nor binding over it, shall be unclean.*[157] For the protection of the covering or the binding is the reproof of disciplinary silence: everyone who is not kept in check by it is rejected as an unclean and defiled vessel.

But it frequently happens that wise men, when they decide that they are not heeded, enjoin silence on their lips. But generally when they see that the sins of the wicked gain strength when they are silent and refrain from criticism, they experience a kind of inner compulsion, so that they burst forth in language of open reproof. And hence when the prophet Jeremias had imposed on himself silence in preaching, saying: *I will not make mention of him, nor speak any more in his name,* he immediately added: *And there came in my heart as a burning fire, shut up in my bones: and I was wearied, not being able to bear it. For I have heard the reproaches of many.*[158] For because he had seen that he was not listened to, he sought silence; but when he beheld evils increasing, he did not persist in that silence. For when he ceased to speak publicly from being weary of speaking, he maintained a flame kindled within him by the zeal of charity.

For the hearts of the just are stirred up when they behold the unreproved deeds of the wicked increase, and they believe that they are themselves partakers in the guilt of those whom they allow by their own silence to grow in iniquity. The prophet David, after he had imposed silence on himself, saying: *I have set a guard to my mouth, when the sinner stood against me; I was dumb, and was humbled, and kept silence from good things,*[159] in the midst of his silence glowed with this zeal of charity when he immediately added: *And my sorrow was renewed. My heart grew hot within me: and in my meditation a fire shall flame out.*[160] His heart grew hot within him because the flame of charity was reluctant to emit words of admonition. The fire burned in the meditation of his heart because disapprobation of the evildoers did not find expression in fiery reproof. For the zeal of charity in gaining strength tempers itself with worthy consolation when it issues forth in words of reproach against the deeds of the wicked in order that it may not cease to reprove what it cannot reform lest it be judged a participant by tacit approval of evildoing.

30

We must consider with great discretion when we must be silent or speak out

You dress up speeches only to rebuke: and you utter words to the wind.[161] We should know that when we are restrained from speaking by excess of fear, we are sometimes confined more than is necessary within the barriers of silence; and while we incautiously avoid faults of the tongue, we are secretly involved in worse lapses. For often while we are immoderately restricted in speech, we engage in a lengthy and unwholesome inner monologue so that thoughts seethe all the more in the mind, the more harsh keeping of indiscreet silence afflicts them. And commonly the more copiously these thoughts spill forth, the more immune they are considered to be since they are not apparent to critics. Whence the mind is sometimes lifted up in pride and regards as weak those persons whom it hears speaking; and when it closes the mouth, it is unaware to what degree it exposes itself to evil by being proud. For it represses the tongue, but it lets the heart soar; and whereas through negligence it never gives heed to itself, it censures all others more freely as it does so more secretly. But for the most part unduly silent people, when they undergo any injustices, enter into more bitter grief the less they have to say about what they are enduring. For if the tongue spoke with composure of the troubles inflicted, grief would escape from consciousness. For closed wounds are more painful: when purulent matter that festers within is discharged, the source of pain is susceptible to treatment. Generally while overly silent men view the offenses of others and yet force the tongue to be silent, they are, as it were, withholding the use of medication after wounds have been discovered. And these become fatal when speech that could release the poison is disallowed. And hence if immoderate silence were not at fault, the prophet would not say: *Woe is me, because I have held my peace.*[162]

Under these circumstances, what is incumbent on us if not to see that the tongue is earnestly kept under strict but balanced control, not relentlessly chained, lest either being let loose, it do us a disservice, or being bound up, it be sluggish in rendering service? For hence it is said by Sirach: *A wise man will hold his peace till he see opportunity,*[163] so that when he considers it opportune, strictness of silence being put aside, by speaking such things as are fitting, he may devote himself to serving a useful purpose. Hence Solomon says: *A time to keep silence, and a time to speak.*[164] To be sure, the times for an interchange are to be weighed with discretion, lest either when the tongue ought to be restrained, it be loosened for unavailing words, or when it can speak to good purpose, it idly withhold itself. This need the Psalmist considered and phrased in a brief petition, saying: *Set a watch, O Lord, before my mouth: and a door round about my lips*[165] For a door is opened and is closed. He then who prayed not that a barrier should be set to his lips, but a door, clearly showed that the tongue ought both to be restrained by self-control, and loosened in case of necessity, so that the voice should open the discreet mouth at the proper time, and on the other hand, silence should on occasion fittingly close it.

Concerning this circumspection it is written: *And lay your finger on your mouth.*[166] The finger signifies discretion since by the finger we tell things apart. Whence the Psalmist says: *Blessed be the Lord my God, who teacheth my hands to fight, and my fingers to war,*[167] by the hands denoting engagement, and by the fingers, discretion. And so the finger is laid on the mouth when the tongue is bridled by discretion so that by what it says, it may not lapse into the folly of sin.

31

Sins of evildoing

The sword is drawn out, and cometh forth from its scabbard, and glittereth in his bitterness.[168] While the wicked man devises snares for plundering his neighbors and in his mind plots evil deeds, he is like the sword still in its scabbard; but when he wickedly executes the evil he has contrived, the sword is drawn forth from its sheath: he too comes to light from the concealment of his thoughts by the wickedness of evildoing. He is shown in action such as he was, hidden in thought. And observe that the text reads: *It is drawn out and cometh forth from its scabbard*, that is, drawn out by Satan but coming forth by the act of the evildoer's own free will. For he that is drawn doubtlessly follows the one that draws him; but he that comes forth is seen acting according to his own will. He then who is both drawn to wicked practices by the old enemy and also is fettered in the desire of them by his own free will, is described as drawn out and coming forth from his scabbard since this thing which proceeded from evil thought to extreme action is attributed both to the wickedness of the one that prompted and of the one that consented by his own will.

The fearfulness of this power is further shown when it is immediately added: *And glittereth in his bitterness.* Lightning, for example, when it comes suddenly from above, when it glitters fearfully before our eyes, displays dazzling brightness, and strikes what stands in its way. Thus it is, certainly, with the wicked man when he has arrogated to himself the glory of the present life: by the same source of his appearing bright with power in the present world, it comes about that he is ultimately struck down. For the wicked man to be, as it were, effulgent is to be radiant in worldly esteem. But because the splendor of that glory is consigned to the eternal punishments of hell, he is already rightly said to glitter in his bitterness. For he that now delights in striking with fearfulness and brightness, as a result afterwards undergoes punishments forever. And indeed it is written of a certain rich man that he feasted splendidly every day.[169] Now it is one thing to show splendor and another to be fulminating, for sometimes there is splendor without striking, but splendor with striking is expressed by the term lightning. He then who being placed in power harms others is not inappropriately referred to as lightning because just as he is raised up against good persons by a sort of glorified light, so is the life of those persons tormented through his instrumentality.

And because the unrighteous know what they should do and disdain such action,[170] of them it is written: *To him, therefore, who knoweth to do good, and doth it not, to him it is sin.*[171] And again: *Let them go down alive into hell.*[172] Those are alive that are aware of the things that are done to them. For the dead neither perceive nor are they aware. And so it is customary for the dead to represent persons that know not, but the living, those that know. Therefore to go down alive into hell is for persons to sin knowingly and consciously.

32

Evildoers run against God with neck raised up

There are some persons who by the just judgment of God are permitted to carry out with worse wickedness that which they wickedly desire to do in opposition to God. Then, while malice inflames and power strengthens them, they are all the more incapable of self–knowledge in their waywardness because in the affluence of worldly goods, they are always powerfully being drawn out of themselves. Concerning their state of mind it is said: *For he hath stretched forth his hand against God, and has strengthened himself against the almighty.*[173] To stretch forth the hand against God is to persevere in evildoing, with contempt for the judgments of God. And because the wrath of God then increases when he allows that to be fulfilled which ought not even to have been conceived in thought, the wicked man is strengthened against the almighty since he is permitted to prosper in his wicked conduct, so that he both does evil things and yet lives in happiness. Of him it is further added: *He hath run against him with his neck raised up.*[174]

To run against God with neck raised up is to commit boldly acts that are displeasing to the Creator. Of the one so acting it is rightly said: *He hath run,* that is, in doing evil he met with no hindrance from adversity. Concerning him it is still further added: *And he is armed with a fat neck.*[175] A fat neck is wealthy pride, which plentiful riches support as with layers of flesh. And so the powerful evildoer is armed against God with a fat neck since, puffed up with temporal possessions against the precepts of truth, he is propped up as by an abundance of flesh. For what is poverty but a sort of leanness, and what is abundance of provisions but the fatness of the present life, an existence which, although the worldly cherish it with full craving, they cannot long depend on? For certainly however many days on earth are granted them, they are, as it were, advancing by so many steps toward their end; they indeed project to great length their pleasurable desires, but suddenly are brought down to the confines of hell. For because even that which is drawn out by the greatest longevity imaginable, if it is brought to an end, is not really long, those wretched persons learn from its ending the brevity of what was not in their permanent keeping.

But they would live prudently if, considering the shortness of the present life, they looked not to the enjoyment but to the termination of it, and thus inferred that what offers passing delight amounts to nothing. For hence it is said by Solomon: *If a man live many years, and have rejoiced in them all, he must remember the darksome time, and the many days: which, when they shall come, the things past shall be accused of vanity.*[176] Hence again it is written: *In all thy works, remember thy last end, and thou shalt never sin.*[177]

33

Evildoers who sow and reap sorrows are consumed by the wrath of God

I have seen those who work iniquity, and sow sorrows, and reap them, perishing by the blast of God, and consumed by the spirit of his wrath.[178] They sow sorrows who act perversely; they reap sorrows when they are punished for this perversity. For the harvest of such sorrow is the retribution of condemnation. But since it is immediately added that those who sow and reap sorrows perish by the blast of God and are consumed by the spirit of his wrath, in this text the reaping of sorrow is revealed to be not punishment as yet, but the further development of wickedness, for the punishment of that reaping in the spirit of God's wrath comes later. Here then they sow and reap sorrows since whatever they do is wicked, and they flourish in that wickedness, as is said of the wicked man by the Psalmist: *His ways are filthy at all times; thy judgments are removed from his sight: he shall rule over all his enemies.*[179] And it is soon after added concerning him: *Under his tongue are labor and sorrow.*[180] Therefore he sows sorrows when he does wicked things, he reaps sorrows when from those acts of wickedness he thrives temporarily. How then is it that by the blast of God they perish who for the most part are permitted to remain here below and in greater prosperity than the righteous? For hence it is said of them again by the Psalmist: *They are not in the labor of men: neither shall they be scourged like other men.*[181] Hence Jeremias says: *Why doth the way of the wicked prosper?*[182] Certainly because, as it is written: *The most High is a patient rewarder,*[183] he often for long bears with those whom he condemns forever. Yet sometimes he moves quickly since he hastens to encourage the faintheartedness of the innocent. Therefore almighty God sometimes permits the wicked to hold sway for long so that the life of the righteous may be more fully cleansed. Yet sometimes he speedily cuts down the unrighteous, and by their ruin he strengthens the hearts of the innocent. For if he were now to strike all who do evil, on whom would he then have to inflict the final judgment? But if he did not now strike anyone whatsoever, who would have believed that God has concern for human affairs? Sometimes then he strikes the wicked to show that he does not let evils go unpunished. But sometimes he is lenient toward the wicked for long, so that he may teach those who take heed what judgment lies in store for them.

But would that those who will not resist temptations to sin cleansed by weeping offenses already committed! Would that they at least realized what they have done and tended the barren fig tree,[184] that is, applied to the unfruitful soul the fertile shedding of tears!

BOOK 3

VICES

Prologue

Sins of thought, word and deed develop into different species that are called vices. And hence the discussion of sin is followed by the third book of Part 1: Vices. Here are considered the eight principal vices singled out by Saint Gregory. And although in this book after the treatment of any one vice there is appended some mention of what can counteract that vice, in the third book of Part 2: Virtues, you will find *in extenso* remedies for the vices so that virtue may combat vice and transfix it with the sword of the spirit.

1

The queen of vices and the leaders of armies who fight against us

He smelleth the battle afar off, the encouraging of the captains, and the shouting of the army.[1] Some of the tempting vices—which fight against us in unseen battle, supporting pride that reigns over them—like captains, lead the way; others follow as an army does. For all faults do not enter the heart with equal access. But while the few leading ones infiltrate an unguarded mind, the lesser troops effect an entrance in legions. For when pride, the queen of sins, has fully laid hold of a defeated heart, she soon turns it over for ruination to seven principal vices as if to some of her captains. And in truth an army follows these captains because there undoubtedly come in their wake clamoring hosts of vices. What we have said is better demonstrated if we enumerate and highlight individually, as best we can, the leaders themselves and their army. Pride is of course the root of all evil, of which it is said, as Scripture bears witness: *Pride is the beginning of all sin.*[2] Moreover, proliferating from this poisonous root as its first offspring are seven capital sins: vainglory, envy, anger, melancholy, avarice, gluttony, lust. For because he grieved that we were held in bondage by these seven derivatives of pride, on that account our Redeemer, full of the spirit of sevenfold grace, joined spiritual battle for our liberation.

But each of these dominant sins has its own army opposing us. For from vainglory arise disobedience, boasting, hypocrisy, contentions, obstinacies, discords, and the acceptance of strange teachings. From envy there spring hatred, whispering, detraction, exultation at the misfortunes of our neighbor and affliction at his prosperity. From anger are produced strifes, high-mindedness, insults, complaining, indignation, blasphemies. From mclancholy there arise malice, rancor, faintheartedness, despair, slothfulness in obeying the commandments, and a wandering of the mind toward unlawful objects. From avarice there spring treachery, fraud, deceit, perjury, restlessness, violence, and hardness of heart in place of compassion. From gluttony are propagated foolish gaiety, scurrility, uncleanness, talkativeness, lethargy of intellect. From lust are generated blindness of mind, inconsiderateness, inconstancy, impulsiveness, self–love, hatred of God, affection for this present world but dread or despair concerning that which is to come. Because, therefore, seven principal vices produce so great a progeny of vices, when they penetrate the heart they bring along the troops of an army in their wake. Of these seven, five are of the spirit and two are carnal.

But all of them are so closely interrelated that they take their origin only from one another. For instance, the first offspring of pride is vainglory, which having vitiated the tyrannized mind, soon generates envy because surely the mind in seeking the power of empty renown feels discontent at the ability of someone else to acquire it. Envy in turn generates anger because the more the mind is injured by the inner wound of envy, the more too is the mildness of tranquility lost, as when a painful part of the body is prodded, on account of the wound the afflicting hand is felt to be more heavily imposed. Melancholy in its turn arises from anger, because the more senselessly the agitated mind gets disturbed, the more it impugns itself as worthless; and when it has lost the steadiness of tranquility, it feeds on nothing but the grief resulting from agitation. Melancholy also leads into avarice because when the disturbed heart has forfeited the advantage of inner joy, it seeks outside for means of consolation and is the more intent on possessing external goods, the less inward joy there is to which it may have recourse. But after these vices of the spirit there remain the two carnal vices, gluttony and lust. But it is plain to all that lust springs from gluttony inasmuch as in the very arrangement of parts of the body, the genitals are placed below the belly. And hence when the latter is inordinately filled up, indisputably abuse of the former is encouraged.

But the captains are well said to encourage the armies to shout because the initial vices penetrate the deluded mind under some appearance of reason, but the countless vices which follow, while they draw it along to every kind of madness, confound it, as it were. by beastly uproar. For the seven initial vices are accustomed to encourage the conquered mind with a semblance of reason when each in turn proclaims what follows.(Vainglory) You ought to aim at greater things so that as you have been able to surpass many in power, you may be able to benefit many also. (Envy) In what respect are you inferior to this or that person? Why then are you not either equal or superior to them? What great things you are able to do, which they are not! They should not then be either superior or even equal to you. (Anger) The things that are done to you cannot be borne patiently; indeed, to endure them with patience is a sin. Because should you not resist them with great indignation, they are afterwards heaped upon you immeasurably. (Melancholy) What reason have you to rejoice when you endure so many wrongs from your neighbors? Consider with what sadness all must be looked upon who are turned against you in such bitter anger. (Avarice) It is quite blameless for you to desire some possessions because you seek not to abound but are afraid to be in want; and what another keeps in a miserly way, you use to better purpose. (Gluttony) God made all things clean, in order to be eaten, and if someone refuses to fill himself with food, what else does he do but spurn the gift that has been granted him? (Lust) Why do you not give wider scope to your pleasure when you know not what may come next for you? You ought not to waste in mere desires the time you have received because you know not how quickly it may pass. For if God had not wished human beings to be united in the pleasure of coition, he would not, at the very beginning of the human race, have made them male and female.[3] All this is the encouragement of captains, which when incautiously admitted into the secrecy of the heart, too familiarly advocates things that are wrong. This encouragement a shouting army in truth follows because when the unfortunate soul, once captured by the principal vices, becomes deranged by abundant iniquities, it is then laid waste with brutal savagery.

But the soldier of God, because he adroitly endeavors to foresee the contests with vices, smells the battle afar off; because while he considers with anxious thoughts, what power the leading evils possess to persuade the mind, he detects by the keenness of his scent, the encouragement of the captains. And because he perceives the profusion of subsequent iniquities, he gets wind of the shouting of the army.

2

Pride

He is king over all the children of pride.[4] It is written: *Pride is the beginning of all sin.*[5] For other vices assail those virtues only by which they themselves are destroyed, as anger attacks patience; gluttony, abstinence; lust, continence. But pride, which is the root of all vices, not satisfied with the destruction of one virtue, takes a stand against all the faculties of the soul and as a general and pestilent disease corrupts the whole body, so that whatever is being done when it attacks, even if ostensibly virtuous, by that action God is not served but only vainglory.

But the mind is sometimes carried away to such self–esteem that by reason of its pride lack of restraint extends to vanity of speech. But ruin follows the more easily, the more unreservedly anyone is exalted in his own mind. For hence it is written: *The spirit is lifted up before a fall.*[6] Hence it is said by Daniel: *The king was walking in the palace of Babylon, and he answered and said: Is not this the great Babylon, which I have built to be the seat of the kingdom, by the strength of my power, in the glory of my excellence?*[7] But in what manner swift punishment repressed this pride then and there is indicated by Daniel: *While the word was yet in the king's mouth, a voice came down from heaven: To thee, O king Nabuchodonosor, it is said: The kingdom shall pass from thee, and they shall cast thee out from among men: and thy dwelling shall be with cattle and wild beasts: thou shall eat grass like an ox, and seven times shall pass over thee.*[8] Observe, because pride of mind showed itself even in direct words, the forbearance of the judge ended at once in his sentence and he overthrew the king the more severely, the more immoderately pride lifted itself aloft; and because the king mentioned in sequence the achievements for which he flattered himself, he heard enumerated the penalties that would be imposed. But it should be understood that this very pride which we are discussing affects some persons in temporal and others in spiritual matters. For one person prides himself on gold, another on eloquence; one on weak and earthly things, another on the highest and heavenly virtues. And yet one and the same thing is happening before the eyes of God, though as it occurs in the hearts of men, it is clothed in their sight with a different garment. For when he who was at first proud of earthly glory is afterwards exalted by his sanctity, pride has never abandoned his heart but approaching him as usual has changed its vesture so that it may not be recognized.

But for all who are inwardly exalted by proud thought there is loudness in their speech, bitterness is their silence, dissipation in their laughter, anger in their sorrow, unmannerliness in their conduct, distinction in their appearance, stateliness in their bearing, spitefulness in their responding. Their mind is ever strong in inflicting insult, weak in enduring it; sluggish in obeying, persistent in wearying others; slothful in those things which it should and is able to do, but always ready for those which it should not or is not able to do. In that which it does not seek of its own accord, it is influenced by no exhortation, but it does seek to be compelled to do that which it secretly longs for, because while it fears to become debased from indulging its desire, it wishes to undergo compulsion even in its own will.

Because then we have said that the minds of men are tempted in one way by carnal and in another by spiritual affairs, in the first instance let them hear: *All flesh is grass, and all the glory thereof as the flower of the field.*[9] In the second, let them hear what is said to some persons after their miracles: *I know not whence you are; depart from me, ye workers of iniquity.*[10] Let the first hear: *If riches abound, set not your heart upon them.*[11] Let the others hear that the foolish virgins, who come with empty oil vessels, are shut out from the marriage inside.[12]

Let all together hear: *God resisteth the proud and giveth grace to the humble.*[13] Let all hear: *Every proud man is an abomination to the Lord.*[14] Let all hear: *Why is earth and ashes proud?*[15] Against the plague of this sickness let us all hear what Truth our instructor teaches, saying: *Learn of me, because I am meek, and humble of heart.*[16] For to this end the only begotten Son of God took upon himself the form of our infirmity; to this end the invisible appeared not only visible, but even despised; to this end he endured the mockery of insult, the reproaches of derision, and the torment of sufferings so that God in his humility might teach men not to be proud. How great then is the virtue of humility since for the sole purpose of truly teaching it, he who is great beyond reckoning humbled himself even to the extent of suffering? For since the pride of the devil occasioned the source of our perdition, the humility of God was made the instrument of our redemption. For our enemy, who was created along with everything else, wished to appear exalted above all. But our Redeemer, remaining great above all things, deigned to become little among all things.

But we more effectively both detect the cause of pride and uncover the foundations of humility if we briefly mention and juxtapose what the author of death and what the Creator of life declare. For the one says: *I will ascend into heaven.*[17] But the other says by the prophet: *My soul is filled with evils: and my life hath drawn nigh to hell.*[18] The one says: *I will exalt my throne above the stars of God.*[19] The other says to mankind expelled from the dwelling place of paradise: *Behold, I come and I will dwell in the midst of thee.*[20] The one says: *I will sit in the mountain of the covenant, in the sides of the north.*[21] The other says: *I am a worm and no man: the reproach of men and the outcast of the people.*[22] The one says: *I will ascend above the height of the clouds; I will be like the most High;*[23] the other: *Who, being in the form of God, thought it not robbery to be equal with God; but emptied himself, taking the form of a servant.*[24] The one speaks by his members, saying: *Let no meadow escape our riot. Let us crown ourselves with roses, before they be withered. Let us everywhere leave tokens of joy.*[25] The other makes a pronouncement to his members, saying: *You shall lament and weep, but the world shall rejoice.*[26] The one teaches the minds that are subject to him nothing else but to aim at the height of loftiness, to transcend all their equals in proudness of mind, to surpass with lofty pride the society of all men, and to rise up even against the might of their Creator, as is said of those very subjects by the Psalmist: *They have passed into the affection of the heart. They have thought and spoken wickedness: they have spoken iniquity on high.*[27] The other facing the spittle, the reeds, the blows, the crown of thorns, the cross, the spear and death, admonishes his members, saying: *If any man minister to me, let him follow me.*[28]

Because then our Redeemer rules the hearts of the humble, and this Leviathan is called the king of the proud, we clearly perceive that pride is the most evident sign of the reprobate, but humility, on the other hand, that of the elect. And when it is known which quality anyone possesses, it is determined under what king he is fighting. For everyone bears in a way a banner of his service by which he plainly shows to the rule of which leader he is subject. Whence it is also said through the Gospel: *By their fruits you shall know them.*[29]

3

Pride as soon as it springs up is to be cut away lest it gain strength

The vice of pride must be pulled up by its roots early on so that when it covertly comes forth it may vigilantly be torn out lest it gain vigor by growth or strength from habit. For it is difficult for anyone to detect in himself inveterate pride because without doubt the more we suffer from this sin, the less we notice it. For pride is generated in the mind in the same way as blindness in the eyes. The more widely it expands, the more forcibly it constricts the light. Pride therefore briefly increasing in the mind and extending itself more broadly, pervasively ruins the sight of the afflicted mind so that the captive spirit can both suffer from the arrogance of pride and yet be unaware of it.

But they are enlightened with the light of the living who turning away from pride and the light of the world, have recourse to the splendor of inward brightness so that they may live where they may see, by sensing it, the true light; where light and life are not different from each other, but where light itself is life; where the light so encircles us outwardly as to fill us inwardly; so fills us within as, being itself unbounded, to circumscribe us outwardly. They are enlightened therefore with the light of the living, which they then behold the more clearly, when they more purely live by means of it.

4

Vainglory

Whoever longs for transitory applause suffers a loss by obtaining what he strives for, as Truth asserts, who says: *Amen, I say to you, they have received their reward.*[30] But this hope of being granted a reward cannot long be fostered since the honor is bestowed for works that are evident, but life is moving on to its close; commendations resound, but together with them the periods of time are quickly nearing an end.

Hence it is written: *His folly shall not please him.*[31] For it is great folly to do what is full of toil and to yearn for the voicing of applause; to attend diligently to the heavenly precepts but to seek the reward of an earthly recompense. For, as I might put it, he that in return for the good he practices looks for human applause is bearing something of great worth to be sold at a mean price; from that by which he could have earned the kingdom of heaven, he seeks the coin of approbation. He therefore sells at a mean price who expends a great deal but gets back very little. But the evil spirits feed on commendations of this sort, making of them a means to serve the purpose of perdition. Hence it is well said by the prophet: *The standing stalk, there is no bud in them, and it shall yield no meal; and if it should yield, strangers shall eat it.*[32] For the stalk is without a bud when life lacks the merits of virtue. The stalk yields no meal when he that thrives in this world understands nothing refined, yields no fruit of good conduct.

But often when meal has been yielded, strangers eat it up because even when good works are done for pretentious show, the wishes of evil spirits are satisfied by them. For those who do not seek to please God by them do not feed the owner of the land but strangers. He also who delights in applause is fed by his own folly, which satisfies him now but shall not do so later: when the time of retribution comes, for the gratification of praise he will receive the sentence of God's rebuke; for the reception of temporal glory he will suffer everlasting torments. Then in truth shall he realize that all that could pass away was as nothing.

Hence it is rightly added: *And his trust shall be like the spider's web.*[33] Just as the spider's web is diligently woven but is destroyed by a sudden gust of wind, so whatever is done with laborious effort for the sake of human praise, the breath of man's applause dispels; and it is as if his labor vanishes with the wind. Words of instruction also, spoken for applause of this kind, stir their hearers to offer praise rather than inducing them to shed tears. So words that issue from a cold heart, not burning with the fire of divine love, do not inflame their hearers with heavenly affection. For that which is not itself afire cannot kindle anything else. Hence their sayings sometimes fail to instruct their hearers and make the very persons that utter them worse by being exalted with praise. So Paul bears witness: *Knowledge puffeth up; but charity edifieth.*[34] Very often also men of this sort chasten themselves with admirable mortification, wear down bodily strength, and as it were while living in the flesh utterly kill the life of the flesh, and by abstinence come so close to death that they live nearly dying every day; but they seek human observers for all this, they look for the glory of admiration, as Truth testifies, by saying: *They disfigure their faces, that they may appear unto men to fast.*[35] For their faces turn pale, the body shakes from weakness, the breast labors with irregular breathing. But meanwhile word of admiration is sought from the lips of neighbors, and no such concerned thought is given to anything other than human esteem. These persons are well represented by the Simon who at the time of our Lord's passion bore the cross by compulsion; of him it is written: *And, going out, they found a man of Cyrene, named Simon; him they forced to take up his cross.*[36] For what we do by compulsion, we do not practice with love as our incentive. And so to bear the cross of Jesus by compulsion is to practice the mortification of abstinence for some motive other than what is called for. Does one not bear the cross of Jesus under compulsion who according to the commandment of the Lord subdues the flesh, but does not love the realm of the spirit? And hence the same Simon bears the cross but does not die because every dissembler afflicts his body with abstinence but yet in the love of glory, does not die to the world.

On the other hand it is well said by Paul of the elect: *And they that are Christ's have crucified their flesh, with the vices and concupiscences.*[37] For we crucify the flesh, with its vices and concupiscences, if we so restrain our appetite that we no longer look for any worldly glory. For he that mortifies the body but yearns for honors has put the cross on his flesh, but from concupiscence lives in a more worldly manner since it often happens that by the appearance of holiness someone unworthily obtains a position of authority which, unless he showed some merit, he would not attain by effort. But that which he gains for enjoyment is passing, and what punishment ensues is enduring. Now his reputation for sanctity rests on the lips of man, but when the judge of what lies within examines the secrets of the heart, no witnesses of external life are summoned.

Hence it is further added: *He shall lean upon his house, and it shall not stand.*[38] His house therefore is delight in approbation: in it he dwells peaceably since in all his works he rests upon this approval within his mind. But this house can not stand, because praise passes away with life, and the applause of men has no standing in the last judgment. Hence also the foolish virgins who had taken no oil in their vessels, because their glory was in the voices of others and not in their own conscience, upset by the presence of the bridegroom, say: *Give us of your oil, for our lamps are gone out.*[39] For to seek oil from our neighbors is to beseech the fame of good works from the testimony of another's speech. For the empty soul, when it finds that it has retained nothing within by all its efforts, seeks an external witness.

But such a one then leans in vain upon this house of applause since no human testimony supports him in the judgment. But when he knows that the testimony of another's lips is wanting to him, he turns to reckoning up his own works. Hence it is added: *He shall prop it up, and it shall not rise.*[40] For that which cannot stand by itself is propped to make it stand; for when men of this kind see life tottering in the judgment, they try to prop it up by the enumeration of their deeds, saying: *Lord, Lord, have not we prophesied in thy name and cast out devils in thy name and done many miracles in thy name?*[41] But the house of praise, supported by all these allegations, shall not rise because the judge says at once: *I never knew you; depart from me, you that work iniquity.*[42]

5

Vainglory and boasting

There are some persons who while they desire to do what is right, first carefully look for witnesses of their deeds and consider thoughtfully if there are others who may see what they are about to do and having seen, can give a fitting report. But if by chance no one should happen to witness their deeds, they surely judge these works to be wasted. And since witnesses are lacking, they themselves relate what they have done. And when they begin to be carried away by applause, they often magnify by fabrication these deeds that they report. But even when they do give true accounts, by the act of reportage they forfeit the good they have done, because when they are rewarded with the desired external recompense, they are dispossessed of their eternal reward.

For by disclosing their good works they point out to the evil spirits, as enemies plotting against them, what to plunder. This eventuality is represented by Ezechias, who on one occasion by a single prayer and in the course of a single night, brought back the sun; later he had his life prolonged when it was already threatened by the end approaching. Now having welcomed messengers of the king of Babylon, he showed them all the goods that he possessed. But he soon heard the prophet say: *Behold, the days shall come, that all that is in thy house shall be carried into Babylon. Nothing shall be left, saith the Lord.*[43] Hence it is said by the Psalmist: *And he delivered their strength into captivity: and their beauty into the hands of the enemy.*[44] For the strength and beauty of proud men are delivered into the hands of the enemy because every good thing that is displayed in the desire of praise is given over to the hidden adversary's right of possession; for he incites his enemies to plunder who brings treasures to their notice. For as long as we are separated from the safety of our eternal country, we are walking along a way with robbers lying in wait. He then that fears being robbed on the journey must hide the possessions that he carries. Wretched are they who by coveting the praises of men fritter away in themselves all the fruits of their labors, and while they seek to show themselves off for others, doom all that they do. When the evil spirits exhort these persons to boastfulness, treating them as prisoners, they strip off their works, as we have said. Wherefore, pointing out the malice of our old enemy host under the image of a certain people, Truth says through the prophet: *He hath laid my vineyard waste, and hath peeled off the bark of my fig tree: he hath stripped it bare, and cast it away: the branches thereof are made white.*[45] For by enemies lying in wait the vineyard of God is changed into a wasteland when the soul that is rich in productivity is ravished by strong desire for the praise of men. The invading hostile nation peels the bark off the fig tree of God because drawing the misguided soul to the desire for applause, to the extent that it is led on to ostentation, it is divested of the covering of humility, and stripped bare and cast away: as long as it was hidden from sight in its good works, it was as it were clothed with its own covering of bark. But when the mind longs for what it has done to be seen by others, it is as though the stripped fig tree had lost the bark that covered it. Here it is properly added: *The branches thereof are made white*, since a person's works, when revealed to the eyes of men, begin to glow; an aura of sanctity is acquired when upright conduct is brought to light. But since, when the bark is removed, the branches of the fig tree wither, it is to be observed with discernment that when the deeds of prideful men are placed before human eyes, the action from which they seek to derive favor is the source of deterioration. Therefore the mind that is presented in a boastful light is rightly called a stripped fig tree because it is both white insofar as it is distinctly seen and on the verge of withering insofar as it is devoid of the protecting bark.

6

Prevention of vainglory

If we perceive the good things that we do, we are commonly led to entertain pride; if we do not know about them, we cannot preserve them. For who would not in some slight degree be made proud by the consciousness of his virtue? Or who again would keep safe within him that good which he is not aware of? What then remains as an antidote to either of these ills except that knowing all the good things that we do, we should not dwell on them in order that we look upon them both as proper and as insignificant? And thus the knowledge of their virtuousness may make the soul attentive to their safekeeping, and the estimate of their lack of importance may not exalt the soul in pride. For the seeking of human approbation acts as a highwayman, who as people are going along a straight road joins them from the roadside in order that the traveler's life may be cruelly taken by the secretly drawn dagger. Because often when the intention to serve a useful purpose is diverted to our own interest—as when human praise is sought—in a horrendous way sin finishes off the identical work which goodness began.

Let the good things we do, therefore, remain hidden if we expect to receive from the great arbiter the compensation for our work. It is thus that he who is Truth says in the Gospel: *Let not thy left hand know what thy right hand doth, that thy alms may be in secret: and thy Father, who seeth in secret will repay thee.*[46] It is hence that it is said by the Psalmist: *All the glory of the daughter of kings is within.*[47] Hence Paul says: *For our glory is this: the testimony of our conscience.*[48] For the daughter of kings is the Church, which is engendered by good works, the preaching of spiritual princes. But her glory is within because what she effects she does not store in mind for the boasting of outward display.

But although the things that we do must be kept concealed, yet Truth says: *Let them see your good works and glorify your Father who is in heaven.*[49] But assuredly it is one thing when in the display of works the glory of the giver is sought, and quite another when on account of the largess of the giver, personal praise is coveted. And hence again in the Gospel by Truth himself it is said: *Take heed that you do not your justice before men, to be seen by them.*[50] Therefore, when our works are shown to men, we must first weigh well, while looking into the heart, what is the purpose of the zeal for such display. For if we seek the glory of the giver, even our works that are made public we keep hidden in his view. But if we desire to win personal praise on account of them, they are already removed from his sight even though they are not widely known by others. And hence when he comes as judge he will say to the foolish virgins: *Amen, I say to you, I know you not.*[51] While he sees in them spiritual corruption, even carnal integrity does not prevail.

Indeed it is most important that those who strive for spiritual progress so seek the glory of their Creator by making their works known as not to experience self-congratulation when praise is bestowed. For then only is a praiseworthy work inoffensively displayed to others when the praise awarded is truly decried in one's own estimation. Since the weak on the whole do not rise above such praise by thoroughly belittling it, the need remains for keeping hidden the good that they do.

7

Envy

Envy slayeth the little one.[52] We can envy only those whom we consider better than ourselves in some respect. Therefore he is a little one who is slain by rivalry, for he bears witness against himself that he is inferior to the one by envy of whom he is distressed. It is hence that our shrewd enemy, envying the first man, deceived him because the devil having lost his state of bliss, knew his present state to be inferior to man's immortality. It is hence that Cain went so far as to murder his brother because when Cain's sacrifice was disregarded, he was angered that Abel, whose offering God accepted, was preferred to himself; and terrified at Abel's being better than himself, he deprived him of his very existence.[53] Hence Esau was stirred up to persecute his brother for, the blessing of the firstborn being lost—which in any case he had himself sold for a dish of pottage—he lamented his inferiority to Jacob, whom he preceded at birth.[54] Hence Joseph's brothers sold him to Ismaelites that were passing by because, the mystery of the revelation being disclosed, they endeavored to resist his advancement lest he might become superior to them.[55] Hence Saul persecutes his servant David by throwing a lance at him for he dreaded being surpassed by David whom he perceived to be daily gaining stature by his virtuous achievements.[56] Thus he is a little one who is slain by envy because, unless he was inferior, he would not deplore the probity of another.

But in these matters it must be kept in mind that though in every vice that is practiced, the venom of our old enemy is poured into the human heart, yet in this wickedness the serpent bestirs his inmost parts and discharges the poison of maliciousness that is to be implanted. In this regard it is written: *By the envy of the devil, death came into the world.*[57] For when the decay of envy has corrupted the vanquished heart, exterior indications show how greatly mad impulses provoke the mind. For the complexion is altered by pallor, the eyes are depressed, the disposition is inflamed; as the limbs are chilled, there is frenzy of emotion, gritting of teeth, and while growing hate is buried in the deeper reaches of the heart, the confined anguish penetrates the senses with dark foreboding. Nothing of its own that prospers gives respite because its suffering distresses the downcast spirit which is harassed by the prosperity of another; and the higher the structure of another's works rises, the deeper the foundation of the envious spirit is undermined so that insofar as others press on to better things, its downfall should be the greater; for by this ruination even that is destroyed which was believed to have been raised in other actions with thorough accomplishment. For when envy has made the mind decline, it consumes all that it encounters which was well done. Whence it is well said by Solomon: *Soundness of heart is the life of the flesh: but envy is the rottenness of the bones.*[58] For what is denoted by the flesh except weak and delicate things; and what by the bones other than strong deeds? And it frequently happens that some with real innocence of heart should appear to be weak in some of their deeds; but some now perform deeds that are marked by vigor in the eyes of men, yet regarding the virtues of others, these persons are inwardly consumed with the plague of envy. And so it is well said: *Soundness of heart is the life of the flesh*, because when inward innocence is preserved, even if there are some outward weak points, yet they are sooner or later overcome. And it is rightly added: *But envy is the rottenness of the bones*, because by the vice of envy even brave deeds of virtue are wasted in the eyes of God. Indeed, the rotting of the bones from envy is the spoiling of even rugged virtues.

8

Repression of envy

It is difficult for a person not to envy in another that which he earnestly desires to obtain, since whatever we receive that is temporal becomes more diminished in each individual the more numerous are they who share in it. And for this reason envy troubles the mind that harbors desires because another recipient deprives it, either in whole or in part, of what it seeks. Let him, therefore, who wishes to be completely free from the plague of envy, hold in esteem that inheritance which no number of joint heirs reduces, which is both one to all and entire for each, and which is shown to be the more plentiful the more the number of those who take possession of it is increased. Therefore the lessening of envy results in the growing predilection for happiness, and its complete demise is the perfect love of eternity. For when the mind is withdrawn from the desire of anything that is divided among a number of recipients, the more love of neighbor is increased, the less fear of loss to self from his advancement is experienced. And if the mind is wholly absorbed in the love of our heavenly country, it is also fully grounded in the love of our neighbor. For while it desires no earthly objects, there is nothing to oppose the love it has for its neighbors. For what else is this charity but the eye of the mind, which if it is affected by the dust of earthly love, is at once deflected and dazzled from its gaze at the inward light? But because he is a little one who loves earthly things, and a great one who yearns for the things of eternity, by means of this distinction we may suitably interpret the text: *Envy slayeth the little one*,[59] because no one perishes from the malady of this plague except the one that is still sickly in affection.

9

Anger

Anger indeed killeth the foolish: and envy slayeth the little one.[60] Since it is written: *But thou, Lord, judgest with tranquillity,*[61] we must particularly take note that as often as we restrain our turbulent emotions by the virtue of mildness, we are trying to return to the likeness of our Creator. For when anger strikes peace of mind asunder, it throws the mind, almost torn to pieces and broken apart, into disorder so that it is not in harmony with itself when it is bereft of the vital force of its pristine likeness. Therefore let us consider how great is the sin of anger, through which when mildness is lost, the likeness of the supernal image is spoiled. By anger wisdom is forsaken so that there is no awareness of what to do nor of what order to follow, as it is written: *Anger resteth in the bosom of a fool,*[62] since it withdraws the light of understanding when its disturbing influence troubles the mind. By anger life is lost although wisdom may seem to be retained, as it is written: *Anger destroyeth even the wise,*[63] for indeed the confused mind is not effective even if it is able to judge anything wisely. By anger righteousness is abandoned, as it is written: *The anger of man worketh not the justice of God.*[64] For while the upset spirit activates its reasoning faculty, all that comes to mind it considers right. By anger all the graciousness of social life is lost, as it is written: *Be not a friend of an angry man: lest perhaps thou learn his ways and take scandal to thy soul.*[65] For he who does not conduct himself temperately and reasonably must like a beast live alone. By anger harmony is disrupted, as it is written: *A passionate man provoketh quarrels, and an angry man poureth forth sins.*[66] For an angry man pours forth sins because he debases even evil men, whom he rashly incites to discord. By anger the light of truth is lost, as it is written: *Let not the sun go down upon your anger.*[67] For when anger produces in the mind the darkness of confusion, God withholds the ray of the knowledge of himself. By anger the brightness of the Holy Spirit is banished. Against this occurrence, it is written according to the old translation: *Upon whom shall my spirit rest, but upon him that is humble and peaceful, and that trembleth at my words?*[68] For when he mentioned the word humble, he at once added the word peaceful. If then anger dispels peace from the mind, it denies that dwelling place to the Holy Spirit, and the soul left empty by his departure, is filled with consternation and shows the dismay that wells up from the inmost depths of its being.

For the heart that is stirred by the incitement of its own anger beats quickly, the body trembles, the tongue stammers, the countenance takes fire, the eyes grow fierce, and they that are well known are not recognized. With the mouth indeed a sound is shaped, but the understanding has no part in it. In what way then does he differ from delirious persons, who is not conscious of his own actions? Whence it very often happens that anger reaches even to the hands, and the further reason departs, the more insolent is the stand anger takes. And the mind has no strength to restrain itself since it is given over into the power of another. And rage puts the limbs to stressful outward exertion insofar as inside it holds captive the mind itself that governs the limbs. But sometimes it does not thrust out the hands, but it turns the tongue into a shaft of malediction. For it requests with entreaty a brother's destruction and wishes God to do what the wicked man himself is either afraid or ashamed to do. And it comes about that both by wish and words he commits murder even when he refrains from hurting his neighbor with his hands. Sometimes when the mind is disturbed, anger as if in judgment imposes silence, and to the extent that it does not express itself outwardly by the lips, inwardly it blazes more fiercely so that the angry man ceases to talk with his neighbor and in saying nothing, says how hostile he is. And sometimes this severity of silence enters into the administering of discipline if at least the rule of discretion is diligently retained in the interior. But sometimes while the incensed mind forgoes the usual conversation, in the progress of time it is entirely cut off from the love of neighbor, and sharper impulses encroach upon the mind; motives also develop for more serious aggravation. And the mote in the eye of the angry man is turned into a beam,[69] while anger is changed into hatred. It often happens that anger, kept within the heart by silence, seethes more violently and silently phrases vehement remarks; it conjures up provocative rejoinders and as if it held jurisdiction in the dispute, issues with animosity a harsher reply. All this Solomon implies in a few words, saying: *The expectation of the wicked is indignation.*[70] And the result is that the troubled spirit finds greater uproar in its silence, and the fury of pent-up anger rages devastatingly. Hence a certain wise man of the past said in effect: The thoughts of the angry man are a generation of vipers; they devour the mind that is their mother.[71]

But we should know that there are some whom anger rather quickly inflames, but it more readily leaves them. Others it is slow in exciting, but it grips them more lastingly. For some, like kindled reeds, while they make a great noise, produce something like a crackling sound when set on fire: they indeed speedily flame up, but then they soon cool down into ashes; others, not unlike the heavier and harder kinds of wood, are slow in beginning to burn, but once kindled, are with difficulty extinguished: they more slowly stir themselves up to fieriness, but retain longer the fire of their rage. Still others, and their condition is worse, are both quick in yielding to the flames of anger, and slow in putting them out. But others both yield to them slowly and part with them quickly. Regarding these four ways of acting the reader sees clearly that the last rather than the first comes closer to the blessing of tranquility, and in evil the third is worse than the second.

10

Repression of irascibility

There are two ways in which anger, being subdued, begins to lose its access to the mind. The first method is that the prudent mind, before it sets out to do something, anticipates all the affronts it is liable to undergo, so that by thinking of the shameful abuse of its Redeemer, it may prepare itself for adversities. When they occur, it meets them with greater courage insofar as by foresight it fortified itself more carefully. For whoever is caught off guard by adversity is akin to one whose enemy finds him sleeping and kills him more quickly because he stabs one who offers no resistance. For he that through watchful care foresees imminent evils is really watching in ambush, awaiting hostile attacks; and he girds himself effectively for victory in that circumstance wherein he was expected to be caught unaware. Consequently, in preparation for any undertaking the mind must dwell shrewdly on potential mishaps so that having them before it at all times, it may constantly be protected against them by the breastplate of patience, and may both by foresight get the better of any opposition and consider an advantage whatever does not go wrong. Now the second way of preserving mildness is—when we notice the sins of others—to keep in mind our own offenses by which we have sinned against our neighbor. For our own frailty, duly considered, makes us overlook the sins of others against us. For that person bears with patience an injustice that is done to him who justly remembers that there may perhaps even now be something on his part that others must bear with. And just as fire is extinguished by water, so is rage rising in the mind suppressed when each person recalls his own misdeeds, for he is ashamed not to forgive offenses who remembers that he himself has often committed offenses, whether against God or against his neighbor, that need to be forgiven.

But in these matters we must keep in mind that the anger caused by hastiness of temper differs from anger prompted by zeal. The first springs from evil, the second from good. For if no anger originated in virtue, Phinees by the sword would not have appeased the force of God's punishment.[72] Because Heli lacked such anger, he implacably stirred up the exercise of heavenly vengeance. For insofar as he lacked ardor against the evil practices of those under his charge, the severity of the eternal ruler was inflamed against him.[73] This disposition is countered by the Psalmist: *Be ye angry, and sin not.*[74] This injunction is not correctly understood by those who believe we should only be angry with ourselves, and not with others as well when sin is committed. For if we are commanded to love our neighbors as ourselves, it follows that we should be as angry with their faults as with our own evil ways. On this point it is said by Solomon: *Anger is better than laughter: because by the sadness of the countenance the mind of the offender is corrected.*[75] And the Psalmist says again: *My eye is troubled through indignation.*[76] For anger arising from evil blinds the eye of the mind, but anger that comes from zeal troubles it, because to whatever extent it is affected even in support of virtue, that state of contemplation which can be attained only by a tranquil heart is ruffled. For that zeal in the cause of righteousness, since it stirs the mind with disquietude, soon detracts from its keenness so that in its troubled state it does not see the higher realities, which it previously beheld in tranquility. But it is brought back to the heights with greater alertness by the same means that dislodged it from its vantage point. For the same unending effort in behalf of virtue before long opens in tranquility broader vistas than those closed off for a while by disturbance. And from the same source whence the mind is confused in its vision, it derives light for seeing more clearly; just as when ointment is applied to the sickly eye, it is fully deprived of light but after a short time regains a truer light thanks to the healing agent that occasioned the brief darkness. But contemplation is never joined to agitation, nor can the disturbed mind behold what it is scarcely able to gaze on even when tranquil; for neither is a ray of sun perceived when driving clouds cover the face of the sky; nor does a troubled fountain pool reflect the image of the beholder, which when calm it shows properly, for inasmuch as its water is rippled, it distorts the appearance of a likeness on its surface.

But when the spirit is stirred with zeal, great care must be taken lest that same anger, which is employed as an instrument of virtue, gain dominion over the mind, or in a matronly way take precedence; let it rather, like a handmaid ready to render service, always go along in the wake of reason. Then in fact is it enlisted more vigorously against evil, when it serves in subjection to reason. For however much our anger may originate in zeal for virtue, if from lack of moderation it has mastered the mind, it promptly disdains rendering service to reason, and the more shamelessly gives itself wider scope, the more flagrantly it rates the defect of impetuosity as a good quality. Whence it is necessary that he who is influenced by zeal for virtue should above all see to it that his anger does not escape control by the mind: in punishing sin, considering time and method, let him with acute analysis rein in the rising agitation of his mind, restrain his ardor, and subject his impetuous emotions to calmness. In order that the punisher of another may become the more just, the more victorious he has been over self, he should correct the faults of offenders in such a way that having first acquired greater patience, he denounces his own temper by rising above it, lest in being immoderately stirred by his zeal for righteousness, he stray from virtue. But as we have said, inasmuch as even a commendable striving for virtue troubles the eye of the mind, it is rightly said here in our text: *Anger killeth the foolish*.[77] In other words: Anger due to zeal disturbs wise men, anger due to sin destroys fools; the first is kept under the control of reason, the other dominates the vanquished mind in opposition to reason.

11

Melancholy

The wicked are always waiting to see the suffering of the righteous and desire to look upon them in distress. And they dig through houses in the dark,[78] when they corrupt by disgraceful discourse the heart of innocent but weak persons at the time of their abasement. But it commonly happens that when they see the good downfallen, suddenly by secret divine command some righteous person who seemed overwhelmed is supported by a temporal power, and the prosperity of the present life smiles on the one whom the darkness of adversity earlier disheartened. As we have said, when the wicked behold the prosperity of that person, they are deeply troubled. For at once they turn again to their own hearts, they bring back before the eye of the mind whatever they recall having done through perversity, they fear that every vice of theirs will be avenged. Thus the same event which caused him who received power to shine caused any wicked person who feared correction to be sad in darkness. And so it is well said: *If the morning suddenly appear, it is to them the shadow of death*.[79] For the morning is the mind of the righteous man, which leaving the darkness of its sin, is already bordering on the light of eternity, as it is likewise said of holy Church: *Who is she who cometh forth as the morning rising?*[80] The more therefore every upright person shining with the light of justice is in the present life raised high with honor, the more the honor becomes the shadow of death in the eyes of the wicked, because they who remember that they have done evil things are in fear of being chastised. For they desire always to have a free rein in their iniquities, to live uncorrected, and from sin to derive joy.

But when a trial of this sort suddenly arises and pierces the mind, it utterly confounds those thoughts. For an unexpected enemy enters what is like an untroubled city, and the necks of proud citizens are laced with a sudden sword-stroke. There ensues nothing but continual lamentation while the captured city of the mind is, in the slaughter, emptied of the glory of its great ones. For only great tribulation holds sway when the tranquil mind is assailed by the inroads of trial. For when the adversity of trial forces itself into the mind, it produces in it a kind of darkness and confounds it with the gloom of its bitterness.

For while the mind, subjected to trial, considers that it is displaced from original stability, it is blinded by a covering of sorrows as by a veil of darkness, and its eye is closed to every ray of joy. And while in turmoil it perceives that it has ceased to be what it had been, it heaps up in itself countless waves and disturbances. At one time it grieves that it has lost its tranquility; at another, it is afraid lest it be ruined in evil deeds. At one time it calls to mind on what a height it had taken a stand; at another, it observes in what a depth of vices it is lying as a result of its pleasure–seeking. At one time it renews efforts to recover its strength; at another, as though already defeated and crushed, it despairs of recovering it.

When such manifold thoughts thus advance upon the afflicted mind, it is as if people rise and overpower it in the night. Such people the prophet surely had presumed he could overcome, not by himself, but with the aid of divine protection when he said: *My protector, and in him will I hope, subduing people under me.*[81] For people are subdued under holy minds when by the latter, foolish thoughts of the people through experience of strict severity are dissolved, so as not to hurry along the steep declines of fancies but, submissive to reason, humbly to leave the heart at rest. Hence, subjected to trial, the mind that endures the agitations of despair falls more quickly into the darkness of melancholy; and he who had thought highly of himself in tranquility, in trouble is thrown into worse disorder by the gloom of his thoughts.

12

Cure of melancholy

Although our Creator is merciful and just, let no one say: Because he is merciful, I sin venially; and let not him who sins declare: Because he is just, I despair of forgiveness of sin. For God remits the sin that is regretted, but let everyone be afraid of sinning because he knows not whether he can properly regret it. Before sinning, therefore, let him fear justice, but after sinning, let him count on mercy; and let him not so fear his justice as not to gain strength from any consolation of hope, nor be so confident of his mercy as to neglect to apply to his wounds the medicine of worthy penitence. But let him always think as well that the one whom he counts on to spare him in mercy, judges also with severity. Therefore let the hope of the sinner rejoice in his mercy, but let the thought of punishment make the penitent tremble under his severity. Let the hope of our confidence, therefore, have also the sting of fear, in order that the justice of the judge may frighten into the correction of his sins the one whom the love of the liberator invites to trust in pardon.

For thus does the mercy of the divine dispensation always restrain us in our pride, support us in our offenses lest we sink into despair. Whence he also warns us through Moses, saying: *Thou shalt not take the upper nor the nether millstone to pledge.*[82]   For by take (*accipere*) we sometimes mean take away (*auferre*). Whence also those birds that are bent on seizing other birds are called accipiters (hawks). Whence the apostle Paul says: *For you suffer if a man devour you, if a man take from you,*[83] that is to say: *if a man take away from you.* But the pledge of a debtor is the confession of a sinner. For a pledge is taken from a debtor when a confession of sin is accepted from a sinner. But the upper and lower millstone are hope and fear. For hope raises the heart on high, but fear thrusts it down lower. But the upper and lower millstone are so inevitably joined together that one is uselessly possessed without the other. Hope and fear, therefore, ought to be constantly united in the breast of a sinner because he both hopes fruitlessly for mercy if he does not also fear justice, and he in vain fears justice if he does not also trust in mercy. Therefore taking as a pledge the upper or the lower millstone is forbidden because he who preaches to a sinner must so deftly organize what he says as not in leaving hope intact to remove fear, nor yet in withdrawing hope to leave the sinner in fear only. For the upper or lower millstone is taken away if by the tongue of the preacher, in the breast of the sinner either fear is disjoined from hope, or hope from fear.

13

Avarice

Of avarice it is written: *The desire of money is the root of all evils.*[84] Whence the one over whom covetousness is said to have dominion is surely shown to be subject to all evils. We should know that avarice sometimes comes unnoticed upon men through pride and sometimes through fear. Thus there are some who while they seek to appear more powerful, are incited to strive for the possessions of others, and there are some who while they are afraid lest the necessary reserves should be wanting to them, open their minds to covetousness and go after the belongings of others when they suspect that their own may not be enough for them.

Hence it is written: *Because he broke in and stripped the house of the poor, he hath violently taken away a house which he did not build: and yet his belly is not filled.*[85] He breaks in and strips the house of the poor, who in addition is not ashamed to despoil through avarice the one whom he crushes by power. He has taken away a house which he did not build. That is to say: He who ought to have built it, over and above takes it away. For the Lord who is to come in judgment shall say to the reprobate: *For I was hungry and you gave me not to eat: I was thirsty and you gave me not to drink: I was a stranger and you took me not in; naked, and you covered me not,* and so on.[86] As a consequence of this sin it is stated: *Depart from me, you cursed, into everlasting fire, which was prepared for the devil and his angels.*[87] If then he is sentenced to so great punishment who is convicted of not having given, what penalty should be imposed on the one who is proved to have stolen? And so he has taken away a house which he did not build because he not only did not give anything of his own, but also took away what belonged to another. So it is fittingly added: *And yet his belly is not filled.* For the belly of the wicked man is avarice because there is collected whatever is swallowed with evil desire. Yet it is plain that avarice is not quenched by the desired possessions but augmented. For after the manner of fire, when it has taken hold of fuel to feed on, it increases, and by the very thing that seems for a moment to put a damper on the flame, it is seen before long to be expanded. And often when almighty God is greatly incensed toward the covetous soul, he first lets it procure all things according to its wish, and afterwards takes them away with a vengeance so that it may endure eternal punishments on account of them.

And hence it is added: *And when he hath the things he coveted, he shall not be able to possess them.*[88] For it is a mark of God's greater wrath when even that thing is granted which is wrongly desired, and from that cause stems sudden retribution because that too was acquired which was coveted in the face of God's wrath. And hence it is said by the Psalmist when the people are described as having wrongfully desired flesh for food: *As yet their meat was in their mouth, and the wrath of God came upon them, and he slew the most of them.*[89] Indeed the judgments of God are usually slower in being manifested when we are prevented from having evil desires satisfied. For the quicker that an evil desire is permitted to be fulfilled, the more speedily it is usually punished. And so by the fact that the wicked person is quickly made to appear great in order to be powerful, action is taken with rapidity that he should not be. For the trees that grow more slowly last many years, and those that flourish in a short time perish more quickly, and in a sense while they are in a hurry to be, they are on the way not to be.

Here is added: *When he shall be filled, he shall be straitened.*[90] First, of course, from avarice he aspires to heap together things he covets, and when he has gathered together a great many in a kind of belly of avarice, by being filled he is straitened because while he is concerned as to how he may keep the things he has acquired, his own fullness itself straitens him. For the field of a certain rich man had brought forth abundant fruit, but because he had no place to store such a harvest, he said: *What shall I do, because I have no room where to bestow my fruits? And he said: This will I do: I will pull down my barns and will build greater.*[91] He then who distressed by his abundance said, *What shall I do?* was upset as if oppressed by the quantity of food. Let us consider with what longings he desired that his land might produce abundant crops. Behold now his wishes are fulfilled, since the land did bear rich fruit. But because storage places are inadequate, the enriched rich man does not know what to do. O impoverishment caused by overabundance! By the fruitfulness of his land the mind of the covetous man is straitened. For when he says, *What shall I do?* he clearly shows that overburdened by the outcome of his desires, he labored under a kind of bundle of supplies. And so it is well said: *When he shall be filled, he shall be straitened*, since the mind of the covetous man which had before sought rest through plenty, was afterwards put to worse trouble for the safekeeping of that abundance.

And hence it is here yet further added: *He shall burn: and every sorrow shall fall upon him.*[92] For first he had sorrow in the wearying of his own concupiscence about how to lay hold of the things coveted: how to get some by flattery, some others by threats; but when having acquired these things, he has attained his desire, another sorrow wearies him, namely, that it is with anxious fear that he guards what he remembers having acquired with great trouble. On every side he fears attackers, and fears to be himself subjected to what he has done to others. He fears someone powerful lest he suffer violence from him; again, when he sees a poor man, he mistrusts him as a thief. He is solicitous too about the things which he has hoarded lest by their inherent frailty they be wasted through neglect. In all these matters then, because fear is in itself punishment, the unhappy man suffers things as great as those he is afraid of suffering. And after these sorrows he is also brought to hell and delivered over to eternal torments. Therefore every sorrow shall fall on him who is consumed both here first by the penalty of coveting, afterwards by the trouble of safekeeping, and elsewhere at some future time by the punishment of retribution.

But it is wonderful security of the heart not to seek the goods of others but to rest content with a sufficiency for each day. From this same security also arises everlasting rest because from a good and quiet state of mind we pass on to eternal joys. On the other hand, the reprobate are both wearied here in desires and hereafter in torments. And from the sorrow of scheming there arises their sorrow of pain since from the burning of avarice they are drawn into the fire of hell.

14

Prevention of avarice

For I have always feared God as waves swelling over me; and his weight I was not able to bear.[93] When swelling waves stand out overhead, and when they threaten that death which they bring down, no concern for temporal things, no enjoyment of the flesh is recalled by mariners. Those very things as well they throw overboard for the sake of which they undertook long voyages; all things are scorned by the mind through love of living. Accordingly he fears God as waves swelling over him who while he desires the true life, despises all things that he here bears in his possession. For as if caught by a tempest, we discard the freight of the vessel when from the mind that is overburdened we remove earthly desires. And the outcome is that the lightened vessel stays afloat which with a full cargo was sinking, because surely the weighty cares of this life drag down the mind. That mind is carried so much the higher amid the waves of temptations, as it is more carefully purged of worldly thoughts. But there is also something else related to the tossing of the sea that ought to be carefully watched. For when a storm arises, first light waves, and afterwards greater surges are stirred up; finally the waves lift themselves on high, and by their very height overturn all the seafarers. Thus in very deed does that last tempest of souls rush on that it may overwhelm the whole world. For now it shows us its beginnings by wars and disasters as by a kind of waves, and as we are daily brought closer to the end, we see heavier torrents of tribulations rushing in upon us. But ultimately, all the elements being in commotion, the heavenly judge when he comes brings the end of all things because at that time surely the tempest lifts the waves to the heavens. Hence it is also said: *Yet a little while, and I will move not only the earth, but heaven also.*[94] Because holy men are vigilantly mindful of this tempest, they fear it as the waves swell daily over them, and by these troubles that belabor the world, they foresee what trials are to follow.

But it is well added: *And his weight I was not able to bear*, because they who view with undistracted mind the coming of the last judgment, see surely that such great terror is impending as they not only dread then to see, but even now dread to foresee. For by the beholding of such great fright the soul trembles with dread, and diverting its attentive gaze, it is unwilling to behold what it foresees. Therefore it is well said: *And his weight I was not able to bear*, because when the mind through reflection sets out to explore the power of divine majesty coming to judgment and the terror of such searching scrutiny, soon fleeing back to itself, it is terrified at what it discovered.

15

Gluttony

He heareth not the cry of the exactor.[95] In this text some wish the belly to be understood by the exactor, for it exacts from us a certain debt since even by nature it requires daily income from human labor to be spent on it. It is more to the point to realize that the vice of gluttony tempts us in five ways: it often gets the start on times of need; sometimes without getting ahead of itself, it seeks more tasteful food; sometimes it looks for dishes that are prepared more carefully; sometimes it finds agreeable both quality of food and timing but exceeds in quantity the standard of moderation; sometimes what it longs for is even inferior, and yet it sins more seriously through the unrest of boundless desire. Jonathan in fact came under his father's sentence of death because in tasting honey he anticipated the time set for eating.[96] And the people brought out of Egypt died in the desert because, despising the manna, it sought flesh for food, which it considered more tasty.[97] And the first fault of the sons of Heli arose from the fact that the servant of the priest at their behest would not accept cooked meat according to the ancient custom but sought raw flesh for him to serve in a more savory way.[98] And when it is said to Jerusalem: *This was the iniquity of Sodom thy sister, pride, fullness of bread, and abundance,*[99] it is clearly shown that she gave up her well–being because, with the sin of pride, she went beyond the measure of moderate nourishment. And Esau lost the glory of the firstborn because he desired mean food, lentils, with great eagerness of longing; and when he put this ahead of selling his birthright he showed with what eagerness he coveted it.[100] For it is not the food but the desire that is at fault. Whence also we frequently take delicacies without blame and taste meaner food not without guilt of conscience. Indeed Esau, whom we have mentioned, lost his birthright because of lentils, and Elias preserved bodily strength by eating flesh in the desert.[101] Whence also the ancient enemy, because he knows it is not food but the desire of food that is the cause of perdition, both subjected the first man to himself not with flesh but an apple,[102] and tempted the second Adam not with flesh but bread.[103] Hence it is that the fault of Adam is commonly committed even when mean and cheap food is taken. For it is not Adam alone who has received the prohibiting command to abstain from forbidden fruit. For when God points out certain substances as injurious to our health, by a kind of prohibition he forbids us to use them. And while we desire and taste what is harmful, what else are we really doing but eating what is forbidden? Therefore nourishment is to be taken which nature requires, not which gluttony suggests.

16

Prevention of the vice of gluttony

There is no measuring up to the conflict of spiritual struggle if the enemy who is stationed within, namely, the appetite of gluttony, is not first conquered; because if we do not overcome those evils which are closer to us, we no doubt go on in vain to attack those which are distant. For war is uselessly waged in the field against external enemies if a traitorous citizen remains within the very walls of the city. The mind also of the combatant is itself by the grievous shame of confusion kept back from the encounter of spiritual combat when, weak in its battle with the flesh, it is wounded and overcome by the weapons of gluttony. For when it sees itself defeated by ignoble rebels, it is ashamed to enter into conflict with greater adversaries.

But some, ignorant of the order of battle, neglect to bring gluttony under control and proceed at once to spiritual engagements. They sometimes perform many acts of great bravery, yet with the vice of gluttony ruling over them, by enticement of the flesh they forfeit all their brave accomplishments; and while the belly is not restrained, all their valorous deeds are toppled at once by the lust of the flesh. Whence it is also written of the victory of Nabuchodonosor: *The chief of the cooks (Nabuzardan) destroyed the wall of Jerusalem.*[104] For by its allusion to the walls of Jerusalem what does Scripture express but the virtues of a soul that is tending to the vision of peace? Or who is understood by the chief of the cooks but the belly, which is served with most diligent care by cooks? The chief of the cooks destroys the walls of Jerusalem because when the belly is not restrained, it endangers the virtues of the soul. Hence it is that Paul was weakening the strength of the chief of cooks, who was besieging the walls of Jerusalem, when he said: *I chastise my body, and bring it into subjection; lest perhaps when I have preached to others, I myself should become a castaway.*[105] Hence he also said beforehand: *I so run, not as at an uncertainty; I so fight, not as one beating the air.*[106] Because when we restrain the flesh, we beat by these blows of our abstinence not the air but unclean spirits; and when we subject that which is within us, we inflict blows on adversaries positioned outside us. Hence it is that when the king of Babylon orders the furnace to be heated, he commands a mass of brimstone, tow, pitch and dry sticks to be supplied.[107] But yet he does not consume in this fire the abstinent youths because although the ancient enemy presents to our view innumerable desires of nutriments in order that the fire of lust may increase, yet the grace of the Holy Spirit inspires holy minds, and they remain unscathed by the fires of carnal concupiscence, so that although the flame may burn so far as to tempt the heart, yet the temptation may not consume as far as to exact consent.

But it is a great task of discretion to give this exactor something and yet to refuse him something, both to restrain gluttony by not giving, and by giving to support nature. This discretion is indicated when it is said: *He heareth not the cry of the exactor.*[108] For the word of this exactor is the necessary demand of nature. But his cry is the appetite of gluttony going beyond the bounds of necessity. But it should be known that pleasure so cloaks itself with the appearance of necessity that an accomplished observer can scarcely discern it. For while necessity asks for a debt to be paid, pleasure secretly provides a longing to be fulfilled; it brings the appetite into danger the more fearlessly, the more it conceals itself under the respectable pretense of satisfying need. But often secretly annexed pleasure ensues in the very course of eating; sometimes, however, it is boldly patent even in trying to take the lead. Still it is easy to discover when pleasure takes precedence over need, but it is very difficult to discern when it secretly allies itself with eating that is necessary. For because it follows the lead of natural appetite, it seems as if it were making its way more slowly in the rear. For at the time when the demand of necessity is met, because in the act of eating pleasure is blended with necessity, it is not known what need requires and what, as has been said, pleasure secretly procures. But we can often tell them apart, and yet, because we know from experience that they are connected, take pleasure, when carried beyond proper bounds, in being knowingly deceived; and while the mind is pleased with itself on grounds of necessity, it is deceived by pleasure. For it is written: *Make not provision for the flesh in its concupiscences.*[109] That therefore which is forbidden to be done through concupiscence is conceded under the guise of necessity.

But often, while we incautiously condescend to necessity, we are catering to concupiscence. And sometimes, while we strive to oppose these desires rather intemperately, we add the stresses of necessity. For it is necessary that everyone so maintain the stronghold of continence as to destroy, not the flesh, but the vices of the flesh. For generally, when the flesh is restrained more than is reasonable, it is weakened even for the practice of good works, so as to be unfit for prayer or preaching while it is intent on stifling completely the causes of vices within itself. As a helper of our inward intention there is the physical entity that is ours: to it belong the emotions of licentiousness; at the same time, it has as its function the carrying out of good works. But often while we attack an enemy in its person, we kill a citizen whom we love; and often while we spare this fellow citizen, we foster an enemy for battle. For our vices become self-assured from the same food by which virtues are nourished and kept alive.

And when a virtue is nourished, the strength of vices is frequently increased. But when intense abstinence weakens the power of vices, virtue also faints and gasps. Whence it is necessary for our inward self to preside as a kind of impartial arbiter between itself and its external counterpart, in order that its outward self may both always be able to perform its appointed ministry and never with unfettered boldness act counter to that duty; and let the inner self not be stirred if the other self whispers any suggestion, provided it is always subdued when the force of authority is imposed.

17

Provision for the flesh is prohibited in its desires, permitted in necessity

Frequently the soul is minded to take the way of righteousness, shakes off sloth, and is transported by desire into heavenly regions so that almost no trace of it seems left here below. And yet when it is summoned to make provision for the flesh, without which the course of the present life cannot be completed, this contingency keeps it trammeled below as if it had not yet made any spiritual progress. When the words of divine truth are heard, the soul is lifted up into love of the celestial region, but when preoccupation with the present life sets in again, it is buried under the weight of earthly cares, and the seed of heavenly hope lies dormant in the soil of the heart because the thornbush of care acquires dense growth. This same bush Truth uproots by itself with the hand of holy exhortation, saying: *Be not therefore solicitous for tomorrow.*[110] And in opposition to this solicitude it is said by Paul: *Make not provision for the flesh in its concupiscences.*[111] Yet in these words of our leader and his warrior we see that the soul is pierced with a mortal wound by the flesh as soon as a balance is not maintained in making provision for it.

Certainly while this mortal life goes on, we cannot wholly dispense with care for the flesh, but it is controlled so that it serves the mind as discretion requires. For whereas Truth forbids us to be anxious for tomorrow, he does not tell us to withhold altogether from things present the attention which he does caution us not to extend into the future. And indeed while Paul will not let provision be made for the flesh in its concupiscences, certainly he does permit it to be made in matters of necessity. Thus the care of the flesh must be restrained under the discreet guidance of careful control so that it may obey and not take charge; may not as a governess rule the soul but being subject to the dominion of the mind, like a handmaid wait in attendance; may come when summoned and when dismissed by intimation of the heart, quickly take leave; may scarcely show itself in the wake of holy thought and never obtrude in the presence of earnest thought. All this is imparted to us in the scriptural account of Abraham's meeting the three angels.[112] For he met them as they were coming, outside the door of his tent, but Sara stood behind the door: just as the man and the master of the spiritual house, that is, our intellect, must in thinking of the Trinity go beyond the confinement of the flesh and, as it were, go forth out of the door of its earthly habitation. But let care of the flesh, as a woman, not appear outside, and let her not venture to seem conspicuous so that being behind her husband, circumspectly concerned only with necessary matters, she may learn not to reveal her presence rashly, but to be governed by reserve. But often when it is said she should not count on herself but put her full trust and hope in God, she is loath to do so and does not believe that without her application earthly resources will be at hand. And hence this same Sara, upon hearing the promises of God, laughs, and is reproached for laughing, but after the reproach she is made to be with child. And she who in the vigor of youth was not able to become pregnant, when weakened by old age conceived in a shriveled womb because when care of the flesh has ceased to have self–confidence, by divine promise it receives against hope what from human reasoning it doubted it would ever obtain. Hence he that is begotten is well called Isaac, that is, laughing, because when it begets trust in heavenly hope, what else does our mind give birth to but joy? Therefore one must take steps lest care of the flesh either goes beyond the limits of necessity, or in what it seeks with moderation, relies on itself. For often the mind is deceived in considering that to be necessary which it desires for pleasure, so that it believes all that is pleasing to have a usefulness to which life has a claim. And often, because the effect matches what is foreseen, the mind is supported in self–confidence. And when it perceives that it has what others lack, it rejoices in reflecting on the greatness of its foresight and is so much the further removed from real foresight, the more unaware it is of the elation it is experiencing. Therefore we should resourcefully consider with constant earnestness and vigilance whether what we execute in deed or what we revolve within is not either externally increasing earthly care so as to encumber the mind, or is at least allowing the spirit to be exalted interiorly by its control of such care. We should take this precaution so that while we show fear of divine judgments with temporal prudence, we may escape the woes of everlasting judgment.

18

Lust

Blessed Job, in characterizing the offense of lust, says: *It is a fire that devoureth even to destruction,*[113] because the guilt of this outrage does not simply stain to the point of defilement but devours to the extent of destruction. And however many other deeds may be good, if the wickedness of lust is not washed away, they are overwhelmed by the immensity of this fault; hence Job added: *And rooteth up all offspring.*[114] The offspring of the soul of course are good works. Yet if over the soul, right order being inverted, the flesh exercises dominion, all the actions that are performed well are consumed by the fire of lust. For in the eyes of almighty God the works of righteousness and of devotion that are seen to be unclean by the infection of corruptness are of no account. For what gain is there if someone dutifully has compassion for a neighbor in need while he undutifully destroys himself, God's dwelling place? If therefore by purity of heart the flame of lust is not extinguished, any virtues that arise are fruitless, as is said through Moses: *A fire is kindled in my wrath, and shall burn even to the lowest hell: and shall devour the earth with her increase.*[115] For a fire consumes the earth with her increase when lust consumes the flesh and all its good deeds. For surely the flame of corruption burns up whatever issues from the fruit of righteousness.

Now the wickedness of lust is committed either in thought or deed. For our crafty enemy when he is unable to bring about the deed, tries to defile secret thought. Hence too it is said to the serpent by the Lord: *Thou shalt creep on the breast and belly.*[116] So the serpent creeps on the belly when the deceitful enemy through the human members subject to him drives lust on to fulfilling the deed, but the serpent creeps on the breast when those whom he cannot defile in the deed of lust, he does defile in thought. Thus to the one about to commit lust in act, the serpent creeps on the belly. But to another considering its commission in the mind, the serpent creeps on the breast. But because through thought commission of the deed comes about, the serpent is rightly described first as creeping on the breast and afterwards on the belly.

The places for the seed of coition are said to be in the loins with men but in the navel with women. Hence it is written: *His strength is in his loins, and his force in the navel of his belly.*[117] Hence it is also that Truth says to his disciples: *Let your loins be girt.*[118] Hence Peter, when he urged that lust be excluded from the heart, said in admonition: *Having the loins of your mind girt up.*[119] Hence Paul, when he said that the priesthood of Levi was tithed by the sacrifice of Abraham in the time of Melchisedech, indicated where Levi was then concealed in the body of his father: *For he was yet in the loins of his father.*[120] But that the seed vessel of lust is with women contained in the navel is attested by the prophet who, reproaching the wantonness of Judaea under the figure of a prostituted woman, says: *In the day of thy nativity thy navel was not cut.*[121] For to cut the navel in the day of nativity is to terminate the lust of the flesh at the time of conversion. For since it is difficult to correct evil beginnings and to improve the shape of something once it has been malformed, Judaea is blamed from her birth as having, while born of God, retained her navel unsevered, because she did not end lustful negligences. Because therefore both sexes are intensely submitted to the power of the devil by the infirmity of lust, his strength is both said to be in his loins against men, and his force in his navel against women.

It must therefore be duly noted that after the devil has once seized the spirit of a man, he immediately strives for the corruption of the flesh. We observe this even in the first man and woman; by covering their nakedness after the commission of pride,[122] they plainly showed that after they had endeavored to arrogate lofty powers to themselves, they soon experienced shame in the flesh.

19

Fornication is differentiated according to the status and commitment of the guilty person

Sometimes, it is true, the guilt of fornication may be not at all different from that of adultery, since Truth says: *Whosoever shall look on a woman to lust after her hath already committed adultery with her in his heart*.[123] The Latin word for adultery used here is derived from the Greek; yet the concupiscence that is forbidden in the text does not specifically concern a married woman. It appears our Lord is saying that by a lustful gaze at an unmarried woman adultery is committed. Yet generally speaking lust is differentiated according to the status or commitment of the guilty person; that is to say intentional concupiscence defiles one in sacred orders, as the sin of adultery defiles a layman. Nevertheless in persons who are alike, the same guilt of lust is differentiated; to the fact that in their case the sin of fornication is distinguished from that of adultery, the tongue of the great preacher bears witness: this is one of the assertions Paul makes: *Neither fornicators nor idolaters nor adulterers shall possess the kingdom of God*.[124] He assigned sentence to several types of guilt, showing how greatly they differ. By this statement of Job: *If my heart hath been deceived upon a woman*,[125] the holy man is revealed not even to have entertained a thought connected with the defilement of fornication. But by this further declaration: *And if I have laid wait at my friend's door*,[126] he clearly makes it known that he was free of the guilt of adultery. But perhaps someone may say about this matter: What does the holy man assert about himself that is extraordinary, if he did preserve himself not only from the guilt of adultery but also from the defilement of fornication? The fact of the matter is that there had not as yet gone forth for the restraining of the flesh the stricter instruction of revealed grace that not only condemns wantonness of the body but also of the heart. There had not as yet appeared the instances of chastity displayed by many living in continence as patterns for imitation; yet blessed Job provided examples of purity that he had not received. But by many even now after the prohibition of God, impurity of the flesh is committed. It follows that because now after the precept with so great fault there is serious transgression, with as great praise previously was there abstinence in this regard.

20

Prevention of lust

No one understands his wrongdoing unless he has begun to be righteous. For he who is turned the wrong way cannot perceive what he is. But he who is conscious that he is a sinner, has begun in some degree to be righteous, and being righteous blames what he had done when unrighteous. And by this accusation of himself he begins adhering to God when, passing a righteous judgment against himself, he condemns in himself what he perceives to be displeasing to God. But some persons do not know that they have sinned because they do not observe men. For if they considered men, they would more quickly acknowledge how much they had fallen beneath men by sin. And although in holy Scripture it is sometimes the custom to represent men as those who savor the things of men, as the apostle says: *Whereas there is among you envying and contention, are you not carnal?* immediately adding: *Are you not men?*[127] yet sometimes it calls men those whom it shows to be unaffected by the bestial impulse of passions. To them the Lord says through the prophet: *And you, the flock of my pasture, are men,*[128] for the Lord in truth feeds those whom carnal pleasure does not affect as it does the beasts. But on the other hand, they who yield to the desires of the flesh are no longer called men but beasts, as is said by the prophet of some who were dying in their sins: *The beasts have rotted in their dung.*[129] Indeed for beasts to rot in their dung is for carnal men to end their life in the stench of lust. For they are said to be no longer men but beasts, of whom it is said by the prophet: *Every one neighed after his neighbor's wife,*[130] and of whom another prophet says: *Their flesh is as the flesh of asses, and their issue as the issue of horses.*[131] And hence it is said by David: *Man when he was in honor did not understand: he is compared to senseless beasts, and is become like to them.*[132] Rightly then are those called men who are supported by reason and justice, and those are named irrational animals who are slaves to pleasure of the flesh.

But the flesh whose pleasure enslaves is called a worm, as Job testifies: *Man that is rottenness and the son of man who is a worm.*[133] And again: *His sweetness a worm.*[134] How great is the blindness of everyone full of lust and devoted to the pleasures of the flesh is clearly shown. For what is our flesh but rottenness and a worm? As for whoever covets carnal desires, what else does he do but love a worm? For our graves bear witness what the substance of our flesh is. What parent, what faithful friend can bear to touch the flesh of one however beloved that is filled with worms? And so when there is concupiscence of the flesh, let it be considered what it is when lifeless, and it is understood what is loved. For nothing has so much power to subdue the appetite of carnal desire, as for everyone to consider what that which he loves while it lives will be when dead. For when the corruption of the flesh is considered, it is seen in a moment that when the flesh is unlawfully coveted, decay is desired. Therefore it is well said of the mind of the lustful man: *His sweetness a worm*, because he who is seething with the desire of carnal corruption longs for the stench of rottenness.

21

Lust arises from pride and is overcome by humility

Who teacheth us more than the beasts of the earth, and instructeth us more than the fowls of the air.[135] The beasts of the earth are they who, from the practice of a carnal life, seek the lowest things; but the fowls of the air are they who scrutinize sublime things with the zeal of a proud curiosity. The former, by their way of life, place themselves below their proper state; the latter, by their searching, exalt themselves beyond their powers. The pleasure of the flesh casts the former down to the very bottom; the willfulness of curiosity lifts up the latter as into matters that are above them. To the former it is said by holy Scripture: *Do not become like the horse and the mule which have no understanding.*[136] The proud effort of the latter is blamed when it is said: *Seek not the things that are too high for thee, and search not into things above thy ability.*[137] To the former it is said: *Mortify your members which are upon the earth: fornication, uncleanness, lust, evil concupiscence;*[138] to the latter it is said: *Beware lest any man cheat you by philosophy and vain deceit.*[139] God teaches us, therefore, being above the beasts and the fowls of the air, that as long as we realize what we are, the weakness of the flesh does not cast us down, nor does the spirit of pride raise us up; we do not by sinking down, fall beneath the lowest things, nor do we become proud by boasting of sublime powers. For he who sins in the flesh is overcome by the appetite of beasts; likewise, he who is exalted in mind is raised up as are the fowls by the mobility of flight.

But if we carefully see to it that both humility of mind and chastity of body are maintained, we soon know that the one is preserved by the other. For pride has often been to many a seedbed of lust because while their spirit raised them as if on high, their flesh buried them in the lowest depths. For they are first secretly raised up, but afterwards they fall openly; for while they swell by the secret impulses of the heart, they fall with evident lapses of the body. In fact, thus exalted, they had to be struck with righteous retribution in order that, having set themselves above men by pride, they might be reduced by their lust to the semblance of beasts. Indeed, *man when he was in honor did not understand: he is compared to senseless beasts, and is become like to them.*[140] For the flight of knowledge lifted them as if on high; Paul said of them what we mentioned earlier: *Because, when they knew God, they have not glorified him as God or given thanks; but became vain in their thoughts.*[141] But how they fell into bestial and more than bestial pleasure he added, saying: *God gave them up to the desires of their hearts, unto uncleanness.*[142] See how the flesh overwhelmed those whom prideful learning had raised up: from the soaring of birds, they fell below the appetites of beasts; they sank beneath themselves by the very means through which they appeared to rise above themselves. We must take heed then, and by every safeguard the mind must be kept free of the swelling of pride. For our thoughts do not fly unburdened past the eyes of God; and through the years no moments of time are spent without being subject to retribution. God thus beholds what exalts the mind within and therefore permits the external strengthening of what will cause its decline. That is first raised up within which is afterwards struck down exteriorly by the corruption of lust. Open punishment surely follows a secret fault in order that inner defects may be punished by external evils and the heart may openly lose the high position which was secretly appropriated. For hence it is said by Osee against the Israelites: *The spirit of fornication is in the midst of them, and they have not known the Lord.*[143] In order to show that the cause of lust burst forth from the sin of pride, Osee proceeded to say: *And the pride of Israel shall answer in his face.*[144] The prophet said in effect: The sin which through pride of mind lay hidden, openly corresponds to the lust of the flesh. Accordingly the cleanness of chastity is to be maintained by the observance of humility. For if the spirit is dutifully humbled before God, the flesh is not raised unlawfully above the spirit. Indeed the spirit has dominion over the flesh committed to it if it acknowledges the obligations of lawful service to the Lord. For if through pride it slights its Creator, it consequently takes on itself combat with its servant, the flesh. Whence also the first one to be disobedient, as soon as he had sinned through pride, covered his nakedness.[145] For because his spirit had

offered affront to God, it soon experienced the shame of the flesh. And because it refused to be subject to its Creator, it lost the right over its subject, the
flesh, which it used to rule, so that the disorder of its own disobedience might
redound upon itself and it might learn, when overcome, what it had lost
through pride.

Therefore let no one consider after he has begun to seek things above
him and is overthrown by carnal pleasure, that he is only then defeated when
he is openly overcome. For if the poison of lust frequently springs from the
root of pride, the flesh then triumphed when the spirit was secretly proud; the
soul then began its fall into the wantonness of beasts when by lifting itself up as
the fowls, it rose higher than it should have. For hence it is that long–lived
continence suddenly comes to an end, that chastity preserved even to old age is
frequently violated. For since humility of heart is neglected, the just judge
turns his gaze even from bodily integrity, and at one time or another because of
open sin proclaims those to be reprobate whom in secret he long endured as
reprobate. For he who has suddenly lost something good held for a long time
has retained something evil; from it he suddenly proceeds to a further evil by
which he was even then estranged from God when he indicated adherence to
him by cleanness of body. Therefore because pride of mind leads to defilement of the flesh, the heart of the reprobate plunges from the flight of birds
into the wantonness of beasts. But holy men, in order that they may not fall
headlong into the whirlpool of lust through bestial appetite, carefully guard
the thoughts of their mind from the flight of pride, and so that they may not by
being foolish sink into the lowest depths, they humbly restrain all their exalted
pretensions.

22

Greed and wickedness; pride and vainglory

Those who are burdened by the weight of avarice are represented as a
plate of lead.[146] To them it is said by the prophet with reproach: *O ye sons of
men, how long will you be dull of heart?*[147] Indeed by lead, whose nature it is to
be heavy, the sin of avarice is especially denoted: greed renders the mind it has
infected so heavy that it can never be lifted up to seek things on high. Hence it
is written in Zacharias: *Lift up thy eyes and see what this is that goeth forth. And I
said: What is it? And he said: This is a vessel going forth. And he said: This is their
eye in all the earth. And, behold, a talent of lead was carried: and, behold, a woman
sitting in the midst of the vessel. And he said: This is wickedness. And he cast her
into the midst of the vessel and cast the weight of lead upon the mouth thereof.*[148]
Concerning this vision of the vessel and the woman and the lead, in order to

show more fully what he had come to know, he went on to say: *And I lifted up my eyes and looked: and, behold, there came out two women, and a wind was in their wings, and they had wings like the wings of a kite: and they lifted up the vessel between the earth and the heaven. And I said to the angel that spoke in me: Whither do these carry the vessel? And he said: That a house may be built for it in the land of Sennaar.*[149] Wishing to show the prophet by what sin especially the human race fell away from him, by the figure of a vessel God indicated the nearly wide open mouth of avarice.

We cited above: *This is their eye in all the world.*[151] We see many men of dull sense, and yet we find them shrewd in evil practices, witness the prophet who said: *They are wise to do evil, but to do good they have no knowledge.*[152] Therefore these persons are slow–witted, but in those things which they desire, they are spurred on by the goads of avarice; and whereas they are blind to what is good, under the encouragement of rewards they are quick in perception for doing evil things. Hence it is rightly said of this avarice: *This is their eye in all the world.* The text continues: *And, behold, a talent of lead was carried.* What is a talent of lead but the weight of sin from that avarice? Next it is said: *And, behold, a woman sitting in the midst of the vessel.* And the angel made known who the woman was, adding: *This is wickedness. And he cast her into the midst of the vessel.* Wickedness is cast into the midst of the vessel because in avarice there is always wickedness involved. *And he cast the weight of lead upon the mouth thereof.* The mass of lead is cast upon the woman's mouth because the wickedness of avarice is burdened by the weight of its own sinfulness.

And I lifted up my eyes and looked: and, behold, there came out two women, and a wind was in their wings. These two women are the two principal vices, that is, pride and vainglory, which are without doubt united to the wickedness of avarice. They are described as having a wind in their wings because they are subservient to the will of Satan in their actions. *And they had wings like the wings of a kite.* Now the kite is always engaged in preying on the young of animals. So these women have wings like the wings of a kite because surely their actions are like those of the devil, who is always plotting against the life of little ones. *And they lifted up the vessel between the earth and the heaven.* Pride and vainglory have this characteristic: they lift up above others in his own thoughts the one infected by them when he is held prisoner; at one time by pursuit of possessions, at another time by the desire of dignities they lift him up close to the height of honor. But he that is between earth and heaven both abandons things below and does not attain the things on high.

Therefore these two women lift up the vessel between earth and heaven because pride and vainglory so exalt the mind taken captive through greed for honor that men disdainfully forsake all their neighbors and boastfully seek the heights. But while such persons indulge in pride and in imagination transcend their fellowmen among whom they dwell, by just decree of God they do not succeed in being united to the heavenly inhabitants. Thus the vessel is said to be lifted up between earth and heaven because avaricious persons through pride and vainglory both look down on neighbors alongside them and by no means take hold of the things above, which are beyond them. *And I said to the angel that spoke in me: Whither do these carry the vessel? And he said to me: That a house may be built for it in the land of Sennaar.* Sennaar means their malodor. And as there is a good odor from virtue, witness Paul who says: *God manifesteth the odor of his knowledge by us in every place, for we are the good odor of Christ unto God,*[152] so conversely is there malodor from vice. *For the desire of money is the root of all evils.*[153] And because everything evil is engendered by avarice, it is fitting that the house of avarice should be built in malodor. And it should be taken into account that Sennaar is a very wide valley in which the building of a tower was begun by men in their pride: when the diversity of tongues was introduced, construction ceased.[154] The tower was called Babylon on account of the confusion of minds and tongues. Justly therefore is the vessel of avarice placed where Babylon, that is, confusion, is being built, because while it is certain that from avarice and wickedness all things evil have their origin, rightly are avarice and wickedness described as dwelling in confusion.

23

War against vices: How we are overcome now by one, now by another

There are some who resolve with practically fixed purpose to resist the vicious faults that lead them astray, but with the crisis of temptation rushing upon them, they do not stand fast in their proposed determination. Thus, when someone, puffed up by the evil boldness of pride, considers that the rewards promised to humility are great, he takes a stand against himself and, as it were, divests himself of the swelling and pompous haughtiness of pride and vows to prove himself humble in the face of any and all insults. But when the affront of a single word has suddenly moved him, he at once returns to his usual haughtiness and is led into such a state of pride that he does not at all remember that he had desired the advantage of humility. Another, troubled with avarice, avidly aspires to increase his holdings. When he sees that all things soon pass away, he halts the grasping vagaries of his mind, determines to seek nothing further, and to hold what he already has only under the control of great moderation. But when things that please him are suddenly presented to his eyes, the mind at once aspiring to obtain them cannot contain itself, seeks an opportunity of getting them, forgets the restraint it had agreed upon with itself, becomes unsettled under the influence of its planning and longing for their attainment. Another is defiled by the corruption of lust and is now held fast by long habituation, but he sees how estimable is the virtuousness of chastity and realizes it is shameful to be conquered by the flesh. Therefore he resolves to check the frailties of his passions and intends to use all his strength to recover from the habit. But when the notion of it is either presented to his eyes or brought back to his memory, struck by a sudden temptation he is at once driven from his previous state of readiness, and he who had raised against it the shield of determination lies pierced with the shaft of self–indulgence, overcome in his weakness by lust as if he had not taken up arms of resolve. Another is set on fire by the flames of anger and is unbridled even to the extent of inflicting insults on his neighbors. But when no cause for wrath crosses his mind, he considers how great is the worth of meekness, how exalted the virtue of patience, and readies himself to be forbearing even in the face of insults. But when any slight inducement to disturbance arises, he is in an instant roused from the marrow to protests and abuse, so that not only does the patience he had promised never occur to him, but the mind is beside itself, not aware of the reproaches it is voicing. And when he has fully satisfied his rage, it is as if he returns after exercise to a state or repose, and he then regains control of himself in the confinement of silence, when not patience but the gratification of his overbearing nature bridles his tongue. With difficulty therefore and belatedly, after insults have been offered, does he restrain himself, because even frothing horses are often curbed not by the hand of the rider but by the boundaries of the field. Therefore it is well said of the reprobate: *The paths of their steps are entangled.*[155] For by intent they indeed seek right avenues but are ever reverting to their accustomed evil ways, and being as if drawn out of themselves, they circle back to themselves, truly desiring good paths but never departing from evil ones. For they wish to be humble, yet without being despised; to be content with what they have, yet without experiencing need; to be chaste, yet without mortification of the body; to be patient, yet without tolerating insults; and when they seek to attain virtues, yet avoid their demands, what else is this than simultaneously to be unacquainted with the conflicts of war in the field and to desire the triumphs of war in the city?

Again, the fact that their ways are described as entangled may be understood in another sense as well. For often some persons vigorously prepare to encounter some vices, but neglect to subdue others; and when they do not take a stand against the latter, they are restoring against themselves the former, which they had subdued. Someone, for instance, has now freed the flesh from lust, but he has not yet withdrawn the mind from avarice; and when he remains earthbound to indulge in avarice and does not abstain from worldly pursuits, under given circumstances he also falls into lust, which he seemed to have already subdued. Another has overcome the hold of avarice but has never subdued the force of lust, and when he is paying the price of fulfilling his lust, his heart also yields to the yoke of avarice, which he had for a long time overcome. Another has now overthrown rebellious impatience but has not yet conquered vainglory; and when on account of the latter he meddles with the honors of the world, hampered by the vexations of dispute he again becomes a captive of his impatience; and while vainglory rouses the mind to self–vindication, on being surpassed it gives in to that which it had overcome. Another has subdued vainglory but has not yet suppressed impatience; and when impatiently he utters many threats to those who oppose him, being ashamed not to carry through on what he says, he is brought back under the yoke of vainglory, and thus vanquished, he sustains defeat in that quarter where he was rejoicing that he had been victor. Thus then do the vices retain a hold over their escapee by mutual assistance, and as one already lost they receive him back under the rule of their dominion and hand him over to each other in turn for vengeance. Thus for the wicked the paths of their steps are entangled because although by mastering one evil habit they free the foot, yet while another habit holds sway, they get their foot caught in the very one that they had conquered.

24
Succession of vices: When one is conquered, another conquers

The terrible ones shall go and come upon him.[156] Those here called terrible ones are evil spirits, who are to be feared and kept at a distance by righteous minds. And since these evil spirits are rightly believed to concern themselves individually with particular vices, when a wicked person in fact abandons for a time some vices and begins to practice others, then surely the terrible ones go and come upon him, since—although some evil habits leave the soul of the wicked—others take possession of it. For you may often see the evil person, established in earthly power, stirred by strong passion and carrying out all that his rage has suggested; and when his fury is gone, soon lust harasses his soul; and when lust is discontinued for a time, pride—as on account of continence—is immediately substituted for lust in his heart, and in order to be feared by others, he seeks to appear terrifying. But when it is to his advantage to speak falsely, putting aside to a degree awesome pride, he is disarming and gentle in speech; and when he has ceased to seem proud, he does not hesitate to become deceitful. Rightly is it said of the one in whose mind vices give way to vices: *The terrible ones go and come upon him*, since by as many vices departing and entering as he is oppressed, by so many evil spirits coming and going is his soul veritably ravaged.

But often the wretched mind is aware of evil that has already passed on but does not perceive evil when it is still being harbored. The mind rejoices in being no longer subject to some vices but neglects to use precaution and to lament that their place has been taken by others, to which perhaps it succumbs more sinfully; and so it is that while some vices pass away and others continually replace them, the heart of the reprobate is possessed without intermission by vices. Hence it is well said by the prophet Joel: *That which the palmerworm hath left the locust hath eaten; and that which the locust hath left the bruchus hath eaten; and that which the bruchus hath left the mildew hath destroyed. Awake, ye that are drunk, and weep.*[157] For what is designated by the palmerworm (a caterpillar), which creeps with all its body on the ground, except lust? The latter so defiles the heart which is possessed that it cannot ascend to the love of heavenly purity. What is expressed by the locust, which flies by leaps, except vainglory, which exalts itself by empty pretensions? What is indicated by the bruchus (the wingless larva of the locust), almost the whole of whose body is concentrated in its belly, except voracity in eating? What but anger is denoted by mildew, which destroys as it makes itself felt? Therefore what the palmerworm has left the locust has eaten, because when the sin of lust has receded from the soul, vainglory often takes its place. For since it is not now subdued by love of the flesh, the soul prides itself as if holy through chastity. And what the locust has left the bruchus has eaten, because often when vainglory—which supposedly came from holiness—is foiled, either the appetite or various ambitious desires are indulged in rather immoderately. For the mind which does not know God is conducted the more perilously to any object of ambition, the more unrestrained it is by any love even of human praise. What the bruchus has left the mildew destroys because often when the gluttony of the belly is restrained by abstinence, the impatience of anger is more cruelly domineering: as mildew, it eats up the harvest by destroying it because the flame of impatience dissolves the fruits of virtues. When therefore vices replace vices, one plague devours the field of the mind when another abandons it.

And now to our text is fittingly added: *Awake, ye that are drunk, and weep,*[158] that is, shake off the sleepiness of your insensibility and resist with watchful lamentations the many plagues of vices that replace one another in the devastation of your hearts.

25

How great a tumult of thoughts oppresses those who are enslaved by vices

All who seek forbidden things or desire to appear important in this world are inwardly hindered by frequent disturbance of thought, and while they stir up in themselves a host of desires, they trample upon the helpless mind in their constant rambling. Thus one person has subjected himself to the rule of lust, and he forms before the eyes of the mind representations of impure acts, and when the realization of the deed is not forthcoming, the act is the more often committed by inward intent; the consummation of pleasure is sought, and the mind being struck powerless, carried this way and that, uneasy and blinded, seeks an opportunity for most vile fulfillment. Therefore that mind, which is disordered by a riotous tumult of thoughts, submits as to a throng. Another person has surrendered to the dominion of anger, and what has he taken to heart but quarrels which do not even exist? Such a person is often oblivious to the present, contradicts the absent, giving and receiving insults within himself, making his retorts more harsh. And while there is no one there to resist him, he makes up disputes interiorly with great outcry. He then who is pressed down by a mighty weight of angry thoughts, contends with an inner mob. Another has given himself over to the rule of avarice and developing an aversion toward his own possessions, covets another's belongings. Generally unable to obtain what he longs for, he spends the day in idleness, but the night in rumination. He is sluggish in useful work, because he is wearied with unlawful concerns; he augments his plans and broadens his capacity for grandiose thoughts; he strives to reach the desired objects and in order to obtain them he seeks the most secret and devious paths for the matter in hand. As soon as he thinks he has found some likely solution for a given situation, he is already jubilant at having practically obtained what he had coveted; and now he is planning what he may even further add to the object when he gets it, and is considering how it might be carefully worked into better condition. Assuming that he now possesses it and is improving its appearance, before long he is giving thought to the trickery of envious persons and pondering what quarrel they may pick with him. He examines his possible reactions, and while he has nothing as yet in his possession, the empty-handed litigant is working hard in defense of the object that he desires. Thus, although he has not any part of the desired object, yet he harbors inwardly the aftermath of covetousness, the exertion of strife. Someone else subjects himself to the tyranny of pride, and while he lifts up his uneasy heart to outdo men, he surrenders to the vice. He

covets ornaments of high honors, seeks to be exalted by his successes, and all
that he desires to be he pictures in his mind. Already it is as though he is sitting
in the judgment seat, sees the obedience of his subjects gratifying him, stands
out above others, inflicts penalties on some persons, rewards those who have
imposed them on others. Already in his imagination he appears in public surrounded by crowds, already notes with what deference he is treated; yet after
dwelling on these honors, he returns to solitude; now he is maltreating some
persons, honoring others; now he is exercising his dislikes upon the first group,
now he is receiving favors from the second. What else but daydreaming is that
person doing who pictures so many fanciful imaginings in his heart? Therefore, since he is burdened by the circumstances of so many eventualities that
he envisions, he certainly carries about within himself hosts of things that are
engendered by his desires. Someone else shuns forbidden objects, yet he
dreads being at a loss for the necessities of life; he is anxious to retain the
worldly goods granted him; he is ashamed to seem lowly among men, and he is
greatly concerned about appearing needy in his living conditions or an object
of contempt in public. He diligently determines what suffices for himself,
what the needs of his dependents may require; and in order that he may properly discharge the duties of patronage toward his dependents, he searches for
patrons whom he may himself depend upon. But while he is joined to them in
such a relationship, he is undoubtedly implicated in their concerns; in this con-
nection, he often consents to illicit acts, and evils which are distasteful on his
own account, he commits for the sake of other objectives which he has not forsaken. For often, while he dreads the lessening of his status in the world, he
gives approval to actions on the part of his patrons which in his own private
judgment he now condemns. While he gives careful thought to what he owes
to his patrons and to his dependents, what gain he may make for himself, what
is advantageous to his relationships, he is in a way beset by a crowding together
of concerns as great as the mass of demands that trouble him.

26
Vices: Whoever offends in one is guilty of all

I was clad with justice: and it clothed me as with a garment.[159] He is clothed
with justice as with a garment who protects himself on every side with good
behavior and leaves no part of his activity exposed to sin. For he that is just in
some deeds and unjust in others, is in a sense covered on one side and stripped
on the other. Nor are those any longer good deeds which are defiled by evil
deeds that supervene. For hence it is said by Solomon: *He that shall offend in
one shall lose many good things.*[160] Hence James says: *Whosoever shall keep the*

whole law, but offend in one point is become guilty of all.[161] This declaration he carefully developed when he added: *For he that said: Thou shalt not commit adultery, said also: Thou shalt not kill. Now, if thou do not commit adultery, but shalt kill, thou art become a transgressor of the law.*[162]

Accordingly, with the eyes of the heart directed all around us, we must watch on every side. Hence it is also rightly said by Solomon: *With all watchfulness keep thy heart, because life issueth out from it.*[163] As he was about to say *watchfulness*, he put first *all*, surely in order that each one might inspect himself on this side and that, and as long as he is in this life, might know that he is faced with spiritual enemies in battle array, lest the reward he is earning by given actions be lost by other deeds, and lest on one side the enemy be blocked, but on another side an entrance be thrown open. For if against plotting enemies a city is fortified by a great rampart, is encircled with strong walls, is defended by a sleepless watch, and yet there be only a single opening left undefended through neglect, at that point surely the enemy, who seemed to be shut out on all sides, enters in. For instance, let us hear with what defense the Pharisee who went up into the Temple to pray had fortified the city of his soul: *I fast twice in a week*, he says; *I give tithes of all that I possess.*[164] He that started with: *I give thee thanks*, did surely employ great defenses. But let us see where he next left an undefended opening for a plotting enemy: *that I am not as this publican.*[165] See how through pride he opened to attacking enemies the city of his heart, which he blockaded in vain by fasting and almsgiving. Vainly are other sections defended when one place with an entrance open to the enemy is not defended. He rightly gave thanks but wrongly exalted himself above the publican. By priding himself he betrayed the city of his heart, which he guarded by fasting and by giving alms. Gluttony was subdued by abstinence, voracity of the belly was destroyed, avarice was overcome by generosity, covetousness was disparaged. With what great effort do we believe this was accomplished? Oh! how many painful efforts affected by one vice lost strength, what great qualities were ruined by the weapon of one sin! Hence there is great need both always to be doing good works and carefully to refrain from dwelling on these same good works, lest if they exalt the mind, they cease to be good, as serving not the Creator but pride.

Concerning this matter, we are not acting improperly if from books—though not canonical, yet written for the edification of the Church—we adduce confirmation. Consequently: Eleazar in battle struck and brought down an elephant, but fell under the beast that he killed.[166] Who then are represented by him whose own victory crushed him but those persons who overcome vices, but by being exalted are felled by the very things they overthrow? For it is as if the one who is exalted by the sin he overcomes, dies under the enemy he slays. Accordingly it must above all be kept in mind that good works cannot be beneficial if evil ones that creep in are not repelled. All that is done perishes if it is not carefully protected by humility. Hence too it is well said of our first parent: *The Lord put him into the paradise of pleasure, to work it and to keep it.*[167] For to *work* something is to do the good that is commanded, but the one upon whom there steals what is forbidden does not *keep* what he has wrought.

BOOK 4

THE RICH

Prologue

The discussion of vices is followed by the fourth book of Part 1, in which detailed consideration is given to the major servile followers of the vices, that is, the rich. While they strain to increase their temporal wealth, their interim pleasures bring them into a perilous state: across beguiling meadowlands they are diverted to the prison of death.

On the contrary, in the fourth book of Part 2, rectors of the Church are discussed; considered to be prominent among those who practice the virtues, they are especially committed to spiritual rather than worldly gain, to be faithful in increasing the Lord's goods.[1] Love like theirs—contrary to the attachment characteristic of the rich—if carefully nurtured, will provide the earnest reader with a remedy for love of riches.

1

God and temporal riches cannot both be loved

Whoever is dominated by the love of earthly things does not find happiness in God. The soul cannot indeed exist without happiness, for it takes delight either in things below or in things above; and the more it is dedicated with soaring devotion to things above, the more disdainful it is in its aversion to those below; on the other hand, the more it is fired with keener interest in things below, the more insensible and deserving of condemnation it is in its tepidity toward those above. For both cannot possibly be loved at the same time on equal terms. Hence the apostle John, knowing that amid the thorns of worldly attachments the harvest of heavenly charity cannot flourish, before he sows the seed of eternal love eradicates from the hearts of his hearers the thorns of earthly affections with the holy dexterity of the sacred word: *Love not the world, nor the things which are in the world.*[2] And next he says: *If any man love the world, the charity of the Father is not in him.*[3] This is as much as to say: Both these loves are not admitted to one and the same heart, nor does the yield of heavenly charity increase in that heart where the thorns of unworthy gratification destroy it. And he enumerates all the gashes resulting from that self-indulgence: *For all that is in the world is the concupiscence of the flesh, and the concupiscence of the eyes and the pride of life, which is not of the Father but is of the world. And the world passeth away and the concupiscence thereof.*[4] Therefore no one oppressed in spirit by the thorns of earthborn love can take delight in God.

Hence it is that under the image of Ephraim it is said by the prophet of a soul weighed down by earthly desires: *Ephraim is become as bread baked under the ashes, that is not turned.*[5] For by our nature as established by God we have the intention that aspires toward God; but from an evil customary mode of life an inclination within us directs the mind toward the present world. But bread under the ashes is cleaner on the side which is concealed underneath, and more soiled on the side which has ashes on it. Whoever therefore disregards the motivation by which he ought to seek God, turns down the cleaner side, as of bread under the ashes; and when he willingly supports worldly concerns, he bears above him what amounts to a heap of ashes. But the bread under the ashes would be reversed if he were to cast off the ashes of carnal desires and let appear above the good intention that he had by long neglect repressed in himself. But a reversal is refused when a mind weighed down with the love of secular concerns neglects to throw off the accumulation of ashes lying upon it; and when it makes no attempt to rise up with right intention, it turns down the cleaner surface.

2

Those who love earthly things labor for temporal gain and soon grow weary in striving for what is spiritual

All who are enamored of this world are strong in the things of earth, weak in the things of heaven. Thus for temporal glory they are willing to work themselves to death, and for everlasting hope they do not even for a short time persist in their effort. For the sake of earthly gain they endure every injustice, and for the sake of a heavenly reward they refuse to bear even the slightest verbal affront. They are strong enough to stand before an earthly judge even for a whole day, but at prayer in the presence of God they grow tired even in the course of a single hour. Often they endure exposure, abjectness, hunger, to acquire riches and honors, and they painfully do without those things they are striving to obtain. But they avoid the more readily seeking with any effort the things that are above, the more slowly they think their labor will be requited.

And yet they cannot either seek when not possessed, or keep once attained, the temporal things they desire without burdensome, care–ridden difficulties: to strive for outstanding glory among their equals; to exact undue respect from inferiors and to show less than due respect to superiors; for the most part to demonstrate power by injustice; always to do what is wicked, and yet—in order not to be charged with wickedness—to be apprehensively on guard. All these things surely annoy the wretched persons, but those annoyances they do not feel, overcome as they are by the love of temporal things. And hence it is rightly said: *And they counted it delightful to be under the briers*,[6] because urged on by the delights of sin, from attachment to the present life they are not aware how bothersome are the things they undergo.

Therefore they rejoice, but under briers, because they take delight in earthly things; yet as long as they are unable to administer temporal matters without distress, these unfortunate persons are rankled by those concerns which weigh upon them. They remain under the briers, and this circumstance they deem delight because at the same time they endure hardships from love of the present life, still, being caught in the toils of excessive desire, they consider the trouble of that endurance to be pleasure. Hence Jeremias, rightly taking upon himself the likeness of the human condition, complains in lamentation: *He hath inebriated me with wormwood*.[7] Any inebriate is insensible to what he is undergoing, but he that is inebriated with wormwood has both imbibed what is bitter and yet does not understand the bitterness with which he is imbued. So the human race, being by the just judgment of God left to its pleasures and consigned by them to voluntary sufferings, is inebriated with wormwood. For these are bitter things which it endures for the love of this life, and yet by the blindness of concupiscence as by the insensibility of inebriation, the bitterness is not understood. Thirsting thus for earthly glory, while finding instead many tribulations, it drinks what is bitter. But because it took this unrestrainedly, through inebriation it is now unable to discern the evil of that bitterness. Thus wicked men for the sake of the glory of this world love even tribulations and on this account willingly submit to drudgery and most docilely place themselves under the yoke of heavy labors. This is well described under the likeness of Ephraim by the prophecy of Osee: *Ephraim is a heifer taught to love threshing*.[8] For a heifer accustomed to the labors of threshing, very often, when set loose, returns of its own accord to the same customary labor. So the mind of the wicked, committed to the service of this world and accustomed to the weariness of temporal things, even if it is left to its own devices, yet is eager to be subject to earthly straining and seeks the usual wretched way of life, the labor of threshing: it is not willing even when it is permissible, to be free from the yoke of worldly servitude. This yoke was removed from the disciples by the Lord, who when he said: *Take heed to yourselves, lest perhaps your hearts be overcharged with surfeiting and drunkenness,* instantly added: *and the cares of this life; and that day come upon you suddenly.*[9] And again: *Come to me, all you that labor and are burdened; and I will refresh you. Take up my yoke upon you and learn of me, because I am meek, and humble of heart*.[10] What is it for the Lord to call himself meek and humble in his teaching except an indication that he proposes level paths for a good life with the rough ways of pursuing pride left behind? But because the minds of the wicked are more pleased by the harsh aspects of pride than by what is agreeable in meekness and humility, they decide it is delightful to be under brambles. For from love of the world they are ready to bear asperities as if they were mild and enjoyable while they struggle in this life to reach the heights of achievement.

The Lord commands desistance from absorption in worldly efforts; he urges the pleasantness of holy tranquility. And yet the frantic mind of the wicked rejoices more on obtaining what is carnally harsh than on having what is spiritually attractive, is more satisfied by the bitterness of fatigue than by the restfulness of quietude. The Israelite people revealed this preference on its part: while it received the sustenance of manna from above, it longed for the fleshpots, the melons, the leeks and onions from Egypt.[11] For what is signified by the manna but the food of grace, having a sweet savor, given from on high for the restoring of the interior life to persons living in true freedom; what by the fleshpots but carnal works, which are effected with difficulty by the toils of tribulations as by fires; what by melons but earthly delights; what by leeks and onions, which very often bring tears to those who eat them, but the distress of the present life—borne by its devotees not without grief—and yet is loved amid the tears? Therefore forsaking manna, they sought together with melons and pieces of meat, leeks and onions, surely because the worldly-minded scorn the pleasant benefits of tranquility, conferred by grace, and for the sake of carnal pleasures they covet the tiring paths of this life, even though fraught with tears; they scorn having a state of life in which they may rejoice in a spiritual manner and seek one in which they may mourn even from a material point of view.

3

The rich will not easily reach the kingdom of heaven, but affection, not fortune, is open to blame

The powerful and the rich have this characteristic: being engrossed with deceitful riches, they neglect the true riches of God; and the less they investigate what is true, the more fully are they attracted to false treasures. And indeed the manifold concern for earthly things is engrossing and blinding. Hence it is that with difficulty is eternal rest attained by the powerful who are surrounded by numberless hosts of lieges and bound with the tight coils of a great variety of concerns. In this regard Scripture says: *A most severe judgment shall be for them that bear rule.*[12] Hence Truth says in the Gospel: *Unto whom-soever much is given, of him much shall be required.*[13] It rarely happens that those who possess gold strive for eternal rest, inasmuch as Truth himself says: *How hardly shall they that have riches enter into the kingdom of God!*[14] Indeed, what joys in the next life can they be hoping for who here yearn for increase of riches? Yet in order that our Redeemer might show this (eternal rest for the rich) to be very rare and to come about only by divine prodigy, *With men*, he says, *this is impossible; but with God all things are possible.*[15]

Therefore those who view themselves as abounding in earthly resources do not seek the true riches of God. And yet fortune is not at fault but affection. For all things that God created are good, but he who misuses good things surely brings it about that as through gluttony of voraciousness, he perishes on account of the bread by which he ought to live. The beggar Lazarus attained rest, but torments afflicted the proud rich man.[16] And yet Abraham was rich, who held Lazarus in his bosom; still, addressing his Creator, he says: *I will speak to my Lord, whereas I am but dust and ashes.*[17] How then did he, who considered himself to be dust and ashes, know what value to assign to riches? Or when did his possessions ever exalt him who had such a mean opinion of himself, the owner of them?

And yet there are some who are not supplied with earthly property and yet tower in their own mind with the arrogance of pride. No fortune uplifts them to the display of power, yet the boldness of their conduct ranks them among the reprobate rich persons. All whom love of the life to come does not humble, the sacred word here calls rich, because in the avenging of judgment there is no distinction between those who show pride in their wealth or in their attitude.

4

The rich disagree among themselves but agree in oppression of the good

And as the tops of the ears of corn they shall be broken.[18] The tops of the ears of corn are the beards. They come out of an ear of corn joined, but growing a little further are separated from one another, shaggy and stiff. In just this way the evil–minded rich appear on the scene of this world's glory. For by a shared nature they are joined to one another, but as they thrive they are on the contrary divided against one another. For one looks down upon another, and a second is inflamed against a third by the firebrands of envy. They, then, who are separated from the unity of charity stand bristling against one another as beards do. What then might I have called the evil–minded rich of this world but typical beards of the human race? While they pride themselves against one another, with one accord they strike against the life of the good, are indeed divided among themselves, yet together bear down upon the grains beneath.

At a given time therefore the beards spring up high, the grains lie hidden, because both the power of the reprobate stands out, and the glory of the elect is not apparent. The former are prominent in the pride of honors, the latter are in the low state of humility. But the time of winnowing will arrive, which will both break the stiffness of the beards and not bruise the solid grains. For then the pride of the wicked is shattered, then the life of the elect becomes clear with all the brilliance of faultlessness because while the unrighteous are torn apart, the effect of this crushing of the beard is that the grains which lay hidden appear. And when the beards are broken, the brightness of the grains is revealed because when the wicked lapse into everlasting punishments, the righteousness of the saints is manifested with the glow of truth. Whence too it is rightly said by John: *Whose fan is in his hand; and he will thoroughly cleanse his floor and gather his wheat into the barn. But the chaff he will burn with unquenchable fire.*[19]

<h2 style="text-align:center">5</h2>

Temporal things are not to be loved or trusted; they are to be possessed for usefulness not pleasure

He who puts his hope in a creature gives up hope in the Creator. Hope had been set in precarious things by that rich man who said: *Soul, thou hast much goods laid up for many years; take thy rest; eat, drink, make good cheer.*[20] But the heavenly voice rebukes this man, saying: *Thou fool, this night do they require thy soul of thee; and whose shall those things be which thou hast provided?*[21] That day was the last on earth for him who had expected many years amid the abundance of his goods, so that in fact he who, while hoarding up means for himself, was looking far ahead, did not see a single additional day. For it is the equivalent of laying a foundation in running waters to wish to base an assurance of hope on perishable things. For while God abides forever, all things pass away. What then is it to attach ourselves to passing things but to flee from him who abides? For who, being seized by the swollen currents of rushing waters, could ever remain fixed himself as the water tumbles down? If anyone is to avoid passing on without trace, his only course is to flee passing things, lest by what he loves he should perforce experience what he seeks to avoid. For he who clings to what is slipping away is surely destined to go the way of what he is grasping. So the first step is not to love temporal things and then not to put trust in such things that are to be possessed for the sake of usefulness, not pleasure; for when one is attached to what is transitory, soon he imperils the condition of his soul. For the surge of the present life drags off the one whom it lifts up; and he is quite unthinking who is tossed about in the water and yet attempts to stand fast. But there are very many who while they never place confidence in transitory things, yet when they are abundantly available to them for necessary purposes, rejoice in the secrecy of their hearts. In this matter there is no doubt that the less anyone is grieved that the things of eternity should be lacking, the more he rejoices that those of time are supplied to him; and the less he grieves that temporal things are lacking, the more surely may he expect that eternal blessings shall be his.

6

Riches are comparable to a dream: at death a rich man takes with him only what he has given to the poor

The rich man when he shall sleep shall take away nothing with him; he shall open his eyes and find nothing.[22] In harmony with that belief the Psalmist says: *All the foolish of heart were troubled. They have slept their sleep: and all the men of riches have found nothing in their hands.*[23] For in order that the rich after death may find something in their hand, they are told before death in whose hands they should place their riches: *Make unto yourselves friends of the mammon of iniquity: that when you shall fail they may receive you into everlasting dwellings*.[24] *The rich man when he shall sleep shall take nothing away with him.*[25] When he died he would take away his goods with him if when he lived, on hearing a petitioner he had taken them to himself; for all earthly things that we part with by keeping, we keep by giving; our retained patrimony is lost; paid out, it remains. For we cannot long continue together with our goods because either we by dying abandon them, or they by perishing in a sense abandon us while living. We must therefore act in such a way that completely perishable things become an imperishable reward.

But it is a matter for great wonder that it is said: *When he shall sleep he shall open his eyes and find nothing.* For in order to sleep we close our eyes and on waking open them. But in this case, because man consists of soul and body, when the sleep of one component is mentioned, the wakings of the other are indicated because when the body falls asleep in death, then the soul awakes in true knowledge. And so the rich man sleeps and opens his eyes, because when he dies in the flesh, his soul is compelled to see what it refused to foresee. Then indeed it wakes up in knowledge of the truth, then it sees that all that it possessed is nothing. Then it finds itself empty, whereas it used to rejoice that compared with other men it was replete with goods. It sleeps and takes nothing away with it, no part at all of the goods that it possessed. For the fault allied with the goods accompany them, although all things for the sake of which the fault was committed are left behind. So then, let him go now and take pride in things acquired, let him be raised above others and pride himself in having what his neighbor does not have. Sooner or later the time will come for him to awake and to learn then how worthless that was which he had possessed in sleep. For it often happens to the needy person while sleeping that in a dream he sees himself rich, is overjoyed that he has what he lacked, and now seeks to disdain those by whom it grieved him to be disdained. But suddenly waking up, he who for a while at least in sleep possessed the semblance of riches, is sorry that he has awakened. For he groans continuously under the weight of poverty and is oppressed by the afflictions of his indigence, all the worse because for a very short time he was rich at least in a barren way. This is indeed the exact state of the rich of this world who are filled with pride because of what they own. They do not know how to make good use of their abundance: they are rich as dreamers are; but on waking up, they discover their poverty because they take nothing away with them to the judgment that is final, and the higher they are now raised up for a brief time, the more severely they reproach themselves in eternity. So let the rich man say: *He shall open his eyes and find nothing*, because he there opens to punishments the eyes that here he kept closed to mercy. He opens his eyes and he finds not the return for kindness because he kept them shut when it was at hand. They too are late in opening their eyes who, as Wisdom testifies, are in the time of their condemnation described as ready to say: *What hath pride profited us? Or what advantage hath the boasting of riches brought us? All those things are passed away like a shadow, and like a messenger that runneth on.*[26] They now learn by their loss that the things which they possessed were worthless and transitory, which so long as they were theirs, seemed to their foolish hearts great and abiding. It was late that the rich man opened his eyes when he saw Lazarus at rest, whom he refused to notice lying at his door.[27] He understood there what here he was unwilling to do: in his condemnation he was forced to acknowledge what it was that he lost when he did not recognize his neighbor in need.

7

The folly of seeking riches and glory, since the rich and the famous die and decay

Your remembrance shall be compared to ashes.[28] All those who by earthly reckoning follow the fashion of the present age, are attempting in all that they do to leave to this world remembrance of themselves. Some through the pursuits of war, some through the towering walls of edifices, some through learned books of worldly lore, are eagerly at work building up for themselves a name to be remembered. But since life itself quickly runs on to an end, what is there about it that will be permanent when in its instability it is rapidly slipping away? For a breeze disperses ashes, as it is written: *Not so the wicked, not so: but like the dust, which the wind driveth away from the face of the earth.*[29] And so the remembrance of the foolish is rightly compared to ashes because it is lodged where it may be carried away by a breath of air. For however much anyone may endeavor to make his name illustrious, his remembrance is stored as ashes are: the wind of mortality snatches it away even more quickly. On the contrary, it is written of the righteous man: *The just shall be in everlasting remembrance.*[30] For by the very fact that he marks his deeds for the eyes of God alone, he sets firm the renown of his name in eternal realms.

The text continues: *And your necks shall be brought to clay.*[31] As sight is signified by the eye, so is pride by the neck. The neck is brought down to clay when every proud man is humbled in death, and the flesh that was extolled decays in corruption. For let us consider what is the condition of the corpses of the rich lying in their graves; what the image of death is in the lifeless flesh; what the decay of corruption is like. And surely these were the very persons who were extolled with honors, took pride in the things they acquired, looked down upon others, rejoiced that they were quite unique. And as long as they never gave thought to where they were going, they knew not what they were. But the neck is brought down to clay because they lie shunned in corruption who exulted in vainglory. The neck is brought down to clay because the decay of corruption proves how vulnerable is worldly power.

8

The rich who labor at heaping up riches are suddenly borne away to eternal punishment

And the dwelling of the wicked shall not stand.[32] A dwelling is constructed in order that the body may be protected from heat and cold. Here by the word dwelling is meant the building up of earthly good fortune by which the wicked are augmenting impermanent shelters to shield themselves from the rigors of the present life as from heat and rain. Thus they take steps to advance in honors, lest they seem unworthy of respect. They accumulate in profusion the good things of earth, lest they waste away in the chill of neediness. They spurn providing for what is to come and are fully intent on not lacking anything here and now. They seek to spread their name in order not to be unknown, and if everything goes according to plan, they regard themselves as invulnerable and are happy with their lot. Thus in their inner stronghold they have surely set up their dwellings. They bear adversities with impatience, they rejoice in prosperity with gaiety. They are concerned only with present circumstances and seek no support in fostering by recollection love for their heavenly home. They rejoice that they have the good things they desire and finding earthly rest in them, by ignoring the soul they inter it amid those things, because felled by the weapon of worldly concern, they bear within themselves the mass of material belongings they add to by searching outside themselves.

And the farther removed they are from the inheritance of the eternal country, the deeper in the earth do they fix the foundations of the heart. It is hence that in the beginning of human existence Enoch is born seventh in the chosen family.[33] It is hence that Cain calls his firstborn son Enoch and gives his name to the city that he built.[34] For Enoch means dedication. And so the wicked dedicate themselves in the beginning, for in this life, which is first, they plant the root of the heart so that they flourish here to their satisfaction and yet wither completely with respect to the country that comes hereafter. But for the righteous, Enoch is born the seventh because the solemn dedication of their lives is kept for the end. It is hence, as Paul attests, that Abraham dwells in tents, for he looks forward to a city with foundations that the heavenly builder constructed.[35] It is hence that Jacob walks humbly, following the flocks of sheep, and Esau coming to meet him proceeds proudly amid the bustle of numerous attendants, because the elect are without pride, and the prosperous reprobate take pride in worldly goods.[36] Hence the Lord says to Israel: *If thou shall choose one from the people of the land and make him king over thee, he shall not multiply horses and horsemen to himself.*[37] And yet as soon as the first king chosen from that people had attained the height of power, he chose for himself three thousand horsemen, immediately progressed into pride, and rushed into further elevating the height he held, because outwardly he could not conceal by an air of equality the fact that his spirit raised his inner self high above others.[38] That rich man had, so to speak, built for himself a fortified dwelling when he said: *Soul, thou hast much goods laid up for many years; take thy rest; eat, drink, make good cheer.*[39] But because his dwelling is not based upon the foundation of truth, he instantly heard: *Thou fool, this night do they require thy soul of thee: and whose shall these things be which thou hast provided?*[40] Therefore it is well said: *And the dwelling of the wicked shall not stand,* because the devotees of this fleeting life, while they diligently seek stature in temporal matters, are suddenly carried off into eternity.

9

Those who seek riches and glory in earthly things: how in the end the latter are scattered

They that fear the hoar frost, the snow shall fall upon them.[41] The frost congeals below, but the snow falls from above. And often some persons, while they fear temporal adversities, expose themselves to the severity of everlasting punishment. Concerning them it is rightly declared by the Psalmist: *There have they trembled for fear where there was no fear.*[42] For one person already longs to defend the truth freely, yet disturbed in his longing, he fears the indignation of an earthly power; and while on earth he fears man who opposes the truth, he undergoes the wrath of heavenly Truth. Another, conscious of his sins, already desires to give to the needy the things he possesses, yet fears lest he himself be in need of what he has given away. When, being alarmed, by holding back he provides worldly reserves, he deprives the soul of the sustenance of mercy, and when he fears suffering need on earth, he cuts himself off from the abundance of heavenly nourishment. Therefore it is well said: *They that fear the hoar frost, the snow shall fall upon them*, because those who fear from below what ought to be despised, undergo from above what ought to be feared; and when they will not disregard what they might have scorned, they meet with judgment from heaven that they cannot bear. Now when they act in this way, they attain the glory of the world in time, but what will they do in the hour of summons, when in terror they abandon at once all the things that they kept here with great fear?

And hence it is rightly added: *At the time when they shall be scattered they shall perish.*[43] For all persons who are ruled by concern for the present life are in disarray by the loss of it, and then they perish outwardly who long since perished within by neglecting the things of eternity. Concerning them it is rightly added: *And after it groweth hot they shall be melted out of their place.*[44] For every wicked person, after it has grown hot, is melted out of his place because in drawing near to the judgment of inner severity when he has already begun to be heated in the knowledge of his punishment, he is severed from that gratification of the flesh to which he had long adhered. Hence it is that it is said by the prophet against the reprobate: *And vexation alone shall make you understand what you hear,*[45] because they never truly understand the things of eternity except when they are already made to undergo for temporal things punishment without recourse. Then the mind is heated and is inflamed with the fires of fruitless penitence; it shall fear being led to judgment and wishfully holds fast to thc present life, but it is melted from its place because abandoning the pleasures of the flesh, its insensibility is dissolved by chastisement.

10

The rich who find consolation now will have none hereafter

But the eyes of the wicked shall decay: and the way to escape shall fail them.[46] Moreover, the eyes of the wicked are the intentions of carnal desires in them. These decay for this reason: they neglect their eternal interests and are ever on the alert only for transitory advantages. For they give thought to acquiring glory, they wish above all things an increase in temporal goods, they are daily advancing toward death with the passing of transient things; but they know not how to consider the things of mortality in accordance with their mortal nature. The life of the flesh is failing as the minutes pass, and yet the desire of the flesh is growing; property acquired is ruined by an instant end, yet the eagerness to possess is unending; but when death snatches the wicked, then indeed their desires are ended with their life. And their eyes surely decay through heavenly avenging because here through self-examination they would not desist from earthly gratification. These eyes of theirs the Psalmist had seen closed in the midst of former enjoyment when he said: *In that day all their thoughts shall perish.*[47] For they meet at once with eternal woes they had never thought about and suddenly lose the temporal goods they had long held and used. Every way of escape shall fail them because their iniquity finds no place to hide from the observation of the strict judge. For now, when the wicked suffer sad[48] or adverse things, they find a hiding place for refuge because they at once have recourse to the enjoyment of earthly objects of desire. For in order that poverty not torment them, they soothe the spirit with riches. Lest the contempt of their neighbors sadden them, they exalt themselves with the trappings of excellence. If the body is surfeited with fastidiousness, it is supplied with a variety of dishes that are served. If the mind is downcast by any incitement of sadness, it is at once relieved by the diversions of pastimes that are proposed. Here therefore they have as many places of refuge as there are delights at their disposal. But some time or other the way to escape shall fail them when their soul, with all else left behind, sees only itself and the judge. Then the pleasure is withdrawn, but the guilt of pleasure remains, and these unfortunate persons suddenly learn by the loss of their possessions that they were perishable things. Yet throughout their corporal existence they never cease to seek what will do them harm.

But when they are afflicted with weariness of spirit, the rich of this world are accustomed to look upon the temporal goods bestowed on them and to banish their sadness. For when they feel themselves affected with a touch of sadness, they look at their steeds, they survey their vessels of gold or silver, they make the round of their property. And while they gladly cast their glances through the array of these temporal things, they overcome the sadness of spirit that has arisen. And hence Truth says to them in the Gospel: *Woe to you that are rich: for you have your consolation.*[49]

11

The many–sided prosperity of the rich that in a moment is drawn down to hell

A good many of the rich are lifted up by riches and when they begin to be powerful they are permitted to continue long in this life. And length of days strengthens in the pride of their power those whose substance uplifts them. And when they have been lifted up by honors and strengthened by riches, together with a large patrimony they have heirs given to them; and lest any internal design inflame anyone's mind and domestic discord detract from the joys of their tranquility, security is bestowed upon them; and while the rod of discipline from above does not strike them, the more they continue in sin, the less they are punished for sin.

In the fields too prosperity smiles on them, as it is written: *Their ox has conceived, and faileth not; their cow has calved, and is not deprived of her fruit.*[50] By common usage ox is masculine and cow feminine, but literary speech assigns to ox common gender. Hence it is here said: *Their ox has conceived, and faileth not; their cow has calved, and is not deprived of her fruit.* This is equivalent to saying that their flock conceives, and what is conceived comes to be born, and by nourishment is reared unto growth.

The fruitfulness of the cattle is followed by that of their household. Whence also it is said: *Their little ones go out like a flock.*[51] And as the masters have honors and possessions bestowed upon them, those in the family enjoy sportive pursuits. Hence there follows: *Their children dance and play. They take the timbrel and the harp, and rejoice at the sound of the organ.*[52] But let us heed what follows so much pleasure on their part: *They spend their days in wealth. And in a moment they go down to hell.*[53] Every length of time during the present life is then known to be but a moment when it is ended. For when each person is brought to the last end, he no longer keeps anything from the past because all periods of time have elapsed; he has nothing in the future because not the minutes of a single hour remain. So the life that could be thus narrowed was but a moment.

Hence it is well written of them: *Suddenly shall they die, and the people shall bow down at midnight, and pass away.*[54] However late the unrighteous are taken out of this life, they are taken away suddenly and in an instant because they know not how to foresee their end by taking thought. That rich man was taken away suddenly who left the barns that he was preparing and found the place of hell that he was not looking for. Whence on account of this ignorance of his blindness it is well said to him: *This night do they require thy soul of thee.*[55] For taken away by night was that soul, which refused to foresee what it could suffer. Whence the apostle Paul rightly says to the disciples who are thinking on future things: *But you, brethren, are not in darkness, that that day should overtake you as a thief. For all of you are the children of light and children of day; we are not of the night nor of darkness* .[56] For the day of death seizes as a thief in the night when it casts out the souls of foolish men, unforeseeing. Whence it is here also fitly added: *And the people shall bow down at midnight, and pass away.* Bowed down they pass away at midnight who, being humbled, are carried off by the blindness of their negligence.

12

Wretchedness of the rich after death

Poverty like water shall take hold on him: a tempest shall oppress him in the night.[57] Let us look now at the need of the rich man in the flames of hell whose abundance was so great when he feasted. For he says: *Father Abraham, have mercy on me and send Lazarus that he may dip the tip of his finger in water to cool my tongue; for I am tormented in this flame.*[58] By these words it is not this that is made known to us—that there is so much fire a single drop of water is then sought as a sufficiency of refreshment—but that he who has sinned by abundance should there be consumed by excessive burning need. For we see in the words of the rich man occasioned by the most precise judgment of God, how fitting a punishment is inflicted for such a sin. For impelled by need, he is there driven to beg for the very least, who here, impelled by covetousness, reached the point of refusing to give the very least. What more exact, more strict retribution can there be? He begged a drop of water, who refused to give crumbs of bread. Poverty like water takes hold of him. Not unsuitably likened to water then is that need which torments in hell, the place which, swallowing up those consigned to the depths below, is usually designated by the name pit. Whence it is said by the prophet speaking in the name of members of the human race: *My life is fallen into the pit.*[59] But in the exultation of those who escaped, it is sung: *O Lord my God, I have cried to thee: and thou hast healed me. Thou hast brought forth, O Lord, my soul from hell: thou hast spared me from them that go down into the pit.*[60]

A tempest shall oppress him in the night.[61] What does he here call the night but the hidden time of sudden departure? And by the word tempest he indicates the whirlwind of the judgment. The Psalmist also attests to this, saying: *God shall come manifestly; our God shall come and shall not keep silence. A fire shall burn before him: a mighty tempest shall be round about him.*[62] Of this tempest Wisdom says through Solomon: *I also will laugh in your destruction and will mock when that shall come to you which you feared; when sudden calamity shall fall on you, and destruction, as a tempest.*[63] And because this ignorance of the coming departure is itself called night, in the night a tempest shall oppress him; that is, the whirlwind of divine judgment, while he is unaware, shall seize him. For it is hence that Truth himself says: *But this know ye, that if the householder did know at what hour the thief would come, he would surely watch and would not suffer his house to be broken open. Be you then also ready; for at what hour you think not the Son of man will come.*[64] Hence also it is said against the evil servant: *But if that evil servant shall say in his heart: My lord is long in coming; and shall begin to strike his fellow servants and shall eat and drink with drunkards, the lord of that servant shall come in a day that he hopeth not and at an hour that he knoweth not.*[65] Therefore it is said: *A tempest shall oppress him in the night.* For because he is not willing to do the good things that he sees, he is caught by the tempest of his destruction that he does not see.

13

The rich feed the devil with their delights

To him the mountains bring forth grass.[66] By mountains is expressed the pride of secular powers, of whom the Psalmist says: *The mountains melted like wax, at the presence of the Lord,*[67] because many who had been puffed up with stubborn pride were melted with great fear when God was manifested in the flesh. Or as the same prophet says again: *The mountains ascend: and the plains descend.*[68] For many persecutors of the Lord come against him in pride, but return from him in humility. And these ascend, as mountains, by the swelling of power, but descend, as plains, brought low of course through acknowledgment of sin.

But because some remain at the height of their pride and refuse to bend humbly to the divine commands, and because they continue to think and to perform wickedness according to the desire of the ancient enemy, it is rightly said of Behemoth in this place: *To him the mountains bring forth grass.* For the proud of the world bring forth grass to this Behemoth because they support him by acting wickedly. To this Behemoth they bring forth grass because they offer him their fleeting and deceiving pleasures. *Men*, says the Apostle, *shall be lovers of themselves;*[69] he included in their description these words: *Lovers of pleasures more than of God.*[70] What then is the grass of the mountains except fleeting pleasure, which springs from the heart of the proud? If in their pride they did not scorn God, they would by no means commit so many wanton acts in their licentiousness. By such grass this Behemoth is no doubt fed, because in longing for their punishment by eternal death, he is appeased by their evil habits. For the rich and proud of this world—even if, at times, hindered by the decree of God's governance, they desist from accomplishing their wicked deeds—multiply wicked aspirations: at one time, to make themselves appear superior to others in wealth and honor; at another, to exercise this power of theirs in striving to harm their neighbors; at another, influenced by wanton emotions, to be unrestrained in frivolities and pleasures. For since they never think of using properly what they have received from God, what else are they doing but struggling against God by means of his gifts? Because therefore this Behemoth always recognizes in the minds of the rich and proud his own desires, he finds a sort of grass on the mountains: restored by it, he fills out the belly of his malice.

Moreover, it is added in the text: *There all the beasts of the field shall play.*[71] What are designated by beasts but unclean spirits; what by the field but the present world? Whence it is said against Ephraim concerning the chief malignant spirit himself: *The beast of the field shall tear them.*[72] Or as Isaias says: *No mischievous beast shall go up by it (the holy way).*[73] But that the world is understood by field, the word of the Lord attests in the Gospel, which says: *But the field is the world.*[74] The beasts of the field, therefore, play in the grass of the mountains because in this world the devils, who have been cast down from above, delight in the evildoing of the proud. The beasts play in the grass when the reprobate spirits lure the hearts of men into unlawful thoughts. For evil spirits, to play is to deceive at one time by false promises the minds of men, made in the likeness of God; at another to foist on them transitory pleasures for lasting ones; at another to make light of lasting punishments as if they were transitory. He had no doubt feared being the plaything of these beasts who said: *In thee, O my God, I put my trust: let me not be ashamed; neither let my enemies laugh at me.*[75]

14

The poor who lust after riches are in the sight of God as guilty as the rich who are reprobates

There are some who in this world have no riches but long to have them; they seek to be raised up although in this world they are unable to obtain what they desire, and while they are not favored with any possessions or honors, yet because of unworthy desires conscience declares them guilty in the sight of the eternal judge. For every such person is often disturbed because he cannot be rich and distinguished. It is written of him: *But another dieth in bitterness of soul without any riches.*[76] Notice the kindred source of dissatisfaction: the rich man emptily rejoices with a proud heart; the poor man more emptily grieves with a proud heart. Concerning both it is now rightly added: *And yet they shall sleep together in the dust, and worms shall cover them.*[77] For to sleep in the dust is to close the eyes of the mind amid earthly desires. Hence it is said to every sinner asleep in his guilt: *Rise thou that sleepest, and arise from the dead; and Christ shall enlighten thee.*[78] But the worms that proceed from the flesh cover them both because carnal cares spread over the mind of the proud person, rich or poor. For in the things of earth the reprobate, poor and rich, although they are not supported by equal prosperity, are still beset by equal solicitude because what the one already possesses with worry, the other longs for with anxiety and since he is unable to get it, he is grieved. So let it be said: *They shall sleep together in the dust, and worms shall cover them,* because although not lifted up together by temporal goods, yet in concern for temporal goods they are both lulled to sleep by dullness of mind. Worms cover them together because either this one in order that he may possess what is coveted, or the other in order that he may not lose what is possessed, has carnal thoughts imposed on him.

15

The pride and iniquity of those who cling to riches

Fatness hath covered his face.[79] Sight is in the face, in proximity to the first more honorable part of the body. Therefore the bent of the mind is not unjustly denoted by the face: the way we turn it determines what we see. And so fatness covers the face because coveted abundance of earthly goods oppresses the eyes of the mind and disfigures in the sight of God what merit there might have been in such goods since it adds the weight of manifold concerns. Yet it is not enough for the rich that they alone be full of pride: in their fatness those united to them must take pride. For there are some who are prideful on being allied with rather prominent patrons whose power induces them to form sides against the destitute.

Hence it is also set forth: *And the fat hangeth down on his sides.*[80] Because fat is the richness of the flesh and we are accustomed to call the sides of the rich those whom we see united to them, the fat hangs down on his sides since everyone that attaches himself to a powerful and wicked man is also swollen by his power even as with the fatness of goods, so that following the wickedness of an evil patron he has no fear of God, he distresses the poor—as many and as much as he is able—and uplifts his heart on the strength of temporal glory. So when there is such a one who sides with a powerful wicked man, on his sides surely the fat hangs down.

16
Inordinate love of relatives—How they should be loved

Consider the paths of Thema, the ways of Saba.[81] Thema is interpreted the south wind; and Saba, a net. By the south wind, which unloosens the limbs it blows on with its warm air, is designated dissolute laxity of life; and by a net, impeded action. For those who irresolutely seek to attain the things of eternity, by their disordered efforts hinder themselves in advancing toward God with unrestricted progress; and when they become snarled in slack practices, they are really stepping abidingly into the meshes of a net.

But there are some who abandon all that they had possessed in the world, who do not strive for glory in the present life, yet being tied with the bonds of earthly relationship, while they imprudently fulfill what love of kindred calls for, inject themselves into matters which together with self–interest, they had already renounced. Hence, because of inordinate love of their relations they enter the precincts of magistrates, concern themselves with disputes about worldly affairs, give up the freedom of interior repose, and resume earthly pursuits that were long forsaken.

But although it is necessary that they who with intense zeal seek to gain the reward of eternal surety should, to please God, render service to as many as they can, still it is in order to please God that they withhold their private services from their relatives. Hence it is that when a disciple said: *Suffer me first to go and bury my father,*[82] he then heard from the lips of Truth: *Let the dead bury their dead; but go thou and preach the kingdom of God.*[83] It is to be noted in this instance that as long as the chosen disciple is held back from the burial of his father, to be pleasing to the Lord it is not permitted for any devout person to do for a deceased father, out of worldly affection, that which, to please the Lord, he ought to do even for strangers. Hence again Truth says: *If any man come to me, and hate not his father and mother and wife and children and brethren and sisters, yea and his own life also, he cannot be my disciple.*[84] In view of the fact that in this text to the hatred of kindred, the hatred of one's own life is annexed, it is clearly shown that we are commanded to hold our relatives as well as ourselves in hatred in such a way that dismissing them in preference to eternal interests and disregarding their earthly service when it is a hindrance, we may learn by the practice of judicious insight both to love them in a suitable way and to hate them in a saving way so that hatred may find a way to spring up through love and we may be able to love more truly through hatred. Hence again it is said through Moses: *Who hath said to his father, and to his mother: I do not know you; and to his brethren: I know you not; and they have not known their own children. These have kept thy word and thy covenant, and observed thy judgments.*[85] For he longs to know God more familiarly who, from love of religion, desires to know no longer those whom he has known in the world. For the knowledge of God is diminished by a serious loss if it is subdivided with a human participant.

We should indeed, even in a temporal way, be of more help to those with whom we are more closely united than to others; for a fire too extends its heat to things nearby, but it first warms the place where it starts. But everyone ought to feel pity for the needs of his kindred in such a way, however, that by such sympathy he does not let the force of his purpose be impeded, so that affection indeed should fill the inmost part of the heart, yet not divert it from its spiritual resolve. For holy men do love family members and see that they have what is needed, but from love of spiritual things they subordinate this attachment within themselves in order to temper it by the control of discretion, so that they may not be led by it, even in a small matter and in the least degree, to deviate from the proper path. As a graphic sign of these men we have the draft animals that, proceeding to mountainous regions under the ark of the covenant, make their way both with dedication and determination, as it is written: *Taking two kine that had suckling calves, they yoked them to the cart, and shut up their calves at home: and they laid the ark of God upon the cart.* And soon after: *And the kine took the straight way that leadeth to Bethsames; and they went along the way, lowing as they went; and turned not aside neither to the right hand nor to the left.*[86] For observe, when the calves are placed in an enclosure, the animals yoked to the cart bearing the ark of the Lord put forth complaints and go their way, lowing from deep within, and yet never shift their steps from the path. Their loving instincts elicit compassion, but they do not turn back. Just so must they go forward who, being placed under the yoke of the sacred law, now carry the Lord's ark in inward knowledge, so as not to be deterred by compassion for the needs of relatives from the way of righteousness they have entered upon. For Bethsames means the house of the sun. Thus to go to Bethsames bearing the ark of the Lord is with heavenly knowledge to draw near to the abode of light eternal. But we then really proceed on toward Bethsames when in treading the path of righteousness, we never stray off to the bordering sides of error, not even out of love for children. Affection for them should indeed rank high in our mind but not turn it about, lest that mind if untouched by affection, be harsh; if unduly touched by misdirection, be neglectful.

17

The feasts of the rich can hardly be enjoyed without sin
Self–indulgence can be compared to a moth

Far be it from us to suspect that the sons of holy Job through fondness for feasts were only concerned with gormandizing. But still we know it to be true that though someone, by the practice of self–control, may not go beyond the bounds of necessity in eating, yet the lively attention of the mind is dulled in feasting, and relaxing with a sense of security, underestimates the intensity of the struggle against temptations. Hence the holy man, since he knew that there can scarcely be feasting without offense, summoned and sanctified his sons: when the days of feasting were done, he has recourse to the purification of a holocaust for each one. He knew, obviously, that plentiful feasts must be cleansed by great purification of sacrifices, and whatever personal stains the sons had contracted at their feasts, the father removed by the offering of a sacrifice. For there are some defects that are almost or even wholly inseparable from feasting. Thus sensuality is the constant accompaniment of banqueting, for when the body delights in the pleasure of refreshment, the heart is relaxed in carefree enjoyment. Whence it is written: *The people sat down to eat and drink, and they rose up to play*.[87]

Moreover, almost always idle talk is a concomitant of feasts: when the stomach is replenished, the tongue is loosened. Whence the rich man in hell is well described as asking for water in these words: *Father Abraham, have mercy on me and send Lazarus, that he may dip the tip of his finger in water, to cool my tongue; for I am tormented in this flame*.[88] He is first said to have feasted sumptuously every day, and then it is related that he sought a drop of water upon his tongue; for, as we have said, because at feasts talk usually flows freely, the fault is indicated by the punishment when Truth asserted that the one he had said feasted sumptuously every day, was most tormented in his tongue. However, nothing is recounted against the rich man with respect to talkativeness, but while the punishment is said to reside in the tongue, we are shown which among others was the most serious offense in his feasting.

But those whose indulgence in a weakness is their downfall are appropriately said to be consumed as by a moth.[89] For a moth damages and makes no sound; so the minds of the wicked, since they neglect to assess their losses, have no real awareness of their impaired condition. For they are forfeiting innocence from the heart, truth from the lips, continence from the flesh, and with the passage of time, life from the sum total of their age. But they do not at all perceive that they are unceasingly losing these endowments while they are wholeheartedly taken up with temporal concerns. Therefore they are consumed as by a moth because they submit to the silent attack of sin while they remain ignorant as to what great losses of life and innocence they sustain.

Hence it is well added: *From morning till evening, they shall be cut down.*[90] The sinner is cut down from morning until evening while from the beginning of his life to the end, he is wounded by committing sin. For at all times by increase of ill will the reprobate redouble blows upon themselves; they are knocked down in this way and tumble to the depths. It is well said of them by the Psalmist: *Bloody and deceitful men shall not live out half their days.*[91] For to live out half our days is to set apart for penitential sorrow a portion of our life equal to that misspent in pleasure, and in so doing make reparation to good purpose. But the wicked never live out half their days because not even in the end of their time do they change their perversity of heart. Paul rightly urges the opposite of this, saying: *Redeeming the time, because the days are evil.*[92] For we redeem the time when by tears we retrieve our past life, which we lost by being undisciplined. But the foolish, deceived by pleasures as long as they love the things they see which belong to time, being hostile to their own best interests fail to see where they are dispatching themselves for all eternity.

According to the measure of each sin, blindness of understanding is engendered in our perception, and according to what each person has committed outwardly, he is made dull of sense in what he might have understood that is internal and invisible. Whence also it is written: *Every man that shall eat the sour grape, his teeth shall be set on edge.*[93] By teeth are understood our inner senses; sin is denoted by the sour grape. For a sour grape is fruit before its time. But whoever wishes to be satisfied with the delights of the present life is like someone in a hurry to eat fruit before its time. Thus the teeth of him who eats the sour grape are set on edge because he who is nourished by delight in the present life has restricted his interior perceptions so that they can no longer eat—that is, understand—spiritual things: by the fact that they gratify themselves in outward things, they are made dull in those of the interior. And as long as the soul is fed with sin, it is unable to eat the bread of righteousness, since the teeth, being set on edge by the habit of sin, cannot partake of what is inwardly tasteful.

BOOK 5

THE REPROBATE

Prologue

The discussion of the rich, considered somewhat conspicuous among those who prove to be false, is followed by the fifth book of Part 1, entitled The Reprobate; in it are treated various iniquities of those who, unbridling their actions to the point of licentiousness, spend the periods of the present life dedicated to the treacherousness of pleasures in fulfilling carnal desires; when these pursuits in brief compass come to an end, the reprobate are borne away to eternal punishments.

Entirely different from the desires of such votaries are those of the just, who are discussed in the fifth book of Part 2, in which you will find a remedy for the excesses of the reprobate if you are determined to follow the morals of the just described there.

1

The firmness of the reprobate and their indigence

The firmness of the reprobate is to love unceasingly transitory things, to hold out continuously against the scourges of the Creator, not even in adversity to desist from love of temporal things, to achieve vainglory even with an impaired way of life, to seek out increases in wickedness, to attack the life of the good not only with words and practices but even with weapons, to put their trust in themselves, to commit iniquity daily without any lessening of desire. Hence the prophet says to the reprobate: *Woe to you that are mighty to drink wine, and stout men at drunkenness.*[1] Hence the Psalmist, making known against the reprobate the voice of the Redeemer represented in his passion, says: *Behold, they have caught my soul: the mighty have rushed in upon me.*[2] And so the reprobate are thoroughly strong, who with so many travails pursue the concupiscence of this world, boldly expose themselves to perils, gladly bear insults for the sake of gain, do not—being overcome by any opposition—shrink from the lust of their appetites, grow obdurate from beatings and for the sake of the world undergo the ills of the world and—as I might put it—in seeking its pleasures are losing them, and yet do not grow weary in the process.

Hence, even the strength of the reprobate is accurately called their need, for while they are filled with vices, they are emptied of the riches of virtues. In their case it often happens that lifted up by the madness of pride, while they do not consider the faults of their lapses, they also fail to see that they are lacking in good deeds. Whence it is said by the voice of the angel to the preceptor of Laodicea: *Thou sayest: I am rich and made wealthy and have need of nothing; and knowest not that thou art wretched and miserable and poor and blind and naked.*[3] He who is lifted up through pride in his sanctity, speaks of himself as rich, but is censured as poor, blind and naked. Poor, certainly, because he has not the riches of virtues; blind, because he does not see the poverty he is suffering; naked, because he has lost his principal garment, but even worse, because he does not know that he has lost it. Therefore because, as we have said, the need of the reprobate is their lack of merits, it is rightly said of the devil: *Want goeth before his face.*[4] For no one is granted recognition of him unless he is first deprived of the riches of virtues. For he takes away good thoughts, and afterwards supplies a clearer knowledge of his own iniquity. Want is thus said to go before his face because, in other words, when he tempts by lying in ambush, he despoils men before he is seen. For on this account it is said of Ephraim by the prophet: *Strangers have devoured his strength and he knew it not.*[5] For by strangers are usually meant apostate angels, who devour our strength when they consume the virtue of the mind by destroying it. This is what Ephraim both endured and did not know, because through the temptation of malignant spirits he both lost the strength of his mind and did not understand that he had lost it.

2

Those who bury themselves in sin rise with difficulty, and when they have become accustomed to sin they are incited even more to sinning

He hath thrust his feet into a net, and walketh in its meshes.[6] He who thrusts his feet into a net cannot get them out when he wishes; likewise he who buries himself in habits of sin does not rise up as soon as he wishes; and he who walks in the meshes of a net, entangles his steps by walking, and when he tries to free himself in order to walk, he is so bound that he cannot succeed. For it often happens that a man won over by the delight of this world, reaches for the glory of its honor, attains the goal of his desires, and rejoices at having obtained what he sought. But seeing that the good things of this world, when not possessed, are held in esteem, and very often, when possessed, seem worthless, he learns how paltry is what he sought. Whence, coming to his senses, he searches for a way to rid himself without fault of what he sees he acquired with fault; but the same standing that entangled him holds him fast, and he cannot without further sins flee from a situation in which he culpably put himself. Therefore he has thrust his feet into a net and walks in its meshes because when he strives to get free, he then sees plainly with what sturdy shackles he is bound. For we do not really know of our duress until, attempting to free ourselves, we metaphorically try to lift our feet.

And hence openly making known his entanglement, he adds: *The sole of his foot shall be held in a snare,*[7] because the end of the matter will surely be connected with sin.

And because the enemy of mankind, when he entangles in sin the life of any individual, eagerly longs for his death, it is rightly added: *And thirst burns against him.*[8] For our old enemy, having ensnared a life in sin, yearns to absorb the death of the sinner. Yet this text can also be understood in another way. For the evil mind, when it sees that it has been involved in sin, seeks with some slight inclination to escape from its snares; but fearing either the threats or reproaches of men, it chooses to die forever rather than undergo a little adversity for a time. Hence it abandons itself fully to vices by which it feels itself already bound once and for all. Therefore he whose life is enveloped in sin even to the end has the sole of his foot held in a snare. But because, mindful that he is fettered with evil habits, on that account he loses hope of freeing himself, by that despair he is more fiercely inclined to the lusts of this world, the ardor of desire rages within him, and the mind having been enmeshed by previous sins, is spurred to greater offenses. And hence it is added: *And thirst burns against him.* For in his mind there is a thirst that burns against him because the more accustomed he is to doing evil things, the more fervently eager he is to assimilate evil. For the unrighteous man to thirst is to lust after the goods of this world. And hence our Redeemer cures the man who has dropsy before the Pharisee's house,[9] and when he was speaking against avarice it is written: *Now the Pharisees, who were covetous, heard all these things; and they derided him.*[10] What does it mean then that the man with dropsy is cured before the house of the Pharisee, if not that by sickness of the body in the former, sickness of the heart in the latter is represented? For if one is sick with dropsy, the more he drinks, the more he thirsts; and every covetous person also increases his thirst by drinking inasmuch as when he has obtained the things he desires, the more he aspires to desire others. For he who by acquiring is made to long for more, increases his thirst by drinking.

3

By the habit of sinning the heart of the reprobate is blinded

We should know that sometimes the eye of the intellect is first darkened, and afterwards the spirit being taken captive, wanders amid externally directcd desires, so that the blinded mind does not know where it is being led and willingly yields to the allurements of the flesh. But at other times the desires of the flesh first flare up and after long enjoyment of forbidden activity, they close the eye of the heart. For often the mind discerns what is right but does not rise up courageously against evil practices and in resisting suffers defeat while—still perceiving just what it is doing—it is overcome by its carnal emotion. For the fact that reasoned vision is commonly first impeded and afterwards through desires of the flesh the mind is enslaved by earthly troubles, Samson attests: taken captive by the Philistines, after he lost his eyes he was forced to turn the millstone,[11] because the evil spirits, after they tear out the inner sight of reason by the goadings of temptation, consign the soul to going around in a circle of outward trials. Again, the fact that often at one and the same time proper external action is abandoned and yet the light of reason is retained in the heart, the prophet Jeremias makes known: relating the captivity of Sedecias, he tells us the sequence of internal captivity in these words: *And the king of Babylon slew the sons of Sedecias, in Reblatha, before his eyes; and the king of Babylon slew all the nobles of Juda. He also put out the eyes of Sedecias.*[12] The king of Babylon is of course our old enemy, the past master of inner confusion, who first slays the sons before the onlooking parent because the devil often so destroys good works that the grieving person who is taken captive perceives their destruction. For the soul frequently laments and yet overwhelmed by carnal pleasures, loses the virtues which it fostered with love; it sees the losses which it suffers, and yet does not raise the arm of virtue against the king of Babylon. But while, with eyes open, it is harmed by committing evil, by becoming used to sin it eventually reaches the point of being deprived of the light of reason itself. Whence the king of Babylon put out the eyes of Sedecias after his sons had first been put to death, because the evil spirit after good deeds have first been put aside, afterwards also takes away the light of understanding. It is fitting that Sedecias suffers in Reblatha, a name that means these many, considering that anyone at last has even the light of reason removed when he is weighed down by bad habit in his manifold iniquity. But in whatever way sin occurs or in whatever circumstances it arises, still the paths of the reprobate are always entangled, so that attached to wicked lusts, they either do not seek any good works, or seeking them with weak purpose the mind does not take deliberate steps in pursuit of such works. For the reprobate either do not set out with right aims or breaking down on the way, they do not attain them. Whence it generally happens that out of weariness they return to their old ways, fling themselves from their high resolve into carnal pleasures, heed only the things that are transitory and neglect those which abide.

Whence it is added: *They shall walk into emptiness, and shall perish.*[13] They indeed walk into emptiness who bring with them nothing of the fruit of their labor. Thus one man exerts himself in acquiring honors, another is bent on increasing his holdings, another yearns to merit praise; but everyone at his death leaves all such things here: he has expended his labor on emptiness who has brought nothing with him into the presence of the judge. Conversely, it is well said in the Law: *Thou shalt not appear empty in the sight of the Lord.*[14] For he who does not offer the wages of a life made worthy by doing what is right, appears before the Lord empty. Hence it is said of the just by the Psalmist: *But coming, they shall come with joyfulness, carrying their sheaves.*[15] For they come to the judgment carrying their sheaves who manifest in themselves those good works by which they may merit life. Hence the Psalmist says again of everyone among the elect: *Who hath not taken his soul in vain.*[16] For he takes his soul in vain who, giving thought to present things only, does not heed those which shall follow him forever. He takes his soul in vain who, neglecting the life of the soul, prefers to it concern for the flesh. But the righteous do not take their soul in vain because whatever they do corporally they apply to their lasting welfare with steady intention, so that when the deed passes away, still the reason for the deed may not vanish but after this life provide rewards. But the reprobate disregard these matters, for walking indeed into emptiness, in seeking life they retreat from it, and in finding it they forsake it.

4

The habit of sinning induces the reprobate to despair

Everyone who, leaving the path of life, casts himself down into the darkness of sins, thrusts himself, as it were, into a well or pit. But if, through offenses of long duration, he is also weighed down by a habit of sin so as to be unable to rise up, he is hemmed in as if by the narrow opening of a well. Whence David the prophet makes entreaty in the name of sinners, saying: *Let not the tempest of water drown me, nor the deep swallow me up: and let not the pit shut her mouth upon me.*[17] For it is as if a tempest of water has carried away the one whom the iniquity of evildoing has shaken from a firm position of righteousness. But if it has not yet prevailed by habituation, it has not been overwhelming. He has already fallen into a well who has done what divine law forbids. But if long habit does not yet weigh him down, the well has not shut its mouth upon him. He escapes therefore the more readily, the less tightly he is hemmed in by habit. Whence the prophet Jeremias, on seeing that through prolonged habit Judaea had been oppressed by iniquities, in her name cries out in lamentation, saying: *My life is fallen into a well, and they have placed a stone over me.*[18] For one's life falls into a well when it is defiled with the stain of iniquity. But a stone is placed over it when the mind is also absorbed by sin through unyielding habit so that if it wishes to rise, it can in no way do so because the heavy mass of evil habit weighs upon it. But because it subjects itself to divine power and is favored by being brought back to the broad place of good deeds from the close confines of evil habit, therefore it is said: *He shall set thee at large out of the narrow mouth.*[19] For whoever, after having borne the yoke of iniquity is brought back by penitence to the freedom of good works, is set at large out of the narrow mouth.

For it is quite like being in the narrowness of a restricted opening to have the wish and not the ability to rise from an overpowering evil habit; to have, at least in desire, an inclination for things above but still to remain in fact amid lesser things; to progress at heart but not to follow through by action and to experience in one's self a certain self-contradiction. But when a soul thus inclined is assisted by the hand of grace uplifting it, out of a narrow opening it is set at large because having overcome its difficulties, it performs the good works which it desires. The prophet David had looked upon the blockage of a narrow way of escape when he said: *Thou hast saved my soul out of distresses. And thou hast not shut me up in the hands of the enemy.*[20] Moreover, he realized that he had been brought safely into a broad area when he added: *Thou hast set my feet in a spacious place.*[21] For our feet are set in a spacious place when we advance toward appropriate goals and are not impeded by any difficulties. For it is as if we are proceeding through a broad area whither we please because we are not straitened by obstacles placed in our way.

The text continues: *(the narrow mouth) which hath no foundation under it.*[22] For as he who is plunged into a well is kept at the bottom of it, so would the tumbling mind remain in the utmost depths if, once having fallen, as long as it is daily plunging into worse offenses, it finds almost no fixed bottom to the well into which it has fallen. For the well would have a foundation if there were any limit to sin. Whence it is elsewhere well said: *The wicked man, when he is come into the depth of sins, contemneth.*[23] For he disregards changing his ways because he has no hope that he can be forgiven. But when he sins still more through despair, he practically removes the bottom of the well so as to find there no halting place.

5

The habit of sinning is like a prison confining the reprobate

If he pull down, there is no man that can build up.[24] Almighty God pulls down the heart of man when he abandons it; he builds it up when he fills it. For he does not destroy man's soul by making war but by departing, because when left to itself it is capable of effecting its own ruin. Whence it commonly happens that when the heart of the hearer, because of competing sins, is not filled with the grace of almighty God, it is in vain that he is outwardly admonished by a preacher, for every mouth that speaks is mute if he who inspires the words that are heard does not make himself heard in the heart. Hence the prophet says: *Unless the Lord build the house, they labor in vain that build it.*[25] Hence Solomon says: *Consider the works of God, that no man can correct whom he hath despised.*[26] Nor is it any wonder if the preacher is not heard by the reprobate soul since sometimes the Lord himself in the things which he speaks is opposed by the morals of the recalcitrant. For hence it is that Cain could be admonished even by the voice of God, yet could not be changed because, as required by the sin of ill will, inwardly God had already forsaken the heart to which outwardly he spoke words that would serve as a divine decree. And it is well added: *If he imprisons a man, there is none that can release,*[27] because by whatever he does that is wrong, what else does man do but make a prison of his conscience so that guilt of soul may oppress him even though no one openly accuses him? When by the judgment of God he is left in the blindness of his ill will, he is as if imprisoned within himself so that he may not find a way of escape that he does not deserve to find. For often some persons long to be free of their evil practices, but because they are burdened by the weight of their deeds, being confined in the prison of evil habit, they cannot get free by themselves. And certain persons, wishing to punish their own offenses, instead of acting rightly as they imagine, commit worse offenses, and the unfortunate outcome is that what they thought was escape they find to be greater imprisonment. Thus for example the reprobate Judas, when he brought death upon himself because of his sin, suffered the punishment of eternal death and aggravated his sin by the way he repented.[28]

Therefore let it be said: *If he imprisons a man, there is none that can release,* for as no man resists his goodness in calling, so no one hinders his justice in forsaking. And so for God to imprison is not to release those who have imprisoned themselves. Hence it is said to Moses concerning Pharaoh: *I shall harden his heart.*[29] For God is said to harden the heart with justice when he does not soften the reprobate heart through grace. And so he imprisons the man whom he leaves in the darkness of his own deeds. For Isaac desired to release from imprisonment his firstborn son when he tried to put him before his brother in blessing him. But the one whom the father preferred, God rejected, and the one whom the Lord preferred, the father blessed even against his will so that he who had sold his birthright for a meal might not receive the blessing of the firstborn that he had forfeited through gluttonous desire: seeking earthly things, pursuing transitory things, he desired to inherit the blessing and was rejected. *For he found no place of repentance, although with tears he had sought it,*[30] for tears have no fruit when they are directed to regretting with sighs things that will perish. And so Isaac could not release his son whom almighty God by a just judgment left in the prison of his hardness of heart.[31]

6

Those hardened in sin who cannot be restrained even by scourges

He who here turns his eyes away from the sight of his guilt cannot hereafter avoid the punishment of hell. But often those who do not fear eternal torments are at least afraid to do evil on account of temporal affliction. But there are some who have become so hardened in wickedness that they do not fear to be severely affected with respect to things they love, provided they can accomplish what they have waywardly planned.

Hence concerning the obduracy of the wicked person it is written: *For what is it to him what befalleth his house after him: and if the number of his months be diminished by one half?*[32] We must not take this to mean that after a wicked person is condemned to everlasting punishment, he shall not think of his house, that is, of his relatives whom he has left, since Truth in person tells us that the rich man who was buried in hell, even in the midst of punishment had concern about his five brothers whom he had left.[33] For every sinner will be wise in punishment who was foolish in sin because, being crushed with pain there, he opens his eyes to reason, which here being devoted to pleasure he kept closed; and by the torturing punishment he is forced to learn wisdom who here with pride blinding him, acted foolishly. However, his wisdom will then no longer benefit him because here, where he should have acted in accordance with wisdom, he wasted the opportunity. For as the highest good here he longs to have offspring of his descent, to fill his house with servants and possessions, and to live long in this corrupt flesh. But if here anything has come within range of desire which, however, he cannot obtain except by offending his Creator, somewhat disturbed in mind he deliberates: if he does anything that involves his Creator's displeasure, his house, children and life are exposed to retribution. But prompted by his pride, he at once becomes willful and he dismisses whatever affliction he may experience in his household or in his life as long as he can fulfill the things he has in mind, and while he lives, he does not cease accomplishing his desires. For suppose his house is adversely affected on account of sin; but *what is it to him what befalleth his house after him?* Suppose for the avenging of his evildoing the length of life that he might have had is shortened; but *what is it to him if the number of his months be diminished by one half?* And thus the sinner prides himself, facing God in the act of his repression of the sinner's pride; not even the retribution that is brought to bear humbles the mind which deliberate obstinacy toward the Lord causes to be persistent in wrongdoing. Also to be noted is how serious a guilt lies in the fault of simultaneously being mindful of the punishment of sin and still despite fear of retribution not yielding to the rule of the Creator.

7

Hardened sinners who are not brought to their senses by fear of God, shame among men or scourges

There are some persons who by the unexpected development of ill will are attracted to doing evil, but they are held back by shame among men. And very often by the fact that they are sensitive to public shame, they examine their conscience and pass judgment against themselves: if they are afraid to do evil because of human reaction, how much more should they not even have considered what is evil because of censure by God? As it happens, these persons correct greater evil by subordinate good, that is, interior sin by exterior shame. There are also persons who after resisting God in their hearts, scorn human judgments much more, and they are not ashamed to carry out boldly all the evil that they seek: secret wickedness entices them to commit sin and outward shame is no deterrent, as it is also said of a certain wicked judge: *Who feared not God nor regarded men.*[34] Hence too it is said of persons sinning with shameless effrontery: *And they have proclaimed abroad their sin as Sodom.*[35] Thus very often there are such wicked persons who are not prevented from doing evil either by fear of God or by human respect; and it is well said to these through blessed Job: *And you are not ashamed to oppress me,*[36] because it was both wrong to have willed evil and worse not to be ashamed of ill will.

For although the mind is disturbed, although conscience is reproachful, yet the wicked person is overcome by his own strong desire and when fear has been stifled, temerity develops from his iniquities. And often when punishment also comes to mind, he shows defiance against God and decides to undergo any afflictions at his hand, relying on the ability in this life to do all that he pleases.

Since therefore he brushes aside even afflictions, it is plain that he is hereafter to be the more subjected to suffering heavier punishments, the more he now spurns the grace of greater foresight. Hence it is written: *If they shall hear and observe, they shall accomplish their days in good, and their years in glory. But if they hear not, they shall pass by the sword: and shall be consumed in folly.*[37]

By good is designated right conduct, by glory, heavenly reward. Therefore
they who strive to obey the divine commands fulfill their days in good, and
their years in glory, because they achieve both an earthly pilgrimage marked by
good deeds and its culmination in blessed reward. *But if they hear not, they shall
pass by the sword, and shall be consumed in their folly*, because punishment
comes upon them by way of tribulation and folly finally consumes them. For
there are some, as we have said, whom not even torments restrain from their
abandoned habits. Of these it is said by the prophet: *Thou hast struck them, and
they have refused to receive correction.*[38] And of them it is said under the figure
of Babylon: *We have cured Babylon, and she is not healed.*[39] And of them it is
again said: *I have killed and destroyed my people, and yet they are not returned from
their ways.*[40] These sometimes come forth worse from scourging because when
struck with pain, they are either more hardened by their unyielding obstinacy
or, what is worse, burst forth even in the bitterness of blasphemy. It is well
said, then, that they pass by the sword and are consumed in folly, for through
their scourges they increase the sins which they should correct because of the
scourging. And they both feel now the punishments of affliction and do not
escape later the sufferings of just retribution. For it is the insensibility of folly
that iniquity has such a hold on them that not even punishment prevents them
from offending.

8

Scornful reprobates and those who believe God does not exist

Who have said to God: Depart from us.[41] Even foolish men do not presume to say this in words, yet all wicked persons say to God, not in words but by
the way they live: *Depart from us.* For when they do those things which almighty God forbids, what else are they doing but fastening their soul against
the almighty? For just as to think of his precepts is to bring him into one's
heart, so to resist his commandments is to keep him out of the dwelling place
of the heart. They say: *Depart from us*, because they refuse to proffer him access to themselves and attack him with wicked deeds even if they seem to offer
praise in words.

Moreover they say: *We desire not the knowledge of thy ways,*[42] by the very
fact that they scorn acquiring knowledge of him. Yet it should be observed that
it is one thing not to have known and another thing to have been unwilling to
know. For he does not know who is willing to learn and cannot. But if someone, in order not to know, turns his ear away from the voice of truth, such a
person is adjudged not to be in ignorance but in contempt. But the way of God
is peace, humility and patience. But because the wicked look down on all

three, they say: *We desire not the knowledge of thy ways.* For while they are prideful in this life, while they are puffed up with honors, while they are covetous even if they are not wealthy, they demean the ways of God by their way of thinking. For because God's way in this world was humility, this very God, our Lord and Redeemer, came to reproaches, to mockery, to the Passion; and he calmly endured the adversities of this world, resolutely avoided good fortune so that he might teach both the prosperity of eternal life as something to be sought and the adversity of the present life as something not to be dreaded. But because the wicked covet the glory of the present life, they shun ignominy. They are described as saying: *We desire not the knowledge of thy ways.* For they are unwilling to know what they scorn to do.

Their words are further continued when it is said: *Who is the Almighty that we should serve him?*[43] For the mind of man, being unfortunately directed outwards, is so spread out in things corporeal as to be able neither to return to its inner self nor to think of him who is invisible. Hence carnal men, spurning spiritual commands, because they do not see God with bodily sight, at some time reach the point of suspecting that he does not even exist. Hence it is written: *The fool hath said in his heart: There is no God.*[44] Whence also it is now said: *Who is the Almighty, that we should serve him?* For very often men strive more to serve men whom they see with bodily sight, than to serve God whom they do not see. For in all that they do, they stretch toward the range of their eyes, and because they cannot stretch the eyes of the body to God, they either scorn paying him homage, or if they begin, they grow weary. For, as has been said, they do not believe him to be whom they do not see with bodily eyes. If they were humbly to seek God, the author of all things, they would discover interiorly that what is not seen is better than what is seen. For they themselves are made up of an invisible soul and a visible body; but if that which is not seen is withdrawn from them, at once that which is seen perishes. But there are some who do not dispute that God both exists and is incomprehensible; yet they seek from him not himself, but his external gifts. When they see that these are lacking in those who obey him, they disdain to obey him themselves.

9

Contrivers of evil deeds and those who rejoice when they do evil

According to the multitude of his devices so also shall he suffer.[45] He who found many ways to incur guilt is tormented by punishment for newfound ways: what he could not understand here, he is hereafter made aware of, when he is given over to punishment. The elect, versed in good works, sometimes apply themselves to do more than the Lord saw fit to command: thus, virginity of the flesh is not commanded but counseled, for if it were commanded then marriage would be considered sinful. Yet many are strong in the virtue of virginity so as to do more, following the counsel, than was mandated. Similarly, the wicked in general are versed in evil ways so that they contrive more evildoing than they could learn from the practice of their predecessors. And hence they are afflicted with the torment of greater retribution since they devised more evil ways that are deserving of chastisement. And so it is well said: *According to the multitude of his devices so also shall he suffer*. For he would not discover new wickedness unless he also looked for it, and he would not seek it unless he was ready to engage in it deliberately. Therefore in his suffering the excess of evil devising is taken into account, and he receives the penalty of condign punishment. And although the pain of all the reprobate is endless, greater torments await those who uncovered many kinds of wicked ways by their desires as well.

It should in addition be observed that some take unending delight in the fact that they are guilty of misconduct. Of these Solomon says: *Who are glad when they have done evil, and rejoice in most wicked things*.[46] And again: *There are wicked men who are as secure as though they had the deeds of the just*.[47] These, without doubt, are not exalted by security but by madness; they are full of pride when they ought to be aggrieved, and by reason of the fact that these unhappy persons perish in exultation, they are mourned by good persons. Indeed, similar to madmen in their perceptions, they consider the insanity that is their chief characteristic to be a virtue. They do not know that it is a result of a disease that they are more unrestrained in their conduct than the sane, and they look upon themselves as if they had grown in strength while they are drawing near to the end of life by increase of sickness. Because they have no sense of reason, they are pitied and they laugh; and the more flushed they are with great exultancy, the more senseless they are and unaware of the malady that afflicts them.

10
Pretenders and crafty persons

Dissemblers and crafty men provoke the wrath of God.[48] After naming dissemblers, he appropriately appended the modifier crafty, for unless they are crafty in mental power, they cannot with consistency make a pretense of the impression they wish to convey. For there are some vices that can easily be practiced even by those of a slower habit of mind. Thus anyone who is slow-witted is able to swell with pride, to yearn with the cravings of avarice, and to yield to lustful impulses, but no one can display the falsity of dissembling unless he has a rather keen natural capacity. For such a person is actually obliged to keep two considerations in balance by constant observation so as to learn craftily both how to conceal what he really is and to make a display of what he is not; to suppress his real faults and to exhibit unreal assets; not to pride himself openly in what he seems to be and to pretend often to decline glory in order to gain greater glory: for, since he cannot attain it by seeking it before the eyes of men, he generally contrives to secure it by drawing back. These tactics then do not suit the simpleminded, for if that is the case they are in fact sophisticated.

But when he spoke of dissemblers and crafty men, he fittingly added, not that they deserve, but that they *provoke* the wrath of God. But to provoke it is willfully to act counter to his commands; to know what is virtuous, but to spurn it; to be able, and yet not willing to do good. For these grow dark within by committing iniquity and are whitened outwardly by display of righteousness. To them it is said by the voice of the Lord: *Woe to you, scribes and Pharisees, hypocrites; because you are like to whited sepulchres, which outwardly appear to men beautiful, but within are full of dead men's bones and of all filthiness. So you also outwardly indeed appear to men just; but inwardly you are full of hypocrisy and iniquity.*[49] Therefore in outward display they maintain what they oppose in their inner life. But thinking evil within, they increase those evils which they conceal outwardly by taking on a different appearance. At last in the presence of the strict judge they cannot, therefore, plead the excuse of ignorance because while they display before the eyes of men every kind of sanctity, they testify against themselves that they do know how a good life should be lived.

Therefore in all that they do or say they show simplicity externally, but they are inwardly being crafty in a refinement of duplicity; they simulate spotlessness on the outside, but they conceal ill will at all times under the appearance of purity. In opposition to them it is well ordered through Moses: *Thou shalt not wear a garment woven of woolen and linen together.*[50] For simplicity is denoted by wool, artifice by linen. And in fact a garment that is made of wool and linen hides the linen inside and has the wool outside. And so he wears a garment woven of woolen and linen together who in the manner of speech or behavior that he uses, conceals within the artfulness of ill will and lets the simplicity of innocence appear outwardly. For since craftiness cannot be detected under the semblance of purity, it is as if linen lies under the thickness of wool.

11

Mistrustful persons

The sound of dread is always in his ears: and when there is peace he always suspecteth treason.[51] Nothing else is more favorable than simplicity of heart because whereas it exhibits inoffensiveness toward others, there is nothing it is afraid to be obliged to suffer from others. For it has its simplicity as a kind of rampart of strength, nor is it apprehensive of undergoing what it has no remembrance of having done itself. Whence it is well said by Solomon: *In the fear of the Lord is confidence of strength.*[52] He also says: *A secure mind is like a continual feast,*[53] for the repose of security is like the continuance of nourishment. But on the other hand, the evil mind is always in ferment since it is either planning mishaps that it may bring about or fearing lest such occurrences be brought upon itself by others, and whatever harm it devises against neighbors, it fears may be contrived by neighbors against itself. It becomes suspicious on all sides, expects trouble from all sides. Everyone that comes to mind is believed to be planning hostile acts. Therefore anyone lacking the repose of security has undoubtedly the sound of dread always in his ears. And it often happens that each one of his neighbors has other things on his mind, having no hostile designs, but when there is peace he always suspects treason, because he who is always acting deceitfully does not imagine that others are straightforward in his regard. And because it is written: *The wicked man, when he is come into the depth of sins, contemneth,*[54] being surrounded with the darkness of his iniquity, he at last loses hope in light.

12

Oppressors

By reason of the multitude of oppressors they shall cry out: and shall wail for the violence of the arm of tyrants.[55] We can rightly say that all the wicked are oppressors, not only those who ravage our external goods but those also who strive by their evil habits and by the example of their reprobate life to destroy our internal merits. For the former seek to assail the things that are outside of us, the latter attempt to prey on us within. The former cease not to rage with love for our goods, the latter with hatred of our virtues. The former envy what we possess, the latter the way we live. The former desire to seize our external goods because they like them, the latter try to overthrow our inner merits because they dislike them. Therefore, as our way of life is superior to the substance of our goods, he is the greater oppressor who attacks our virtues by his wicked conduct rather than he who diminishes our goods by violently oppressing us. The more formidable opponent has withdrawn nothing from our subsistence, but he has set before us an example of perdition. He has imposed on us, therefore, a more weighty oppression, the more he has stirred our untroubled heart by temptation. Although he has not won us over to conduct such as his, yet he has forced on us the conflict of temptation. We sustain therefore a heavy oppression from his manner of life because we undoubtedly suffer within that which we must overcome with difficulty. And because there are hosts of those who torment us, it is well said: *By reason of the multitude of the oppressors, they shall cry out.*

But because what they cannot accomplish by words they endeavor sometimes to effect by force, it is rightly added: *And they shall wail for the violence of the arm of tyrants.* He who desires to frighten us also when urging us to sin, now rages against us with the arm of tyranny. For it is one thing to recommend vices by one's way of life; to bring force to bear by terrorizing is another. For when we have before us examples of evil, we are subjected in a way to the din of the oppressor; but when force is used against us to compel us to sin, we carry about a tyrant within us.

13

Hypocrites

The hypocrite, who in the Latin tongue is called *simulator*, dissembler, aims not to be but to appear just, yet shuns being seen for what he is and before the eyes of men clothes himself with a certain covering reputation for uprightness. Hence it is said in the Gospel: *Woe to you, hypocrites; because you are like to whited sepulchres, which outwardly indeed appear to men beautiful, but within you are full of dead men's bones and of all filthiness. So you also outwardly indeed appear to men just; but inwardly you are full of covetousness and iniquity.*[56] Therefore concerning them is is written: *Can the rush be green without moisture or a sedgebush grow without water?*[57] A rush or a sedge denotes the life of the hypocrite, which has an appearance of greenness, but has no fruit of usefulness; dry in barrenness of deed, it is green with sanctity in name only. But a rush or sedge does not grow without water, because hypocrites receive grace for the doing of God's good works, that is, to perform signs, expel demons from possessed bodies, by the gift of prophecy know beforehand things to come; yet they are void of the fruit of the grace received because in the thought of their heart they seek not the glory of the giver but their own applause. And the fullness of the gift becomes for them the increase of condemnation, for when at the judgment they say: *Lord, Lord, have not we prophesied in thy name,* and so on, the Lord will say: *I never knew you;*[58] because hypocrites seek their own praise from their good works, they do grow green in the water, but are still barren.

Hence it is well added: *When it is yet in flower, and is not plucked up with the hand, it withereth before all herbs.*[59] The rush in flower is the hypocrite in commendation. The sedge springing up with sharp corners, in its flower cuts the hand that plucks it, because the hypocrite in the midst of applause—if anyone dare to rebuke him for his wickedness—is disdainful and at once with asperity cuts off the attacker. For he desires not to be holy but to seem holy; and when he is rebuked, he breaks out in abuse, and strives to show he is innocent, invoking not his own actions but the offenses of others. Hence Solomon: *Rebuke not a scorner lest he hate thee.*[60] For it is not the affronts of the scorner that are to be feared by the just man, but rather his becoming worse after he is drawn into hatred.

And it should be observed that the good qualities of the just, since they begin from the heart, increase until the end of life. But the activity of hypocrites, since it is not rooted in the heart, comes sooner to an end. Hence: *It withereth before all herbs.* For according to the flesh, even the just are herbs, as the prophet says: *All flesh is grass.*[61] But the rush is said to wither before all herbs, for while the righteous persevere in goodness, hypocrites languish along the way of life. For although the deeds of the just come to an end together with the life of the flesh, the rush precedes this withering because before the end, the hypocrite abandons any good works that were manifest. These are *as grass upon the tops of houses, which withereth before it be plucked up,*[62] because the hypocrite still dwells in the present time when he forsakes the works of goodness that are likened to the state of being green. Who it is that corresponds to a rush or a sedge is shown when it is added: *Even so are the ways of all that forget God.*[63] In all his deeds the hypocrite expects paying of honor, being feared by his betters, being called holy by men. But these tokens cannot abide, for his mind is not set on that glory which is endlessly possessed. Hence the text continues: *And the hope of the hypocrite shall perish.*[64] For there are some persons who, as long as they cannot obtain the glory of the present world by the ways of the world, affect a semblance of holiness, assume the guise of reverence, wish to be considered followers of the ancient Fathers. And although they do not seek to acquire the merits of the Fathers, they do attempt to obtain positions and titles of power; and when, as it often happens, they cannot get them peacefully, they also have recourse to the disruption of peace and concord.

14

Justification of their own sins a special practice of hypocrites

Let that night be solitary.[65] There are some persons who not only do not lament the evil they do, but also do not cease to praise and defend it; and without doubt a sin that is defended is doubled. And in opposition to this practice it is said: *My son, hast thou sinned? Do so no more.*[66] For he adds sin to sin who also supports what he has evilly done; and he does not let the night be solitary who to the darkness of his fault adds the support of vindication. It is hence that the first man, when called to task concerning the night of his misconduct, refused to have that night be solitary because while by the examination he was called to repentance, he added the support of justification, saying: *The woman, whom thou gavest me to be my companion, gave me of the tree, and I did eat;*[67] implicitly turning the fault of his offense against his Creator, he as much as said: You, who gave me the woman, gave me the occasion of sinning. Hence it is that in the human race the branch of this sin is protracted from that root to the present time so that what is evilly done may also still be justified.

Hence it is written: *Shut close up with scales pressing upon one another.*[68] It is said that the body of the dragon is covered with scales so that it may not be quickly penetrated with shafts. In like manner the whole body of the devil, that is, the host of the reprobate, when rebuked for its iniquity, tries to excuse itself with all possible evasions and in a way holds before it scales of defense so that it may not be pierced with the arrow of truth. For whoever, when rebuked, seeks to excuse rather than lament his sin, is covered as if with scales when impugned by holy preachers with the sword of the word. He has scales and therefore the arrow of the word has no path for transfixing his heart, for it is repelled by carnal resistance lest the sword of the spirit be embedded in him.

It should not be overlooked that although these scales of defense cover almost the whole human race, they press especially upon the minds of hypocrites and crafty men. For they shun the more vehemently confessing their own faults, the more foolishly they are ashamed of being seen by men as sinners. And so feigning holiness is rebuked, and their hidden wickedness is discovered; their pretense relies on the scales of justification and repels the sword of truth. Whence it is well said by the prophet against Judaea: *There hath the lamia lain down and found rest for herself; there hath the ericius had its hole.*[69] For hypocrites are designated by the lamia, but by the ericius all the wicked who conceal themselves by various defenses. For the lamia is said to have a human face but the body of a beast. Thus also in the first impression which all hypocrites produce, there is something in the order of sanctity, but what next appears is the body of a beast, because the deeds which they perform under the semblance of goodness are intensely unworthy. But by the name ericius is designated the defense of wicked minds, for clearly when an ericius is being caught, his head is seen, his feet appear, and all his body is in view; but once he has been seized, he gathers himself up into a ball, draws his feet inward, hides his head; and the whole body that was just seen, is all lost at once in the hands of the one that holds it. It is precisely thus with wicked minds when they are caught in their own excesses. For the head of the ericius is seen, because it is observed with what beginnings the sinner approached sin. The feet of the ericius are seen, because it is known by what steps the wickedness of the sinner has been perpetrated; and yet the wicked mind, by suddenly proffering its excuses, draws its feet inward because it conceals all the stages of its iniquity. It withdraws its head, because by its extraordinary defenses it shows that it did not even begin anything wicked; and it remains as a ball in the hand of the one that holds it, because he who rebukes, suddenly losing all that he had previously known, simply has before him the sinner wrapped up within his own conscience; and he who had just seen the whole by uncovering it, being ridiculed by the evasion of a wicked justification, is completely without evidence. There is then in the reprobate a counterpart for the lair of the ericius, because the wicked mind, wrapping itself within itself, hides in the shadows of its self-justification.

15

Justification of the sins of others

The shades cover his shadow.[70] All the wicked are shadows of the devil: as long as they are engaged in imitating his iniquity, they appropriate from his form a reflected image. But as the reprobate are his shadows in the plural, so each sinner is his shadow in the singular. But when the wicked oppose the teaching of the just, when they do not permit any wicked person to be corrected by them, the shades of this Behemoth cover his shadow because whenever sinners are conscious of a given sin in themselves, they justify some other sinner in that sin. His shades cover his shadow when those who are rather wicked justify by their perverse encouragement the actions of the very wicked. In doing this they are undoubtedly concerned lest while the fault in which they are implicated is corrected in others, they may at some time be set right. They are shielding themselves, therefore, when they protect others because they foresee that their own conduct is subject to attack in the same way they see others confounded by unrestricted reproof. And thus it happens that while the sum total of sins is justified, it is also increased; and the guilt of each person is the more easy to incur, the more difficult is its punishment. For the offenses of sinners gather so much greater increase, the longer they are allowed through the defense of the powerful to remain unpunished. But such persons, whether they are looked upon as inside or outside holy Church, reveal themselves as more flagrant enemies of God, the greater patrons they are of vices. For by their justification they fight against him who is displeased with those practices which they increase by defending them. This conduct through the prophet the Lord rightly refutes under the image of Babylon, saying: *Thorns and nettles shall grow up in its houses, and the thistle in the fortresses thereof.*[71] For what do we understand by nettles but the itchings of thoughts, and what by thorns but the prickings of vices? Nettles therefore and thorns sprout up in the houses of Babylon because in the disorder of a reprobate mind there arise thoughts and desires, which inflame, and lead to sinful deeds, which sting. But they who follow this course have others even more wicked than themselves as their defenders. Whence in the text just above he went on to say: *And the thistle in the fortresses thereof.* For the thistle becomes thick with such a crown of thorns that it hardly can be touched because of its sharpness. The nettle and the thorn therefore grow up inside, but both of them are reinforced outside by the thistle because, assuredly, smaller offenders commit all kinds of evil, but they have greater and more depraved defenders. Whence it is rightly said in the first text above: *The shades cover his shadow.* For when a greater sinner justifies a lesser wicked person, a shade actually darkens a shadow so that it may not be irradiated with the light of truth.

16

The stubborn unity of the reprobate in justifying one another's sins

The scales of sinners are both hardened and joined together lest they be penetrated by any breath of life from the mouth of preachers. For those who are joined by a similar guilt are also by evil justification brought close together in stubborn agreement in order that they may protect one another with mutual defense of their sins. For everyone fears for himself when he sees another being admonished or corrected and therefore takes a united stand against the words of accusers because in protecting another, he protects himself. It is therefore rightly written of them: *One is joined to another, and not so much as any air can come between them,*[72] because while they in turn shield one another in their iniquities by their justification, they by no means permit the breath of holy exhortation to enter in.

But he specifies still more plainly their deadly agreement, saying: *They stick to one another and they hold one another fast and shall not be separated.*[73] For they who might be corrected if separated, when united continue in the obstinacy of their iniquities, and day by day become the more easily separable from the knowledge of righteousness, the less separable they are from one another by any rebuke. For as it is usually harmful if unity among the good is lacking, so is it ruinous if it is not absent from the wicked. For unity strengthens the wicked while it makes them agree, and it makes them the more incorrigible, the more unanimous they are. Concerning this unity of the reprobate it is said by Solomon: *The congregation of sinners is like tow heaped together.*[74] The prophet Nahum says of it: *As thorns embrace one another, so is the feast of those who drink together.*[75] For the feast of the reprobate is the delight of temporal pleasures. In this feast they undoubtedly drink together who become intoxicated together with the allurements of their delight.

17

Arrogant people and the four signs by which the swelling of arrogant persons is pointed out

It is no slight cause for condemnation to pride oneself on an advantage that is given in common; to know the source of a gift and not to know how the gift he has received should be used. For there are four signs by which every kind of pride of the arrogant is pointed out: either they think that they possess any good quality from themselves; or if they believe that it is given them from above, they think that they have received it as a result of their own merits; or they boast of possessing what they surely do not have; or having despised others, they desire to be seen as the only ones to possess what they do have. For he boasted that he possessed his good qualities from himself to whom it is said by the Apostle: *What hast thou that thou hast not received? And, if thou hast received, why dost thou glory, as if thou hadst not received it?*[76] Again, the same apostle warns us not to believe that any gift of grace is given us for our precedent merits, when he says; *By grace you are saved through faith; and that not of yourselves, for it is the gift of God; not of works, that no man may glory.*[77] He also says of himself: *Who before was a blasphemer and a persecutor and contumelious. But I obtained mercy.*[78] By these words he clearly declares that grace is not given according to merits, when he taught us both what he deserved on his own for his evil deeds, and what he received through God's goodness. Again, some persons boast that they have what they really do not have, as the divine voice speaks of Moab through the prophet: *I know his pride, and his arrogance, and that his virtue is not according to it.*[79] And as is said to the angel of the church of

Laodicea: *Because thou sayest: I am rich, and increased with goods, and have need of nothing; and knowest not that thou are wretched and miserable and poor and blind and naked.*[80] Finally, some wish, with contempt for others, to be seen as the sole possessors of the good qualities that they have. Whence also the Pharisee on that account went down from the temple without being justified, because by ascribing to himself as exclusively his the merit of good works, he put himself above the prayerful publican.[81] The holy apostles also are restrained from this sin of pride; for on returning from their preaching and saying with pride: *Lord, the devils also are subject to us in thy name,*[82] lest they rejoice in this singular gift of miracles, the Lord at once answered them, saying: *I saw Satan like lightning falling from heaven.*[83] For Satan had said with special pride: *I will exalt my throne above the stars of God; I will sit in the mountain of the covenant, in the sides of the north; I will be like the Most High.*[84] And the Lord, in order to repress pride in the hearts of his disciples, related in wondrous fashion the ruinous judgment which the past master of pride himself underwent, so that they might learn from the author of pride what they had to fear from the sin of arrogance. Into the fourth kind of pride, then, the boasting of the sole possession of anything, the mind of man frequently falls. Yet in that respect it approaches more closely to a resemblance of Satan, because whoever rejoices at the special possession of any good quality, whoever wishes to appear more exalted than others clearly imitates him who, having scorned the blessing of the company of angels, fancying his place in the sides of the north, and proudly seeking to be like the most high, tried by his evil desire to rise to the peak of superiority.

18

How brief is the glory of the wicked, which is suddenly dissolved into nothing

They are lifted up for a little while but they shall not stand.[85] The glory of the wicked, since it is generally prolonged for a great number of years, is by the minds of the weak considered to be long and rather stable. But when a sudden end discontinues it, such glory is shown beyond doubt to have been short, because the end by setting a limit makes it known that what could pass away was trivial. And so they are lifted up for a little while and do not stand because from the very fact that they seek to seem lofty, by pride they become far removed from the true essence of God. For they are not able to stand because they are distinguished from the permanence of the eternal essence, and they undergo this first defeat since by glorying in self they sink into themselves. For hence it is said by the Psalmist: *When they were lifted up, thou hast cast them down,*[86] because their inward collapse is proportionate to their false extrinsic rise. Considering this shortness of temporal glory, he says again: *I have seen the wicked highly exalted, and lifted up like the cedars of Lebanon. And I passed by, and lo, he was not.*[87] Hence again he says: *For yet a little while, and the wicked shall not be.*[88] Hence James says: *For what is your life? It is a vapor which appeareth for a little while.*[89] Hence the prophet, reflecting on the brevity of carnal glory, gives notice, saying: *All flesh is grass, and all the glory thereof as the flower of grass.*[90] For the power of the wicked is likened to the flower of grass because the glory of the flesh, while it glitters, is subject to decline; while it is lifted up inwardly, discontinued by a sudden end it lies prostrate. For in the same way, by the blowing of breezes straw is carried on high, but by a sudden downfall is brought back to earth. Thus smoke is lifted up to the clouds, but suddenly while swelling out it is dispersed. Thus vapor from below, growing thick is raised aloft, but the ray of the sun when risen dispels it as if it had not existed. Thus on the surface of the grass the moisture of the dew of night is sprinkled, but by the sudden heat of the light of day it is dried up. Thus the fragile drops of water, raised when showers begin, vie with one another as they make their appearance, but as they break open they vanish more quickly, the more they swell and rise higher. And when they grow large so as to be seen, by growing they see to it that they shall not stand.

19

The reprobate who even at the point of death assign everything that they must forsake as if still destined to be theirs

The mind of the condemned is inhibited by such love for the period of the present life that they long to live here forever: if it were possible, they would like to have their span of life never end. For they dislike thinking about the future, they place all their hope in transitory things, they covet only what passes away. And whereas they give too much thought to transient things and have no hope in those that will abide, their internal vision is so confined in insensible blindness that it is never directed to eternal light. Whence it often happens that trouble already affects the body and approaching death takes away the power of their life–force, yet they never cease being concerned about worldly matters. And already the avenger is carrying them off to judgment, and yet they themselves, preoccupied with the proper arranging for temporal interests, are only thinking how they may still share in the life of this world. Everything that they must forsake they assign as if still destined to be theirs, because the hope of living is not shattered at the very moment when life is ending. They are already being brought to judgment by decree, yet they still cling to ownership by concern. For by the shameless soul, death is still believed to be far off even when it is perceptible. And the soul is so disjoined from the flesh that by maintaining itself in undue love for present things, when it is led to everlasting punishment, it does not even know where it is being led; and in leaving all that it refused to love within bounds, it suddenly finds boundless things that it never imagined.

For those men love the life of the flesh as abiding who do not consider how infinite is the eternity of the life to come, and since they give no thought to the permanency of the everlasting state, they consider their place of exile to be their native land, darkness to be light, motion to be immobility, for they who know nothing of greater things can by no means pass judgment on the least of things. And it is for this reason that the reprobate person is inept at evaluating the onward movement of the present life because out of love for that life he has come to idolize it.

20

The reprobate, by fulfilling their desires, are led through pleasant meadows to prison

Is not destruction to the wicked, and aversion to them that work iniquity?[91] The end of the wicked under consideration here is attended by prompt comforting of the good. For while by the destruction of the former, the latter perceive the evil they themselves escape, they regard as slight whatever adversity they undergo in this life. Therefore let the reprobate now go and satisfy their desires for pleasures: in their final condemnation they are destined to learn that in living wickedly they had affection for death. But let the elect be afflicted by temporary lashing so that scourges may correct the deformity of those whom fatherly affection ordains for an eternal inheritance. For now the righteous person is scourged and corrected by the lash of discipline because he is being prepared for the Father's legacy. But the unjust person is released to his own pleasures because the more temporal good things are allotted to him, the more definitely are eternal blessings denied him. The unjust person, hastening to a deserved death, partakes of unrestricted pleasures, just as calves that are to be slaughtered are left in more open pastures. But on the contrary, the righteous person is restrained from the enjoyment of passing pleasure in the same way that the calf assigned to a purposeful life of labor is held under the yoke. In this life earthly goods are withheld from the elect, just as sick persons for whom there is hope of recovery are not allowed by the physician to have everything they desire. But to the reprobate are given the good things which they long for in this life, as to the sick who are incurable nothing that they desire is denied. Therefore let the righteous consider what are the evils that await the wicked and not envy their fleeting happiness. For what is there that the just should esteem in the enjoyments of the wicked when they themselves are by a rough road making their way to the regions of salvation, and the wicked are like those passing through pleasant meadows to the bottomless pit? Therefore let the just man say: *Is not destruction to the wicked and aversion to them that work iniquity?* The word aversion would have a harsher sound if the translator had kept it in its original form. For what we call aversion is among the Hebrews termed anathema.[92] So at the end there will be aversion to the wicked when they perceive themselves to be anathema in regard to the inheritance of the strict judge because here they scorned him by evil practices. Therefore, let the unrighteous person flourish: he is alien to the flowering of the eternal inheritance.

But he is the more frightfully buried in torments, the higher he is lifted up in sins, for to be borne aloft is momentary, but to be punished is perpetual: he who is honored along the way will be condemned on his arrival. And he is as one coming to prison through pleasant meadows who is advancing toward ruin through the amenities of this world. At the time of death any of the unsteadfast can consider that the glory of one who is destined to die is of no account. For then even they forswear that glory who until death pursue it with steadfast affection.

BOOK 6

PUNISHMENT OF THE REPROBATE
Prologue

The punishment of the reprobate is discussed in the sixth and last book of Part 1; it is placed right after the treatment of the reprobate and their wicked deeds because militant activity of this kind has a suitable recompense. As the Apostle says: *The wages of sin is death.*[1]

However, contrary to the punishment of the reprobate is the glory of the just, which is examined in the sixth and last book of Part 2; because if you seek a preventative for the sufferings of the reprobate, you can find none more appropriate than the blessedness of the just.

1
Eminence of the judge on the last day and terror of the judgment

And who shall be able to behold the thunder of his greatness?[2] This thundering of his coming the psalmist David echoes, saying: *God shall come manifestly: our God shall come and shall not keep silence. A fire shall burn before him; and a mighty tempest shall be round about him.*[3] Of the same coming Isaias says: *Behold the day of the Lord shall come, a cruel day and full of indignation and of wrath and fury, to lay the land desolate; and to destroy the sinners thereof out of it.*[4] This day the prophet Sophonias foretells, saying: *The great day of the Lord is near: it is near and exceeding swift. The voice of the day of the Lord is bitter: the mighty man shall there meet with tribulation. That day is a day of wrath, a day of tribulation and distress, a day of calamity and misery, a day of darkness and obscurity, a day of clouds and whirlwinds, a day of the trumpet and alarm.*[5] The terror then of the strict judgment which Sophonias terms the trumpet, blessed Job calls thunder. Joel also considering it, says: *Let all the inhabitants of the land tremble: because the day of the Lord cometh, because it is nigh at hand, a day of darkness and of gloominess, a day of clouds and whirlwinds. For the day of the Lord is great and very terrible: and who can stand it?*[6] But how incomprehensible and unimaginable is that greatness with which he is to come in his second appearance we to some extent estimate rightly if we ponder with careful consideration the significant circumstances of his first coming. Undoubtedly the Lord came to die in order that he might redeem us from death, and the weakness and hardships of our flesh he endured in his own body. Before he came to the gallows of the cross, he let himself be bound, spit upon, struck by blows with the hand. Notice to what abuses he consented to be brought for our sake, and yet before he permitted himself to be seized, he questioned his captors, saying: *Whom seek ye?* They at once answered him: *Jesus of Nazareth.* And when he unexpectedly said to them: *I am he,* uttered in a tone of most unassuming response, *they went backward and fell to the ground.*[7] What then shall he do when he comes to judge the world who by a single utterance prostrated his enemies even when he was being brought to judgment? What is that judgment which he will administer as immortal, who in a single statement could not be withstood when he was about to die? Who will be able to sustain his wrath whose very meekness could not be borne? Therefore let the holy man consider and say: *And seeing we have heard scarce a little drop of his words, who shall be able to behold the thunder of his greatness?*[8]

2

Greatly should one fear the last judgment in which Christ will not pass over the least commandment

And that he himself that judgeth would write a book.[9] To the people still fearing the Law was handed down by a servant, but upon loving children the grace of the Gospel was conferred by the Lord.[10] Coming for our redemption, he established the New Covenant for us, but examining us with respect to the precepts of that covenant, he is also to come one day as judge. He who is Truth itself says: *The Father judgeth no man, but hath given all judgment to the Son.*[11] And thus he will then be the guarantor of judgment who is now the writer of the book, in order that he might then exact with strictness what he now commands with compassion. For in similar fashion we see every day that teachers assign to the young the rudiments of letters with persuasion but examine them with severity; and what is imparted with gentleness is subject to inquiry with the rod of discipline. For now the precepts of divine revelation sound mild, but in answering for them we shall find them harsh. Now there is a gentle warning of exhortation, but then shall follow the strict justice of the judge, because it is certain that he will not pass over the least commandment without close examination. Thereby it is apparent that he who judges is the one who wrote the book.

Hence it is written: *Flee then from the face of the sword, for the sword is the revenger of iniquities. And know ye that there is a judgment.*[12] Everyone who is accountable for wicked matters—including disdain for the fear that is to be mentioned—does not know that there is a judgment of God. For if he did know that this was something to be feared, he would not do things that deserve to be punished at that time. For there are very many who nominally know that there is a final judgment, but by acting wickedly they certify that they are unaware of it. For he who is not terrified by this as he should be, does not yet know with what whirlwind of fright it will come. For if he had known enough to gauge the gravity of the terrible scrutiny, surely in fearing it he would guard against the day of wrath. Therefore to flee from the face of the sword is to assuage the sentence of strict censure before it is manifest. For the formidableness of the judge can be countered only before the judgment. Now he is not seen but is appeased by prayers. But when he shall take his place at that dreadful inquest, he is to be both visible and implacable, because the deeds of the wicked he has long borne in silence, he shall requite all together in wrath. Whence it is necessary to fear the judge now, while he does not yet administer judgment, while he is longsuffering, while he still tolerates evils that he sees, lest when he has once extended his hand in the retribution of punishment, he strike the more severely in judgment, the longer he waited before judgment.

3

The classifications of the condemnable and of those about to be judged at the judgment

There are two divisions, namely, the elect and the reprobate; but both are comprised of two classes. For some are judged and perish; others are not judged and perish. Some are judged and reign; others are not judged and reign. They are judged and perish to whom it is said in our Lord's assertion: *For I was hungry and you gave me not to eat; I was thirsty and you gave me not to drink. I was a stranger and you took me not in; naked and you covered me not; sick and in prison and you did not visit me.*[13] To them it is previously declared: *Depart from me, you cursed, into everlasting fire, which was prepared for the devil and his angels.*[14] But others are not judged in the last judgment and perish. Of them the prophet says: *The wicked shall not rise again in the judgment,*[15] and the Lord declares: *But he that doth not believe is already judged,*[16] and Paul says: *Whosoever have sinned without the law shall perish without the law.*[17] Therefore even all unbelievers rise again, but to torment and not to judgment. For their case is not then examined because previously they come in sight of the strict judge with the condemnation of their unbelief. But those who retain their profession of faith but have not works that accord with it, are convicted so that they perish: but they who have not received the sacraments of the faith, do not hear the reproach of the judge at the last inspection, for already judged by the darkness of their unbelief, they do not deserve to be convicted by the verbal censure of him whom they had scorned: the former do at least hear the words of the judge who have kept at least the words of his faith; the latter in their

eternal condemnation do not hear the words of the judge because they withheld their reverence for him even nominally. The former perish by the law
because they sinned under the law; to the latter no mention of the law is made
in their condemnation because they made no attempt to have anything to do
with the law. For there is no need for anyone who could not be restrained by
the law to be dispatched by the law.

It is also to be observed that the reprobate see Christ as judge not in the
form of his divinity but only in his humanity, in which he could be recognized
whom their own evil deeds, then brought to mind, cause to be reflected in their
sight so that they may not see the brightness of his divinity.

But of the class of the elect some are judged and reign who wash away
with their tears the stains of their life, who redeeming their former evils by
their later deeds, conceal from the eyes of their judge under the cover of almsgiving whatever impropriety they may at any time have committed. To them
the judge will say at his coming: *I was hungry, and you gave me to eat; I was thirsty,
and you gave me to drink; I was a stranger, and you took me in; naked, and you
covered me; sick, and you visited me; I was in prison, and you came to me.*[18] He
prefaces these words by saying: *Come, ye blessed of my Father, possess you the
kingdom prepared for you from the foundation of the world.*[19] But others are not
judged and reign who leaving all things heard from the Lord: *You who have left
all things and have followed me, when the Son of man shall sit on the seat of his
majesty, you also shall sit on twelve seats, judging the twelve tribes of Israel.*[20]

4

Hell : How it is a region of darkness and wretchedness

*Before I go, and return no more: to a land that is dark and covered with the
mist of death.*[21] What is denoted by the land that is dark except the hideous
confines of the infernal region? They are covered by the mist of eternal death
because it separates the damned forever from the light of life. The infernal
region is not improperly called a land. For all are held fast who are imprisoned
by it. It is indeed written: *One generation passeth away and another generation
cometh: but the earth standeth forever.*[22] Thus the vaults of hell are rightly said
to be a land that is dark, for all whom they engulf for chastisement they torment not by fleeting suffering or phantoms of the imagination, but keep in the
unyielding punishment of perpetual damnation. Yet these precincts are sometimes designated as a pit, as the prophet attests who says: *They have borne their
shame with them that go down into the pit.*[23] Thus hell is called both a land because it holds fast all who enter, and a pit because it swallows up those it has
once seized, agitated and trembling in overflowing torments: but the holy man,

either in his own voice or that of mankind, requested that before he departs, he may lament his sorrow.[24] This is not because he that laments his sin is to go to the land that is dark, but because everyone that neglects lamentation assuredly does go there. Thus the creditor says to the debtor: Pay your debt before you are imprisoned for your debt. Yet he is not imprisoned if he does not delay paying what he owes. Here too it is rightly inserted: *and return no more*, because the mercy of him who spares no longer sets free those whom his justice in judging once condemns to the places of punishment.

These places are still more accurately described when it is said: *A land of misery and darkness*.[25] Misery has reference to pain, darkness to blindness. Therefore that land which holds in custody all those banished from the sight of the strict judge, is presented as a land of misery and darkness, for pain torments externally those, cut off from the true light, whom blindness darkens inwardly. Still, the land of misery and darkness may also be understood in another sense. For this land as well in which we are born is indeed a land of misery but not of darkness, because we here suffer the many misfortunes of our fallen nature; yet while we are in this land, we do still return to the light through the grace of conversion, as Truth exhorts us, who says: *Walk while you have the light, that the darkness overtake you not*.[26] But that other land is one both of misery and of darkness, for everyone who has been cast there to suffer its punishment, never again returns to the light.

5

The fire of hell and the classification of the damned according to the quality of merits

Where (dwelleth) the shadow of death and no order.[27] As external death separates the flesh from the soul, so internal death sets the soul at variance with God. Therefore the shadow of death is the darkness of separation because each condemned person, since he is beset by everlasting fire, is deprived of internal light by darkness. But it is the nature of fire to produce both light and burning, whereas the fire that punishes past sins has a burning effect but no light. For hence it is that Truth says to the reprobate: *Depart from me, you cursed, into everlasting fire, which was prepared for the devil and his angels*.[28] And again, presenting in the person of one individual the collective whole, he says: *Bind his hands and feet, and cast him into the exterior darkness*.[29] Accordingly, if the fire that torments the reprobate could have light, he that is rejected would not be described as cast into darkness. Hence too the Psalmist says: *Fire hath fallen upon them, and they have not seen the sun*.[30] For fire falls upon the wicked, but as it falls the sun is not seen, for those whom that flame of hell afflicts it

blinds to the vision of the true light so that both the pain of burning fire torments them externally and the affliction of blindness darkens them inwardly.
Thus they who have failed their Creator both in body and in heart are to be
punished in body and heart at the same time. They are to suffer punishment in
both ways who while they lived here, indulged their wicked pleasures both
ways. Whence it is well said by the prophet: *They went down to hell with their
weapons.*[31] For the weapons of sinners are the members of the body, with
which they carry out the evil desires they think of. Hence it is rightly said by
Paul: *Neither yield ye your members as instruments of iniquity unto sin.*[32] Therefore to go down to hell with weapons is—together with those same members
whereby they satisfied the desires of pleasure—to undergo the torments of
eternal punishments: in this way pain engulfs on all sides those who now, enslaved by their pleasures, make war on all sides against the righteousness of
him who judges justly.

But greatly to be wondered at is the assertion: *Where no order (dwelleth).*
For almighty God, who punishes evils rightly, does not in any way permit even
torments to be inordinate because the very punishments that emanate from
the scales of justice cannot be inflicted without order. How then will there be
no order in punishments insofar as the retribution of punishment is visited
upon each of the condemned according to the measure of his guilt? For hence
it is written: *The mighty shall be mightily tormented, and a greater punishment is
ready for the more mighty.*[33] Hence it is said in the condemnation of Babylon: *As
much as she hath glorified herself and lived in delicacies, so much torment and sorrow give ye to her.*[34] If then the punishment is divided according to the measure
of the sin, it is certainly clear that order is maintained in the penalties. And
unless meritorious acts affected the amount of torments, the judge who is to
come would not assert that he will say to the reapers: *Gather up first the cockle
and bind it into bundles to burn.*[35] For if no order will be observed in punishment, why is the cockle that is to be burned bound in bundles? But
undoubtedly to bind up bundles to be burned is to join like to like of those to be
given over to eternal fire so that all whom a similar sin defiles, an equal punishment may bind together, and they who were defiled by iniquity that is not
disparate may be afflicted by torments that are not dissimilar. Therefore condemnation may destroy together those whom pride uplifted together; and all
whom ambition puffed up in no unlike degree, no unlike degree of suffering
may afflict; and an equal flame of punishment may torment those whom an
equal flame of sin set on fire with lust. For as *in my Father's house there are many
mansions*[36] according to diversity in virtue, so a dissimilarity in guilt subjects
the condemned to a difference of punishment in the fires of hell. Although

there is one hell for all, yet it does not set fire to all in one and the same singularity. For as we are all affected by one sun, yet we are not all warmed beneath it in one assemblage—for it is certainly according to the composition of the body that the burden of the heat is felt—in the same way there is also for the condemned one hell that punishes, yet it does not burn all in one manner, for the difference here on earth that is occasioned by an unequal degree of healthiness in bodies is reproduced in hell by an unequal set of offenses. How then is it said that there is no order in the punishment by which without doubt everyone is tormented according to the measure of his sin?

In fact, after the holy man referred to the shadow of death, he mentions what great disorder there is in the souls of the condemned, since the pains that come well ordered by justice are undoubtedly far from well ordered in the heart of those withering away. For as we have said just above, while each one of the condemned is burned with flames, he is wasted by the fire of blindness inwardly, and consigned to a state of pain, he is thrown into disorder both inside and out so that he is tormented by his own confusion being worse confounded. Thus to rejected souls there will be no order in their punishment, because in their death the same confusion of mind rages more fiercely. By the awesome power of the judge, equity ordains this condition so that a punishment seemingly without order may confound the soul. Or, at least, order is said to be lacking in his punishments because when certain factors appear as penalties, their proper character loses its identity.

6

The fire of hell which gives light to some and no light to others, and the damned who are punished along with the devil

And (where) everlasting horror dwelleth.[37] In the torments of this life, fear has pain, pain has no fear, because pain does not torment the mind when it has already begun to suffer what it feared. But hell is both darkened by the shadow of death and inhabited by everlasting horror because they who are consigned to its fires both undergo pain in their punishments and are ever stricken with dread in the shattering distress of pain so that they both suffer what they fear and unceasingly fear what they are suffering. For it is written concerning them: *Their worm shall not die and their fire shall not be quenched.*[38] Here, the flame that burns gives light; there, as we showed above by the words of the Psalmist (57, 9), the fire that torments blocks the light. Here, fear departs when endurance of what was feared has begun; there, pain lacerates and fear distresses. Thus in a terrible way the lot of the condemned will be pain with fear, flame with darkness. Thus, indeed, the weight of supreme justice must be fclt by the condemned so that for those who while they lived did not hesitate to be out of harmony with the will of the Creator, in their future ruin the very torments will be in discordance with their dispositions to the extent that the more they are in conflict, their sufferings are increased, and as they appear in varying forms are felt in many ways. Yet these punishments both torture beyond their strength those immersed in them and preserve them, drying up in them the forces of life in order that the limit may so afflict life that torment may affect it without limit because it is both hastening to an end through torments and expiring, goes on endlessly. Thus for these unhappy souls there comes about death without death, an end without end, expiring without expiration, because death is living, and the end is ever beginning, and expiring cannot be terminated. Therefore because death both destroys and does not kill, pain torments but does not dispel fear, the flame burns but does not disperse the darkness, in the light of all that is inferred from knowledge of the present life, the punishments are irregular because they fail in all respects to retain their characteristics.

Though the fire of hell gives no light for comfort, yet—in order that it may inflict more torture—it does give light for another purpose. For the reprobate shall see, by the flame lighting them, all their followers with them in torment out of love for whom they committed faults, since they who had carnal affection for their life against the precepts of the Creator are for the increase of their condemnation afflicted by the ruin of those persons. This we surely infer from the testimony of the Gospel, in which as Truth declares, that rich man whose fate it was to enter the torments of eternal fire, is described as remembering his five brothers: he asked Abraham to send them a warning lest a like punishment should torment them if they ever joined him.[39] Thus it is beyond doubt clear that he who remembers his absent brethren to the heightening of his pain might shortly thereafter even see them in his presence to add to his punishment. But what wonder is it if he looks upon the reprobate being burned together with himself who to the increase of his suffering saw in the bosom of Abraham that Lazarus whom during life he had scorned? If therefore to him there appeared the patriarch in order that his pain might increase, why should we not believe that he can see undergoing punishment those whom he had loved in opposition to God? From this account it follows that those whom the reprobate now love inordinately, by a singular provision of judgment, they will then see as companions in suffering so that the relationship which was preferred to the Creator may intensify the penalty of their own punishment when it is condemned before their eyes by a like retribution. Therefore the fire that torments in darkness must be believed to preserve light for anguish. And if we cannot prove this from direct testimony, then it remains for us to show it to be true from a parallel source.

For three Hebrew youths, when the fires of the furnace were kindled at the command of the king of Chaldaea, were cast into it with hands and feet tied. Yet when that king, having compassion, sought them in the fire of the furnace, he saw them walking about with their garments unharmed.[40] Here it is clearly understood that by wonderful dispensation of the Creator the property of fire, being moderated into a different capability, at the same time did not touch the garments but burned the bonds, and for those virtuous young men the flames grew cold for inflicting torment and blazed for loosening them from their bonds. Thus as fire is able to burn for the elect as a means of relief and yet lacks the power to burn in punishment, so in the parallel case the flame of hell does not shine upon the reprobate for the sake of consolation, yet does give light for punishment, so that the fire of torment may both glow with no brightness for the eyes of the condemned and for the increase of their pain may show how those who had their affection are tormented. And what wonder is it if we believe that the fire of hell supplies at the same time the affliction of darkness and of light when we know by experience that the flame of torches also burns and is darksome? Then the voracious flame burns those whom carnal pleasure now defiles, then the endlessly yawning abyss of hell engulfs all whom empty pride now exalts, and they who by any vice satisfied here the will of the crafty tempter, being then rejected, enter into torments with their leader.

And although the nature of men and of angels is far different, the one punishment enfolds those whom the same guilt unites in sin. This fact is made known precisely and with brevity by the prophet who says: *Assur is there and all his multitude: his graves are round about him.*[41] For who is designated by the name of Assur, the proud king, if not that old enemy falling through pride, who—because he draws many into sin—descends with all his multitude into the vaults of hell? Moreover, graves conceal the dead. And who else suffers more bitterly than he who, scorning his Creator, abandoned life? Obviously, when human hearts take to themselves this dead being, no doubt they become his graves. But his graves are round about him because all in whose souls he now buries himself at their desire, hereafter he joins to himself by torments. And since the reprobate now admit evil spirits within themselves by committing unlawful deeds, then the graves will burn together with the dead.

This, we know, is the punishment that awaits the damned, and with Scripture instructing us, we are in no doubt as to how great the fire of damnation is, how great the darkness in that fire, how great the fear in that darkness. But what good is it to know these things in advance if it is not our lot to escape them? Therefore with the whole thrust of our mind we must see to it that while we have a period of immunity, by striving to live well we escape the torments that punish the wicked. For hence it is said by Solomon: *Whatsoever thy hand is able to do, do it earnestly; for neither work, nor reason, nor knowledge, nor wisdom, shall be in hell, whither thou art hastening.*[42] Hence Isaias says: *Seek ye the Lord while he may be found: call upon him while he is near.*[43] Hence Paul says: *Behold, now is the acceptable time; behold, now is the day of salvation.*[44] Hence he says again: *Whilst we have time, let us work good to all men.*[45]

7

The damned suffer in body and soul from corporeal and undying fire

He shall be punished for all that he did, and yet shall not be consumed.[46] For he suffers punishment in torment for those desires to which he unlawfully adhered in the world, and consigned to penalizing flames, he is always dying since he is always kept alive in death. For he is not consumed in death because if the life of someone dying were consumed, his punishment also would end with life; but in order that he may be tormented without end, he is forced to live without end in punishment, so that for him whose life here was dead in sin, death there may live in punishment. We may say then: *He shall be punished for all that he hid, and yet shall not be consumed,* insofar as he is tormented and not destroyed, he dies and lives, he is withering away and surviving, he is always finishing and is without end. These things are very terrible just to hear about; how much more terrible to go through them!

Moreover, because the multiple wickedness of the reprobate requires that they can never be without punishment, it is properly said concerning them that they shall suffer desolation and hunger when, being condemned in the last judgment, they are deprived of the sight of the bread that is eternal. For it is written: *Let the wicked be taken away, that he see not the glory of God.*[47] And the Lord himself says: *I am the living bread, which came down from heaven.*[48] Thus at the same time desolation and hunger torture those who not only feel external torments but are also perishing within from the plague of starvation. Hell lays waste because it burns; hunger kills because the Redeemer hides his face from them. For they justly have their recompense both inwardly and outwardly because the condemned sinned by thought and deed. And since they sinned in spirit and flesh conjointly, they are there likewise tormented in spirit and flesh. Hence it is said by the Psalmist: *Thou shalt make them as an oven of fire in the time of thy anger: the Lord shall trouble them in his wrath; and fire shall devour them.*[49] For an oven is heated within; but he who is devoured by fire begins to be consumed from the outside. Thus in order that the words of Scripture might show that the reprobate burn both ways, it attests that they are at once devoured by fire and made as an oven of fire, so that by fire they are tormented in the body, and by grief burn in spirit.

And because at the coming of the judge their multitude is sequestered from his sight, inwardly indeed conscience is inflamed with longing and outwardly the body suffers from the fire of hell. While it is a corporeal fire and the reprobate cast into it are bodily burned, it is neither kindled by human effort nor kept alive by fuel, but being once set afire it lasts undyingly; it neither needs kindling nor does it lack heat. *A fire that is not kindled shall devour him,*[50] since the justice of the Almighty, foreseeing future events, from the beginning of the world created the fire of hell which for the punishment of the wicked would start once and for all, but without tinder never lose its heat.

8

Punishment of some begins here and will last forever. The meaning of God judgeth not twice upon the same thing

And he shall cast upon him, and shall not spare.[51] As often as God corrects the sinner by affliction, he casts the scourge in order that he may spare. But when by striking he brings to an end a life that persists in sin, he casts the scourge but does not spare. For he who cast the scourge so that he might spare, at some time or other casts it in order that he may not spare. For in this life the more the Lord is intent on sparing, the more he scourges while waiting to see the outcome, as he himself says to John by the voice of the angel: *Such as I love, I rebuke and chastise.*[52] And as it is said elsewhere: *For whom the Lord loveth, he chastiseth; and he scourgeth every son whom he receiveth.*[53] But conversely it is written of the scourge of condemnation: *The sinner hath been caught in the works of his own hands.*[54] Of him the Lord—when he sees a host of people transgressing incorrigibly, whom he now regards not as sons under discipline but as enemies under severe affliction—says through Jeremias: *I have wounded thee with the wound of an enemy, with a cruel chastisement.*[55] And what is said in our text, *He shall not spare,* is also expressed by Jeremias in other words: *Why criest thou for thy affliction? Thy sorrow is incurable.*[56] Hence the elect always see to it that they return to righteousness before the wrath of the judge is undyingly kindled, lest surprised by the last scourge, life should end together with sin. For the scourge will then remove the sin when it changes the way of life, since it does not atone for the actions of those whose ways it does not change. Therefore every divine affliction is either a purifying of the present life in us or a beginning of the punishment that follows. For with respect to those who profit from the scourge it is written: *Who framest pain in commandment.*[57] For the wicked person who is scourged and set aright, refused to listen to the commandment; the pain he did heed. Therefore the pain is framed in commandment for the one who is restrained from evil deeds by pain rather than by the commandment. But concerning those persons whom scourges condemn and do not set free, it is said: *Thou hast struck them, and they have not grieved: thou hast bruised them, and they have refused to receive correction.*[58] For such persons their scourges begin in this life and continue in eternal affliction. Hence the Lord says through Moses: *A fire is kindled in my wrath, and shall burn even to the lowest hell.*[59] For as far as the present affliction is concerned, it is rightly said: *A fire is kindled in my wrath*; but with respect to eternal damnation, it is properly added immediately: *And shall burn even to the lowest hell.* Although it is usually said by some persons that it is written: *God judgeth not twice upon the same thing,*[60] they do not heed what is said by the prophet of the wicked: *And with a double destruction destroy them,*[61] nor what is written elsewhere: *Jesus, having saved the people out of the land of Egypt, did afterwards destroy them that believed not.*[62] If we agree with those who maintain that a sin cannot be punished twice, this must be understood of persons afflicted on account of sin and dying in their sin because their punishment began here and is completed hereafter, so that to the unrepentant there is one affliction, which begins here in time but is consummated in eternal punishment: thus to those who flatly refuse to mend their ways, the inflicting of present scourges is the actual beginning of the torments to come.

Hence it is written: *And he shall distribute the sorrows of his wrath.*[63] For he who reserves eternal sorrows for the wicked person in retribution, sometimes also pierces his soul here with temporal sorrow because both here and hereafter too he strikes, distributing the sorrows of his wrath upon the unrighteous. For neither does present punishment that does not divert the mind from its evil desires free him from eternal chastisements. And hence it is said by the Psalmist: *He shall rain snares upon sinners: fire and brimstone and storms of winds shall be the portion of their cup.*[64] In mentioning snares, fire, brimstone, and storms of winds, he introduced indeed many sorrows; but because the sinner who is not converted by them is called to eternal punishments, he did not at this time call those sorrows his whole cup but a portion of his cup, since the suffering begun indeed here through sorrows, is consummated in everlasting punishment.

9

The damnation of infants who die immediately upon birth and before they have been reborn [through the sacrament of baptism]

And he shall multiply my wounds, even without cause.[65] There are some who are withdrawn from the present light before they reach the stage in life at which spiritual worth can be demonstrated. Because the sacraments of salvation do not free them from original sin and here they did nothing meritorious on their own, hereafter they are liable to torments. One wound they have is to be born in corruption, and another, to die in the flesh. But insofar as after death there does come death eternal, by a mystical and just decree their wounds are multiplied even without cause. For they are subject to everlasting torments who committed no sin by their own will. For hence it is written: *And the infant of a single day is not pure in his sight upon earth.*[66] Hence Truth himself says: *Unless a man be born again of water and the Holy Ghost, he cannot enter into the kingdom of God.*[67] Hence Paul says: *We were by nature children of wrath, even as the rest.*[68] How then does someone—who adds nothing of his own, exposed to ruin by the guilt of birth alone—fare at the last judgment as far as the determination of human understanding is concerned, unless he is wounded even without cause? And yet in divine severity it is just that mortal progeny, like an unfruitful tree, should preserve in the branches the bitterness it drew from the root.

10

The folly of thinking that the reprobate will not be condemned forever

There are some persons who neglect to put an end to their sins on this account: they suppose that the future judgments in their regard will some time or another have an end. To them we briefly reply: If at any time the punishments of the reprobate will be ended, the joy of the blessed should also be ended at some time. For Truth himself says: *These shall go into everlasting punishment; but the just into life everlasting.*[69] Therefore if what he has threatened is not true, neither is what he has promised true. But they say: Sinners he threatened with eternal punishment in order to restrain them from committing sins, because he ought to threaten, not inflict, punishments on his creature. To this we reply more promptly: If he has made false threats in order to convert people from unrighteousness, he has also made false promises to encourage them

in righteousness. And who can tolerate the madness of those who, while by
their assertion they cause people to expect that the punishments of the reprobate are terminated, also set aside by their assertion the rewards and
remunerations of the elect? Who can tolerate the madness of those who try to
affirm that what Truth has threatened concerning eternal fire is not true, and
who, while intent on declaring the Lord to be merciful, do not shrink from
proclaiming him deceitful?

But they say: A fault that has an end should not be punished without end.
Almighty God is certainly just, and what is not committed by eternal sin should
not be punished with eternal torment. We reply to them with little hesitation
that they would be correct if the just and strict judge at his coming considered
not the hearts but only the deeds of men. For the wicked have sinned in a limited way because they lived within a limit. For they would have liked to live
without end in order that they might abide in their sins without end. For they
have a greater desire to sin than to live; and they therefore wish to live forever
here in order that they may never abandon sin as long as they live. It pertains
then to the justice of the strict judge that they should never lack punishment
whose mind never desired in this life to be free from sin; and that no end of
punishment should be granted to the wicked person because as long as he was
able to do so, he did not wish to put an end to his guilt.

But they say: No just person delights in cruelty, and a negligent servant is
directed by his just master to be chastised in order to be corrected of his neglect
of duty. Therefore he is chastised for some purpose since his master takes no
delight in his suffering. But for what purpose will the wicked burn forever who
have been consigned to the fires of hell? And because it is certain that the
merciful and almighty God does not delight in the tortures of the wicked, why
are these outcasts tortured if they do not make amends? We reply to them
quite quickly that because almighty God is merciful, he does not delight in the
torture of the unfortunate, but because he is just, he is not appeased by the
endless punishing of the wicked. But all the wicked are punished by eternal
suffering, and indeed by their own iniquity; and yet they are afflicted by fire for
some purpose, namely, in order that the just may see in God the joys that they
experience, and perceive in the wicked the punishments they have escaped, so
that they may realize they are the more indebted to divine grace, the more they
see the evils—that by its help they were able to avoid—being punished eternal-
ly.

But they say: And where is their holiness if they will not pray for their
enemies—whom they will then see burning—since it is said especially to them:
Pray for your enemies?[70] But we reply at once: They pray for their enemies at

the time when they are able to convert their hearts to fruitful penitence and save them by this conversion. For what else may we pray for in behalf of our enemies except what the Apostle says: *That God may give them repentance, and they may recover themselves from the snares of the devil by whom they are held captive at his will?*[71] And how will prayers be offered for them when they cannot in any way be turned from iniquity to works of righteousness? There is, therefore, the same reason for not praying for men condemned to eternal fire as there is now for not praying for the devil and his angels who have been assigned to eternal punishment. This is now the reason that holy men do not pray for unbelieving and wicked men who are dead; for they avoid having the merit of their prayer set aside in the sight of the righteous judge, since it is in behalf of those whom they know to be already consigned to eternal punishment. For if even now the just when alive do not feel pity for the unjust who are dead and condemned—since they know that they themselves are still suffering from their flesh what will be subject to judgment—how much more severely do they then consider the torments of the wicked when, divested of every sin of corruption, they will adhere more closely and firmly to righteousness? The force of severity so engages their mind—by reason of the fact that they cling to the righteous judge—that they are not at all pleased with whatever is not in accord with the exactness of that intrinsic model.

11

On the day of judgment, in the sight of all, the devil with the reprobate will be cast into Gehenna

And in the sight of all he shall be cast down.[72] When the eternal judge appears with terror, when legions of angels are at his side, when the whole ministry of heavenly powers is present, and all the elect are brought to this spectacle, the cruel and mighty devil is brought captive into the midst and with his own body—that is, with all the reprobate—is given over to the eternal fires of hell, when it is said: *Depart from me, you cursed, into everlasting fire, which was prepared for the devil and his angels.*[73] O what a spectacle that will be when to the eyes of the elect will be presented this most huge monster, which—if seen earlier during their time of warfare—might have terrified them too much! But it is so ordered by the secret and wonderful decree of God that he is now conquered by his grace, unseen by the combatants, and that then he is beheld by the joyful victors as already captive. But the just then realize more fully how much they are indebted to divine assistance when they have seen so mighty a beast whom they have now conquered in their weakness, and perceive in the huge size of their enemy, how much they owe to the grace of their defender.

The apostle Peter says: *God spared not the angels that sinned, but delivered them, drawn down by infernal ropes to the lower hell, unto torments, to be reserved unto judgment.*[74]

PART TWO

BOOK 1

THE GRACE OF GOD
Prologue

The second part of this work is made up of six books which communicate to the attentive reader the remedy for the ills that are discussed in the six books of the first part and that you will find mentioned at the beginning of each book.

Therefore the first book of this second part takes its name from divine grace since no one of sound mind doubts that grace is the ideal remedy for counteracting the suggestions of the devil, dealt with in the first book of the first part. And just as the devil's suggestions antecede and stir up evil in us, so does God's grace, without which we cannot do anything virtuous, mercifully prompt and anticipate all the good that we do.

1

The grace of God that redeemed man and showed the way of life

The Redeemer of the human race, having been made through flesh the mediator between God and man, alone appeared just among men and yet, subjected to the punishment of sin although sinless, both showed man that he should not sin and rescued him from God's wrath: he gave examples of innocence; he took upon himself the punishment due to wickedness. Therefore by suffering, he rebuked the sin of man, inspiring righteousness; and by undergoing death, he moderated the wrath of the judge. And he put his hand between one and the other, since he both gave examples to men for them to imitate and in himself manifested to God deeds by which he might be reconciled toward humans. For before him there was no one who interceded for the faults of others while being faultless himself. Therefore no one could prevent eternal death in the case of others insofar as guilt of his own impeded him. Thus there came unto men a new man, one who spoke against sin, befriended the guilty; he performed miracles, he suffered hardship. He did this too, more marvelously, by his very miracles: he reformed hearts of sinners by meekness rather than by terror.

Hence also it is written: *Let him take his rod away from me; and let not his fear terrify me.*[1] For through the Law, God held the rod when he said: If anyone does such and such, let him die the death. But becoming incarnate, he took away the rod since he showed the paths of life with meekness. Whence it is said by the Psalmist: *Set out; proceed prosperously and reign.*[2] For he did not wish to be feared as God, but let it be known that he wished to be loved as Father. Paul says this clearly: *For you have not received the spirit of bondage again in fear; but you have received the spirit of adoption of sons, whereby we cry: Abba, Father.*[3]

Hence too it is fittingly added here: *I will speak, and will not fear him.*[4] For the holy man, who beholds the Redeemer of the human race coming in meekness, does not choose fear of the Lord but affection for the Father; and he looks down on fear, because through the grace of adoption he ascends to love. Hence John says: *Fear is not in charity; but perfect charity casteth out fear.*[5] Hence Zacharias says: *That, being delivered from the hand of our enemies, we may serve him without fear.*[6] Therefore fear was unable to raise us from the death of sin, but the infused grace of meekness elevated us to the firm condition of life. This is appropriately denoted by Eliseus when he raised the child of the Sunamitess. When he sent his servant with a staff, the dead child was not restored to life, but coming in his own person and stretching himself upon the dead body, and bringing together his limbs and those of the child, and walking to and fro, and breathing into the mouth of the dead child seven times, at once revived him to the light of life through the ministry of compassion.[7] For God, the Creator of mankind, in a sense grieved for his dead son when with compassion, he viewed us killed by the sting of iniquity. And since he made known the terror of the Law by Moses, in a way he sent the rod by a servant. But the servant could not raise the dead body with the staff because, as Paul attests: *The law brought nothing to perfection.*[8] But when he came in his own person and stretched himself in humility upon the corpse, he brought his limbs for those of the dead body to be patterned after his: *Who, being in the form of God, thought it not robbery to be equal with God; but emptied himself, taking the form of a servant, being made in the likeness of men; and in habit found as a man.*[9] He walks to and fro, because he calls Judaea close at hand and the gentiles afar off. He opens his mouth seven times over the dead body because by the announcing of the divine gift, he communicates the spirit of sevenfold grace to those lying prostrate in the death of sin. And afterwards the body is raised to life because the child, whom the rod of terror could not raise up, has been brought to life by the spirit of love.

2

God's grace and man's free will

The innocent shall be saved: and he shall be saved by the cleanness of his hands.[10] If this prediction is taken to refer to the recompense of the heavenly kingdom, it is supported by truth because when it is written concerning God: *[He] will render to every man according to his works*,[2] the justice of the eternal judge saves that man at the last judgment who is here set free from unclean deeds by God's mercy. But if a man is believed to be saved here by the cleanness of his own hands in the sense that by his own deeds he becomes innocent, surely it is an error; for if grace from above does not keep us from being culpable, assuredly no one faultless will ever be found to be rewarded. Whence it is said by the truthful voice of Moses: *And no man of himself is innocent before thee*.[12] And so heavenly mercy first effects something in us without our help so that our own free will also ensuing, the good which we now desire may be effected with our participation; yet the good that comes from grace that is granted, God so rewards in us at the last judgment as if it had emanated only from ourselves. Because the goodness of God makes us innocent in advance, Paul says: *But by the grace of God I am what I am*, and since our free will follows this same grace, he adds: *And his grace in me hath not been void; but I labored more abundantly than all they;* insofar as he saw that he was nothing of himself, he says: *Yet not I*, and yet since he found that he was something together with grace, he added: *But the grace of God with me*.[13] For he would not have said, *with me*, if together with prevenient grace, there had not been free will accompanying it. Therefore in order to show that he was nothing without grace, he says: *Yet not I*, but to show that with grace he had acted through free will, he added, *but the grace of God with me*. Thus the innocent shall be saved by the cleanness of his hands, because he who is antecedently given grace so that he may become innocent, when he is brought to judgment, is rewarded on account of merit.

3

God chastises those whom he is solicitous to bring back to health

Blessed is the man whom God correcteth.[14] The foremost virtue is not to effectuate what is forbidden, that is, sin; the next virtue is to rectify somehow sins that have been committed. But for the most part we not only fail to avoid sins that are imminent, but we do not even acknowledge them when they are committed. And the mind of sinners is wrapped in deeper darkness, the more oblivious it is to the defect of its own blindness. Hence it very often happens, by the liberality of God's gift, that punishment comes after transgression, and scourges open the eyes of the transgressor, which self-assurance was blinding in the midst of evils. For the sluggish soul is struck by a blow that it may be stirred up so that he who has lost, by being self-confident, the firm condition of uprightness, may, being afflicted, consider where he lies prostrate. Thus the severity of the correction becomes the source of light. And hence it is said by Paul: *But all things that are reproved are made manifest by the light*,[15] for proof of returning health resides in the force of the pain. Hence it is that Solomon says: *Because healing will make the greatest sins to cease*.[16] Hence again it is said: *For whom the Lord loveth, he chastiseth, and he scourgeth every son whom he receiveth*.[17] Hence the Lord addresses John by the voice of the angel, saying: *Such as I love, I rebuke and chastise*.[18] Hence Paul says: *Now all chastisement for the present indeed seemeth not to bring with it joy but sorrow; but afterwards it will yield to them that are exercised by it the most peaceable fruit of justice*.[19] Therefore although pain and happiness cannot come together, yet it is now rightly said: *Happy is the man whom the Lord correcteth*, for insofar as the sinner is oppressed by the pain of correction, he is sometimes instructed in happiness with which pain does not interfere.

Our text continues: *For he woundeth, and cureth: he striketh, and his hands shall heal*.[20] In two ways almighty God wounds those whom he is solicitous to bring back to health. For sometimes he strikes the flesh and softens hardness of heart by fear of him. Thus by wounding he recalls to health when he afflicts his elect outwardly, that they may live inwardly. Whence he also says by Moses: *I will kill and I will make to live. I will strike, and I will heal*.[21] For he kills that he may cause to live, he wounds that he may heal, since he for this reason administers blows outwardly in order that inwardly he may heal the wounds of sins. But sometimes, even if scourges seem to cease externally, he inflicts wounds internally since he strikes the hardness of the heart with the desire of himself; yet in striking, he heals, because when we are pierced with the shaft of his fear, he recalls us to a sense of righteousness. For our hearts are unsound when they are not wounded by any love of God, when they do not feel the trials of their pilgrimage, when they do not experience the least degree of sympathy for the infirmity of their neighbor. But they are wounded that they may be healed since God strikes insensible minds with the arrows of his love and at once endows them with sensibility through the fervor of charity, and hence the spouse says in the Canticle of Canticles: *For I am wounded with love*.[22] For the unsound soul reclining on the pallet of this exile in blind self–confidence, neither saw the Lord nor sought to see him; but on being struck with the arrows of his love, it is wounded deeply by a sense of devotion, burns with the desire of contemplation, and in a wondrous way is vivified by a wound after lying lifeless in an apparent state of well–being. It is ardent and breathless, and yearns to see the one who has been shunned. By being stricken, then, the soul is led back to health, called back by the overthrow of self–love to the security of inward rest.

There are, however, various kinds of blows. For example, there is the blow by which the sinner is struck that he may be punished when he does not forsake his sin; whence it is said to Judaea: *Thy sorrow is incurable.*[23] There is another kind of affliction with which the sinner is struck that he may be reformed, as is said to a man in the Gospel: *Behold, thou art made whole; sin no more, lest some worse thing happen to thee.*[24] With another kind of affliction a person is struck, not that a past offense may be corrected, but that he may not offend in the future; hence Paul: *Lest the greatness of the revelations should exalt me, there was given to me a sting of my flesh, an angel of Satan, to buffet me.*[25] By still another kind of affliction a person is struck neither to reform past faults nor to prevent future ones, but in order that—by unexpected healing which follows affliction—the healer whose power is made known may be loved more ardently; and when an innocent person is afflicted by the scourge, through patience the sum total of merits may be augmented for him. This is clearly understood in the case of the man born blind, concerning whom Truth makes this reply: *Neither hath this man sinned, nor his parents; but that the works of God should be made manifest in him.*[26] Moreover, we must carefully observe that when we are neither corrected by blows nor do we obey precepts, God stirs and shames us by examples: not only by examples of those bound by the Law, but also of those who had no law to restrain them from sin.

Since indeed divine providence has encompassed us, all excuse is circumvented, access to human subterfuge is blocked on all sides. Job, a man of the gentiles, simple and upright and fearing God, a man without the Law, is brought into the midst in order that the perversity of those who are under the Law may be brought to shame. Hence the prophet: *Be thou ashamed, O Sidon, saith the sea.*[27] In Sidon we have a figure of the steadfastness of those subject to the Law, and in the sea, a figure of the life of the gentiles. Accordingly: Be thou ashamed, O Sidon, says the sea, because the life of those subject to the Law is reproached by the life of the gentiles; and by the conduct of those living in the world, the conduct of those who have made the vows of the religious life is put to shame, as long as the latter do not, even under vows, observe the duties they hear imposed in precepts; and the former by their manner of life keep those observances to which they are not bound by legal injunctions.

4

Many return to penitence when they are unable to carry out evil desires

When the elect are weakened and rush into their desires, they are frequently restrained by the hand of divine favor so as to procure no results from their pitiable purpose. And when strong hostility to their wishes arises, they are frequently corrected by this frustration, and through the wondrous rule of inward disposition, a change of their evil will comes about through conversion, while because of their weakness perfection is denied them. For hence it is that under the image of each soul, the Lord says to Judaea, weak and walking in evil ways: *Behold, I will hedge up thy way with thorns and I will stop it up with a wall: and she shall not find her paths, and she shall follow after her lovers and shall not overtake them, and she shall seek them and shall not find. And she shall say: I will go and return to my first husband, because it was better with me then than now.*[28] For the ways of the elect are surrounded with thorns as long as they find the stabs of misfortunes in what they desire in this world. As if by a wall that is interposed, the Lord hinders the ways of those whose desires are opposed by the difficulty of fulfillment. Their souls truly seek their lovers and find them not, when by following malignant spirits, they do not lay hold of those worldly pleasures which they desire. But it is properly added, as a result of this difficulty, that she soon says: *I will go and return to my first husband, because it was better with me then than now.* For the Lord is the first husband, who united to himself the chaste soul by the intervening love of the Holy Spirit. And the mind of each one then yearns for him when it finds various bitternesses, as thorns in those delights which it desires in this world. For when the mind has begun to be hurt by the adversities of the world it loves, it then understands more fully how much better it was for it with its first husband.

Therefore adversity frequently corrects those whom an evil will perverts. Whence also it is greatly to be feared lest favorable happenings should take place when unjust things are desired, because an evil which is also supported by the success of accomplishment is corrected with greater difficulty.

5

The mercy of God who calls to penitence and judges the ungrateful with severity

Will God hear his cry, when distress shall come upon him?[29] His cry in the time of distress God does not hear, because in the time of tranquility he himself did not hear the Lord crying aloud in his precepts. For it is written: *He that turneth away his ear from hearing the law, his prayer shall be an abomination.*[30] And so the holy man, seeing that everyone who now disdains to do what is right, ultimately has recourse to words of petition, puts the question: *Will God hear his cry?* By these words he surely comes close to the words of our Redeemer, who says: *At last come the foolish virgins, saying: Lord, Lord, open to us. And he answering, said to them: Amen, I say to you, I know you not.*[31] Thus such great severity will be exercised then, insofar as now greater mercy is dispensed, and then with strictness judgment upon persons not reformed is issued by him who now patiently directs forbearance to transgressors. For hence the prophet says: *Seek ye the Lord while he may be found: call upon him while he is near.*.[32] Now he is not seen and is near; then he shall be seen and shall not be near. He has not yet appeared in judgment, and if he is sought, he is found. For in a remarkable way when he appears in judgment, at the same time he can be seen and cannot be found. Hence Solomon refers to wisdom both urging pleasantly and judging severely, saying: *Wisdom preacheth abroad: she uttereth her voice in the streets.*[33] The wording he also implies, adding: *O children, how long will you love childishness, and fools covet those things which are hurtful to themselves, and the unwise hate knowledge? Turn ye at my reproof: behold, I will utter my spirit to you, and will show you my words.*[34] There we have the expression of gentle urging. Let us see now in what way the severity of him who censures is made known so that last of all, the strictness of him who punishes may be exercised. *Because I called*, he says, *and you refused. I stretched out my hand, and there was none that regarded. You have despised all my counsel, and have neglected my reprehensions.*[35] Let him now say how he will strike those whom he bears with so much long-suffering, who do not turn back to him: *I also will laugh in your destruction, and will mock when that shall come to you which you feared, when sudden calamity shall fall on you, and destruction, as a tempest, shall be at hand: when tribulation and distress shall come upon you. Then shall they call upon me, and I will not hear: they shall rise in the morning and shall not find me.*[36] By the mouth of the most wise Solomon, then, all details concerning celestial judgment are carefully expressed: it first calls us gently, afterwards censures mightily, and in the end condemns irrevocably.

6

The graciousness of God in allowing time for penitence and in not withholding his gifts even from the ungrateful

Because the merciful Creator does not abandon the work of his hand, he both endures the sins of men by his wisdom and often abates them by their conversion. When he looks upon hardy and insensible minds, he deters them at one time with threats, at another with blows, at another with revelations, in order that those who have become hardened by most pernicious self-sufficiency may at least be softened by salutary fear: thus they may at long last come to their senses and feel shame that they have long tarried. For the Lord, knowing that he judges more severely the last part of our life, on that account purifies the elect more carefully at the end. For it is written: *The Lord shall judge the ends of the earth*.[37] Therefore he watches the more earnestly over our last moments, the more he considers that on them the beginnings of the life to come depend. He mercifully sees to it, by bringing his kindness to the fore, that even those sinners are welcomed who have been converted late in the day.

And he who on the last day is revealed as the one who inflicts punishment was himself for long the silent witness of sin. For hence it is that the prophet says: *I am the judge and the witness*.[38] Hence it is said elsewhere: *I have always held my peace, I have kept silence, I have been patient. I will speak now as a woman in labor*.[39] For a woman in labor with pain brings to light what she has long borne cumbrously concealed. And so after a long silence, like a woman in labor the Lord breaks his silence because what he now bears silently in himself, he finally reveals as one with pain in the punishing of judgment.

Therefore it is to be borne in mind that God in his graciousness grants sinners a period of time for penitence. But because they do not use these intervals for the fruits of penitence but in the service of iniquity, they forfeit what by divine mercy they might have gained. Although almighty God knows beforehand the time for each individual until death, when his life is brought to an end, no one could die at any time but the actual time when he does die. For even if almighty God at times changes his sentence, his foresight never wavers. For though it is recorded that fifteen years were added to the life of Ezechias, the duration of his life was increased from that time when he deserved to die.[40] For God in his providence foresaw his life span ending at that point later on when he did withdraw Ezechias from the present life.

In passing, it should be attentively noted that even from the ungrateful, God does not withhold his gifts in order that either being ashamed because of the graciousness of their Creator, they return to a state of goodness, or they refuse altogether to return. In the latter case, they may be hereafter more severely punished because here they repaid evils for God's more generous benefactions, so that harsher penalties should then chastise those whose wickedness here even gifts did not surmount.

7

Those who abuse the time for penitence

The divine dispensation bears with the iniquity of anyone who sins and is still alive in order that he may be restrained from iniquity. But he who is shown mercy for a rather long time, and yet is not restrained from evil, receives indeed the benefit of heavenly patience, but with the fetters of his guilt is on account of that benefit binding himself more tightly. For because the periods of time allowed for penitence he devotes to sin, the strict judge finally turns from granting proofs of mercy to punishing. Hence it is said by Paul: *Knowest thou not that the benignity of God leadeth thee to penance? But, according to thy hardness and impenitent heart, thou treasureth up to thyself wrath, against the day of wrath and revelation of the just judgment of God.*[41] Hence Isaias says: *For the child shall die a hundred years old, and the sinner being a hundred years old shall be accursed.*[42] This is equivalent to admonishing us as follows: The life of a child indeed is drawn out to great length, in order that childish ways may be corrected, but if he is not even by great length of time restrained from committing sin, this length of life that was granted out of mercy results in towering denunciation. Hence when we become aware that we are holding back a rather long time, we feel obliged to fear those periods of mercy dispensed to us as proofs of condemnation, lest by the clemency of the judge, the punishment of the sinner be increased, and by the agency whereby anyone might be snatched from death, he should more ruinously move toward death. This outcome does quite often occur because the eye of the mind is not at all detached from present things. For the sinner is disinclined to reflect upon the ways of the Redeemer, and so he ceaselessly grows old in his own paths.

Hence it added: *For his eyes are upon his ways.*[43] For the sinner looks attentively at his own ways because he is intent on thinking only of those things, on seeing only of those things, which may support him for temporal advantage. Hence it is that Paul says: *For all seek the things that are their own; not the things that are Jesus Christ's.*[44] For the way of the haughty is pride; the way of the thief, avarice; the way of the unchaste, carnal concupiscence. Thus every evildoer directs his gaze on his own ways since he aims only at vices so that by these he may be content. Whence it is said by Solomon: *The eyes of fools are in the ends of the earth,*[45] because they keep in view, with entire occupation of the mind, only what they may achieve to fulfill an earthly desire. But the sinner would not direct obsessive attention to worldly ways if he fastened the eyes of the mind on the holy paths of the Redeemer. Whence it is again said by Solomon: *The eyes of a wise man are in his head,*[46] that is to say, with undivided effort in accord with faith, the wise man keeps in mind the one of whom he is conscious that he is a member.[47]

8

For those who abuse the time of penitence long–sufferance ends with swift reckoning

His eyes are upon the ways of men: and he considereth all their steps.[48] God is believed not be keeping watch at the time when the wicked person is committing, unpunished, as much evil as he can. He is thought not to be observing the deeds of the unrighteous because he delays just condemnation, and his great forbearance is regarded as a sort of carelessness. The wicked person himself also believes he is not observed by God when he sins, as often as he sins without being punished. To him it is said by a certain wise man: *Say not: I have sinned, and what harm hath befallen me?*[49] He is unwilling to correct the wickedness for which he has not suffered suitable punishment: and the more mercifully he is granted clemency, the more irresponsibly is he spurred on to sinfulness; and ignoring the patience of heavenly sufferance, he is led to increase his guilt by that factor which should have induced him to correct it, as is said by holy Job: *God hath given him place for penance: and he abuseth it unto pride.*[50] Often, too, because he does not suffer immediately the punishment he deserves, he judges that his behavior is not displeasing to God. So let him go now and brazenly venture into every kind of blasphemy; let him carry to its fullness the iniquity of his pleasures; let him plunder the goods of others and be surfeited with the oppression of the innocent, and because he is still unpunished, let him go on thinking that his ways are not observed by God, or what is worse, that they are approved by him! A day will surely come, bringing with it unending and unexpected affliction, and he will then realize that God sees all things when he sees himself condemned by an unprovided death to retribution for all his deeds. Then in suffering he will open the eyes he long kept closed in sin. He will perceive that the righteous judge has observed everything at a time when his perception comes too late for him to ward off the just deserts of his sins. Therefore the unrighteous person who has long been treated leniently is carried away suddenly because *the eyes of the Lord are upon the ways of men, and he considereth all their steps.* This is as much as saying that God does not in the last analysis leave unpunished those sins which he has long considered with patience. See how he has suddenly seized the lawbreaker and has terminated with punishment the sins he endured with forbearance. Let no one say, then, that God does not notice human behavior: long–sufferance ends with swift reckoning.

9

How much we are indebted to the Redeemer. who vouchsafed to us through penitence escape from the devil's jaw

Or will you bore through his jaw with a buckle?[51] The Lord bores through the jaw of Leviathan with a buckle because by the ineffable power of his mercy he so hinders the malice of the ancient enemy that sometimes even those already seized are set free and in a sense they fall from his mouth who after committing sin, return to innocence. Who in fact, once grasped by his mouth, could escape his jaw if it were not bored through? Did he not hold Peter in his mouth when the denial was made?[52] Did he not hold David in his mouth when the plunge into so great an abyss of lust took place?[53] But when both of them returned to life through penitence, this Leviathan somehow let them slip through the opening in his jaw. Therefore they are withdrawn from his mouth through that opening, who after committing such great wickedness, come round again by penitence. But what man keeps away from the mouth of this Leviathan so that he does nothing unlawful? On the contrary, it is hence that we know how much we are indebted to the Redeemer of mankind because he not only prevented us from going into the mouth of Leviathan but also enabled us to get away from his mouth; by piercing that jaw he did not deprive the sinner of hope but gave him a way of escape, so that he might at least afterwards escape death who, off guard at first, was not afraid of being grasped by death. Therefore the heavenly healing art everywhere comes to our aid, because it both gave man injunctions against sin, and yet when he sinned gave him remedies against despair. So the greatest care must be taken that no one through pleasure in sin be seized by the mouth of Leviathan; and yet, if he has been seized, let him not despair, because if he fully laments his sin, he finds an opening in Leviathan's jaw as a way of escape. The sinner is even now being ground by his teeth, but still, if a way of escape is sought, an opening is found in the jaw. He who chose not to take care lest he be seized, even when seized has a way of escape. Let everyone then who is not yet seized, avoid his jaw; but let everyone who has already been seized seek for an opening in the jaw.

Let the hope of our expectation, therefore, have also a touch of fear, in order that the justice of the judge may frighten into the correction of his sins the one whom the love of the liberator invites to trust in pardon. For hence it is said by a certain wise man: *Say not: The mercy of the Lord is great; he will not remember my sins.*[54] For he first speaks of his mercy and then of justice, saying: *For mercy and wrath quickly come from him.*[55] Divine clemency, therefore, boring through the jaw of Behemoth, comes to help the human race in every situation, mercifully and powerfully, because there was no abstention from giving it caution and admonition when free, nor withdrawal from it of the remedy of escape when captured. For the sins of such persons as David and Peter are included in Scripture so that the downfall of eminent persons may be a warning for the rest. But the penitence and pardon of both are made known so that the recovery of the fallen may be the hope of the vacillating. Let no one be conceited about his constancy when David falls. Neither let anyone lose hope should he fall from grace when David rises.

10

Those who are pricked by compunction but never draw back from iniquity or immediately return to it

There are some persons who when they renew their concern for the interior life, contemplate the justice and righteousness of God, and in prayer and weeping tremble with fear, but after the time of contemplation has passed, they return boldly to their wickedness as if, being placed behind God, they were not seen by the eye of his righteousness. And so these persons within themselves in secret accept God's person as if he saw with bodily sight: when they are seen by him, they flatter him with their tears, and when they are out of his sight, their way of life deteriorates. They should be afflicted all the more for their evildoing because in the secret of their hearts they know the righteous judgments of God.

Hence it is written: *As soon as he shall move himself, he shall trouble you: and his dread shall fall upon you.*[56] But righteous men fear God before his wrath is set in motion against them: they fear him unmoved, lest they should feel the effects of his being moved. But, on the contrary, the wicked then at last fear to be disciplined when they are under the lash, and terror then rouses them from the inactivity of their dullness when punishment disturbs them. And hence it is said by the prophet: *And vexation alone shall make you understand what you hear.*[57] For when they have begun to be afflicted with punishment for having disdained and neglected God's precepts, then they understand what they have heard. And the Psalmist says: *When he slew them, then they sought him.*[58] Therefore for reprobate hearts fear does not beget rest, but punishment brings forth fear.

Often, however, the sinner—knowing with how much guilt he is burdened—attempts a breakthrough so as to rid himself of guilt with determination and full conversion, and he does not succeed. Thus he is unable to *lament his sorrow,*[59] for he both sees the guilt of his sinfulness and yet by reason of the weight of earthly encumbrance he has no opportunity for remorse. He is unable to lament his sorrow who strives indeed to resist evil habituation, yet is weighed down by the ever–increasing desires of the flesh. The presence of this sorrow had inflicted anguish upon the spirit of the prophet when he said: *My sorrow is continually before me, for I will declare my iniquity: and I will think for my sin.*[60] But the bonds of his sin being loosed, he knew that he was released, who rejoiced saying: *Thou hast broken my bonds: I will sacrifice to thee the sacrifice of praise.*[61]

Therefore God releases us to lament our sorrow at the time when he both shows us the evil things we have done and helps us to lament these things when we are aware of them. He sets our transgressions before our eyes and with the merciful hand of grace loosens the bonds of our heart in order that our soul may reach out to the liberating power of penitence and, released from the shackles of the flesh, may freely move along the path of love toward its Creator. But it commonly happens that we ourselves censure our way of life and yet willfully do what we rightly reprove in ourselves. The spirit lifts us up to righteousness, the flesh restricts us to habit. The soul resists self–love, but is made captive by beguilement.

Moreover, when a right intention issues a call to conversion but the infirmity of the flesh still revokes this intention, the soul—fettered as if by some kind of bonds—is obstructed. For we often see that many desire indeed a life of holy conduct, but they fear at one time impending misfortunes and at another future adversities, so as to be unable to reach this goal. While with wariness they look out for definite evils, they are unwarily held back by the shackles of their sins. For they envision many things happening during the course of their life, in the face of which they are afraid they cannot stand firm. Of them Solomon well says: *The way of the slothful is as a hedge of thorns.*[62] For when they seek the way of God, the opposing conceptions of their fears standing in the way as thorns of hedges, wound them. But since this obstacle does not usually obstruct the elect, Solomon rightly added: *The way of the just is without offense.*[63] For whatever adversity may have blocked their way of life, the righteous do not stumble against it because with the spring of eternal hope and of internal contemplation they leap over the obstacles of temporal adversity.

11

It is necessary to do things well in life, because in death the soul is given over in eternity to a good or evil spirit

My eye shall not return to see good things.[64] The eye of the dead does not return to see good things because once the soul is separated from the flesh, it does not come back to perform good deeds. Hence it is that the rich man, whom the fire of hell was tormenting, realized that he could not restore himself by activity. For he did not seek to benefit himself, but his brothers who were left behind: *I beseech thee, father Abraham, that thou wouldst send Lazarus to my father's house—for I have five brethren—that he may testify unto them, lest they also come into this place of torment.*[65] For even counterfeit hope usually refreshes the sorrowful soul. But the reprobate, so that they may feel their punishment more severely, lose even hope of pardon. Hence when the rich man was givcn over to chastising flames, he did not seek to help himself, as we have said, but his brothers since he knew that he would never be without the torments of fires as well as the added punishment of despair. Hence Solomon says: *Whatsoever thy hand is able to do, do it earnestly: for neither work, nor reason, nor wisdom, nor knowledge shall be in hell, whither thou art hastening.*[66] So the eye does not return to see good things since the soul, receiving its retribution, is not recalled to the practice of serviceability.

The text continues: *Nor shall the sight of man behold me.*[67] For the sight of man is the mercy of the Redeemer, which softens the hardness of our insensibility when it looks upon us. Hence it is said in the Gospel: *And the Lord·turning looked on Peter. And Peter remembered the word that Jesus had said. And Peter, going out, wept bitterly.*[68] But the sight of man does not look on the soul when divested of the flesh because it does not set free after death the one whom grace does not convert to forgiveness before death. For hence Paul says: *Behold, now is the acceptable time; behold, now is the day of salvation.*[69] Hence the Psalmist says: *For his mercy is for the present age,*[70] in the sense that over the one whom mercy does not rescue now, justice alone holds sway. Hence Solomon says: *If the tree fall to the south, or to the north, in what place soever it shall fall, there shall it be.*[71] For when at the time of death of the human being, either the Holy Spirit or the evil spirit receives the soul departing from the confines of the flesh, he will keep it with him forever without any change, so that once exalted, it shall not tumble into torments, and once plunged into eternal torments, it shall not later come within reach of redeeming help. Therefore it is well said: *And the eye of man shall not see me*, insofar as the one whom the grace of the Redeemer does not now look upon to correct, it shall not then be concerned to shield from ruin. For he who comes in severity to judgment both sees not, in order to save, and yet sees, in order to afflict, since the one on whom he does not look with mercy in the present life, by looking on him hereafter he brings to ruin through judgment. For now any sinner casts away the fear of God and yet lives, blasphemes and yet prospers, because the merciful Creator in seeing does not wish to punish the one whom he wishes to correct by waiting for him, as it is written: *Thou overlookest the sins of men for the sake of repentance.*[72] But when the sinner is looked upon hereafter, he shall be no more, because when the strict judge precisely examines his deserts, the guilty one is not equal to the torments.

The text continues: *Thy eyes are upon me, and I shall be no more.*[73] This likewise accords ever so much with the voice of the righteous, whose anxious mind is ever intent on the judgment to come. For they have fears for everything they do, when they circumspectly consider before how great a judge they

will stand. They contemplate the power of his immensity, and they consider
with how much guilt stemming from their own weakness they are bound. They
count the evils they have done and in contrast to them they sum up the benefits
of the Creator. They reflect how strictly he judges wicked deeds, how accurately he examines the good; and they foresee without ambiguity that they will
perish if they are judged without mercy, for they see that even the fact that we
seem to live righteously is a fault if, when he takes account of our lives, the
mercy of God does not overlook it. For hence it is written in the Book of Job:
The stars are not pure in his sight,[74] for strictly judged in his presence these faithful persons also bear stains of defilement that are conspicuous amid the purity
of holiness.

12

Those who reflect on the brevity of life hasten more quickly to penitence

*For, behold, short years pass away: and I am walking in a path by which I shall
not return.*[75] Everything that passes is short, even if it should seem to be rather
slowly terminated. Moreover, we are walking in the path of death and shall
not return by it, not because we are not brought back by rising again to the life
of the flesh, but because we do not come again to the labors of this mortal life,
or to earn rewards by our labors.

The text continues: *My spirit shall be wasted.*[76] The spirit is spent by the
fear of judgment because the more the minds of the elect sense that they are
nearing the final judgment, the more apprehensively they are shaken by self-
examination; and whenever they find in themselves any carnal thoughts, they
dispel them by the fervor of their penance; and they do not allow their
thoughts to wander about in carnal delight, since they judge and punish themselves more thoroughly, the more imminent is the coming of the just judge
they await. As a result, they always expect an early death, whereas the minds
of the reprobate wickedly activate many plans because they consider themselves destined for a long life. Therefore the spirit of the upright is wasted, but
the spirit of the wicked thrives. For the more the latter swell with pride, the
less their spirit is drained of fretfulness; but the righteous, while they dwell on
the shortness of their life, refrain from sins of pride and impurity.

And hence it is added: *My days shall be shortened and only the grave
remaineth for me.*[77] For he who considers what he will be in death, always becomes uneasy about his conduct, and because of the fact that he practically
ceases to live in his own eyes, he truly begins to live in the eyes of his Creator.
He seeks nothing that passes away, he opposes all the desires of the present

life, and imagines himself at the threshold of death, because he is quite aware
that he is destined to die. For a perfect life is the mirror image of death: while
the righteous carefully conjure it up, they escape the snares of sins. Hence it is
written: *In all thy works remember thy last end, and thou shalt never sin.*[78] And
hence blessed Job, seeing that his days are shortened, reflects that only the
grave remains for him.

13

The misery and brevity of the present life

Man, born of a woman, living for a short time, is filled with many miseries.[79]
In sacred Scripture woman is used either for the sex, or for frailty: for the sex,
as where it is written, *God sent his Son, made of a woman, made under the Law,*[80]
but for frailty, as where it is said by a certain wise man, *Better is the iniquity of a
man, than a woman doing a good turn.*[81] For any strong and discreet person is
called a man, but a woman is perceived as of weak or indiscreet disposition.
And it often happens that even a discreet person suddenly falls into sin, and
that another weak and indiscreet person displays good behavior. But he that is
weak and indiscreet is sometimes exalted by what he has done well, and falls
more gravely into sin; but any discreet person even because of the evil he
judges that he has done, returns with firmer attention to the rule of strictness,
and reaches greater heights of righteousness as a result of the occasion on
which he seemed to have fallen from righteousness for a time. In this matter it
is rightly said: *Better is the iniquity of a man, than a woman doing a good turn,*
since even the fault of the strong becomes an occasion of virtue, and the virtue
of the weak, an occasion of sin. Therefore in this context by the name of a
woman, what else but frailty of disposition is denoted when it is said: *Man born
of a woman?* It is as if it were more openly asked: What strength shall he have
in himself, who was born in frailty?

Living for a short time, and filled with many miseries. Observe that by the
holy man's words the punishment of man is briefly expressed, since his life is
shortened and his misery extended. For if we consider with exactness all that is
involved here, it is punishment and misery. For it is misery to minister to the
corruption of the flesh in things necessary and permitted: clothing is required
against cold, food against hunger, coolness against heat. Health of the body is
maintained only with great care; even when guarded it is lost; when lost it is not
recovered without great difficulty, and yet when restored is always uncertain:
what else is this but the misery of mortal life? We love our friends, suspecting
they may be offended with us; we fear our enemies and certainly are not at ease
concerning those whom we fear; we often talk to our enemies as confidingly as

to friends, and sometimes take the honest words of our friends and perhaps those of the ones that love us very much, as the words of enemies; and we, who never wish either to be deceived or to deceive, make the more serious mistake by our caution: again, what else is this but the misery of human life? When the heavenly country has been lost, rejected man delights in his exile, is weighed down with cares, and yet leaves unnoticed his thinking how burdensome it is that there is so much on his mind; he is deprived of interior light, and yet in this life wishes to put up with his blindness for a long time: what is this but misery, designed to be our punishment? But although he desires to stay here for a long time, still he is impelled by the onward movement of mortal life to depart from it.

The holy man rightly adds: *He cometh forth like a flower, and is destroyed, and fleeth as a shadow, and never continueth in the same state.*[82] For as a flower he comes forth since he flourishes in the flesh; but he is destroyed since he is reduced to corruption. For what are men, born in the world, but a species of flowers in a field? Let us direct our interior gaze over the expanse of the present world, and we see it is filled with as many flowers as there are human beings. So life in the flesh is the flower in grass. Hence it is well said by the Psalmist: *Man's days are as grass: as the flower of the field, so shall he flourish.*[83] Isaias too says: *All flesh is grass, and all the glory thereof as the flower of the field.*[84] For man comes forth like a flower from concealment, and of a sudden appears openly, and in an instant is by death drawn from open view back into concealment. The verdure of the flesh exposes us to view, but the dryness of dust retracts us from sight. Like a flower we appeared, who were not; like a flower we wither, who appeared only for a time.

And since man is daily being wrenched toward death moment by moment, it is rightly added: *And fleeth as a shadow, and never continueth in the same state.* For since infancy gives way to childhood, childhood to youth, youth to manhood, manhood to old age, old age to death, in the course of the present life he is forced by the very stages of his growth into those of his decline, and is ever falling behind for the very reason he thinks he is extending his span of life. For we cannot have a fixed state here: we have come only to pass on; and this very fact of our living means that we are day by day departing from life.

14

The unstable contradictory quality of this life in which we are affected now by one thing and now by its contrary

Leaving the safe refuge of humility and indulging in pride, man came under the yoke of weakness: by giving support to the boldness of his heart, he became subject to it, since he who refused to submit to divine commands, yielded obeisance to his own needs. We shall show this to better effect if we list those burdens, first of the flesh and then of the spirit, which he sustains after this submission.

For to say nothing of the fact that he endures pain and that he struggles for breath during fever, the condition of our body that is called health is constrained by its own illness. For the body declines through idleness, it becomes weak from work; failing by not eating it is refreshed by food so as to hold out; growing lethargic by sustenance it is relieved by abstinence so as to be vigorous; it is bathed in water so as not to be dry, it is rubbed with linen cloths so as not to be weakened by too much immersion; it is invigorated by labor so that it may not be dulled by rest, it is restored by rest so that it may not give way under the exertion of labor; weary from keeping watch it is renewed by sleep, overpowered by sleep it is roused to activity by staying watchful lest it be further wearied by resting; it is covered with clothing lest it be chilled by the distress of cold, fainting from the heat it sought it is revived by the blowing of breezes. And since it finds troubles where it sought to avoid them, being badly impaired, its medicine—so to say—is what makes it sick. Therefore fevers set aside and pains arrested, our health itself is sickness, always in need of a cure. All the comforts we seek to foster life, we welcome as so many medicines for our sickness. But the very medicine itself turns out to be injurious, since clinging a little too long to the remedy we sought, we are more adversely affected by what we prudently provide for our recovery. Thus was self–confidence to be offset, thus was pride to be brought low. For because we once arrogated a high spirit, see how we daily carry about clay that comes apart.

That spirit of ours as well, separated from the secure enjoyment of interior solitude, is now led on by hope, now troubled by fear; now weakening is cast down by grief, now by a false gaiety is alleviated. It prizes transitory objects and is continually afflicted by the loss of them, since it is also unceasingly being altered by a rushing flow of events. Subject to changeable things, it also undergoes changes itself. For seeking what it does not have, it is solicitous to obtain it, and when it has begun to acquire possession, it is discontented with the acquisition of what it sought. Often it loves what it had despised, and despises what it used to love. Effort is required for it to learn the things of eternity, but it quickly forgets them if it ceases to exert itself. It takes a long search for it to find out a little concerning the things that are paramount, but relapsing into its customary ways, not even for a little while does it retain the things it has discovered. Wishing to become learned, it overcomes its ignorance with difficulty, and having become knowledgeable, it has a greater struggle against intellectual pride. Not without difficulty does it subject to itself the tyranny of the flesh, yet it is still inwardly subject to sinful thoughts whose outward manifestations it has already conquered and restrained. It extends itself in search of its Creator, but when it is impeded, the familiar uncertainty of earthly things complicates the search. It desires to determine how, being incorporeal, it rules over the body, and it fails. It wonderingly investigates something it is unable to explain, and not knowing the answer, is surpassed by the reality it discreetly examines. Viewing itself as both expansive and restricted, it does not know how to appraise itself truly, since if it were not expansive it would not be looking into matters of such great scope; and again, if it were not restricted, it would at least find the answer to its inquiry.

Well therefore is it said: *Thou hast set me opposite to thee, and I am become burdensome to myself,*[85] because while exiled man endures both annoyances from the flesh and perplexities in the spirit, surely he is quite burdensome to himself. On every side he is oppressed with sicknesses, on every side he is weighed down with infirmities, so that he who, having abandoned God, believed that he was sufficient unto himself for his rest, might find in himself nothing but an uproar of disorder and might seek to flee from himself after this discovery; but having spurned his Creator, he might not have anywhere to flee. A certain wise man, having rightly reflected on the burdens of that infirmity, declares: *A heavy yoke is upon the children of Adam, from the day of their coming out of their mother's womb until the day of their burial into the mother of all.*[86]

15

Aware that life is short, we prepare for the next life

It often happens that as long as the present life is loved as if it were to last a long time, the soul breaks away from eternal hope, and diverted by prevailing circumstances, regresses through the obscurity of hopelessness. And while it thinks that the period is long which remains for it to live, suddenly upon leaving this life it is confronted by the eternal verities that it cannot evade. Hence it is said by a certain wise man: *Woe to them that have lost patience.*[87] For surely they have lost patience who, while they count on staying long among things visible, abandon hope of the invisible. And while the mind is fixed on what is present, life is ended, and they are suddenly brought to unforeseen punishments which, deceived by their expectations, they believed would either never or tardily be their lot. Hence Truth says: *Watch ye therefore, because you know not the day nor the hour.*[88] Hence again it is written: *The day of the Lord shall so come as a thief in the night,*[89] for since in approaching to seize the soul it is not seen, it is compared to a thief in the night. Therefore death, being always on its

way, must be all the more feared because the time when it is about to come
cannot be known beforehand. Whence even holy men, since they constantly
ponder the shortness of life, live as if dying daily, and prepare themselves the
more thoroughly for the things that will last, the more they are ever reflecting
that by reason of their coming to an end, transitory things are of no account.
For hence the Psalmist, seeing the life of the sinner elapsing at a quick rate,
says: *For yet a little while and the wicked shall not be.*[90] Hence again he says:
Man's days are as grass.[91] Hence Isaias says: *All flesh is grass, and all the glory
thereof as the flower of the field.*[92] Hence James rebukes the spirit of the overconfident, saying: *For what is your life? It is a vapor which appeareth for a little
while.*[93] Therefore it is rightly said: *Wait a little while,*[94] since both what follows
without limit is immeasurable and what comes to an end lasts a little while. For
that should not seem long to us, which by the passage of its particular period is
tending not to be; while it is being drawn out from moment to moment, its particular moments are driving it to what they put off; and the reason it is
perceived to be held onto is the same that causes it to be relinquished.

16

We ought always to be prepared for death because it is uncertain when we will die

Thou hast appointed his bounds which cannot be passed.[95] None of the
things that happen to men in this world takes place apart from the secret design of almighty God. For God, foreseeing before all ages every future
happening, decreed how each one should be ordered throughout the ages. It is
indeed determined for man either to what extent the prosperity of the world
shall fall to his share or to what degree adversity shall strike him, lest either
immeasurable prosperity exalt the elect or excessive adversity weigh them
down. It is also established how long each one shall remain in this mortal life.
For although almighty God added fifteen years to the life of king Ezechias, he
foresaw that the king would die at the time when he permitted the death.[96] In
this matter a question arises as to how it should be said to the king by the
prophet: *Give charge concerning thy house, for thou shalt die, and not live.*[97] For
to him, following his tears, more life was allotted after sentence of death was
declared. But the Lord said by the prophet at what time he merited death;
however, by the liberality of mercy, God deferred death for him until the time
that he foreknew before all ages. And the prophet, therefore, was not deceptive because he made known the time of death as that when the king deserved
to die; and the decisions of the Lord were not overturned, insofar as the fact
that the years of life would increase through God's bounty was also foreor-

dained before all ages. And the period of life, which was added contrary to public expectation, was secretly ordained without extension of foreknowledge.

The days determined in advance for each individual by the hidden foreknowledge of God can neither be increased nor diminished unless it happens that they are so foreknown as either to be longer because of most virtuous works or shorter because of most wicked ones, just as Ezechias acquired increase of days by the shedding of tears and as it is written concerning the unrighteous: *Death meets the undisciplined.*[98] But often the wicked person, although in the secret foreknowledge of God extended periods of his life are not predestined, since he desires to live in a carnal way, he imagines that many years are in store for him. And because he cannot procure what he longs for, it is as if he perishes before his days are fulfilled.[99]

For he should not have been proud, even if he could have had the number of his years established so that, knowing how long he would live, he might know beforehand when to withdraw himself from pride. But since the present life is always uncertain, stealthy death should always be the more feared insofar as it can never be foreseen. And he rightly indicates that the pride of the wicked is tyranny, as it is written: *And the number of years of his tyranny is uncertain.*[100] For he is in the proper sense called a tyrant who unrightfully rules in a commonwealth. But it should be recognized that every proud person in his own way exercises tyranny. For the rule that sometimes a person exercises in a republic—in this case, by usurping the power of high office—another exercises in a province, in a city, in his own family, still another exercises within himself in the thought of his own heart by concealed wickedness. And the Lord does not probe how much evil any such person may be able to do, but how much he wishes to do. Furthermore, when external power is lacking, there is a tyrant within the one whose iniquity exercises rule; for although he does not oppress his neighbors outwardly, yet inwardly he seeks to have power to oppress them. And because almighty God considers the hearts of men, the wicked man has already done in the eyes of God what was coveted. However, our Creator willed that our end be hidden from us in order that remaining uncertain when we may die, we may always approach death in a state of readiness.

BOOK 2

PENITENCE

Prologue

Since the antecedent remedial grace of God calls sinners to repentance, accordingly the discussion of divine grace is followed by the book on penitence: second in the sequence of Part 2 is this remedy for what is second in Part 1 and is of course entitled Sin.

And as sin is committed in three ways—by thought, word, and deed—instruction is given here concerning a threefold remedy, so that for sinful thought the curative of compunction is discussed; for sin by speech, oral confession; for sin by evil deed, almsgiving. Indeed the real penitent must have these attributes: true contrition of heart, unfeigned confession, and complete *de facto* reparation.

1

Penitence and why it should be practiced in sackcloth and ashes

He hath rushed in upon me like a giant.[1] The enemy is easily resisted if prolonged consent is not given to him either in many falls from grace or in a single fall. But if the soul has grown accustomed to yield to his persuasions, the more frequently it subjects itself to him, the more intolerable it makes him, so that it is unable to struggle against him, because without doubt the wicked adversary fights against it like a giant when it is hampered by evil habit. Yet holy Church, even after sins have been committed, generally brings the minds of the faithful back to penitence and washes away sinful actions by the power of voluntary reparation.

Hence it is added: *I have sewed sackcloth upon my skin, and have covered my flesh with ashes.*[2] What is to be understood by sackcloth and ashes but penitence; what by the skin and the flesh but sin of the flesh? Therefore since certain persons after a sin of the flesh return to penitence, it is as if sackcloth is sewn upon the skin and the flesh covered with ashes, because the sin of the flesh is covered by penitence so that it may not be seen for its punishment in the consideration of the strict judge. But holy Church, when she retrieves her weak members from sins and leads them to the remedy of penitence, without doubt helps them with her tears so that they may regain health to receive the grace of their Creator, and she grieves for the strong because she has not done what she did in her weak members.

Hence is it rightly further added: *My face is swollen with weeping.*[3] Clearly, the face of holy Church represents those placed in positions of governance who come first into view, in order that their aspect may be the honor of the faithful people, even if some bodily disfigurement is hidden from sight. These personages who are given charge over the people lament the sins of the weak and so practice penitence for the faults of others as for their own.

It is customary to practice penitence in ashes and sackcloth, as is said in the Gospel: *If in Tyre and Sidon had been wrought miracles that have been wrought in you, they would have long ago done penance in sackcloth and ashes.*[4] For by sackcloth is denoted the coarseness and the irritation of sin; by ashes, the dust of the dead. And thus it is customary to use both of these in penitence, in order that by the irritant of sackcloth we may realize what we have done by sin and in the dust of ashes may consider what we become through judgment. Let disturbing sins then be brought to mind by sackcloth, let the just punishment of sins, which follows the sentence of death, be recalled by ashes. For since afflictions of the flesh arose after sin, let man consider in the coarseness of the sackcloth what he has done through pride, let him consider in the ashes to what end he has come through sin.

2

We should practice penitence for sins lest the judge discover something that has gone unpunished

Let the day perish wherein I was born, and the night in which it was said: A man–child is conceived.[5] By day is understood the pleasure of sin, and by night, the blindness of mind through which man lets himself be overthrown in committing sin. And therefore he wishes the day may perish so that all the persuasiveness observed in sin may be destroyed by the powerful instrumentality of divine justice. He also wishes the night may perish so that what the blinded mind also does in yielding consent be forgotten through the censure of penitence.

But we must inquire: Why is man said to be born in the day, conceived in the night? Holy Scripture uses the designation man in three ways, namely with reference sometimes to nature, sometimes to sin, sometimes to frailty. Man is, for instance, so called with reference to nature where it is written: *Let us make man to our image and likeness.*[6] He is called man with reference to sin where it is written: *I have said: You are gods, and all of you the sons of the Most High. But you like men shall die.*[7] That is to say: You shall die like transgressors. And hence Paul says: *For, whereas there is among you envying and contention, are you not carnal and walk you not according to man?*[8] That is to say: Do not you, who are motivated by conflicting considerations, still sin because of blameworthy human nature? He is called man with reference to his weakness, as it is written: *Cursed be the man that trusteth in man*,[9] that is to say, in weakness. Therefore man is born in the day, he is conceived in the night, since he is not carried away by the pleasure of sin until he is first made weak by the deliberate darkness of his mind. For he first becomes blind in his thinking, and then he gives in to sinful pleasure. Therefore let it be said: *Let the day perish wherein I was born, and the night in which it was said: A man–child is conceived*, that is, let the pleasure perish which has carried him away into sin, and the rash weakness of his mind which dimmed his sight to the point of obscuring evil consent. For a man not warily on guard in the course of the allurements of pleasure, rushes blindly into the night of most pernicious evildoing. Therefore shrewd vigilance must be exercised so that when the occasion of sin initiates entrapment, the mind may decipher to what ruin it is being drawn.

And hence it is fittingly added: *Let that day be turned into darkness*.[10] For the day is turned into darkness when at the very beginning of pleasure, it is seen to what a destiny of destruction sin is abruptly leading us. We turn the day into darkness when, severely chastening ourselves, we harrow the delights of evil enjoyment by the harsh lamentations of penitence, and when with weeping we reproach any sinful pleasure we experience secretly in our hearts. For because no believer is unaware that the thoughts of the heart will be precisely examined at the judgment, as Paul testifies, saying: *Their thoughts between themselves accusing or also defending one another*,[11] searching himself, the believer examines his conscience before the judgment in order that the strict judge may be the more calm in his coming when he sees already appropriately reproved shortcomings that are in issue.

And hence it is rightly added: *Let not God regard it from above*.[12] God regards the things which he searches out when he judges; he does not regard those he considers expiated and thus overlooks at the judgment. Therefore, this day—in other words, this sinful pleasure—is not regarded by the Lord if it is expiated by self–determining atonement, as Paul testifies who says: *If we would judge ourselves, we should not be judged*.[13] Therefore, for God to regard our day is, at the judgment, to institute against our souls a search of every sinful gratification; at this inquiry he then certainly strikes harder the one who is perceived to have spared himself more indulgently. And the text appropriately continues: *And let not the light shine upon it*.[14] For the Lord, appearing at the judgment, shines his light upon all that he reproves. For what is not then recalled by the judge is as if hidden under a kind of darkness. It is indeed written: *But all things that are reproved are made manifest by the light*.[15] In a way, darkness hides the sins of penitents of whom the prophet says: *Blessed are they whose iniquities are forgiven: and whose sins are covered*.[16] Therefore, since everything that is covered is as if hidden in darkness, what is not singled out by punishment does not shine with light on the day of the last judgment. For our deeds that he would not then wish to punish, the mercy of God knowingly keeps hidden in some way. But everything which is at that time manifest in the sight of all, is shown in light. Therefore, let this day be turned into darkness in such a way that by penitence we suppress all the evil that we do. Let not the Lord regard this day, and let not the light shine upon it, in this sense, namely, that while we suppress our own sin, he himself may not rebuke it with the chastisement of the final judgment.

But the judge himself will come who searches all things, blames all things deserving reproach. Because he is everywhere present, there is no place of refuge. But because he is appeased by the tears of our self–correction, that person alone finds a place for flight who after committing sin, hides himself now in penitence.

3

The fear of those truly practicing penitence Both sins against faith and sinful deeds are subject to condemnation

Whosoever committeth sin is the servant of sin,[17] for surely anyone who gives in to evil desire puts himself, formerly free, under the rule of wickedness. But we renounce this master when we struggle against the evil which had made prisoners of us; when we forcibly resist habit, and in opposition to it, suppressing evil desires, defend the innate right of freedom; when by penitence we overcome sin and cleanse the stains of defilement with our tears. But often the mind indeed already deplores the evils it recalls having done, already not only abandons its misdeeds but even chastises them with most bitter lamentations, yet while it remembers the things it has done, it is alarmed by oppressive fear of judgment. It already has a complete change of heart, but does not yet completely attain a state of security, for while it considers how great is the severity of the final judgment, it wavers in anxiety between hope and fear, for it knows not, when the just judge comes, which evil deeds he will count, which ones he will remit. For it remembers what evil it has committed, but it does not know whether it has suitably lamented its guilt, and it is afraid that the greatness of the sin exceeds the extent of penitence. And often Truth does already remit the sin, yet the troubled soul as long as it is solicitous for itself, is fearful about forgiveness, because it is written: *And [let] his sin [pass] even to hell*.[18] For that sin is brought even to hell which before the end of the present life is not amended by renouncement and penitence. Concerning that sin it is truly said by John: *There is a sin unto death; for that I say not that any man ask*.[19] For a sin unto death is a sin even until death, because obviously pardon of sin that is not corrected here is sought in vain.

Concerning such a sinner the text further declares: *Let mercy forget him*.[20] Almighty God's mercy is said to forget him who has forgotten almighty God's justice, since whoever does not fear him now as just, cannot hereafter find him merciful. Without doubt this sentence is directed not only against him who abandons the preachings of true faith, but also against him who, abiding in the right faith, lives a carnal life since the punishment of eternal censure is not evaded whether there is sinfulness in faith or practice. For although the kind of condemnation is different, yet for guilt which is not cleansed by penitence no means of acquittal is of assistance.

4

The judgment of the just against themselves, lest they be judged in the future

While we are able, let us obliterate from the sight of the eternal judge our evil thoughts and more evil deeds; let us bring before our internal vision whatever evil we have committed through the sin of presumption. Let not our weakness favor itself and treat itself gently regarding the sins that it calls to mind. But the more conscious it is of evil, let it be the more beneficently severe with itself, let it conjure up the future judgment, and whatever sins it knows must be severely dealt with by the sentence of the judge, let it dutifully deal with by the penitence of conversion.

It is written: *For it is no longer in the power of man to enter into judgment with God*.[21] This verse calls for greater consideration, the more acutely hurtful is neglect of what it makes known. What is indicated here, of course, is not that judgment which punishes by eternal retribution, but that which, conceived in the mind, removes guilt by conversion. For whoever is afraid of being condemned at the last judgment has no desire to enter into it. Therefore, since it is said: *For it is no longer in the power of man to enter into judgment with God*, it is clearly shown that there is a kind of judgment which is at some time or other desired even by the condemned and the reprobate. And this is none other than that of which the apostle Paul speaks: *If we would judge ourselves, we should not be judged*,[22] and of which it is said by the prophet: *There is no judgment in their steps*.[23] and of which David says: *The king's honor loveth judgment*,[24] so that of necessity he who now honors God by faith carefully judges what conduct is incumbent on him. Hence it is again written: *Be judged before him, and expect him.*[25] He is truly judged before the Lord who beholds the Lord in his heart and in his presence examines his conduct with careful attention. For he expects the Lord the more confidently who daily examines his life with greater diffidence. For he who comes to the Lord's final judgment is no longer judged before him, but by him. Of this judgment the Lord also through the prophet speaks to the forgetful soul: *Put me in remembrance, and let us plead together: tell if thou hast any thing to justify thyself.*[26]

For the mind of everyone must consider with careful attention its pleas before God, and the pleas of God against itself; it must weigh circumspectly either what good things it has received from him, or what unsuitable return it has made for his gifts by wicked living. This examen is continually made by the elect from day to day. Whence Solomon well says: *The thoughts of the just are judgments.*[27] For they approach the chambers of the judge in the inmost part of their own heart; they consider how severely he who is long–suffering ultimately punishes; they are apprehensive because of their past deeds; and they make amends by their tears for the faults they know they have committed; they fear the exact divine judgments even in those matters which they cannot perhaps fathom in themselves. For they see there is perception by divine insight of what they, through human limitation, do not see in themselves. They do perceive mentally the strict judge who, the later he comes, chastens all the more severely. They contemplate also the assembly of the holy Fathers seated with him and reproach themselves for having disregarded either their example or their pronouncements, and in this secret forum of inner judgment, straitened by the indictment of their own conscience, they purge by penitence what they have committed through pride. For there they sum up all that they lack in integrity; there they muster before their eyes everything for which they should weep; there they look attentively at whatever can be decreed by the wrath of the strict judge; there they suffer as many punishments as they are afraid of suffering; and at this judgment carried out in the mind no process is neglected which is necessary for prosecuting more fully the ones who are found guilty. For the conscience accuses, reason judges, fear puts in bonds, and pain punishes. And this judgment is all the more corrective, because it breathes fire inwardly, undeterred by external interference. For when anyone has initiated this investigative action against himself, he is the prosecutor who arraigns, he is the accused who is arraigned; he hates himself, as he remembers himself to have been; and in the person of his present self, prosecutes judicially his former self; and a dispute is begun by him in his mind against himself, producing peace with God. This disputation of the heart the Lord was seeking when he said through the prophet: *I attended and hearkened; no man speaketh what is good. There is none that doth penance for his sin, saying: What have I done?*[28] He was appeased by this dispute of the human heart when he spoke these words to his prophet of king Achab, who reproved himself: *Hast thou not seen Achab humbled before me? Therefore, because he hath humbled himself for my sake, I will not bring the evil in his days.*[29]

Since, therefore, it is now in our power to undergo an inward judgment of our mind against ourselves, by self-examination let us accuse ourselves, and punish our former selves by penitence; let us not cease to judge ourselves while it is in our power; let us carefully heed what is said: *For it is no longer in the power of man to enter into judgment with God.*[29a] For it is usually characteristic of the reprobate to be always doing wrong, and never to correct what they have done. For they disregard with blinded mind everything that they do and do not admit what they have done, except when they have been punished.

5

A penitent ought to weep bitterly for those sins he committed with pleasure

He who recalls his evil deeds shows himself how justly he is to be condemned. Whence it happens that he reproaches with daily shedding of tears every sin which he is mindful that he has committed, and the more he is now able to perceive what is righteous, the more ardently he desires with expression of sorrow to punish his unrighteousness.

Hence it is written: *After (the light) a noise shall roar.*[30] For the Lord undoubtedly turns into sorrow the life of the one whom he has supplied with enlightenment; and the more he makes known to the enlightened mind eternal punishments, the more insistently he calls upon it to show sorrow for its past wickedness; and a man grieves at what he has been because he now begins to discern the goodness which was not his; he hates himself, as he remembers himself to have been; he loves the person he knows he should have been, and now loves only the bitterness of penitence because he carefully considers by what great pleasures he has sinned through self-indulgence. Therefore it is well said: *After (the light) a noise shall roar*, because when God enters the soul, it is clear beyond doubt that the lament of penitence immediately follows, in order that the soul which formerly rejoiced in its iniquity with regrettable delight may now delight in healthful sorrow. But the more abundantly a sin is lamented, the deeper is the knowledge of truth that is attained, because the previously defiled conscience is renewed by a baptism of tears to behold the light within.

Hence after the roaring of penitence it is fittingly added: *He shall thunder with the voice of his majesty.*[31] For God thunders with the voice of his majesty when to us who have now been well prepared through sorrow, he makes known how great he is in the heights above. For thunder proceeds as if from heaven when the favor of grace strikes with sudden fear as we languish in carelessness and neglect, and when lying prostrate, we hear a sound from above; for thinking of things of earth, we are suddenly frightened at the terrifying sentence from above; and our mind, which formerly was benumbed and excessively at ease with the lowest things, is now duly alarmed and concerned with things above.

6

When we are devoted to temporal cares, we easily forget to weep for sins

Let us examine all that we do and blame whatever in us violates the rule of uprightness in order that this accusation may justify us before the strict judge. For we are the more quickly acquitted in this judgment of our conscience, the more strictly we consider ourselves guilty. And we must not hesitate to avail ourselves of the opportunities for self–examination offered to us because, after the duration of this life, there is no occasion to do so. It is indeed not idly said: *For it is no longer in the power of man to enter into judgment with God.*[32] For we are reminded of what we cannot then do in order that we may not now neglect what we can do. But see how matters that constantly arise occupy our minds and deter our conscience from self–examination. For our mind is distracted by those visible things it considers, and when it is busy outwardly, it forgets what is going on within itself. But the divine voice pierces it with its terrible sentences, as with some kind of fasteners, to keep it vigilant so that man, at least when moved by fear, may be frightened by secret impending judgments that he leaves unnoticed when overcome by torpor. For the mind is weighed down, banefully accustomed to the happenings of the old life, and as if asleep is stilled by external matters with which it is familiar; having already exhausted itself in attending to visible things, it has sunk into oblivion with respect to the consideration of inner realities. Hence it is now necessary that the mind which is distracted by visible objects, should be afflicted with invisible judgments, and since it has been overthrown by taking undue delight in outward objects, it should, at least when afflicted, attend to what it has neglected. But see how holy Scripture pierces somnolent hearts with a kind of terror in order that they may not cling to those external things that flow away but have ruined eternal prospects within them: it indicates what is decreed by the secret sentence lest inordinate thought be given to these outward matters.

For as we do not perceive how our limbs grow, our body develops, our appearance is altered, our hair changes from black to white—all these things take place in us without our notice—so does our soul undergo changes by reason of the concerns that engage our attention in the course of the span of life; and we do not realize it unless by calm and careful observation of our inner state, we measure our gains and losses day by day.

In exercising this vigilance both the examples of the Fathers and the precepts of holy Scripture assist us greatly. For if we look at the conduct of the saints and heed the divine commands, we are inspired by contemplating the former and listening to the latter, and our heart is not constrained by torpor when it is encouraged to follow them. Whence it is well said by Moses: *The fire on the altar shall always burn, and the priest shall feed it, putting wood on it every day in the morning.*[33] For the altar of God is our heart, in which the fire is ordered always to be kept burning because from it the flame of love must constantly blaze heavenwards. And on it the priest is to put wood every day, lest it should go out. For everyone who is endowed with faith in Christ is certainly made a sharer with the High Priest, as the apostle Peter says to all the faithful: *But you are a chosen generation, a kingly priesthood.*[34] And as the apostle John says: *Thou hast made us to our God a kingdom and priests.*[35] Therefore the priest, nurturing the fire on the altar, must put wood on it every day; that is, every faithful person must never cease gathering together in his heart, along with the examples of those who have gone before, the attestations of holy Scripture, in order that the flame of love may not decrease within it. For serving up either the examples of the Fathers or the precepts of the Lord in fostering our love is akin to giving nourishment to the fire.

But the fact that we are delivered from the depths of this life, when aided by the divine counsels and the examples of our forebears, is forthrightly signified by the prophet Jeremias being cast into a dungeon; for ropes and old garments are let down in order to lift him out of it.[36] For what are symbolized by the ropes but the precepts of the Lord? For when we are involved in evildoing, in a way they both bind us fast and snatch us away, they tie and draw us, they confine and raise us up. But lest the ropes cut into the prophet when he is tied and drawn up, old garments are let down at the same time because the examples of the ancient Fathers strengthen us in order that the divine commands may not cause us dismay, and from their example we assume with confidence that we are able to do what we recoil from because of our weakness.

Let everyone understand what sin has wrought; let him wreathe his mind with grief and clear away all smugness of heart by the whirlwind of penitence. For unless such a disturbance were to crush the heart as it regains self–knowledge, the prophet would never have said: *With a vehement wind thou shalt break in pieces the ships of Tharsis.*[37] For Tharsis means the exploring of joy. But when the strong windstorm of penitence falls upon the mind, it dispels from it all seeking after blameworthy joy so that it is now disposed to do nothing but weep, favors only what may provide it with salutary fear. For it keeps in mind on the one hand, the strictness of justice, on the other, the deserts of sin; it sees what punishment is in store for it if it is denied divine leniency, which is usually moved by present sorrowing to set aside eternal punishments. Therefore a vehement wind breaks into pieces the ships of Tharsis when a strong force of compunction with wholesome disquietude disturbs our minds, which have devoted themselves to this world, as ships are dedicated to the sea.

But we should understand that when we leave sins unpunished, we are seized by the night; but when we correct them with the censure of penitence, we seize upon the night that we have wrought.[38] But the only time sin of the heart is brought under our rightful control is when it is repressed at the start. And hence it is said by the voice of God to Cain, engaged in evil thoughts: *Thy sin will be present at the door, but the lust thereof shall be under thee, and thou shalt have dominion over it.*[39] For sin is present at the door when it is knocking in one's thoughts, and the lust thereof is under a person and he has dominion over it, if the wickedness of the heart, when perceived, is quickly warded off, and before it grows into obduracy, is subdued by a refractory mind.

7

All sin meets with human or divine punishment

I feared all my works, knowing that thou didst not spare the offender.[40] If there is no sparing of the offender, who is saved from eternal death since no one is found free of sin? Or does he spare a penitent but not a delinquent? Because when we lament aloud our offenses, we are no longer offenders. Otherwise how is it that when Peter denies him, the Lord looks on Peter, and by the look of the denied Redeemer he is brought to tears? How is it that when Paul sought to abolish the name of our Redeemer upon earth, he was favored with words of Christ from the heavens? But sin was still punished in both apostles: of the former it is written in the Gospel: *Peter remembered the word of the Lord, and going out, wept bitterly,*[41] and of Paul, Truth himself who called him says: *I will show him how great things he must suffer for my name's sake.*[42] Therefore God never does spare the offender since he never leaves sin unpunished. For either man himself being penitent punishes it or God making a claim against man exacts reparation. Thus there is no sparing of sin, since it is not forgiven without punishment. So David after admitting his guilt was entitled to hear: *The Lord also hath taken away thy sin,*[43] and yet being afterwards scourged with many afflictions and made a fugitive, he discharged the obligation of the sin that he had committed. So we by the saving water are cleansed of the sin of our first parent, and yet in expiating the guilt of that sin, although freed from it, we still undergo the death of the flesh.

Hence it is written: *If I be washed as it were with snow–waters, and my hands shall shine ever so clean: yet thou shalt plunge me in filth; and my garments shall abhor me.*[44] For snow–waters are the lamentations of humility. Indeed this virtue, since it surpasses all others in the eyes of the strict judge, becomes white as it were by the external appearance of outstanding merit. For there are some who show grief but not humility, because under affliction they weep, yet in the midst of those tears they either take a haughty position against the way of life of their neighbors, or they rise in opposition to the governance of their Creator. The waters that such persons have at their disposal are not snow–waters, and they cannot be clean because they are not washed in the tears of humility. But he had washed himself clean from sin with snow–waters who said with confidence: *God does not despise a contrite and humbled heart.*[45] For they who are intractable in their grumbling harrow their heart indeed but refuse to be humbled. Nevertheless, snow–water may also be understood in another sense. For the water of a spring or a stream arises out of the earth, but snow–water descends from the sky. And there are very many who rack themselves with prayerful expressions of sorrow, yet with all their labored lamentation they toil only for earthly desires; they are spurred on in their supplications, but they seek the joys of transitory happiness. Therefore snow–water does not wash them, because their tears come from below. For it is as though they who are urged on in their prayers by worldly things are bathed in earth–water. But they who weep because they long for heavenly rewards are washed clean in snow–water since spiritual compunction spreads over them. For when they seek the everlasting fatherland with tears, and stirred with longing for it express their sorrow, they receive from on high what cleanses them.

8

Grief of the penitent and contemplation of strict judgment

When, troubled by fear of divine judgment, we lament some evil things we have done, stirred up by the simple force of our sorrow to examine ourselves more diligently, we find in ourselves other things to regret even more.

For often what remains partially hidden in our insensibility is brought to our notice with greater precision in our sorrow. And the troubled mind finds out more surely the evil it has done and was not fully aware of; the discrepancy reveals to it more plainly how far it has deviated from the peace of truth, since its guilt, which while secure it did not remember, it discovers in itself when disturbed. For the increasing bitterness of penance forces upon the attention of the ashamed heart the unlawful things it has committed, portrays the strict judge confronting these lapses, hurls threats of punishment, strikes the soul with dread, disconcerts it with shame, rebukes the illicit passions of the heart, disturbs the repose of its criminal self–assurance. The spirit of penitence sums up the gifts the Creator has bestowed upon the sinner, the evil things he has done in return for the divine gifts: he was wondrously created, had sustenance freely provided, was endowed with the essence of reason at his creation, was called by the grace of his Creator, even when called refused to respond, the mercy of the one calling did not neglect him even when deaf and resisting, he was granted gifts of enlightenment, even after receiving these gifts he blinded himself by wicked deeds, was purified of the blind mistakes by the scourges of fatherly solicitude, by means of these lashes was restored to the joys of well-being by the remedy of mercy, being subject to certain non–grievous faults does not cease sinning even during these scourgings, the sinner not being abandoned by heavenly grace even when it was lightly esteemed. Therefore since grief rebuked the disturbed mind with such severity, at one time by a review of the gifts of God, at another time by reproaches of the sinner's conduct, this bitterness has a voice of its own in the heart of the righteous which speaks to them the more pointedly, the more it is inwardly heeded.

While the saints by certain insights see how precise are the judgments of God, they are as it were disturbed in their nighttime repose by the vision of a dream. For they behold how strict is the judge who is coming: while with the power of infinite majesty he lights up the secret recesses of hearts, he brings back all sins into view. They reflect on how great is that shame of being disgraced in the sight of the whole human race, of all the angels and archangels. They consider carefully what pain is to follow that shame when at the same time guilt ravages the undyingly dying soul and hell fire the imperishably perishing flesh. Therefore when the mind is shaken by such a terrifying concept, it is not unlike a horrid trance experienced during sleep.

9

The bitterness of present penitence does away with the punishments of the wrath to come

He who maintains servile fear of the Creator of mankind certainly does not love him. For then only do we offer true homage to God when we have no fear of him owing to the hopefulness of our love, when affection not fear motivates our good works, when perverseness is no longer pleasing to our mind, even if it were permitted. For whoever is restrained by fear from the practice of wrongdoing would act in a perverse manner if he were at liberty to do so. Therefore he is by no means truly righteous who is still not free from the desire of perversity. And we do not render true service to God if we keep his commandments out of fear rather than love. But when our mind is inflamed by the love of his kindness, it is relieved of all desire for the present life, for the soul is stirred against self so that it may accuse itself of the sins which it formerly justified, having no knowledge of the things above.

But it often happens that when we commit sin, we also judge by discerning the things we do. The mind itself brings what it does to trial, but inasmuch as it fails to abandon this in desire, it is ashamed to acknowledge it. But once it bears down upon carnal pleasure with the whole weight of its judgment, it asserts itself with a bold voice of acknowledgment by self–accusation. But there are some who admit their sins in plain words but yet do no know how to be sorry in confessing them. And they speak with pleasure of things that they ought to lament.

But he who truly hates his sins must speak of them in the bitterness of his soul. Hence it is written: *I will speak in the bitterness of my soul.*.[46] For it is necessary that bitterness punish whatever the tongue reproaches by judgment of the intellect. For the bitterness of present penitence does away with the punishments of the wrath to come. God judges man in this life in two ways: either by present ills he already begins to impose upon him the torments to come, or by present scourges he does away with the torments to come. For unless the just judge afflicted some both here and hereafter according to their sins, Jude would not have said: *The Lord did afterwards destroy them that believed not,*[47] and the Psalmist would not say of the wicked: *Let them be covered with their confusion as with a double cloak.*[48] For by a double cloak is meant a lined garment. And so they are covered with a double cloak who according to the deserts of their guilt are afflicted with both a temporal and an everlasting punishment. For chastisement delivers from torment only those whom it changes. For those whom present ills do not amend, they lead to the ills that are to come. But if there were not some whom present punishment saves from eternal punishment, Paul would not have said: *Whilst we are judged we are chastised by the Lord, that we be not condemned with this world.*[49] Hence it is said to John by the voice of the angel: *Such as I love, I rebuke and chastise.*[50] Hence it is also written: *For whom the Lord loveth he chastiseth; and he scourgeth every son whom he receiveth.*[51]

10

God keeps in a sealed container, as it were, the sins that penitence has not washed away

Thou indeed hast numbered my steps: but thou sparest my sins.[52] God numbers our steps when he takes note of each one of our deeds for the sake of retribution. For what is indicated by steps but each act on our part? Thus almighty God both numbers our steps and spares our sins since he both accurately considers our actions and yet remits them for penitents. He both sees obduracy in those who sin and yet softens it into penitence by his prevenient grace. But he numbers sins when he induces us to undergo a change of heart and to be sorry for all our offenses. And he mercifully remits them insofar as while we ourselves punish them, he himself does not include them in the last judgment, as Paul testifies, who says: *If we would judge ourselves, we would not be judged.*[53]

Hence it is further added: *Thou hast sealed up my offenses as it were in a bag, but hast cured my iniquity.*[54] Our sins are sealed as it were in a container since what we do openly, unless cleansed by subsequent penance, is kept as if under cover in the secrecy of God's judgment to be brought forth finally from its sealed container and divulged at the judgment. Hence it is said by Moses: *Are not these things stored up with me, and sealed in my treasures? In the day of vengeance I will repay them.*[55] But when for the evil things that we have done we are lacerated by the scourge of discipline and atone for them by penance, he seals up and cures our iniquity, since he neither leaves things unpunished here nor reserves them to be punished in the judgment. Therefore he seals offenses because he takes note of them with exactness here to chastise them, but he cures them because he fully remits them through lashes. Hence the iniquity of his persecutor (Saul/Paul) whom he threw to the ground, he also sealed up and cured when he said concerning him to Ananias: *This man is to me a vessel of election, to carry my name before the Gentiles and kings and the children of Israel. For I will show him how great things he must suffer for my name's sake.*[56] For he still threatens him with future sufferings on account of past transgressions; thus surely was what he had done wrong kept sealed up in God's heart. But undoubtedly in this sealing he had cured the transgressions, since he called him a chosen vessel. Or, surely, our offenses are sealed up in a sack when the evil things that we have done we think about continually with a heedful heart. For what is the heart of man but the sack of God? While we earnestly look into it to see by how many sins we transgress, we carry our offenses sealed up as it were in the sack of God. David kept his sin sealed up in a sack, who said: *I know my iniquity: and my sin is always before me.*[57]

11

The sinner ought to examine sins diligently and cease not to be rid [of them] by weeping

Let every sinner examine with close attention his earthly thoughts, consider the weight amassed by his old way of thinking, and cease not to rid himself of it by tears. Whence also Isaac is appropriately described as having dug wells in a foreign land.[58] From this incident we learn, faced with the hardship of this pilgrimage, to penetrate the depths of our thoughts and until the water of true wisdom is forthcoming, not to let our inquiry slacken in removing what is earthly from the heart. Yet the philistine inhabitants, plotting against Isaac, fill up his wells: likewise, when unclean spirits see us zealously digging into our hearts, they thrust upon us the accumulated thoughts of temptations. Accordingly, our mind must always be cleared and unceasingly dug up lest the area of our thoughts, if left unexplored, should be heaped upon us to form a mound of evil deeds. Hence it is said to Ezechiel: *Son of man, dig in the wall,*[59] that is, break through hardness of heart by frequent attacks of self–examination. Hence the Lord says to Isaias: *Enter thou into the rock and hide in a pit from the face of fear of the Lord and from the glory of his majesty.*[60] For we indeed enter the rock when we penetrate the hardness of our heart and are hidden in a pit from the face of fear of the Lord if, casting out worldly thoughts, we are concealed from the wrath of the strict judge in humility of mind.

Hence the people of Israel are commanded by the Lord through Moses to place a paddle in their belt when they go out for the necessities of nature, and to cover in a pit what they were relieved of.[61] For burdened as we are by the weight of a corruptible nature, certain superfluities of thought issue from the mind as does excrement from the body. But we must carry a paddle in our belt in order that being always ready to censure ourselves, we may have about us the sharp stimulus of compunction to pierce unceasingly the area of our mind with the spur of penitence and to conceal the fetidness issuing from us. For the bodily waste is covered by a paddle in a pit when the superfluity of our mind, examined with precise reproof, is concealed from the eyes of God by the stimulus of compunction.

But God is not unaware of the evil thoughts of men and does not forget their evil deeds unless they are obliterated from his sight by penitence.

12

The sinner ought to have a two–fold sighing in penitence: for the good undone and the evil done

Every sinner must in his penitence have a two–fold sorrow: he has failed to do the good that he should have done and has done the evil that he should not have done. For hence it is that it is said by Moses of him who took an oath to do something either ill or good, and has violated it through forgetfulness: *Let him offer of the flocks an ewe lamb, or a she–goat, and the priest shall pray for him and for his sin. But if he be not able to offer a beast, let him offer two turtle doves, or two young pigeons, one for sin, and the other for a holocaust.*[62] For to take an oath is to bind ourselves with a vow of servitude to God. And when we promise good works, we pledge ourselves to do good. But when we vow abstinence and the affliction of our flesh, we swear to do ill to ourselves for the time being. But because no one in this life is so nearly perfect, however devoted to God he may be, as not to sin in ever so small a degree in regard to these pious vows, an ewe lamb of the flocks or a she–goat is ordered to be offered for his sin. For what is signified by the ewe lamb but the innocence of the active life? What is signified by the she–goat, which often feeds while hanging suspended on the highest and remotest cliffs, but a contemplative life? Therefore he who sees that he has not fulfilled what he has promised and proposed, should the more earnestly prepare himself for the sacrifice to God either by the innocence of good works or by the lofty food of contemplation. And an ewe lamb of the flocks is fitly ordered to be offered, but a she–goat not of the flocks, because an active life is the lot of many, a contemplative life the lot of a few. And when we do those things that we see many are doing or have done, we offer as it were an ewe lamb of the flocks. But when the power of the person offering is not equal to an ewe lamb and a she–goat, there is added as a remedy for the penitent that two young pigeons or two turtle doves may be offered. We know that young pigeons or turtle doves utter moans instead of a song. Therefore what is indicated by two young pigeons or two turtle doves but the two–fold groaning of our penitence, so that when we are not equal to offering good works, we may grieve in two ways, both because we have not done right and have also done evil things? Whence also one turtle dove is ordered to be sacrificed for a sin offering but the other for a holocaust. For a holocaust means entirely burnt.

Therefore we sacrifice one turtle dove for a sin offering when we grieve for our fault, but we make a holocaust of the other when, because we have neglected good works, thoroughly inflaming ourselves, we are glowing with the fire of grief.

13

Compunction

Divine inspiration at one time spurs us on with love, at another time with terror. Sometimes the Lord shows us how unimportant present things are and stirs up the desire to love eternal things; sometimes he first points out the things of eternity so that afterwards temporal things may become worthless. Sometimes he discloses to us our evil deeds, and thence draws us on even to the extent of grieving for the evil deeds of others as well. Sometimes he presents to our gaze the misdeeds of others, and reclaims us from our own wickedness when we are spurred on in a surprising way.

Sometimes we also consider either open scourges or hidden judgments, and are constantly disposed to weep. Hence it is fittingly written: *And teaching, he instructeth them with discipline,*[63] because to a mind that torments itself with penitence, the sorrows of compunction are like the wounds of blows. Hence Solomon, rightly joining together the force of each kind of blow, says: *The blueness of a wound wipeth away evil, and stripes in the more inward parts of the belly.*[64] For by the bluish color of a wound he implies the discipline of bodily blows. But blows in the more inward parts of the body are the internal wounds of the mind, which are inflicted by compunction. For as the stomach is distended when filled with food, so is the mind raised up when enlarged with wicked thoughts. Therefore the lividness of a wound and blows in the more inward parts of the body wipe away evil, because at the same time external discipline does away with faults, and compunction lances the expanded mind with the punishment of penitence. But they differ from each other in this respect, that the wounds of blows cause pain, the sorrows of compunction are morally attractive. The former afflict and torment, the latter restore when they cause affliction. Through the former there is grief in affliction, through the latter there is joy in grief. Still, because compunction itself wounds the mind, it is not incongruously called discipline.

There are in fact four properties whereby the mind of a righteous man is strongly affected by compunction: when he either calls to mind his sins, considering where he has been; or fearing the sentence of God's judgments and examining himself, he gives thought to where he shall be; or carefully observing the evils of the present life, with sorrow he reflects where he is; or he contemplates the blessings of the heavenly fatherland and because he does not yet possess them, mournfully perceives where he is not.

For no one would outwardly lament what he is if he had not been able to perceive inwardly what as yet he is not. For when we realize that we were created intact but were deceived by deadly consent to the persuasion of the devil, we become aware that what we made ourselves is one thing, and what we were made is another: blameless by nature, but corrupted by our own fault. Filled with compunction as a result, we seek to nullify what we have done so that we may be renewed in accord with the way we were created.

When grace from above comes to us, immediately it urges us on to yearn with tears for its increase. For our mind, touched by the inspiration of the Holy Spirit, at once awakens to reflection about its ruin, bestirs itself in the pursuit of heavenly things, takes fire with the fervor of highest love, gives thought to the ills which oppress it on all sides, and weeps while making progress, having earlier rejoiced while losing ground. Therefore it is well said to the Creator: *And returning thou tormentest me wonderfully.*[65] For when almighty God in visiting our soul lifts it to love of him, he makes it more sorrowful in tears. It is as if the soul were to say plainly: In leaving me you do not influence me because you render me insensible, but when you return, you torment me because when you come to me, you show me how pitiable I am. And hence the soul does not say it is tormented judicially, but wonderfully, since while the soul is borne on high by tears, with joy it marvels at the pain of compunction, and it is pleased to be so affected because it sees that by affliction it is raised on high. But because we often tire of holy desire, God in his goodness presents to us examples of the righteous so that when our soul observes the gains of others, it may be ashamed of its sloth.

Hence the text continues: *Thou renewest thy witnesses against me, and multipliest thy wrath upon me.*[66] God's witnesses are they who by holy works bear witness what rewards are in store for the elect. Hence those who have suffered for the sake of truth, we call in Greek martyrs, that is, witnesses. The Lord renews his witnesses against us when he displays the lives of the elect in opposition to our wickedness for the purpose of censuring, so that we who are not moved by precepts may be stirred up, and in longing for what is right, our mind may consider nothing difficult that it sees fully accomplished by others. And it often happens that when we observe the good actions of another's life, we are concerned about the deficiencies of our own life.

Hence it is added: *And thou multipliest thy wrath upon me.*[67] God's wrath is said to be multiplied upon us since by the lives of the righteous we fail to learn what great wrath shall come upon us hereafter if we do not amend our ways. For we see the elect of God both acting dutifully and enduring many hardships. Whence it is inferred to what extent the strict judge will hereafter afflict those whom he condemns if he so torments here those whom he loves, as Peter testifies, who says: *The time is that judgment should begin at the house of God. And if first at us, what shall be the end of them that believe not the gospel of God?*[68] But when we are encouraged by the progress of a brother and then estimate the severity of the judge because of our indolence, we must from now on chasten whatever we blame in ourselves as deserving condemnation. Hence the text continues: *And pains war against me,*[69] because while we behold the admirable deeds of the righteous, we chastise with pain our life, which by comparison with theirs is displeasing, so that whatever defilement our deeds have caused in us, our tears may wash clean, and if the guilt of taking pleasure in them still defiles us somewhat, the pain of sorrow may wipe away the stain.

14

Confession

Wherefore I will not spare my mouth.[70] He spares his mouth who is ashamed to confess the evil he has done. For to put the mouth to work is to employ it in the confession of sin that has been committed. But the just man does not spare his mouth because forestalling the wrath of the strict judge, he vents his rage upon himself in words of self-accusation. Hence the Psalmist says: *Let us come before his presence with confession.*[71] Hence it is said by Solomon: *He that hideth his sins shall not prosper: but he that shall confess and forsake them shall obtain mercy.*[72] Hence it is again written: *The just man is first accuser of himself.*[73] But the mouth is not opened in confession except when—at the thought of the strict judgment—the spirit is straitened by fear. And hence it is then fittingly added: *I will speak in the tribulation of my spirit.*[74] For tribulation of the spirit sets the tongue in motion, so that the voice of confession assails the guilt of evildoing. It is also to be borne in mind that often even the reprobate confess sins but consider telling them with tears to be of little value. But the elect reproach with tears of severe censure their sins that they reveal in words of confession. Hence it was proper that after blessed Job pledged himself not to spare his mouth, he then mentioned tribulation of the spirit. It is as though he made clear acknowledgment, saying: The tongue tells of guilt in such a way that the spirit, free of the sting of sorrow, roves among other things, but in speaking of my sins, I expose my wound; and in thinking about my sins for their amendment, I seek the cure of the wound by the medicine of sorrow. For he who makes known the evil he has done but disdains weeping for what he has disclosed, in effect reveals the wound by pulling back the clothing but applies no remedy to the festering sore. Therefore it is necessary that sorrow alone should extort the voice of confession, lest the wound being exposed but neglected, should—the more freely it is now touched through being known by someone else—be worse infected. On the contrary, the Psalmist had not only disclosed the wound of his heart but was also using on it, thus uncovered, the remedy of sorrow, when he said: *I declare my iniquity: and I will think for my sin.*[75] For by declaring, he revealed the hidden wound, and by his thinking for it, what else did he apply to the wound but a remedy? But to the mind that is distressed and carefully giving thought to its own ills, there arises a strife for and against self. For when it incites itself to the sorrows of penitence, it tears itself apart with secret rebuke.

15

A person ought to recognize his sin and to reveal it by the voice of confession

If as a man I have hid my sin, and have concealed my iniquity in my bosom.[76] For these are the proofs of true humility: both for a man to know his wickedness and when known, to reveal it by the voice of confession. But on the contrary, it is the common failing of the human race both to commit sin by succumbing to temptation and to hide what is committed by denying it and when proven guilty, to go further astray by self–justification. For from that fall of the first man we derive these accretions of wickedness, and from it we also acquire the very root of sin. For thus Adam, when he had touched the forbidden tree, hid himself from the face of the Lord amidst the trees of paradise.[77] In the account of the attempt to hide, which could not of course succeed, it is not the intended result but the intention itself that is pointed out. When he was accused by the Lord of having touched the forbidden tree, he answered: *The woman, whom thou gavest me to be my companion, gave me of the tree, and I did eat.*[78] The woman also when questioned, answered forthwith: *The serpent deceived me, and I did eat.*[79] They were interrogated in order that by confession they might wipe out the sin which by transgressing they had committed. Whence too that tempter, the serpent, who was not to be restored to forgiveness, was not questioned concerning the sin. Thus man was asked where he was so that he might reflect upon the offense and by confessing it be aware how far he had departed from the face of the Creator. But both chose to have recourse to the mitigations of defense rather than of confession. And while the man chose to palliate the sin through the woman, and the woman through the serpent, they added to the fault that they tried to vindicate: Adam indirectly implicating the Lord because he who had made the woman had himself appeared to be be the author of their sin; and Eve referring the sin to the Lord who had placed the serpent in paradise. For they who had heard from the mouth of the deceitful devil: *You shall be as Gods,*[80] because they were not able to be like unto God in divinity, as an addition to their error they tried to make God like unto themselves in transgression. Therefore in this way, while they attempted to defend their guilt, they managed to cause the sin to be made more monstrous when examined than it had been when committed.

Hence now also the branches of the human race still derive bitterness from this root, and when anyone is accused of a moral fault, he takes cover under words of self-defense as under proverbial leaves of trees and flees from the presence of his judge as if to dark refuges of self-justification as long as he does not wish to have his deed known. By this concealment he has not hidden himself from the Lord, but the Lord from himself. For his aim is that he should not see him who sees all things, not that he himself should not be seen; whereas for every sinner the beginning of enlightenment is the humility of confessing, since he now refrains from excusing himself who is not ashamed to admit the evil that he has done, and he who by defending himself might have been accused, by accusing himself defends himself most quickly. And hence to dead Lazarus, who was held down by a great weight, it is not said: Be restored to life, but: *Come forth.*[81] By this rising again that was effected in his body, is signified how we are revived in the heart, when it is said to the dead man: *Come forth*, so that being dead in his sin and buried under the weight of evil habit—because he lies hidden within his conscience through wickedness—he should go forth from himself by confession. For to the dead man it is said: *Come forth*, that from excusing and concealing sin he may be called forth to accusing himself with his own lips. Hence the prophet David, in coming to life from that death marked by so great guilt, as it were went forth at the voice of the Lord when, being rebuked by Nathan, he accused himself of what he had done.[82]

16

The signs of true confession

And I have concealed iniquity in my bosom.[83] It is quite often the custom in sacred Scripture to use the word bosom for the mind, as for example it is said by the Psalmist, speaking for the Church about our persecutors, who are joined to us indeed by nature but disjoined in life: *Render to our neighbors sevenfold in their bosom.*[84] It is as though he said plainly: Let them receive in their minds what in raging against us they do to our bodies, so that just as they punish us externally to some degree, they may themselves be punished internally to a higher degree. Therefore since the bosom is understood as the privacy of the mind, to conceal iniquity in the bosom is to hide it in the recesses of conscience, not revealing it by confession but cloaking it by defense. On the contrary, James says: *Confess therefore your sins one to another; and pray one for another, that you may be saved.*[85] Solomon also says: *He that hideth his sins shall not prosper: but he that shall confess and forsake them shall obtain mercy.*[86]

But herein we should realize that men very often both confess their sins and are not humble. For we know many who, when no one accuses them, confess that they are sinners, but when by chance they are rebuked for their sin, they seek the protection of defense that they may not seem to be sinners. If when these persons assert guilt of their own accord, they knew with true humility that they were sinners, they would not deny what they had confessed when they are accused by others. Here, the marks of true confession require that when anyone calls himself a sinner, he not contradict another who also says that about him. For because it is written: *The just man is first accuser of himself,*[87] he does not so much seek to appear a sinner but rather a just man, who simply acknowledges himself to be a sinner when no one accuses him; but when another reproaches the evil that we have done, he tests the truth of confession. If we proudly defend what we have done, it is clear that for our part we fictitiously called ourselves sinners. Whence it is above all incumbent on us that the evil things we have done, we both confess of our own accord and do not disown them when others accuse us of them. For it is the fault of pride that what anyone on his own deigns to admit about himself he disdains to have said to him by others.

17

Alms and how they should be given

If I have despised anyone passing by because he had no clothing and the poor man that had no covering: if his sides have not blessed me, and if he were not warmed with the fleece of my sheep.[88] Because he does not despise the poor, he displays the virtue of humility; and because he covers him, a sense of duty. These two virtues ought to be so joined as always to be supported by mutual assistance insofar as humility, when it shows respect for a neighbor should not abandon the grace of generosity, and justice, when it is generous, should not partake of pride. Thus toward the need of a neighbor, let justice sustain humility, humility sustain justice, so that when you see a sharer of human nature lacking the necessities of life, you should neither through injustice fail to cover him, nor through pride fail to respect the one you cover. For there are persons who as soon as they are asked for basic wants by their needy brothers, intending afterwards to grant them alms, first direct to them words of disparagement. Although such persons in material things perform charitable service, they forfeit the grace of humility, so that in large part it seems that they are now making up for the slight inflicted when after abusive remarks they give alms. And it is not a work of great merit that they give the things requested because by the actual giving they scarcely make amends for intemperate speech. To these persons it is well said in the book of Ecclesiasticus: *When thou givest any thing, add not grief by an evil word.*[89] And again: *Lo, a word is better than a gift, and both are with a justified man,*[90] that is, alms should be extended through dutifulness, and a kind word through humility. But on the other hand, others able to do so are not eager to support their needy brothers with alms, but only to patronize them with innocuous words. These persons the holy preaching of James strongly rebukes when he says: *And if a brother or sister be naked and want daily food, and one of you say to them: Go in peace, be ye warmed and filled; yet give them not those things that are necessary for the body, what shall it profit?*[91] These persons the apostle John admonishes, saying: *My little children, let us not love in word nor in tongue, but in deed and in truth.*[92] Therefore our love must always be shown both by respectfulness of speech and by the service of generosity.

But it is of great effectiveness in subduing a person's pride in giving if when he gives worldly things, he considers carefully the words of the heavenly Teacher when he says: *Make unto you friends of the mammon of iniquity; that when you shall fail, they may receive you into everlasting dwellings.*[93] For if by friendships we obtain everlasting dwellings, undoubtedly we should consider when we give that we are offering presents to protectors rather than bestowing gifts on the needy. Hence it is said by Paul: *Let your abundance supply their want, that their abundance also may supply your want.*[94] In other words, we must carefully consider that those whom we now see in need, we shall at some time see in abundance, and we who are looked upon as rich shall—if we neglect to give alms—at some time be in need. Therefore he who now gives temporal support to a poor man will hereafter receive from him everlasting supports in the same way, so to speak, that ground is cultivated for its yield and pays back more abundantly than it has received. As a result, pride should never arise from charitable giving because surely the rich person by what he bestows on the poor man is seeing to it that he himself is not poor in eternity. Therefore blessed Job that he might accurately show with what deliberation humility and compassion were united in him, says: *If I have despised anyone passing by because he had no clothing and the poor man that had not covering: if his sides have not blessed me, and if he were not warmed with the fleece of my sheep.* That is to say: In the love of neighbor, repressing by one and the same dictate both the evil of pride and of injustice, humbly seeing anyone passing by, I did not despise him and I mercifully warmed him. For whoever through haughtiness of pride elevates himself above the one to whom he gives anything, by priding himself inwardly is guilty of an offense greater than the reward he merits by giving material goods, and he himself is made bare of interior good when in clothing the naked he despises him, and so brings it about that he is rendered worse than his own self the more he considers himself better than his neighbor in need. For he is less in need who is without a garment than he who is without humility. Hence when we see sharers of our nature without external things, we must reflect how many interior good things we lack, so that our self–esteem does not put us above the needy when it is shrewdly observed that need is more real the more it pertains to the inner self.

And because there are some who cannot extend their feelings of compassion to persons unknown to them but show mercy only to those whom they have come to pity by constant acquaintance and thus let familiarity mean more than nature—giving things necessary to particular persons not because they are men, but because they are acquaintances—it is well said by blessed Job at this point: *If I have despised anyone passing by because he had no clothing.* For to an unknown neighbor he shows himself compassionate since he speaks of anyone passing by, because to the upright mind nature is more meaningful than acquaintance. For that matter, anyone who is in need, by the very fact that he is a man, is no longer unknown to him.

18

[Alms] ought to be given without delay to the poor who ask for them with true humility

If I have denied to the poor what they desired, and have made the eyes of the widow wait.[95] By these words the holy man is shown to have taken care of not only the need of the poor but also what they wished to have. But what if the poor wished those things which perhaps it was not advantageous to receive? Or, because in sacred Scripture the humble are usually called poor, are only those things which the poor wish to receive to be judged those which the humble seek? And surely it is required that whatever is asked for with true humility should be given without hesitation, that is, whatever is sought not from desire but from necessity. For it is indeed very prideful to desire anything beyond the limits of need. And hence it is said to persons seeking with pride: *You ask and receive not, because you ask amiss.*[96] Therefore because they are truly poor who are not urged on by the spirit of pride—as Truth makes clear when he says: *Blessed are the poor in spirit* [97]—it is well said here by holy Job: *If I have denied to the poor what they desired*, since they who desire those things which it is clear are not advantageous for them because they are filled with a spirit of pride, are indeed not poor. But blessed Job, insofar as he called the poor humble, did not withhold whatever the poor man desired to receive from him, because in truth every humble person did not even desire to receive what he should not have. But when Job points out his spirit of generosity by showing that he had concurred in the desire of the poor, it is necessary that we inquire whether he had dimmed the light of mercy by tardiness in giving. Hence he adds: *Or made the eyes of the widow wait*. He did not want the petitioning widow to wait in order that not only by the gift but also by the readiness of the gift he might increase the merits of good deeds. Hence it is written elsewhere: *Say not to thy friend: Go, and come again, and tomorrow I will give to thee, when thou canst give at present*.[98] Now there are some who are accustomed to bestow much outwardly, but rejecting the amenity of a shared social life, they refrain from having the poor as their companions in a social relationship.

Hence blessed Job, that he might make known not only that he had given much outwardly but also had received sociably in his own presence all the needy, adds directly: *If I have eaten my morsel alone, and the fatherless hath not eaten thereof*.[99] In other words, judging that anyone detracted from considerateness if he ate alone what the Lord of all created in common, he was minded to carry on this common fellowship within his domestic walls with those persons by whom the rewards of eternal retribution may be advanced. Whence the holy man describes himself as having had as his companions at table not some neutral person but the fatherless. But whether he himself developed these unusual feelings of compassion or obtained them from the grace of his Creator, let him make known.[100]

19

Alms have worth when sin is lamented and renounced

As often as we give alms after sin, in a way we pay a price for evil deeds. And hence it is said by the prophet concerning him who does not give alms: *He will not give to God his ransom, nor the price of the redemption of his soul*.[101] But sometimes the haughty rich oppress those below them, seize the things of others, and yet to some extent give to others, and while they belittle many, they sometimes give protective assistance to some persons, and for the iniquities that they never abandon they seem to offer a price. But the price of alms frees us from sins only when we lament and renounce the sins we have committed. For he who wishes both always to sin, and as it were always to give alms, gives a price in vain, since he does not redeem his soul, which he does not restrain from vices. Hence it is written: *Let him not believe, being vainly deceived by error, that he is to be redeemed with any price*.[102] For the alms of the proud rich man have no power to redeem him: his plundering of the poor man, carried out at the same time, will not allow his alms to rise up before the eyes of God. This text may probably be understood in another sense, since often proud rich men, when they give alms, do so not for the desire of eternal life, but for the extending of temporal life; they believe that they can delay death by donations, but *let him not believe, being vainly deceived by error, that he is to be redeemed with any price*, because by the gift he granted he cannot manage to evade the destiny that is due to him whose wickedness brings his life to an end.

But he righteously does what is kindly who first learns to do what is just, so that the stream of mercy conferred on our neighbors has its source in the spring of justice. For there are many who perform apparent works of mercy in behalf of their neighbors, but do not abandon deeds of injustice. If they truly strive to show mercy to their neighbors, they should first have been merciful to themselves by living justly. Hence it is written: *Have mercy on thy own soul, pleasing God*.[103] Therefore he who wishes to show rightful mercy to his neighbor must find the model of discernment in himself. For it is written: *Thou shalt love thy neighbor as thyself*.[104] How, then, is he dutiful toward another by showing mercy, who by still living unjustly becomes merciless to himself? Whence it is said by a certain wise man: *He that is evil to himself, to whom will he be good?*[105] Obviously, in order that the mercy to be shown toward the needy may be in fact appropriately extended, there are two essentials to be coordinated, that is, the man that is to give and the thing that is to be given. But the man is by far and beyond comparison better than the thing. Therefore he who gives a material possession to a needy neighbor, but does not keep his own life free from evil, gives his property to God, but gives himself to sin. That which is of less significance he offered to the Creator, and that which is of greater importance he reserved for wickedness.

20

It does no good to give alms with the hand unless ill will is dismissed from the mind

The stranger did not stay without, my door was open to the traveler.[106] Paul is the authority for the description of charity as patient and kind.[107] By patience it endures calmly the wrongs of others; by kindness it employs mercifully its own worldly goods. Whence blessed Job patiently put up with friends who spoke ill of him and kindly welcomed to his home travelers and strangers. To his friends he gave good example, to the others he gave help in their need: in his meekness he was not stirred to anger against the former; in his mercy he was ready to be of assistance to the latter. For the holy man, contemplating by the spirit of prophecy the Redeemer of mankind, also put his instructions into practice, notably these counsels: *Forgive; and you shall be forgiven. Give; and it shall be given to you.*[108] For our giving pertains to the things that we have outwardly, but our forgiving to the abatement of the pain inwardly contracted by the offense of another. But it should be known that he who forgives but does not give, although he has not done his utmost, yet has fulfilled the better part of mercifulness. But he who gives but never forgives does not practice mercy at all, because a gift is not accepted by almighty God from a hand that is extended by a heart bound in wickedness.

For the soul that offers alms must first be made clean because everything that is given to God is requited according to the disposition of the giver. Therefore every stain of evil must we wiped clean from our inner self by a change of heart because an offering cannot appease the judge unless it is acceptable through the purity of the one who offers it. Whence it is written: *The Lord had respect to Abel, and to his offerings. But to Cain and his offerings he had no respect.*[109] For sacred Scripture does not say: The Lord had respect to the offerings of Abel, but to the offerings of Cain he had no respect, but it first says that *he had respect to Abel* and then added: *And to his offerings.* And again it says that *to Cain he had no respect*, and then: *Nor to his offerings.* For according to the heart of the giver is the thing that is given received. Therefore the Lord found pleasing not Abel because of his offerings, but because of Abel the gifts offered. For we read that the Lord regarded the person who gave before the things he gave.

21

He who has sinned against us is to be forgiven immediately when he begs for pardon

For thou hast taken away the pledge of thy brethren without cause.[110] In holy Scripture by the term pledge is signified sometimes the gifts of the Holy Spirit, but sometimes the confession of sin. Thus pledge is understood as the gift of the Holy Spirit, as is said by Paul: *God hath given the pledge of the Spirit in our hearts.*[111] For we receive a pledge so that we may hold a guaranty concerning a promise that is made to us. Therefore the gift of the Holy Spirit is called a pledge because by it our soul is strengthened to assurance of inward hope. Again by the name pledge confession of sin is customarily understood, as it is written in the Law: *If thy brother should owe thee anything and thou should take a pledge from him, restore the pledge before sunset.*[112] For our brother becomes our debtor when any neighbor is shown to have trespassed against us. For sins we call debts. Whence it is said to the servant when he sinned: *I forgave thee all the debt.*[113] And in the Lord's Prayer we say daily: *Forgive us our debts, as we also forgive our debtors.*[114] Moreover, we take a pledge from our debtor when from him who is known to have sinned against us, we now have a confession of his sin by which we are asked to forgive the sin that was committed against us. For he who confesses the sin he has committed and begs pardon has already, as it were, given a pledge for his debt. This pledge we must restore before sunset because, before the Sun of justice shall set in us, we must pay back the acknowledgment of pardon to the one from whom we received the acknowledgment of transgression, so that he who is mindful that he has transgressed against us, may be made aware that his transgression we have now forgiven.

BOOK 3

VIRTUES

Prologue

As Saint Gregory says: Hearts that are full of evil things do not easily accept the good seed. Hence it is said to Jeremias: *Lo, I have set thee this day over the nations and over kingdoms, to root up and to pull down, and to waste and to destroy, and to build and to plant.*[1] He is indeed commanded first to pull down and then to build, first to root up and then to plant, because the foundation of truth is not properly laid unless the structure of error is torn down.[2] Therefore the discussion of penitence, by which the vices are rooted up, is not inconsistently followed by the book in which the virtues to be planted are discussed. This third book of Part 2 explains the remedies for the vices dealt with in the third book of Part 1.

1

Virtues that are incomplete without some other accompanying virtue

There are some of God's gifts without which life is not acquired, and there are others by which holiness of life is proclaimed for the advantage of others. For humility, patience, faith, hope, charity are divine gifts without which men cannot attain life. But the grace of prophecy, healing, diverse kinds of tongues, the interpretation of speeches are divine gifts, yet are such as show forth the presence of his power for the amendment of all observers.[3]

Therefore some goods are of the highest, others of an intermediary nature. For the highest goods are faith, hope, charity. When these are truly possessed they cannot be directed to evil. But goods of an intermediary nature are prophecy, doctrine, the power of healing, and the rest, which are so placed between one and the other, that sometimes the heavenly fatherland only, but sometimes earthly glory is sought by their help. Therefore we call these virtues intermediary which we direct to whatever our mind seeks for its use when possessed just as it uses worldly riches. For through earthly riches, some pride themselves in boastful display, others perform works of mercy for their needy neighbors. Therefore when external praise is sought through doctrine and prophecy, the height of earthly glory is striven for as if through material riches. But when doctrine and prophecy are employed in striving for souls, the riches we have received are dispensed as it were to our needy brethren. Therefore

because the unwary mind absconds from the hand of the giver by means of
those gifts which it boasts of possessing, we must with vigilant foresight see to it
that our vices are first overcome and our gifts are afterwards circumspectly
held in our possession. For if the mind heedlessly gives itself over to them, it is
not uplifted by their help but is rejected as if already rewarded for its former
labors. Whence also it happens that insofar as the virtue we possess is appropriated for the sake of transitory praise, it is no longer virtue because it is an
instrument of vice.

He who is supposed to be strong in any particular virtue is truly strong
only when he is not subject to vices in another respect. For if he is subjugated
by vices of another kind, not even that is solid in which he was believed to stand
firm. For each individual virtue is so much the less, the more the others are
lacking. For it has often happened that we see some who are modest but not
humble, some apparently humble but not merciful, some seemingly merciful
but not at all just, some in appearance just, but trusting in themselves rather
than in the Lord. And it is certain that there is not even true chastity in the
heart of one who lacks humility, since with pride corrupting him inwardly, he
commits fornication: loving himself, he is untrue to the love of God. And humility is not true if mercy is not joined to it, because humility is not worthy of
the name when it is incapable of being prone to compassion at the affliction of
a brother. Nor is it true mercy which is not in keeping with the virtuousness of
justice, for what can be defiled by injustice is beyond doubt unable to feel pity
for itself. Neither is it true justice which puts its trust not in the Creator of all
things, but perhaps in itself or in created things, since as long as it withdraws
hope from the Creator, it destroys in itself the priority of original justice.
Therefore one virtue without others is either nonexistent or imperfect. To
speak—as it has seemed proper to others—of the first four virtues, namely,
prudence, temperance, fortitude and justice, they are all the more nearly perfect, the more they are mutually joined to one another. But separated, they
cannot be complete: prudence is not real which is not just, temperate and
strong; temperance is not complete which is not strong, just and prudent; fortitude is not entire which is not prudent, temperate and just; justice is not true
which is not prudent, strong and temperate.

2

Humility, which is the remedy against pride

Since humility is the source of virtue, that virtue truly flourishes in us
which abides in its own root, that is, in humility. For if it is uprooted, without

doubt it withers away because it loses the moisture of charity that deep within gives it life.

Therefore let us see what great gifts of virtue David received and how he persevered in all of them with unshakable humility. For in whom would it not stir up pride to break the mouths of lions, to tear apart the arms of bears, to be chosen when his elder brethren had been set aside, to be anointed for ruling when the king had been rejected, to topple with a single stone Goliath who was dreaded by all, to bring back after the destruction of the Philistines the many foreskins stipulated by the king,[4] to receive at last the promised kingdom and to have power over the whole people of Israel without opposition?[5] And yet when he had the Ark of God brought back to Jerusalem, mingled with the people he dances before the Ark as though forgetful that he had been chosen before all.[6] And because, as is believed, it had been the custom of the people to dance before the Ark, the king whirls around in the dance as an obeisance to God. Behold, the one whom the Lord chose particularly shows slight self-esteem before the Lord both by making himself equal with the least and by displaying unassuming behavior. The power of his reign is forgotten, he has no fear of demeaning himself in the eyes of his people by dancing, he does not bear in mind before the Ark of the one who had given him honor that he had been placed in honor above the others. Before God he performed even the most commonplace actions in order to enhance by his humility the brave deeds he had accomplished before men. I do not know what others think of his deeds; I am more astonished when David dances than when he engages in battle. For by fighting he subdued his enemies, but by dancing before the Lord he conquered himself. When Michol, the daughter of Saul, still inspired with pride at her royal descent, despised David in his humbled condition, saying: *How glorious was the king of Israel today, uncovering himself before the handmaids of his servants, and was naked, as if one of the buffoons should be naked*, she immediately heard: *As the Lord lives, I will play before the Lord, who chose me rather than thy father*. And a little later he says: *I will both play and make myself meaner than I have done, and I will be little in my own eyes*.[7] It is as though he said plainly: I desire to become ignoble before men because I seek through humility to keep myself noble before the Lord.

3

Simplicity is the antithesis of vainglory and its remedy

For the simplicity of the just man is laughed to scorn.[8] It is the wisdom of this world to keep the heart secret by stratagems, to conceal thought with words, to portray things that are false as true, to falsify those that are true. This indeed is the practical wisdom that is acquired by the young through practice, that is learned at a price by children; those who are knowledgeable in it, filled with pride, look down on other men; those who are uninformed about it, being subdued and fainthearted, admire it in others, by whom this wicked duplicity under a disguised name is held in esteem as long as wrongheadedness is called urbanity. Its devotees are taught to seek high places of honor, to rejoice in attaining vain temporal glory; to repay time and again the troubles brought on by others; when resources are at hand, to yield to no opponents; when the advantage of power is lacking and a malicious action cannot be accomplished, to effect in an unobjectionable way a resemblance of it. But on the other hand, it is the wisdom of the upright to feign nothing through false show, to convey meaning by words; to love true values as they are, to keep clear of the false; to perform good deeds without reward, to bear ills more gladly than to cause them; to seek no revenge for wrong, to consider suffering insult for the sake of truth to be a gain; to judge themselves less worthy than all men even when they live more worthily than all. For they are aware that the good qualities which are commonly known can hardly be present in them without great risk. And although they believe themselves to be wise, yet they would wish to be wise without being so reputed and are in every case very much afraid of publicity about what they have to say. And they seek, if possible, to be silent as long as they perceive that silence is safer for many, and consider those to be more fortunate whom a lower position in holy Church conceals in silence; and yet in order that holy Church be defended, they feel forced to take on themselves the task of speaking because they are impelled by the force of charity, but with great desire seek the relief of silence. This latter state they preferably maintain; its opposite they enter into from a sense of duty.

But this simplicity of the righteous is mocked because by the worldly-wise the goodness of simplicity is thought to be foolishness. For undoubtedly everything that is done disinterestedly is considered folly by them, and whatever activity truth favors sounds silly to worldly wisdom. For what is more nonsensical to the world than to reveal by words what one is thinking, to feign nothing by cunning deceit, to take no revenge for affronts, to pray for calumniators, to seek poverty, to give up one's possessions, not to resist a robber, to offer the other cheek to an assailant? Whence that illustrious and wise man of God speaks pointedly to the lovers of this world: *We shall sacrifice the abominations of the Egyptians to the Lord our God*.[9] For the Egyptians abhor eating the flesh of sheep, but what the Egyptians loathe, the Israelites offer up to God, since that simplicity of conscience which those fond of vainglory scorn as most mean and common, the righteous turn into a sacrifice of virtue. And the upright, when they worship, offer in sacrifice purity and meekness to God: this the reprobate abhor and consider to be folly.

But there are some who in the good actions that they perform are not single–minded insofar as they seek by means of them not an inner reward but external signs of approbation. Hence it is well said by a certain wise man: *Woe to the sinner that goeth on the earth two ways.*[10] For the sinner goes two ways when at the same time what he does is godly, and the purpose he has in mind is worldly. For there are in addition some who are simple in such a way as not to know what is right, who while they do not know how to be on guard through uprightness, cannot be innocent through simplicity. Hence Paul says: *But I would have you to be wise in good and simple in evil.*[11] And again: *Brethren, do not become children in sense, but in malice be children.*[12] And the Lord in the Gospel: *Be ye wise as serpents and simple as doves,*[13] so that the astuteness of the serpent may instruct the simplicity of the dove, and the simplicity of the dove may temper the cunning of the serpent. Hence the Holy Spirit appeared not only in the form of a dove, but also in the form of fire.[14] For by the dove simplicity is indicated, and by fire, zeal. Therefore all who are filled with the Holy Spirit are devoted to the meekness of simplicity in such a way that they are inflamed with zeal of righteousness against the offenses of sinners.

There are also other simple persons who penetrate the depths of understanding because they do not think it beneath them to put into practice even the least things they have learned, and while they aid understanding with action, they lift themselves above the level of the naturally gifted. Hence it is well said by Solomon: *The stellio (lizard) supporteth itself on hands and dwelleth in kings' houses.*[15] For commonly birds, which wings lift up in flight, dwell in bushes, and the lizard, which has no wings for flying, supporting itself on what the text calls hands, has access to the dwelling of royalty, for often some who are talented, while they grow sluggish from inattention, persist in evildoing, and the simple persons, with no wing of talent to aid them, are supported by the constancy of their effort in scaling the ramparts of the eternal kingdom. Therefore while the lizard supports itself with hands, it dwells in kings' houses, since the simple man, by earnestness of endeavor, reaches a height that the clever man does not attain.

4

Charity is the fulfillment of the law and the remedy against envy

That he might show thee that his law is manifold.[16] The law of God must be interpreted as charity, through which the mind discerns how the precepts of life are to be observed in practice. Concerning this virtue Truth says: *This is my commandment, that you love one another.*[17] And Paul says: *Love is the fulfilling of the law.*[18] And again: *Bear ye one another's burdens; and so you shall fulfill the law of Christ.*[19] For the beginning of the law is the love of God and the love of neighbor. But the love of God is distinguished by three traits. For we are commanded to love God with our whole heart, and with our whole soul, and with our whole strength,[20] so that he who desires to please God must leave for himself nothing of his self. But the love of neighbor is expressed in two precepts since it is said by a certain just man: *Do that to no man which thou hatest.*[21] And Truth says: *All things therefore whatsoever you would that men should do to you, do you also to them.*[22] By the one an evil disposition is restrained, by the other a kind disposition is enjoined.

For when anyone guards against doing to another what he does not want done to himself, he attentively takes heed lest pride lift up his soul even to contempt of neighbor, lest ambition distort his thinking, lest lust defile his heart, lest anger cause irritation and lead to insults, lest envy hurt another, lest talkativeness lure the tongue and draw it on to invectives, lest ill will stir up hatred and provoke imprecations. Again when he thinks how he may do for another what he expects to be done by the other for him, he considers how he may return good things for evil and better things for good; how he may accomplish the following: to extend the favor of goodwill to those dulled by the curse of ill will, to bring the quarrelsome peacefully together, to bind the acquiescent together in the desire of true peace, to present necessary things to those in need, to show to those who are going astray the path of righteousness, to comfort the afflicted by encouragement and sympathy, to restrain by remonstrance those inflamed with worldly desires, to soften the threats of the powerful by reasoning, to lighten the difficulties of the oppressed by all the means at his disposal, to exercise patience with those who offer patent opposition, to demonstrate to those who are inwardly prideful discipline together with patience, to have mildness so temper vigilance in relation to misdeeds of those under our charge that it never weakens the pursuit of justice, to have zeal bent on punishment in such a way that it does not go beyond the bounds of propriety, by benefits to stimulate the ungrateful to love, by services to preserve in love all who are grateful, to be silent about misdeeds of neighbors when they cannot be corrected, to be very much afraid that silence is consent when faults may be amended by speaking up, to tolerate what he overlooks by silence in such a way that none of the poison of indignation is hidden in his mind, to exhibit the service of goodwill to the ill–disposed in such a way as not to depart through kindness from the exigency of righteousness, to employ for the benefit of his neighbors all that he can but by doing so not to be swelled with pride, to draw back from the precipice of pride in the good deeds he performs and yet not become slack in doing good, to so dispose of things which he possesses as to be conscious of how great is the generosity of his heavenly rewarder lest in giving earthly things he devote more thought to his poverty than is necessary and in the offering of the gift sadness obscure the light of cheerfulness.

Therefore the law of God is properly called manifold for, although charity is one and the same, it stirs the mind that is imbued with it to innumerable works in manifold ways. Furthermore, the diversity of the law Paul rightly intimates, saying: *Charity is patient, is kind; envieth not, is not puffed up; dealeth not perversely, is not ambitious, seeketh not her own; is not provoked to anger, thinketh no evil; rejoiceth not in iniquity, but rejoiceth with the truth.*[23]

5

Through charity friends are to be loved in God and enemies for the sake of God

It is usually shown in two ways if charity really fills our heart, namely, if we love our friends in God and our enemies for the sake of God. But it should be recognized that the love of our enemy is really preserved when we are neither distressed by his advancement nor made happy by his downfall. For often in a semblance of love for an enemy the mind is deceived and judges that it loves him if it is not hostile to his life. But either the advancement or the fall of an enemy quietly and accurately determines the strength of love. For in this matter the mind of man does not know itself to the full unless he finds that the one whom he supposes to be an adversary has by regression or advancement changed the quality of his condition in life. For if he is distressed by the prosperity and happy at the calamity of the one who hates him, it is clear that he does not love the one whom he does not wish to be better and by desire he pursues hostilely—even when his position in life is stable—the one by whose fall he is gratified.

But meanwhile it should be observed that usually without loss of charity we experience both gladness at the misfortune of an enemy, and again without the guilt of envy, sadness at his good fortune, when we believe that some are rightly raised up as he falls and we fear that many are unjustly repressed as he advances. In this case neither does his adversity nor his advancement any longer govern our mind if right thinking concerns itself not with what happens to the individual but with the effect this has on others. But for maintaining this perspective, the control of precise discernment is most necessary, lest in carrying out our own distastes we be deceived by the apparent advantage to others.

For if there should not be any rejoicing at the death of an enemy, the Psalmist would not say: *The just shall rejoice when he shall see the vengeance on the ungodly*.[24] For it is one thing to tolerate an ungodly man, and another to tolerate an enemy. For there are many enemies who are not ungodly, and there are some ungodly persons who do not seem to be inimical to us in a special way. But the mind of man judges everyone whom it tolerates as an enemy to be also ungodly and wicked because in its appraisal malice, as accuser, magnifies the faults of the enemy. But with whatever shameful deeds he may be burdened, he is believed to be less wicked if he is not judged to be an adversary. On this point a distinction is to be made: it is one thing for our enemy to harm us, and another to harm himself and others. For if he is good to others, perhaps he cannot without our fault be injurious to us; nor should there now be total rejoicing in the downfall of the one whose hostile actions it is certain we alone have endured. But when the enemy of ourselves and of many persons is frustrated, our heart must be glad for the relief of our neighbors rather than for the fall of our enemy.

For it is necessary when an adversary perishes that we should closely consider both what we owe to the downfall of the sinner, and what we owe to the justice of the vindicator. For when almighty God strikes any evil man, there must be sorrowing over the wretchedness of the fallen one and rejoicing at the justice of the judge, so that both the punishment of the perishing should be cause for grief, and again the equity exhibited by God in judging should be an occasion for joy; thus we may neither remain enemies to a man in his perishing nor be found ungrateful to God in his judging.

6

Patience is the antithesis of anger and the remedy against it

He who is unwilling to practice patience, more swiftly through impatience renounces social life. For only through patience can concord ever be preserved. For frequently in human relations there arises a situation that may lead to the minds of men being mutually severed from their unity and affection; and unless the mind prepares itself to endure unpleasantness, undoubtedly a given limb does not remain part of a corporate whole. Hence it is that Paul says: *Bear ye one another's burdens, and so you shall fulfill the law of Christ*.[25] Hence also Truth says: *In your patience you shall possess your souls*,[26] because without doubt all our conduct, whatever its apparent virtues may be, goes awry unless through the bonds of charity patience is preserved. For he forfeits his own good deeds who refuses to put up with the evil deeds of others. Being wounded by the heatedness of an angry spirit, a person draws back from love, and when he does not endure external oppression, he darkens himself inwardly by loss of the light of charity; nor does he now see where to place the foot of good conduct who has lost the eye of love. For no one is perfect who in the face of slights from his neighbors is not patient. For he who does not bear with composure the wrongs of others, by his impatience indicates that he is far removed from complete goodness. For he refuses to be like Abel, who was not disturbed by the malice of Cain.[27]

Thus on the threshing floor the grains are pressed under the chaff, thus the flowers make their appearance between thorns, and with the rose that is fragrant grows the thorn that is piercing. For the first man had two sons, but one was reprobate, the other elect.[28] Likewise of the three sons of Noe, and the two sons of Abraham and of Isaac as well, one was reprobate.[29] Similarly, of the twelve sons of Jacob, one—although inoffensive—was sold and eleven through wickedness were the sellers.[30] Among the twelve apostles also one was found to be reprobate.[31] For thus to a just man there is joined a malicious sinner, just as in the furnace to the gold there is added chaff along with fire so that as the chaff burns, the gold may be purified. Therefore they are truly good men who can stand fast in goodness even among evildoers. Hence too it is said to holy Church by the voice of the spouse: *As the lily among thorns, so is my love among the daughters.*[32] Hence the Lord says to Ezechiel: *And thou, O son of man, art among unbelievers and destroyers, and thou dwelleth with scorpions.*[33] Hence Peter pays tribute to the life of blessed Lot, saying: *And he delivered just Lot, oppressed by the injustice and lewd conversation of the wicked. For in sight and hearing he was just, dwelling among them who from day to day vexed the just soul with unjust works.*[34] Hence Paul praises the life of his disciples, and in praising strengthens it, saying: *In the midst of a crooked and perverse nation, among whom you shine as lights in the world, holding forth the word of life.*[35] Hence through John the angel of the church of Pergamus bears witness in the words: *I know where thou dwellest, where the seat of Satan is. And thou holdest fast my name, and hast not denied my faith.*[36]

7

Hope is the antithesis of melancholy and the remedy against it

Hope lifts the mind to eternity, and therefore it is not preoccupied with any of the external ills that are endured. Hence it is written: *And to the needy there shall be hope.*[37] No one hopes for what he sees.[38] He then is properly said to hope who closes his eyes to the glory of this world and opens them to the love of the heavenly homeland. Therefore holy Church mingles for the faithful hope and fear regarding the goodness and justice of the Redeemer, so that they may not either rashly rely on mercy or desperately dread justice. For with the words of her founder she comforts and summons to hope those who are fearful, saying: *Fear not, little flock, for it hath pleased your Father to give you a kingdom.*[39] And again: *Rejoice in this, that your names are written in heaven.*[40] Similarly, when he says: *My sheep hear my voice; and I know them; and they follow me. And I give them life everlasting; and they shall not perish for ever. And no man shall pluck them out of my hand.*[41] And again: *He that shall persevere unto the end, he shall be saved.*[42] He who fears is also reassured when it is said to the good thief: *This day thou shalt be with me in paradise.*[43] And again when it is said: *If a man put away his wife, and she go from him and marry another man, shall he return to her any more? Shall not that woman be polluted and defiled? But thou hast prostituted thyself to many lovers. Nevertheless return to me, saith the Lord.*[44] In like manner when it is said: *Therefore, at the least from this time call to me: Thou art my father, the guide of my virginity.*[45] And again: *Return, O rebellious Israel, and I will not turn away my face from you: for I am holy, saith the Lord, and I will not be angry for ever.*[46] On the other hand those presuming on the mercy of God he terrifies, when he says: *Watch ye; and pray that you enter not into temptation.*[47] And again to the presumptuous he brings fear when he says: *I saw Satan like lightning falling from heaven.*[48] And again: *They shall show great signs and wonders, insomuch as to deceive (if possible) even the elect.*[49] Likewise when he says: *The Son of man, when he cometh, shall he find, think you, faith on the earth?*[50] The presumptuous person is frightened as well when Judas falls from the glory of apostleship into the pit of hell. Of him it is said in the setting forth of a declaration: *I have chosen you twelve, and one of you is a devil.*[51] Similarly when it is said: *Why criest thou for thy affliction? Thy sorrow is incurable.*[52] Likewise when it is said: *Thy father was an Amorrhite and thy mother a Cethite.*[53] And again when he prevents the prophet from interceding, saying: *Do not take up praise and prayer for them: for I will not hear them in the time of their cry to me, in the time of their affliction; because if Moses and Samuel shall stand before me, my soul is not towards this people.*[54] Therefore the fearful are summoned to hope and the presumptuous are instilled with fear in such a way that the elect may not act on a presumption of his justice and not despair on account of their past iniquity.

8

True compassion for the neighbor is the remedy for avarice and is its antithesis

Very often men give many things to the poor not because they love those who are poor, but because if they do not give, they fear the wrath of the heavenly judge: if these persons were not afraid of God, they would have been unwilling to give their possessions. And indeed in good works the first step for beginners is for the one who does not yet know how to love his neighbor as himself, to now begin nevertheless to fear heavenly judgments. Therefore, because it is one thing to do a good deed as something ordained but another to do it also as a matter of predilection, in order to make known the intent of his assistance holy Job says: *I was the father of the poor*.[55] He affirms thereby that he was not a protector or a neighbor or helper of the poor, but the father; for indeed by the great kindness of charity, he turns the devotedness of mercy into natural affection, so that through love he saw as sons those over whom through tutelage he was set as father.

For although it is true compassion to come to the aid of a neighbor's suffering by generosity, yet sometimes when externals are abundantly at hand to bestow, the hand of the giver comes upon the gift more readily than his mind encounters sympathy. Hence it is necessary for us to recognize that he gives in an ideal way who together with what he proffers to the afflicted, also makes his own the state of mind of the afflicted in order that he may first transfer the suffering of the sorrowing person to himself and then assuage his sorrow by an act of service. For often, as we have already said, the abundance of material things is what identifies the giver of a benefit rather than the virtue of compassion. For he who is fully compassionate toward the afflicted commonly even gives to the persons in need what puts himself, if he gives it, in straitened circumstances. And the compassion of the heart is at its full when we are not afraid to take upon ourselves the distress of want on behalf of a neighbor in order that we may free him from suffering.

In truth, this model of goodness the mediator between God and man gave to us. When he could have helped us even without dying, yet he willed to come to the aid of mankind by dying because he naturally would have loved us less if he did not take upon himself even our wounds; and he would not have shown the force of his love for us unless what he was to free us from, he did not himself suffer for a time. For he found us subject to suffering and death, and he who brought us into existence out of nothing, clearly had the power to rescue us from suffering even without his death. But in order that he might show how great is the virtue of compassion, he saw fit to become for our sake what he did not want us to be, so that in his own person he should temporarily undergo death that he would dispel from us forever. Could he not, while remaining invisible to us in the riches of his divinity, have enriched us with wonderful virtues? Assuredly, but in order that man might regain interior riches, God thought it fit to appear poor externally. Hence also the admirable preacher, in

order that he might stir the depths of our compassion to the grace of unselfish-
ness, said: *Being rich, he became poor for your sakes.*[56] Paul also says: *Not that
others should be eased, but you burdened,*[57] undoubtedly introducing these
words in deference to the weak because some not being able to suffer need, it
is somewhat permissible to give less, rather than after being generous, to murmur on account of the harshness of need. For that he might stir the minds of
his listeners to great endeavor of liberality, a little later he introduced these
words: *Now this I say: He who soweth sparingly shall reap also sparingly.*[58] We say
too that sometimes it means more to sympathize from the heart than to give,
because everyone who completely sympathizes with one in need considers all
that he gives to be of less value. For unless goodwill surpassed the hand of the
person giving, the same great preacher would not have said to the disciples:
Who have begun not only to do, but also to be willing, a year ago,[59] for it is easy in
good deeds to obey even grudgingly. But this great virtue had been manifest in
the disciples: the good that was commanded them, they had been willing to do
even before the command.

Therefore, since the holy man knew that in the sight of almighty God the
dedication of the mind is sometimes greater than the giving of a gift, he says: *I
wept heretofore for him that was afflicted: and my soul had compassion for the poor
man.*[60] For in bestowing external things, he gave an object outside himself.
But he who imparted to his neighbor tears and compassion, gave him something of his self. But on this account we say that compassion is more than the
gift, because for the most part even he who has no compassion gives something
or other, but he who truly has compassion never withholds what he sees that
his neighbor needs.

9

Fasting is the remedy for gluttony and is its antithesis

*My harp is turned to mourning: and my organ into the voice of those that
weep.*[61] Since the organ gives its sounds by means of pipes and the harp by
strings, the harp can represent right conduct and the organ holy preaching. For
by the pipes of the organ we appropriately understand the mouths of those
who preach, and by the strings of the harp the design of those living aright.
While the intent of the latter is projected to the next life by mortifying the
flesh, it is as if the tightened string in the harp resounded in the admiration of
observers. For the string is dried so that it may sound a suitable note on the
harp, because holy men also chastise their body and bring it into subjection, [62]
and are drawn from things below to those above. It is also to be kept in mind
that if the string in the harp is less taut, it does not sound; if too taut, it sounds

shrill, because surely the virtue of fasting is altogether lacking if a man does not restrain his body as much as he can, or is excessive if mortification is immoderate. For by fasting the vices of the flesh are to be eliminated, not the flesh; and everyone ought to govern himself with such control that at the same time the flesh may not be unrestrained so as to sin, and yet may be able to function in the service of righteousness. It is helpful in this matter to observe with what great skill in instruction the great preacher tends the souls of the faithful like strings outstretched on the harp, some drawn more by tightening, others relieved of tension by loosening. For to some he says: *Not in rioting and drunkenness, not in chambering and impurities.*[63] And again he says: *Mortify your members, which are upon the earth.*[64] Yet to the most beloved fellow preacher he writes, saying: *Do not still drink water, but use a little wine for thy stomach's sake, and thy frequent infirmities.*[65] Thus the former strings by drawing he stretches, lest by not being stretched they fail to sound, but the latter string he frees from tautness, lest the more it is stretched, the less sound it gives.

10

Chastity is the antithesis of lust and is its remedy

Gird up thy loins like a man.[66] Holy Scripture is accustomed to calling those persons men who indeed follow the ways of the Lord with firm and steady steps. Hence it is said by the Psalmist: *Do ye manfully, and let your heart be strengthened.*[67] Hence Paul says: *Lift up the hands which hang down and the feeble knees.*[68] Hence Wisdom in the book of Proverbs says: *O ye men, to you I call.*[69] In other words: I do not speak to women, but to men, because they who are of frail mind cannot understand my words. But to gird up the loins is to restrain lust either in deed or in thought. For the pleasure of the flesh is in the loins. Hence it is said to holy preachers: *Let your loins be girt, and lamps burning.*[70] For by the loins is designated lust, but by lamps the brightness of good works. They are commanded therefore to gird their loins and to hold lamps. It is as if they heard openly: First, restrain lust in yourselves, and then set forth examples of your good works for others. But since we have known that blessed Job was endowed with such great chastity, why is it said to him after so many scourges: *Gird up thy loins like a man,* that is, as a strong man restrain your lust, unless there is one lust of the flesh, by which we corrupt our chastity, but another lust of the heart, by which we boast of our chastity? Let it therefore be said to him: *Gird up thy loins like a man,* in order that he who had first overcome the lust of corruption, might now restrain the lust of pride, lest being proud of his patience or his chastity, he become inwardly more harmfully lustful before the eyes of God, the more patient and chaste he appeared before the eyes of men. Hence it is well said by Moses: *Circumcise the foreskin of your heart,*[71] that is, after you have restrained lust in the flesh, remove excess in thought.

Even other good qualities are of no avail if in the sight of the secret judge they are not made acceptable by the evidence of chastity. For all the virtues are raised to a great height in the view of the Creator by mutual aid, so that because one virtue without another is either nonexistent or minimal, they should be reciprocally supported by being joined together. For whether humility neglects chastity or chastity gives up humility, before the author of humility and chastity, either a proud chastity or an unchaste humility is unable to benefit us.

11
Faith

In the hearts of the elect wisdom is begotten as first of all the endowments that follow: it is brought forth as firstborn offspring by the gift of the Holy Spirit. This wisdom is surely our faith, as the prophet testifies, saying: *Unless you shall believe, you shall not understand.*[72] For we are then truly wise so as to understand when we give the assent of our belief to all that the Creator says. But if wisdom is not first begotten in our hearts, all other gifts cannot be good although they may seem to be such. For it is written: *Without faith it is impossible to please God.*[73]

Therefore he is properly said to be wicked who is devoid of religious devotion. For of such persons the prophet says: *The wicked shall not rise again in judgment.*[74] There are many, however, who have their eyes opened in faith, yet they have kept them closed in their works. Hence it is well said of Judaea: *Her watchmen are all blind,*[75] because in truth they did not see in practice what they perceived in principle. Hence it is also written of Balaam: *Who falling hath his eyes opened.*[76] For falling in works, he kept his eyes opened in contemplation. Even so, those too who open their eyes in faith and are imperceptive in works, placed because of their worthy appearance within the Church, are by reason of their wicked conduct found outside the Church. Of them it is well written elsewhere: *I saw the wicked buried; who also when they were yet living were in the holy place, and were praised in the city, as men of just works.*[77]

But some persons keep faith deep within themselves but do not zealously live according to faith. For they contradict by their conduct what they revere by belief. By divine judgment it is often their fate to lose through desultory living their salutary belief. For they are constantly defiled by wicked deeds and are not concerned that the vengeance of just judgment can be inflicted upon this conduct. And frequently, when they neglect the right way of life, they fall into unbelief although chastisement does not press upon them. When they do not suppose that a strict judgment threatens them, when they imagine that they can sin and not be punished, how can they either be or be called faithful? For to believe that fitting punishment cannot be inflicted on their unamended deeds is to have lost their faith. Therefore because they scorn to practice conduct that is a credit to faith, they lose even the faith that they seemed to possess. Over them in the guise of Jerusalem are uttered by the prophet words of ravaging enemies by whom—alas!—it is said: *Rase it, rase it, even to the foundation thereof.*[78] For Paul says: *Other foundation no man can lay, but that which is laid; which is Christ Jesus.*[79] Destroying enemies, then, make Jerusalem void, even to the foundation, when evil spirits, having first destroyed the structure of good works, remove also the firm grounding of religion from the hearts of the faithful. For works are built on faith, as a building on a foundation. Therefore to have been rased even to the foundation is, good works having been demolished, to have cast aside the strength of faith. Hence also it is said to Judaea by Jeremias: *The children also of Memphis and Taphnes have deflowered thee even to the crown of the head.*[80] For to be thus ravished is, after the practice of evil deeds, to be corrupted in the sublimity of faith itself. For when wicked spirits involve the soul of anyone in evil works but cannot vitiate the integrity of his faith, they still defile the inferior members, as it were, but do not affect the head. But whoever is corrupted in the faith is indeed defiled even to the crown of the head. For a malignant spirit reaches, so to speak, from the inferior even to the higher members when, defiling external conduct, it corrupts with the disease of unbelief the pure loftiness of the faith.

12

Fear

Fearing God, and avoiding evil.[81] To fear God is not to neglect any good things that should be done. Hence it is said by Solomon: *He that feareth God, neglecteth nothing.*[82] But because there are some who practice good deeds, yet in such a way that they are not deterred from certain evil practices, after Job is said to be one fearing God, it is still rightly recorded that he was one avoiding evil. For it is written: *Decline from evil and do good.*[83] For those good deeds are not acceptable to God that are stained in his sight by the admixture of evil deeds. For hence it is said by Solomon: *He that shall offend in one shall lose many good things.*[84] Hence Paul says: *A little leaven corrupteth the whole lump.*[85]

Moreover, it is written of fear: *Behold, the fear of the Lord, that is wisdom: and to depart from evil is understanding,*[86] as though it were plainly stated: Man, turn back to your own self; search thoroughly the secrets of your own heart. If you find that you fear God, surely it is clear that you are full of this wisdom. If you are not able to learn what it is in itself, you do, however, now know what it is in you. For what is feared in itself by the angels, in you is called the fear of the Lord. Because it is certain that you possess it if there is no uncertainty about your fearing the Lord. Hence also it is said by the Psalmist: *The fear of the Lord is the beginning of wisdom*,[87] because wisdom then begins to penetrate a heart when it disquiets that heart by fear of the last judgment. Therefore divine speech accommodates itself to our littleness just as a father speaking to his little child, of his own accord in order that he may be understood, uses baby talk. For because we cannot penetrate the nature of wisdom, what it is in itself, by the condescension of God we have heard what it is in us when it is said: *Behold, the fear of the Lord, that is wisdom*. But because he really understands the force of divine fear who refrains from all improper behavior, it is rightly added: *And to depart from evil is understanding*.

13

Obedience

And every man gave him one ewe, and one earring of gold.[88] By a ewe innocence is designated; by an earring, obedience. For by a ewe is expressed an innocent mind, but by an earring, hearing adorned with the grace of humility.

But because an appropriate opportunity has offered itself for propounding the virtue of obedience, it is fitting to discuss it with somewhat greater deliberation and care, pointing out how great is its merit. For obedience is the one virtue that implants other virtues in the mind and preserves them when planted. Hence also the first man received a precept to observe: if he willed obediently to submit himself to it, he would attain without labor to eternal blessedness.[89] Hence Samuel says: *Obedience is better than sacrifices; and to hearken rather than to offer the fat of rams, because it is like the sin of witchcraft to rebel: and like the crime of idolatry to refuse to obey*.[90] For obedience is rightly preferred to sacrifices because by the latter the flesh of another, but by the former our own will, is immolated. Anyone therefore the more readily appeases God, the more, having repressed in the sight of the Lord the pride of his own will, he sacrifices himself with the sword of the commandment. On the other hand, disobedience is said to be the sin of witchcraft in order to emphasize how great a virtue is obedience: therefore by its opposite it is better shown how worthy of praise it is to be considered. For if to resist is like the sin of witchcraft and to be unwilling to comply like the crime of idolatry, obedience is the one virtue that possesses the merit of faith, without which anyone is convicted of being an unbeliever, although he may seem to be a believer. Hence it is said by Solomon in speaking of obedience: *An obedient man shall speak of victories*.[91] For an obedient man indeed speaks of victories because when we humbly submit to the voice of another, we overcome ourselves in our heart. Hence Truth says in the Gospel: *Him that cometh to me, I will not cast out, because I came down from heaven, not to do my own will but the will of him that sent me*.[92] How can this be? If he were to do his own will, would he reject those who come to him? But who is not aware that the will of the Son is not at variance with the will of the Father? But since the first man went forth from the joy of paradise because he wished to do his own will,[93] the second man, coming for the redemption of men, when he shows that he does the will of the Father and not his own will, taught us to persevere inwardly. When therefore he does not his own will but that of the Father, he does not cast out those who come to him because while by his own example he subjects us to obedience, he closes our way of escape. Hence again he says: *I cannot of myself do any thing, but as I hear, I judge*.[94] For obedience is enjoined on us to be observed until death. But if he judges as he hears, he too obeys when he comes as judge. Therefore lest obedience until the end of our life should appear to us full of hardship, our Redeemer points out that he practices it even when he comes as a judge. What wonder is it then if sinful man is subjected to obedience in the short period of the present life, when the mediator between God and man does not abandon it even when he rewards the obedient?

But it should be known that evil should never be committed through obedience, but sometimes a good deed that is being performed should, through obedience, be discontinued. For the tree in paradise that God forbade man to touch was not evil. But in order that man, who was rightly created, might prosper by the better merit of obedience, it was proper that the Creator should forbid him even what was good, insofar as his conduct might be more truly virtuous, the more humbly he showed that he was subject to his Creator by forgoing even what was good. But it should be observed in this regard that it is said: *Of every tree of paradise thou shalt eat: but of the tree of knowledge of good and evil thou shalt not eat*.[95] For it is necessary that he who does not allow those subject to him one good thing, should permit many, lest the disposition of the person who obeys should thoroughly deteriorate if it is enfeebled from having been utterly denied all good things. But the Lord granted all other trees of paradise for food when he prohibited eating from one, in order that his creature, whom he did not wish to see destroyed but sustained, might be restrained the more easily from one, the more copiously he might partake of the rest.

But because sometimes the favorable but at other times the unfavorable features of worldly matters are imposed on us, we should be greatly aware that sometimes if obedience concerns something in our own favor, it is of no value, but sometimes if it does not at all concern something in our own favor, it is of very slight value. For when success in this world is enjoined, when a higher position is imposed, he who obeys by accepting them makes void for himself the virtue of his obedience if he is eager for these things with longing of his own. For he is not controlled by the rule of obedience who in obtaining the good things of this life caters to his own ambitious desire. Again, when contempt for the world is enjoined, when reproaches and insults are imposed, unless the mind desires even these things of itself, it reduces the merit of its obedience because it stoops reluctantly and unwillingly to those things which are despised in this life. For obedience suffers a loss when one's own wishes do not to some extent accompany the mind in submitting to the reproaches of this world. Obedience then should both in adversity have something in its favor, and again in prosperity should have nothing at all in its favor in order that in adversity it may be more praiseworthy, the more it is united even in desire to the divine ordinance, and in prosperity may be more upright, the more entirely it is divorced in its mind from the present glory that it obtains from God.

But we set forth more clearly the importance of the virtue if we relate the deeds of two men of the heavenly domain. For Moses, when he was pasturing sheep in the desert, was called by the Lord, speaking in the fire through an angel, to preside over the deliverance of all the multitude of the Israelites.[96] But because he was humble in his own mind, he was frightened at the glory of such authority and immediately had recourse to his weakness as a defense, saying: *I beseech thee, Lord, I am not eloquent from yesterday and the day before; since thou hast spoken to thy servant, I have more impediment and slowness of tongue.*[97] And, having put himself aside, he asks for another, saying: *Send whom thou wilt send.*[98] Behold, he is speaking with the one who made his tongue, and in order not to undertake the power of such great authority, he gives as a reason his lack of eloquence. Paul had also been divinely admonished that he must go up to Jerusalem, as he himself says to the Galatians: *Then, after fourteen years, I went up again to Jerusalem, taking with me Barnabas and Titus. And I went up according to revelation.*[99] And when on his journey he had met with the prophet Agabus, he heard from him what great adversity awaited him in Jerusalem. For it is written that Agabus, entwining Paul's girdle about his own feet, said: *So shall they bind at Jerusalem the man whose girdle this is.*[100] But Paul immediately answered: *I am ready not only to be bound, but to die also in Jerusalem for the name of Jesus.*[101] *Neither do I count my life more precious than myself.*[102] Going up then to Jerusalem according to the command of revelation, he knows his future sufferings, and yet he willingly seeks them; he hears of things to fear, but yet he more ardently desires them. Moses therefore has nothing in his favor relating to prosperity because he resists in his prayers being set over the people of Israel. Paul is even led by his own wish to suffering because he acquired knowledge of the evils that threaten him, but yet in his devotedness of spirit he is prepared for more acute sufferings. Moses wished, although God commanded him, to decline the glory of present power; Paul, when God assigned difficulties and hardships, strove to prepare himself for harsher sufferings. We are taught then, with the unbending virtue of both these exemplars leading the way, that if we truly endeavor to obtain the reward of obedience, we must struggle for the prosperity of this world only by command, but that we must war against its trials with dedication.

14

Perseverance

We must see to it that when we overcome evil habits, we are not thrown off balance by exuberant good habits, lest perhaps they run on in a perfunctory manner, lest for lack of watchfulness they be weakened, lest from error they go astray, lest enfeebled by weariness they forfeit the merit of past endeavor. For in all things the mind must keep close watch over itself and persevere in thus providing its surveillance. For to do good is of no avail if it is discontinued before the end of life, just as it is unavailing for him to run fast who stops before he reaches the goal. For hence it is that it is said of the reprobate: *Woe to them that have lost patience.*[103] Hence it is that Truth says to his elect: *You are they who have continued with me in my temptations.*[104] Hence Joseph, who is described as having remained righteous among his brothers until the end, is the only one said to have had a coat reaching to his ankles.[105] For what is signified by such a coat but conduct complete in every detail? For it is as if the stretched-out coat covers the body when good conduct covers us in God's sight even to the end of life. Hence it is that we are instructed by Moses to offer upon the altar the tail of the sacrifice,[106] in order, of course, that every good action we begin we may also consummate with perseverance to the end. Therefore what is begun well is to be done every day, so that since evils are repelled by engaging in combat, the victory of goodness may be maintained with constancy.

15

We must earnestly pray for the virtues which we have lest they decrease

The good things we do, while they produce a pleasant frame of mind, at the same time commonly bring on freedom from care together with inactivity,

and contaminate us through pride. Therefore it is necessary to examine whatever is done lest things which are evil be considered good, and lest those which
are not complete be considered sufficient. For often we are deceived either in
the quality of what is evil or the quantity of what is good, matters that are better resolved by praying than by examining. For when the mind is raised aloft by
compunction, it surveys more surely what is beneath it.

Hence it is written: *And Job rising up early offered holocausts for every one of
them*.[107] We rise up early when being suffused with the light of compunction,
we leave the night of the mind. We offer holocausts for each one when we
offer up sacrifices of prayer for each virtue, lest wisdom exalt; lest understanding through profundity lose its way; lest counsel, while it multiplies, lead to
confusion; lest fortitude, while it gives confidence, prompt precipitation; lest
knowledge without love swell the mind; lest piety veer from the right path; and
lest fear, while it is unduly alarming, may plunge one into despair.

Furthermore, holocaust means whole burnt. Therefore to offer a holocaust is to light up the whole soul with the fire of compunction: only those
know how to do this who fortify their soul with a sturdy guard. Hence Isboseth
perished suddenly; we read concerning him that he had for a doorkeeper not a
man but a woman. His enemies—when the doorkeeper who was cleansing
wheat had fallen asleep—secretly took ears of corn and stabbed him in the
groin.[108] The doorkeeper cleanses wheat when the mind distinguishes the virtues from the vices. Should it cease to be watchful, the way is opened for evil
spirits, who enter in and take the ears of corn because they destroy the germi-
nation of good thoughts, and they stab the groin because they slay the virtues
of the soul by the pleasure of the flesh: hence the name Isboseth, meaning a
man of confusion. Such a man is not provided with a strong guard, since while
he believes he is practicing virtues, he does not remove vices that stealthily
intrude. Hence Solomon says: *With all watchfulness keep thy heart, because life
issueth out from it*.[109] Therefore virtues, beginning with the original intent, are
to be given careful consideration and the assistance of prayer lest they fail.

16
Dispositions during prayer

A salutary remedy, when the soul reproaches itself while remembering
sin, is first to express sorrow for the act of transgression, so that when the stain
of offense is washed away by tears, the visage of the heart at prayer may be seen
unspotted by our Creator. But we must take great care lest as long as the sin
that is deplored is again committed, those very expressions of sorrow lose
weight in the sight of the just judge. For we must earnestly call to mind what is

said: *Repeat not the word in thy prayer.*[110] By this saying the wise man forbids not our asking often for pardon but repeating our sins. In plain words: When you have wept over your misdeeds, never again do anything that is to be lamented in prayer a second time.

Therefore in order that the face may be lifted up unspotted in prayer, whatever can be faulted in the act of prayer must be carefully reviewed before the hours for prayer, and when the mind ends its prayer, let it be prompt to maintain itself just as it desires to appear to the judge at the actual time of prayer. For the mind often dwells on unclean and forbidden thoughts during the periods not devoted to prayer. And when the mind has lifted itself up to prayerful exercises, harking back, it is exposed to recollections of the things with which it was occupied in leisure time. And the soul is now as it were incapable of lifting up its face to God because in its soiled condition it is ashamed of tainted thought. Often we willingly concern ourselves with worldly cares. And when after such preoccupation we apply ourselves to prayerful pursuits, the mind cannot lift itself to heavenly things because the weight of earthly solicitude has thrust it downwards, and the face appears unclean in prayer because it is besmirched by the mire of earthly thought.

However, sometimes we free the heart of all superfluous matters and resist unlawful thoughts even when we are not engaged in prayer, yet because we ourselves commit sins rather infrequently, we somewhat sluggishly put aside the offenses of others, and the more earnestly our mind is afraid of sinning, the more severely it is opposed to harm done to itself by another. Hence it happens that someone is found slow to grant pardon to the same extent that by continuing to improve, he has become cautious about committing sin. And to the degree he himself fears to transgress against another, he seeks to punish the more severely what transgression there has been against himself. But what worse defect can be devised than this blemish of resentment, which in the sight of the judge does not disfigure charity but destroys it? For every sin stains the life of the soul, but resentment harbored against our neighbor slays it. For it is driven into the soul like a sword, and the secret inmost parts are slashed by its blade; and unless it is first drawn out of the pierced heart, no part of divine aid is obtained in prayer, for the healthful medicines cannot be applied to wounded limbs if the iron is not first withdrawn from the wound. Hence it is that Truth himself says: *If you will not forgive men their offenses, neither will your heavenly Father forgive you your offenses.*[111] Hence he admonishes, saying: *When you shall stand to pray, forgive, if you have aught against any man.*[112] Hence he says again: *Give; and it shall be given to you. Forgive; and you shall be forgiven.*[113] Hence to the formulary of petition he allied provisory forbearance, saying:

Forgive us our debts, as we also forgive our debtors,[114] so that really the benefit we ask of God with compunction, we first with change of heart extend to our neighbor. Therefore we then truly lift up our face without spot, when we neither commit offenses nor from selfish ill will withhold acquittance of those which have been committed against ourselves. For in the hour of prayer our mind is burdened with severe disturbance if either its own activity disfigures it, or resentment stored up against another's malice is subject to reproach. When anyone has cleared away these two blights, he is at once liberated from the ills that are connected with them.

17

Prayers of petition

When God is not sought in prayer, the mind soon grows weary in praying since when a man happens to ask for something which God according to his hidden decree refuses to grant, he who is unwilling to give what is prized is himself brought into disfavor. But the Lord desires that he himself be loved more than the things he has made, and that things eternal be prayed for rather than temporal ones, as it is written: *Seek ye first the kingdom of God and his justice; and all these things shall be added unto you.*[115] But since he does not say: shall be given, but *shall be added*, he clearly shows that what is the chief gift is one thing, and superaddition another. For since the eternal world must be what we strive for, but the temporal world what we make use of, the former comes as a gift and the latter as a surplus. And yet often when men ask for temporal goods but do not seek eternal rewards, they request the thing that is added and do not desire that to which it is should be added. Nor do they consider it to be an answer to their prayer if here they are poor in temporal things and hereafter live forever rich in blessedness; but bent on visible things alone, as has been said, they refuse to acquire the invisible by taking the trouble of asking for it. If they sought the things above, they would already garner the fruit of their labor because when the prayerful mind yearns for the vision of its Creator, aflame with divine longings it is united to what is heavenly, removed from what is earthly; it becomes expansive in the zealous attachment of eagerness to gain insight, and while achieving it, is set afire. And to love things above is in itself to ascend on high; and while with great ardor the mind aspires heavenwards, in a wondrous way it is afforded a foretaste of what it longs for.

18

True prayer is more a function of the heart than of the mouth

Real petitioning resides not in words but in heartfelt thoughts. For our desires not our words give more effective access to God's august hearing. For if we seek eternal life with the mouth and nevertheless do not desire it with the heart, in crying out we keep silence. But if we desire in the heart, even when our mouth is still, in being silent we cry out. It is hence that the people in the wilderness make a great noise with their voices, and Moses is silent amidst the clamor of words, and yet while keeping still he is heard by the ear of divine mercy, since to him it is said: *Why criest thou to me?*[116] Therefore, inside in the desire is the secret cry that does not reach the ears of men and yet fills the hearing of the Creator. It is hence that the voice of Anna going to the temple was indeed silent, and yet she sent forth ever so many expressions of her desire.[117] Hence the Lord says in the Gospel: *Enter into thy chamber and, having shut the door, pray to thy Father in secret; and thy Father who seeth in secret will repay thee.*[118] For, having shut the door, he prays in his chamber who while his mouth is silent, pours forth the heart's affection in the presence of the Father of mercy. And the voice is heard in secret when there is a crying out in silence by holy desires. Hence also it is rightly said by the Psalmist: *The Lord hath heard the desire of the poor; thy ear hath heard the desires of their heart.*[119]

Often, however, in the very sacrifice of prayer, persistent thoughts force themselves on us and are able to carry off or demean what we are sacrificing in ourselves to God with tears. Hence when Abraham at sunset was offering sacrifice, he was confronted with fowls coming down which he diligently drove away lest they carry off the sacrifice that had been offered.[120] So let us when we offer sacrifice to God upon the altar of our heart, keep from it unwelcome intruders lest evil spirits and untoward thoughts carry off what our mind hopes it is offering expressly to God.

19

Prolonged prayer / Intercession for adversaries

There are some within holy Church who offer to God long prayers but do not live as petitioners, for they strive after heavenly promises in their petitions but are disengaged from them in their deeds. These sometimes reach the point of tears in their prayer, but after the time of prayer when pride has stirred their mind, they at once swell with the arrogance of pride; when avarice moves them, they soon seethe with the fires of covetous thought; when lust has tempted, they sigh at once with unlawful desires; when anger has vexed them, before long the flame of folly has dispelled their peace of mind. Therefore, as we have said, they both shed tears in prayer and yet having ended their prayers, when they are assailed by sinful suggestions, they do not remember that they experienced tearful desire for the heavenly kingdom. This fact Balaam clearly stated concerning himself; he says, on beholding the dwellings of the just: *Let my soul die the death of the just; and my last end be like to theirs.*[121] But when the time of compunction passed, he gave counsel against the life of those whom he had asked to resemble even in death,[122] and when he found an occasion for avarice, he immediately forgot the state of innocence he desired.

Therefore a prayer which the perseverance of continual love does not sustain, has not the import of virtue. On the other hand, it is well reported of Anna, when she wept: *And her countenance was no more changed to a different form,*[123] precisely because her mind did not put aside after her prayers by indulging foolish joy what at the time of prayer the earnestness of sighing sought for. But by some the effort of prayer is changed over to the service of worldly business. Of them Truth says in the Gospel: *Who devour the houses of widows under the pretense of long prayer. These shall receive greater judgment.*[124] But the emptiness of prayer in contrived words is plainly pointed out. For truly to pray is to voice with compunction bitter sighings and not well–arranged words.

Moreover, anyone deserves to be heard more quickly in his own behalf, the more devoutly he intercedes for others. For he makes his prayers for himself of greater avail if he offers them also in behalf of others. For that sacrifice of prayer is more willingly received which in the sight of the merciful judge is enhanced by love of neighbor. And a person really crowns the sacrifice if he offers it even for his enemies. For hence it is that Truth, the teacher, says: *Pray for them that persecute and calumniate you.*[125] Hence again he says: *When you shall stand to pray, forgive, if you have aught against any man; that your Father also, who is in heaven, may forgive you your sins.*[126]

20

Prayer and action must provide mutual assistance

It should be recognized that everyone at variance in practice with the precepts of the Lord, as often as he hears them, is reproached and confounded by his own heart because he recalls what he has failed to do. For his conscience accuses him of whatever wrong it judges him to have done. Hence the prophet David makes entreaty, saying: *Then shall I not be confounded, when I shall look into all thy commandments.*[127] For greatly confounded is every man when either by reading or hearing he reflects on the precepts of God that by his way of life he has disregarded. For hence it is declared by the voice of John: *If our heart does not reprehend us, we have confidence towards God*.[128] That is to say: If we do what he commands, we obtain what we ask for.

For in the sight of God two things must work closely together: action should be supported by prayer, and prayer by action. For hence it is that Jeremias says: *Let us search our ways, and seek and return to the Lord. Let us lift up our hearts with our hands to the Lord in the heavens*.[129] For to search our ways is to examine what is inmost in our thoughts. But he lifts up his heart with his hands who strengthens his prayer by works. For he who prays and disregards action, lifts up the heart but does not lift up the hands. But whoever acts and does not pray, lifts up the hands and does not lift up the heart.

BOOK 4

PRELATES

Prologue

Those in the Church who excel in the virtues are rightly given charge of others and by divine dispensation are called to lead them. Hence the discussion of virtues is directly followed by the fourth book of Part 2 entitled Prelates (Rectors).

Moreover, this book is presented as a corrective for the fourth book of Part 1. The discussion in that book concerns the rich who figure rather prominently among the reprobate as those who crave temporal gain and disregarding spiritual concerns, amass worldly riches. But in the present book we consider rectors who, among those sons of the Church more outstanding in virtue, devote themselves to winning souls and spurning earthly desires, seek to increase the Lord's wealth.[1]

1

Prelates and rectors of churches who are supported by their benefices are required to preach the word of God

Everyone who by private right rules a domestic household or for the common good is placed over loyal subjects, by having title to guide those entrusted to him figuratively holds land to be cultivated.[2] It is indeed for this purpose that anyone by divine dispensation is given charge of others, that the mind of those under his care, like an expanse of land, may be made fruitful by the seed of his teaching. However, there are some who being placed over holy people, obtain a livelihood through bountiful ecclesiastical benefices but do not render the services of exhortation that are due.

In contrast to them the example of holy Job is proposed when it is said by him: *If I have eaten the fruits thereof without money.*[3] For to eat the fruit of the land without money is to receive funds from the Church but not to present to it the expected preaching. Ostensibly, of this default in preaching it is said by the voice of the Creator: *Thou oughtest therefore to have committed my money to the bankers, and at my coming I should have received my own with usury.*[4] And so he eats the fruit of the land without money who receives the Church's benefits for sustenance but does not render to the people the service of exhortation. What do we pastors say to these charges, who while we herald the coming of the strict judge, take upon ourselves the function of a messenger but derive our sustenance from the Church in silence? We exact all that is required for our corporal needs, but we do not disburse what we owe spiritually to those committed to our care. Observe how holy Job, bearing so many temporal obligations, in the midst of countless duties, attended to the imparting of instruction. And he did not eat the fruit of the land without money because he surely dispensed sound counsel to those from whom he received the means of subsistence. For he who is placed in charge of others, whether they are many or fewer in number, owes this to almighty God: to require due service from those under his care and to give careful attention to what he also owes them in the way of constant guidance. For what are all those united by divine dispensation in mutual service under the one true Lord but servants of one another? Therefore since he who is subordinate shows deference, the duty of discourse is assumed by the superior. Since the subordinate obeys, he who is in charge must respond with conscientious supervision. As a result, while we earnestly endeavor to serve one another now by charity, we are one day to triumph together with the Lord in common rejoicing. But there are some who, by reason of the fact that they discharge the duty of preaching, begrudge to others the gift that they have and therefore no longer enjoy true possession of it. To them it is rightly said by James: *But if you have bitter zeal, and there be contentions in your hearts; this is not wisdom descending from above; but earthly, sensual, devilish.*[5]

Hence also when it is here said: *If I have eaten the fruits thereof without money*, it is rightly added: *And have afflicted the soul of the tillers thereof.*[6] For they are the tillers of this land who, being placed in a lower echelon, with all the earnestness they can muster and the greatest possible effectiveness, cooperate in the service of preaching for the instruction of holy Church. Not to afflict the tillers of this land is not to begrudge their labors lest a rector of the Church, while he arrogates to himself alone the right of preaching, with envy gnawing at him, even impugns others who preach properly. For the devoted mind of pastors, because it seeks not its own glory but that of the Creator, wishes all that it does to be assisted by all. For the faithful preacher desires—if it can be accomplished—that the truth that he alone is not able to promulgate, the mouths of all should voice. Hence when Joshua wished to stand in the way of the two who remained in the camp and prophesied, it is rightly said by Moses: *Why hast thou emulation for me? O that all the people might prophesy, and that the Lord would give them his spirit!*[7] For he was willing for all to prophesy since he did not begrudge to others the gift that he had.

2

Young men and those who submit to the vices by pleasurable consent may not share in the care of souls

Those who are still engaged in a struggle against their vices must not preside over the teaching of others. It is for this reason, according to the word of divine dispensation, that the Levites minister in the tabernacle from their twenty–fifth year, but from their fiftieth become the guardians of the sacred vessels.[8] For what is indicated by the twenty–fifth year, when the prime of youth begins, but the struggles against each vice? And what is expressed by the fiftieth year, in which occurs the jubilee rest, but the inner tranquility when the struggle is subdued? But what is symbolized by the vessels of the tabernacle but the souls of the faithful? Therefore the Levites minister in the tabernacle from their twenty–fifth year and become guardians of the vessels from their fiftieth, to show that they who by pleasurable consent nourish the rivalries of the vices that are still on the offensive, should not presume to take charge of others; but when they have overcome the assaults of temptation, being thus confirmed in inward tranquility, they may then share in the care of souls. But who can fully subdue these assaults of temptation when Paul says: *I see another law in my members, fighting against the law of my mind and captivating me in the law of sin that is in my members*?[9] But it is one thing bravely to endure struggles, another to be weakly vulnerable to attack. In the first instance virtue is tried lest it be overconfident; in the other it is altogether overcome lest it remain steadfast. He then who knows how to endure bravely the trials of the contest, even when he is shaken by temptation, is serene on the towering stronghold of peace; for he perceives that the contests with the vices, even within him, are under his control, since he does not consent to them by yielding to pleasure.

3

Administration should not be undertaken out of cupidity but out of necessity

A man must not undertake to guide others who does not know how to lead them in living well lest he who is chosen to correct the faults of others may himself commit sin which it is his duty to restrain. Let rectors then take care to live for themselves and those under their care; to hide within their mind the good they do and yet by it supply an example of good conduct for the benefit of their disciples; to correct their faults by censuring them and yet not pride themselves on the severity of this correction; to let slight reproof suffice for certain faults and yet not relax the bonds of discipline by this leniency; to take no notice of other faults and yet not allow them to increase by overlooking them. These tasks are laborious, and unless divine grace provides support, not easy to perform. But it is rightly said by the book of Wisdom of the coming of the strict judge: *Horribly and speedily will he appear: for a most severe judgment shall be for them that bear rule.*[10] Since therefore it is common for the sin of pride to result from the power of leading, and pride itself is regarded as ungodly by the strict judge, it is well said of the Lord by Eliu: *Who calleth rulers, ungodly.*[11] For when they are proud of their authority, by their example they lead those under their charge to irreverence.

A person then who is given preferment to rule over men must be extremely careful to take his place on the cathedra of humiity within the sanctuary of his mind. And when others stand before him as he judges, let him constantly have in mind the one before whom as judge he is later to stand and be judged for these matters, so that the more anxiously he trembles now before the one whom he does not see, he may behold with greater assurance when he has seen him. Therefore let him who is perhaps scarcely able to offer reparation to the strict judge merely for his own soul, consider that at the time of rendering account to God he is responsible, so to speak, for as many souls as he had persons under his rule. If this thought continually plagues his mind, it represses every swelling of pride. And a foresighted ruler will more unlikely be called either an apostate king or an ungodly ruler, the more cautiously the power he has received is regarded not as an honor but a burden. For he who is now pleased to be a judge, is not then pleased to behold the judge. For the faults that are committed through love of wielding power cannot be numbered. But then only is authority properly exercised when it is held in check not by loving it but by fearing it. And in order that it may be duly administered, it is proper first of all that not cupidity, but necessity, prescribe it. But once received, it should not be abandoned through fear, nor should it be esteemed as an object of desire, lest anyone as if through humility show greater pride in spurning through avoidance the dictate of divine dispensation, or cast off the yoke of his heavenly ruler because his private authority over others pleases him. Therefore, when power is received, it must not willfully be loved but patiently endured, so that at the time of judgment it may be a source of salutary relief, whereas it now makes itself felt as a burdensome duty.

4

A prelate who delights in ruling and who rejoices in his exceptional distinction falls into the sin of apostasy

Often we are aware that many of those who rule exact an inordinate fear from those under their charge, not so much for the Lord's sake as in the Lord's place. For inwardly they glorify themselves with pride of heart and scorn all under them in comparison with themselves. And they do not regard them with condescension but rule them domineeringly because in truth they pride themselves with lofty thoughts and do not consider those over whom they happen to rule to be their equals. Against this pride it is said in the book of Ecclesiasticus: *Have they made thee a ruler? Be not lifted up: but be among them as one of them.*[12] The Lord also, reproving this pride in pastors, says through the prophet: *But you ruled over them with rigor and a high hand.*[13] For the good counsels they address to their subjects, they express as though ordering rather than advising them, because in fact to say anything to them as if they were on equal footing, they consider beneath them. For they delight in their singular eminence, and not in the equality of their status. But because the Lord examines carefully the arrogant hearts of rulers, it is well said against them: *Who saith to the king: Thou art an apostate.*[14] For every haughty ruler falls into the sin of apostasy as often as he delights in ruling over men, rejoices in his exceptional distinction. For he considers not the deity under whom he himself is and rejoices that it is not as though he were in a state of equality with his equals. But whence is it that this root of vices springs up in the heart of rulers unless it is in imitation of the one who, having scorned the companies of angels, said: *I will ascend above the height of the clouds, and will be like the most High?*[15] Therefore since every ruler, as often as he prides himself on ruling over others, just as often is severed, by falling into pride, from subjection to the supreme ruler, and because when he scorns his equals who are subject to him, he does not acknowledge the supreme dominion of the one under whom all are equal, it is rightly said: *Who saith to the king: Thou art an apostate.*

But since, ruling by domineering, they lead their subjects to irreverence by the example of their pride, it is fittingly added: *Who calleth rulers, ungodly.*[16] For they would lead them into the way of reverence if they presented examples of humility to the eyes of their subjects. But he is an ungodly leader who deviates from the way of truth, and while he is falling headlong himself, invites his disciples to precipices. He is an ungodly leader who advocates the way of error by examples of pride. Paul was afraid of being an ungodly leader when he kept in check the loftiness of his power, saying: *Nor sought we glory of men, neither of you nor of others, whereas we might have been burdensome to you, as the apostles of Christ; but we became as little ones in the midst of you.*[17] He had become as a child in the midst of them because he was afraid lest he set examples of pride if he claimed among the disciples the honor of his high rank. He was afraid in truth lest if he sought for himself the power of pastoral authority, the flock committed to him proceed alongside precipices and lest he, who had undertaken an office of devotion, lead the disciples to ungodliness.

It is therefore necessary for a person in high station to be attentive to the examples he sets his subjects, and to know that he is living for all those over whom he is placed, and to be especially watchful not to pride himself on being placed over others lest he should exact too immoderately the privileges of rightful authority, lest the rule of discipline be converted into the severity of pride, lest by the power of restraining his subjects from perversity, he pervert all the more the hearts of all who observe him, and lest, as has been said, he become a mentor of infidelity by means of his status among the faithful.

5

Powerful prelates should recognize that they are equal in condition to those placed under their charge

God doth not cast away the mighty, whereas he himself also is mighty.[18] In the course of this mortal life some things are harmful in themselves, some because of circumstances: among the first group are sins and shameful acts; among the second, temporal power or the bond of marriage. For marriage is good, but those things which grow up around it through worldly cares are injurious. Hence Paul says: *But he that is with a wife is solicitous for the things of the world; how he may please his wife.*[19] Hence also, recommending to certain persons better options, he deters them from marriage and says: *But this I say, not to cast a snare upon you, but for that which is decent and may give you power to attend upon the Lord, without impediment.*[20] Therefore while that which is not harmful is embraced, something harmful is commonly engaged in because of circumstances, just as frequently we journey along a straight and clear road, and yet our clothing is entangled by thornbushes growing along the way. We do not stumble on a clear road, but alongside there develops what inflicts harm. Great also is temporal power that being well administered has merit in the sight of God, and yet sometimes from standing out above others appears pretentious through intellectual pride, and while all things are placed at its disposal, while its commands are speedily carried out according to its wish, while all its subjects extol with praise its good deeds—if there are any—but do not oppose perverse deeds with any attestation, while they commonly praise even what they ought to reprove, the mind, being led astray by considerations that are beneath it, is unreasonably borne aloft, and while it is surrounded externally with excessive applause is devoid of inner uprightness, and forgetting itself, is carried away by the remarks of others and believes itself to be such outwardly as it said to be and not such as it should inwardly see itself. It scorns those subject to it and does not acknowledge them to be equals in the order of nature, and believes that it has also outstripped by the merits of its life those whom it has surpassed by dint of the power of rank. It considers that it is wiser than all those whom it sees itself surmounting in power. And it is in this way led even to resembling the one of whom it is written: *He beholdeth every high thing, and he is king over all the children of pride.*[21] And of his outward appearance it is said: *A generation, whose eyes are lofty and their eyelids lifted up on high.*[22] It is formed in the likeness of him who aspiring to a unique height and scorning a life in the company of angels, says: *I will ascend above the height of the clouds. I will be like the most High..*[23] Therefore by a wondrous judgment it inwardly finds the lowest point of downfall while externally it raises itself to the highest point of power. For man in truth becomes like an apostate angel when he disdains to be like his fellowman. Thus Saul mounted from the worthiness of humility to immoderate pride at the height of his power. He was indeed raised up through humility, rejected through pride, as the Lord bears witness, who says: *When thou wast a little one in thy own eyes, wast thou not made the head of the tribes of Israel?*[24] Prior to his power he had seen that he was little, but supported by temporal authority he no longer saw himself in that light. For preferring himself in comparison with others, he supposed himself great in his own right. But wondrously, when little in his own sight, he was great in the sight of the Lord; and when great in his own sight, in the Lord's sight he was little. The Lord through his prophet forbids us to be great in our own sight, saying: *Woe to you that are wise in your own eyes, and prudent in your own conceits.*[25] And Paul, warning us not to be great in our own opinion, says: *Be not wise in your own conceits.*[26] Therefore while the mind is puffed up through the multiplicity of those subject to it, it lapses into the lust of pride, the very prominence of its power exploiting it.

But for a random entity not to be good is one thing; for anyone not to know how to use good things properly is another. For power is good in its proper sphere, but it requires a careful mode of living in a ruler. Therefore he exercises it properly who has learned both how to maintain and how to fight against it. He exercises it properly who knows how to raise himself by it above his faults, and with it to become adjusted in equality with others. For the mind of man is commonly not subservient even when not supported by any power.

How much more then does it exalt itself when power is added to it? And yet it is prepared to correct the defects of others with appropriate faultfinding. Hence also it is said by Paul: *For he is God's minister, an avenger to execute wrath*.[27] Therefore when the administering of temporal power is taken upon oneself, vigilance must be exercised with the greatest care in order to discover how to derive from it what is helpful and to resist its temptations, and to preserve oneself, while possessing it, equal with others, and yet by the zeal for punishment to invoke jurisdiction over those who do wrong. We understand this prudence more fully if we consider some instances of ecclesiastical power. Peter, for example, although holding by divine authority the highest post in the Church refused to be treated with undue deference by Cornelius, a man of good deportment who was prostrating himself before him, and recalled that they were alike, saying: *Arise; I myself also am a man*.[28] But when he discovered the sin of Ananias and Sapphira, he soon showed with what great power he had been endowed over the others. For by a word he brought to an end their life, the conduct of which he discerned through the all–searching Spirit,[29] and reasserted himself to be paramount in the Church in opposition to sin because when the honor had been powerfully conferred on him, he took no cognizance of it among his worthy brethren. In their regard, holiness of conduct merited a fellowship of equality; toward the offenders, his zeal for punishment unleashed his rightful power. Paul did not take cognizance of his being placed in charge of his worthy brethren when he said: *Not because we exercise dominion over your faith; but are helpers of your joy*—immediately adding—*for in faith you stand*.[30] That is to say: We do not exercise dominion over your faith by reason of the fact that you stand in faith. For we are your equals when we know that you are standing firm. It was as though he were unaware that he was placed in charge of his brethren when he said: *We became little ones in the midst of you*,[31] and again: *And ourselves your servants through Jesus*.[32] But when he detected a fault that needed correction, he reasserted that he was their master, saying: *What will you? Shall I come to you with a rod?*[33]

The highest of positions is therefore rightly administered when a ruler uses his authority over vices rather than over his brethren. For all men were created equal, but that some are entrusted to others to be governed is not occasioned by nature but by wrongdoing. Therefore rulers ought to reign over the vices on account of which they are given charge over others; and when they correct offenders, let them carefully see to it that they chastise their faults with discipline by the authority of their power, but by preserving humility let them acknowledge that they are equal with those brethren who are corrected. In fact, it is frequently fitting that in secret we should regard more favorably than ourselves those whom we correct. For their faults are chastened through us with the forcefulness of discipline, but in the faults we ourselves commit, we are not chastened by anyone with even a word of rebuke. Therefore we are under greater obligation to the Lord, the more we sin without human punishment. But our discipline renders those subject to it more free from divine punishment, the more punishment for their faults it inflicts here below.

6

Humility must be restrained by a prelate lest the rights of administration be weakened

A prelate must maintain humility in his heart and discipline in his work. And he must meanwhile be earnestly on guard lest the rights of administration be weakened while the virtue of humility is intemperately observed, and lest while the prelate humbles himself more than is fitting, he be unable to restrain the conduct of his subjects under the bond of discipline. Therefore let us remain outwardly true to what we undertake for the benefit of others, and inwardly to the self-knowledge we possess. But still let those also who are entrusted to us become aware, through indications that discreetly come to light, what our true selves are like so that they may observe what to fear from our authority and what to imitate in our humility. But having maintained the authority of our rule, let us constantly turn our gaze to our inward being and untiringly consider that we are created equal with others, not that—for the time being—we have been placed over others. For the more lofty is our power outwardly, the more it should be inwardly restrained lest it dominate our thinking, animate the mind with love of power, lest at last the mind be unable to control that power to which it submits in its desire to exercise authority.

David indeed had known how to control the power of his reign: by humbling himself he overcame all pride in his power, saying: *Lord, my heart is not exalted*; and adding in an increase of humility: *Nor are my eyes lofty*; also adding: *Neither have I walked in great matters*; and after examining himself further with very thorough inquiry, saying: *Nor in wonderful things above me*.[34] And bringing to an end all his thoughts from the bottom of his heart, he also subjoined the words: *If I was not humbly minded; but exalted my soul*.[35] Notice that he frequently repeats the sacrifice of humility, offered from his inmost heart, and by again and again acknowledging it does not cease making the offering and repeatedly speaking of it, shows it to the eyes of his judge. What is this? And how had he known that this sacrifice he was offering in the sight of God with such repetition of words was pleasing to him, unless pride is usually associated with the powerful and haughtiness almost always connected with the wealthy, because quite often surfeit of temperament reinforces conceit?

But it is unusual when humility of demeanor abides in the person of the peerless. Hence we must conclude that whenever powerful persons think humbly they attain a peak of remote and almost inaccessible virtue, and they rightly appease the Lord more readily with this virtue, because powerful though they are, they humbly offer him that sacrifice which the powerful can scarcely offer. For it is a most rare art of living to attain a crowning point and to suppress vainglory, to be indeed in a position of power and not to be conscious of one's power. Therefore let anyone placed over others desire to serve and not to rule. For what is reprehensible is swelling pride and not position of power. God confers power, but the ill will of our mind causes pride. Therefore let us take away what we have contributed, and the things we possess by God's generosity are good.

But the saints know that our fathers of old are recorded to have been not so much kings of men, as shepherds of flocks. And when the Lord said to Noe and his sons: *Increase and multiply, and fill the earth*, he adds: *And let the fear and dread of you be upon all the beasts of the earth*.[36] For he does not say: be upon the men who are to come, but: *be upon all the beasts of the earth*.

Man being placed by nature over irrational animals but not over other men, therefore it is said to him that he should be feared by the beasts but not by men because wishing to be feared by an equal is to be prideful against nature.

Hence the angel, when worshiped by John, declares himself to be a creature, saying: *See thou do it not, I am thy fellow servant, and of thy brethren*.[37] Hence the prophet, when he is carried away to see sublime things, is called son of man, so that being borne to heavenly realms, he might remember that he was a man. It is as though the divine voice admonishes him in plainer words, saying: Remember what you are lest you be exalted by those regions to which you are taken, but moderate the loftiness of the revelation by remembrance of your condition.

7

Prelates are to blend gentleness and severity

When I sat as a king, with his army standing about him, yet I was a comforter of them that mourned.[38] From this passage it can be discerned how by good rulers both full power of ruling and kindness of consoling are mingled. For he says: *And when I sat as a king with his army standing about him*: see the authority of governance; *yet I was a comforter of them that mourned*: observe the ministry of kindness. But discipline or mercy is much deprived if the one is maintained without the other. But toward their subjects there must be in rulers both mercy justly giving comfort and justice kindly dealing wrath. It is hence that to the wounds of that half–dead man who was brought by the Samaritan to an inn, both wine and oil are applied,[39] so that the wounds should be drawn together by the wine and be soothed by the oil; just as everyone who has the duty of healing wounds may by wine apply the sting of strictness, and by oil the beneficence of kindness, so that by the wine what is corrupt may be made clean, and by the oil what is to be healed may be eased. Gentleness is to be blended with severity, and a certain moderation is to be observed in each component so that those being cared for may not either be made worse by much harshness or be unrestrained by excessive kindness. This accord surely that ark of the tabernacle signifies in which along with the tables of the law there are the rod and manna together,[40] because when there is the knowledge of sacred Scripture in the breast of a good ruler, if there is the rod of severity, let there also be the manna of gentleness. Hence also David says: *Thy rod and thy staff comforted me*.[41] For we are struck by the rod, and we are sustained by the staff. So if there is the strictness of the rod that it may strike, let there also be the comfort of the staff that it may sustain. Therefore let there be love but not that which has a softening effect; let there be vigor but not that which grates; let there be zeal but not that which rages to excess; let there be kindness but not that which spares more than is beneficial. It is advantageous to observe in the breast of Moses mercy joined with severity. Let us watch him loving kindly and raging strictly. Surely when the people of Israel in the sight of God incurred the guilt of an almost unforgivable offense so that its leader heard the words: *Go, get thee down; thy people hath sinned*,[42] as though the voice of God said to him: It has fallen into such a sin it is henceforth no longer my people, and added: *Let me alone, that my wrath may be kindled against them, and that I may destroy them: and I will make of thee a great nation*,[43] repeatedly presenting himself for the people he led as a barrier to the vehemence of God in his anger, Moses says: *Either forgive them this trespass, or if thou do not, strike me out of the book that thou hast written*.[44] Therefore let us consider with what deep emotion he loved that people for whose life he begged to have himself struck out of the book of life. But yet let us consider that he who is constrained by such great love of his people, is inflamed against its sins with just as great zeal for righteousness. For as soon as by the first request he obtained pardon of the offense so that they should not be destroyed, approaching that people he says: *Put every man his sword upon his thigh. Go, and return from gate to gate through the midst of the camp, and let every man kill his brother, and friend, and neighbor. And there were slain that day about three and twenty thousand men*.[45] Observe that he who begged for the life of all even with his own death, took the life of a certain number with the sword. Inwardly he burned with the fires of love; externally he was inflamed by the zeal of severity. So great was his kindness that he did not hesitate to offer to die himself for the people in the sight of the Lord; such was his severity that those whom he had feared to see slain by divine power, he did himself slay with the sword of judgment. He so loved those over whom he was placed that for them he did not even spare himself, and yet the offenders whom he loved he so penalized that even when spared by the Lord he destroyed them. In each case he was a forcible emissary; in each case, an admirable mediator: the cause of the people he stated before God by prayers; the cause of God he stated before the people with swords. Inwardly loving, he withstood the wrath of God by entreating; externally raging, he consumed sin by destroying. He quickly comes to the aid of all by staging the death of some. And therefore almighty God listened sooner to his faithful servant acting for the people, because he saw what the servant was about to inflict on the people for God. Therefore in the governance of the people Moses effected a unification so that discipline did not lack mercy, nor mercy discipline.

8

The administration of a prelate must be such that he may be revered when cheerful and held in affection when stirred up

Some persons are so strict that they even lose all friendly consideration, and some are so mild that they forfeit the rights of strict rule. Hence by all rectors both characteristics are to be most diligently maintained so that neither in the power of discipline do they abandon the friendliness of a mild disposition, nor again in gentleness do they abandon severity of discipline: they are neither to grow callous from lack of compassion when they chastise the contumacious, nor to weaken the strength of discipline when they encourage the hearts of the weak. Therefore let vigor of discipline control mildness, and mildness adorn vigor, and so let the one be made acceptable by the other that vigor is not rigid and mildness is not negligent.

For such must be the administering of governance that he who is in command should conduct himself toward those under him with such moderation that both when cheerful he may be revered and when stirred up he may be held in affection, so that neither excessive levity should render him ineffective nor unrestrained severity make him offensive. For often we crush those under our charge when we uphold the force of justice more than is suitable. This force will surely no longer be that of justice if it is not kept under just control. And often we release subjects from the fear of discipline if our rule is marked by a slack rein on gaiety because while they see us lighthearted, as it were, in our free moments, they themselves boldly feel free to be easygoing in unsound ways. But in order that the visage of the ruler may even when joyful be feared, it is necessary that he should himself unceasingly fear the stern look of his Creator. For with difficulty is the mind, known by those under its charge to afflict itself continually for the love of God, credited with lightsomeness. For if one with constant fervor of spiritual desire seeks things above, it is brought into very great question concerning him that he sometimes becomes merry before men. For when the elders are themselves followers of pleasure, the reins on frivolity are loosened for the young. For who would keep himself under the control of authority, when even the very ones who are given the right of control unbend in enjoyment? For what is done by the young for the sake of pleasure must be checked by the control of the elders.

9

Prelates, when they are lifted up by the prosperity of this world, fail unrestrainedly in thought, word and deed

Have I not dissembled? Have I not kept silence? Have I not been quiet?[46] Although all of us, from every station in life, sin in thought, word, and deed, the mind is carried away in these three ways more unrestrainedly when it is exalted with worldly good fortune. For when it sees that it surpasses others in power, with pride it thinks highly of itself. And when the authority of its word is not opposed by anyone, the tongue is unbridled and wags dangerously. And while the mind is allowed to do what it likes, it considers what it likes to be justly permitted. But holy men, when they are supported by worldly power, subject themselves to greater discipline of the mind, the more they realize that through the insensibility of power, in a way they are being urged to indulge rather freely in forbidden acts. Thus they prevent their hearts from contemplating their own glory, they restrain their tongues from immoderate talk, they guard their actions from the deviance of restlessness. For often they who are in power forfeit the good things that they do because of their proud thoughts, and while they consider themselves to be helpful for all purposes, they detract from the merit even of the service they have rendered. For in order that a man's deeds may be more meritorious, they must always seem of no great worth in his own opinion lest an action that is good exalt the heart of the benefactor and by doing so dispossess through pride the author of the deed more perhaps than it helps those for whose benefit it was performed. For hence it is that the king of Babylon, while he was ruminating in the pride of his heart, saying: *Is not this the great Babylon which I have built?* was suddenly turned into an irrational creature.[47] For he lost what he had become because he would not humbly disregard what he had done. And because in the pride of his heart he extolled himself above men, he lost what he had in common with men, human understanding. And often they who are in power give utterance at random to insulting language directed to their subjects, and this asset—that they wield power with vigilance—they lose by reason of their impudence of speech, clearly considering with insufficient fear the words of the judge that he who shall say to his brother without cause: Thou fool, shall be in danger of hell fire.[48] Often they who are in power, while they are unable to refrain from lawful actions, fall into those that are unlawful and unreserved. For he does not descend to unlawful things who circumspectly restrains himself at times even from lawful things. Paul rightly makes it known that he was bound by this restraint when he says: *All things are lawful to me; but all things are not expedient.*[49] And in order to show with what great freedom of mind he was liberated by this bond, he further declared: *All things are lawful to me, but I will not be brought under the power of any.*[50] For when the mind seeks fulfillment of the desires that it has fostered, it is convicted of being enslaved to the things by the love of which it is overcome. But Paul, to whom all things are lawful, is brought under the power of none because by restraining himself even from lawful things, he rises above those things, the enjoyment of which would weigh him down, by spurning them.

Therefore, in order to instruct us, blessed Job makes known what he was like when in power, saying: *Have I not dissembled?* For power that is possessed must both be kept in mind to be useful and disguised to avoid pride, so that he who makes use of it to advantage must know he possesses it, and in order not to be prideful, must appear to be unaware of it. Now, to show what he was like in speech, Job adds: *Have I not kept silence?* Finally, to show what he was like with respect to forbidden deeds, he also adds: *Have I not been quiet?* But the expressions *keep silence* and *be quiet* may well be more closely examined. Thus, to keep silence is to withhold response of the mind to the call of earthly desires. Again, tumult of the heart is a forceful source of great outcry.

Among the quiet are also those installed in power when they intermittently put aside the clamor of earthly matters for the love of God lest while the lowest concerns unceasingly prevail, the heart should entirely abandon the highest. For they know that the mind cannot be lifted up to things above if it is continually engaged in those below with tumultuous care. For what would that mind so engaged gain concerning God which even when disengaged strives with difficulty to apprehend anything about God? But it is well said by the Psalmist: *Be still and see that I am God.*[51] For he who neglects to be still before

God deliberately keeps the light of divine vision from his eyes. Hence also it is said by Moses that those fish that have no fins should not be eaten.[52] For the fish that have fins usually make leaps above the water. Thus they only are assimilated to the body of the elect in the manner of food who while they ply the depths, sometimes by leaps of the mind mount to things on high lest they always be hidden in the deeps of care and be reached by no breath of the highest love as of the free air. Therefore they who are engaged in temporal affairs then only deal properly with external things when they have recourse with solicitude to those of the interior, when they have no affection for the external din of disquietude but rest within themselves in the bosom of tranquility.

For the minds of the wicked do not cease to stir up within them the disturbances of temporal affairs even when not dealing with them. For they keep pictured in imagination the things they love, and although they are not externally active, yet inwardly they are exerting themselves under the weight of an uneasy quiet. And if the management of these same things should be granted to them, they entirely forsake their inner selves and follow these temporal and fleeting concerns with the unremitting steps of thought along the predetermined path. But religious minds do not seek such things when lacking and bear them with difficulty when present, for they fear having to go outside themselves by the care of external things. This is duly signified by the life of the two brothers concerning whom it is written: *Esau became a skillful hunter, and a husbandman: but Jacob a plain man dwelt in tents,*[53] or as is said in the earlier translation: *He dwelt at home.* For what is represented by Esau's hunting but the life of those who, unrestrained in external pleasures, follow the flesh? He is also described as a husbandman, for those who love this world cultivate the external to the same extent that they leave uncultivated their internal interests. But Jacob is called a plain man, dwelling in tents or at home, because, in truth, all who avoid being dissipated in external cares remain plain men in outlook and in the abode of their conscience. For to dwell in tents or at home is to restrain oneself within the secret recesses of the heart and not to waste oneself externally in desires, lest while people aspire to a host of exterior things, they turn away from themselves by the diversion of their thoughts. Therefore let him who was tried and strengthened in prosperity say: *Have I not dissembled? Have I not kept silence? Have I not been quiet?* For, as we have said above, when ephemeral prosperity smiles on such persons, they dissemble the favor of the world as though unaware of it, and with forceful determination they inwardly suppress the source of apparent self–satisfaction. But they keep silence since they are not unruly troublemakers. For all evildoing has its particular vociferation in the secret judgments of God. Hence it is written: *The cry of Sodom and Gomorrha is multiplied.*[54] And they are quiet when not only are they not carried away by any disturbing demand of temporal desires, but they also refrain from undue preoccupation with the necessary concerns of this present life.

10

Prelates need great discretion since those who govern management of things are exposed to the thrusts of the devil

The Chaldeans made three troops, and have fallen upon the camels, and taken them. Moreover they have slain the servants with the sword. And I alone have escaped to tell thee.[55] By camels, which have a clean characteristic since they ruminate, and an unclean one since they do not cleave the hoof,[56] are meant the good stewardships of temporal things: the more extensive the office is, the more does the enemy multiply his plots against us. For everyone who is put in charge of the management of temporal affairs is more extensively exposed to the thrusts of the hidden opponent. For some things a steward tries to do with a view to the future, and often while he cautiously foresees future circumstances with precision, he incautiously fails to see present dangers. Often while he is intent on present matters, he is inattentive to the anticipation of pressing events. Often when he does some things slothfully, he neglects what should be done with care. Often when he displays undue vigilance in his activity, by the restlessness of his way of acting he does greater harm to the interests of his office. But sometimes he strives to put restraint upon his tongue, yet is prevented from keeping silence by the requirements of his task. Sometimes while he gives himself greater latitude in conveying necessary information, he also makes known what he should not have communicated. But for the most part he is involved with so many variations of thought that he is hardly able to encompass the things which, looking ahead, he shifts about in his mind; and while he accomplishes nothing concrete, he labors diligently under great mental stress. For since the deliberations that occupy him are burdensome, even while disengaged and resting from external work, he is still wearied. For commonly the mind as if confronting things about to happen, devotes all its energy to the encounter; great heat of contention is generated, sleep is put to flight, night is turned into day, and while the bed supports the body seemingly at rest, a given matter is being thrashed over with strident disarray in the forum of the mind. And it frequently happens that none of the things foreseen comes to pass, and all that intense thought, laboring in complete conviction of the sequel, proves vain and ebbs away. And the mind is longer diverted from necessary concerns as it dwells to a greater extent on eventualities. Therefore since the evil spirits at one time level a blow against the interests of our stewardship by urging a hesitant or a headlong mode of action, at another time create confusion by suggesting a reluctant or fulsome use of speech, and almost always impose an excessive bulk of thought, the Chaldeans in three troops have taken the camels! For it is akin to making three troops against the camels to devastate the efforts of earthly stewardship at one time or another by unjustifiable deed, by excess of speech, by unregulated thought, so that while the mind is striving to devote itself effectually to practical management, it is cut off from consideration of itself and is the more unaware of the harm it inflicts on itself, the more inappropriate attention it gives to the affairs of others. But rightly does the mind, when undertaking the cares of stewardship, consider what is due to self and what to neighbors, and does not by excess of concern for others neglect its own interests nor by watching its own welfare, put aside the interests of others. But still very often while the mind is diligently careful about both—while it applies itself with great solicitude both for itself and for the matters that have been entrusted to it—if unexpectedly disturbed by some critical point that develops in a given case, it is so taken by surprise that all its precautions are suddenly frustrated. And thus the Chaldeans strike with the sword the servants watching over the camels. Yet one returns, for as such things are going on, the glint of discretion strikes the eyes of the mind, and the soul, coming to its senses, realizes what inner loss has been occasioned by the sudden access of provocation.

11

Prelates should entrust external affairs to be managed by those who have obtained wisdom in these matters; if such persons are not available, prelates themselves should perform such services

He who gives thought to the benefits of eternal recompense must seek every opportunity to merit such reward. For hence it is said by Solomon: *He that feareth God neglecteth nothing.*[57] Hence also Paul says: *Prepared unto every good work.*[58] But in these cases we should bear in mind that sometimes in our actions lesser good things are to be passed over in favor of greater ones. For who could be unaware that to bury the dead is a meritorious work? And yet to one who had asked to be given time to bury his father, it was said: *Let the dead bury their dead; but go thou and preach the kingdom of God.*[59] Thus this filial service had to be esteemed less than the duty of preaching, because by the former he would bury in the earth persons dead in the flesh, by the latter he would raise to life persons dead in the soul. By the prophet it is also said to the chiefs

of the synagogue: *Seek judgment. Relieve the oppressed.*[60] And yet the apostle
Paul says: *Set them to judge who are the most despised in the Church.*[61] For he was
inflaming the hearts of his hearers to the goodness of wisdom, to different
kinds of tongues, to searching also into the mysteries of prophecy, saying: *Be
zealous for spiritual gifts, but rather that you may prophesy.*[62] But because they
would not receive spiritual gifts if earthly matters had weighed them to the
ground, he indicated long beforehand: *Set them to judge who are the most despised in the Church.*[63] It is as though he said in plain words: Those who are of
less merit in the Church and are not strong with any power of great gifts should
judge concerning temporal matters, so that by whom great good cannot be
supplied, lesser good may be provided. These he at once calls despised and yet
wise, when he says: *Is it so that there is not among you any one wise man that is able
to judge between his brethren?*[64] From this fact what is to be inferred if not that
they are to try earthly cases who have received wisdom in external things? But
they that have been enriched with spiritual gifts surely should not be involved
with earthly matters, so that while they are not obliged to administer good
things of a lower order, being trained they may be able to serve the interests of
higher things.

But great care must be taken that they who shine forth with spiritual gifts
should not wholly forsake the affairs of their weak neighbors, but that they
should entrust these matters to be managed by others who are qualified.
Hence also Moses assigned to the people seventy men in his stead, so that the
more he withdrew from external affairs, the more fervidly he might concern
himself with things of the interior. And so it becomes possible for those in the
highest posts to progress toward spiritual endowments when things that are of
least importance do not beset their minds, and again those in the lowest positions in the Church are not deprived of worthy endeavors while in external
matters they find rewarding activity. For holy Church is constituted by a unity
of the faithful just as our body is made one by the unity of its parts. Thus there
are some members in the body which serve in perceiving light, others which are
not separated from contact with earth. The eye, of course, is directed to the
light, and in order that it may not be blinded, it is guarded from dust. But the
foot then rightly performs its function when it is not averse to contact with the
dust of the earth. These members of the body, however, by sharing their functions with each other are mutually joined together so that the foot should run
for the eyes, and the eyes should do the watching for the feet.

In just such a manner should the members of holy Church be both distinct
in office and united in charity so that the highest persons may see the way
ahead for those who are devoted to concerns of earth, so that for instance the

foot may walk by the light of the eyes, and again that whatever is done by those concerned with the affairs of earth may be applied to the service of the higher members, so that the foot, whose way is descried for it, may step not for itself only but for the eyes as well. Therefore while they serve one another in turn by reciprocal stewardship, in a marvelous way it comes about that since all the elect, working for one another, do what is in their power, those works also become their own which they themselves are unable to perform.

But meanwhile we should bear in mind that when there is a lack of persons to minister fittingly to the exterior needs of their neighbors, those too who are endowed with spiritual gifts must with good grace be of service to their weakness and as far as propriety permits, attend with the accommodation of charity to their earthly necessities. And it must not weary the mind if its inclination to be intent on the contemplation of the spiritual is sometimes directed, as though diminished, to dealing with the least concerns, when that Word by whom every creature is maintained, in order that he might benefit mankind, having assumed the nature of man, was willing to be made a little lower than the angels.[65] Therefore what wonder is it if man for man's sake diminishes himself, when the Creator of men and angels for man's sake took the form of man? And yet the inclination is not diminished when it is thus contracted, because it penetrates things above more acutely, the more humbly for the love of the Creator it does not shun things below. What is there that is unworthy of us or difficult, if we direct the mind above and below, when we wash the face of the body with the same hand with which we shoe the foot?

12

Prelates are able to carry out external duties with an ordered mind if they do not seek them with disordered affection

No one fully receives wisdom if he does not strive to withdraw himself from all disturbance of worldly actions. And hence it is said elsewhere: *The wisdom of a scribe cometh by his time of leisure: and he that is less in action shall receive wisdom.*[66] And again: *Be still and see that I am God.*[67]

But how are we to account for the fact that most of the ancient Fathers both vigorously retained this inner wisdom and outwardly administered the affairs of the world in the customary manner? Do we call Joseph deprived of the attainment of this wisdom who in the time of famine, taking upon himself the concerns of all Egypt, not only furnished provisions to the Egyptians but by the adeptness of his administration also preserved the life of foreign people who sought help?[68] Was Daniel devoid of this wisdom who when he was made by the king of the Chaldeans in Babylon chief of the magistrates, was engaged in greater duties by the higher degree of dignity that set him above others?[69] Since then it is plain that very often even the good are involved in worldly matters with no earthly self-interest, we clearly recognize that in this way the citizens of Jerusalem sometimes render public services to Babylon just as the citizens of Babylon are often employed in service to Jerusalem. For there are some persons who preach the word of life for the display of wisdom, minister the aid of alms from a desire of vainglory. And indeed the things they do seem to be proper to Jerusalem, but yet they are citizens of Babylon.

In this way, then, it sometimes happens that they who love only the heavenly country seem to be under the dominion of earthly concerns. Their service, nevertheless, is distinguished from the practices of the wicked for the most part in action, but sometimes before the heavenly judge in thought only. For full of wisdom from above, they discern how they may both be working at one thing outwardly and be applying themselves to another thing inwardly, so that if perhaps by God's secret appointment any worldly concerns are imposed upon them, apart from their initiative, they may yield to God whom they love and may from love of him interiorly desire only to see him, but for fear of him may externally carry out with humility what is imposed upon them, so that they both desire to be devoted to God by the grace of loving affection and again fulfill the duties imposed upon them by their state of servitude. And when activities cause an externally noisy state of affairs, inwardly most peaceful repose is maintained in love; and the disturbances of employment outwardly creating a din, reason as presiding judge makes inward adjustment and with tranquil governance regulates the things which on all sides are less tranquil. For as strength of will keeps control of carnal emotions, so very often the love of tranquility effectively governs the upsets that employment imposes because external duties, if they are not sought with disordered affection, can be executed with a mind not confused but regulated. For holy men do not seek these duties but lament their being imposed by inscrutable appointment, and although with a higher aim they are shunned, with a submissive mind they are endured. These concerns such men are most eager to avoid if possible, but fearing the secret dispensations of God, they take hold of what they flee from and execute what they avoid. For they have recourse to their conscience and there debate what the secret will of God ordains, and being conscious that they must be subject to the highest dictates, they submit pride of heart to the yoke of divine dispensation. But when anyone is so minded, whatever disturbances hold sway externally they never reach his inner being. And so the result is that there is one state maintained internally by desire and another maintained externally by duty, and that with this wisdom hearts are filled, no longer troubled and confused, but composed.

13

If prelates are very much attached to worldly concerns, those under their charge are made worse by their example

Some persons inquire why it is that while rectors, at least for the benefit of those under their charge, are very much attached to worldly concerns, many in the Church deteriorate through their example. Who can deny that this is very true when he sees worldly concerns more carefully attended to by pastors than heavenly interests? But these activities are not unjust if the customs of rulers are ordered in accordance with the merits of those under them. For sins committed secretly and willfully require that unworthy example be presented to them by their pastors in order that by a righteous judgment the proud man, who deviates from the way of God, may falter through the leadership of his pastor along the way in which he is proceeding. Hence it is also said by the prophet, with the zeal of one who is foretelling, not with the wish of one who is cursing: *Let their eyes be darkened that they see not: and their back bend thou down always,*[70] as if he were to say: Let those who are in charge, as those pointing out the paths of human action, not have the light of truth, in order that their subjects who follow them may be bent down by the handicaps of their sins and lose all semblance of uprightness. And this we know was undoubtedly the fact in Judaea when, at the coming of our Redeemer, the multitude of the Pharisees and priests closed the eyes of their mind to the true light, and the people walking according to the examples of its rulers, wandered in the darkness of unbelief.

But it can reasonably be asked how it is written that the Lord makes the hypocrite reign when by the prophet he complains particularly of this matter, saying: *They have reigned, but not by me: they have been princes, and I knew not.*[71] For who that thinks rightly may say that the Lord does what he did not know? But because for God to know is to approve, and not to know is to disapprove, hence he says to some whom he disapproves: *I know you not whence you are; depart from me all ye workers of iniquity.*[72] And sometimes for God to do something is his allowing in his anger that to be done which he forbids: hence he asserted that he hardened the heart of the king of Egypt,[73] because in fact he allowed it to be hardened. In a wondrous way God both makes hypocrites reign and knows them not: he makes them by permitting; he knows them not by rejecting them. Hence it is necessary with respect to everything which is desired in this life, that the divine will should first be probed. And when the ear of the human heart seeks to sense it, what should be known is that he speaks not in words, but in deeds. Therefore when a position of authority is offered, it is necessary for a man first to examine whether his way of life is suited to the post, whether his conduct is at variance with the honor, lest the just ruler of all should afterwards not heed prayers in tribulation because he is oblivious to the assuming of high office that is the source of tribulation.

14

Justice is not to be sold nor defended for a price

When the intention of service is in a dreadful way diverted to our own interests, sin completes the identical work that goodness began. Often even from the very beginning, thought seeks one thing, the deed discloses another.

Often not even the thought itself proves faithful to itself since it dangles one object before the mind's eye and is from afar designedly questing after another. For very often some persons seek earthly rewards; they support justice, and consider themselves innocent, and rejoice in being defenders of righteousness. If the prospect of monetary reward is withdrawn, instantly they cease from their defense of justice; and yet they think of themselves as defenders of justice and tell themselves they are upright, yet do not as just persons seek righteousness but money. Against this stance it is well said by Moses: *Thou shalt follow justly after that which is just*.[74] For he follows unjustly after that which is just who is stirred to the defense of justice not by the pursuit of virtue but by his love for temporal reward. He follows unjustly after that which is just who is not afraid to offer for sale that justice which he pleads. And so justly to follow after what is just is in the espousal of justice to seek that same justice. We often do right things and do not look for rewards nor for applause from our fellowmen. But yet the mind being built up in self-confidence, scorns to please those from whom it seeks nothing, belittles their opinions, and drives itself precariously free along the precipices of pride. And it is the worse overwhelmed beneath sin from the same source whence it boasts: that its sins are subdued, that it is subject to no covetous desires.

Often while we examine ourselves more than is called for, by our very desire of discernment we are the more undiscerningly led astray, and the acuteness of our mind is dulled the more it strives to perceive; for he too, who rashly gazes at the direct rays of the sun, impairs his vision and is rendered sightless from the very act of trying to see too much.

15

A prelate ought not to judge rashly unexamined matters nor to pass judgment precipitately

And the cause which I knew not, I searched out most diligently.[75] We must carefully see to it that in passing judgment we are never precipitate, that we do not rashly judge unexamined matters, that no adverse hearsay affects us, that what is said far and wide we do not believe without proof. These things surely we shall be afraid of doing if we consider more closely the actions of our Creator, for in order that he might deter us from hasty pronouncement of sentence, although all things are naked and open to his eyes,[76] yet he refused to judge the evil deeds in Sodom he heard of, since he says: *The cry of Sodom and Gomorrha is multiplied, and their sin is become exceedingly grievous. I will go down and see whether they have done according to the cry that is come to me: or whether it be not so, that I may know.*[77] Under these circumstances why does the omnipotent and omniscient Lord seem before the trial to hesitate, if not in order to give us an example of deliberation lest we presume to believe the misdeeds of men before we prove them? Observe how through his angels he comes down to establish misdeeds and immediately strikes the evildoers. And he who is patient, who is mild, of whom it is written: *But thou, Lord, judgest with tranquillity,*[78] of whom it is again written: *The Lord is a patient rewarder,*[79] finding them involved in such guilt, as it were, put aside patience and declined awaiting the day of final judgment for punishment but with the fire of judgment anticipated in their case the day of judgment. Observe how the evil he seemingly believed with difficulty when he heard of it, he still punished without delay when he established it to be true. Surely his purpose was to give us an example that more severe crimes are both to be believed with difficulty when they are heard of, and punished more quickly when they are verified.

16

Prelates must not plunge into an atrocious action through impatience or anger

Holy men, although they appear to be set above men by the glory of power, nevertheless inwardly offer to the Lord by their sorrow the secret sacrifice of a contrite heart, since *A sacrifice to God is an afflicted spirit.*[80] But all the elect by inward reflection are skilled in fighting against the temptations of external superiority. If they set their heart on their exterior good fortune, they assuredly would not be righteous. But because the human heart cannot be at all tempted to even the slightest degree of pride in material riches, they contend inwardly against this prosperity lest they yield—I do not say to pride—but to love of that prosperity. To have yielded in great measure to that love is equivalent to rendering the mind captive to its desires. But who that has a taste for earthly things, embracing temporal objects, would not believe blessed Job to be happy amidst so many signs of prosperity when health of body, the life of his children, the preservation of his household, the unimpaired condition of his flocks, were all granted to him? But that in all these circumstances he did not rejoice, he himself testifies when he says: *I went mourning*.[81] For to the holy man still placed in this state of pilgrimage, all that is present in abundance without the vision of God is indigence, because when the elect see that all things are theirs, they lament that they do not see the Creator of all things, and to them all else is too little since the sight of the uncreated is still lacking. And the grace of heavenly dispensation exalts them outwardly in such a way that inwardly the mourning of charity, the teacher, still holds them under discipline. Through it in fact they learn that in return for the things which they receive exteriorly they should always be more humble interiorly, should keep the mind under the yoke of discipline, should never by the boldness of power break forth into impatience. Hence also it is fittingly added: *Without indignation I rose up, and cried in the crowd*.[82] For often the disturbances of seditious men exasperate the spirit of their rulers, and by inordinate emotions they go beyond the bounds of their position.

And very often they who are placed in charge, unless in the expression of the heart they are restrained by the forbiddance of the Holy Spirit, spring forth into the fierceness of enraged retribution, and as much as they have power to do, consider themselves at liberty to do unto their subjects. For impatience is almost always in league with power and even rules over that power, when evil, as its subject, for power carries out the dictates of impatience. But holy men inwardly lower themselves more under the yoke of patience than their relatively higher outward position over people, and they display truer external dominion, the more humble servitude to God they internally maintain. And for this reason they often bear with certain persons more fully, the more they have it in their power to inflict punishment upon them, and in order never to pass over into unlawful actions, they very often are unwilling to carry out in their own behalf even what is lawful; they endure the protests of those under their charge, they rebuke out of love those whom they countenance with mildness.

17

Avoiding irascibility in correcting people

Let not anger overcome thee to oppress any man.[83] Everyone by whom the vices of others are to be corrected must first carefully examine himself lest while punishing faults of others, he himself should be overcome by his ardor for punishment. For fierceness, under pretense of justice, frequently confounds the mind; and while it seems to rage with zeal for righteousness, it satisfies the frenzy of its wrath and considers that it justly performs whatever its anger wickedly dictates. Hence also it frequently transcends the standard of punishment because it is not restrained by the moderation of justice. For it is fitting that when we correct the faults of others, we should first measure our own, that the mind should first subside from its own fierceness, allaying within itself the ardor of its zeal with calm equanimity, lest if we are led on by rash fury to chastise vices, we ourselves sin in correcting sin, and lest we, who are determining and censuring a fault, commit one by taking intemperate disciplinary action. Moreover, the result is not correction but rather the oppression of the offender if in punishment our anger goes beyond what the offense deserves. For in the correction of faults, anger must be under the control of the mind and not in command of it, so that it does not initiate and dominate the judicial process, but follows and serves it, administering the proper sentence that is handed down, not one that anger preconceives. Therefore it is well said: *Let not anger overcome thee to oppress any man*, because surely if he who is striving to correct is overcome by anger, he oppresses before he corrects. For while he is more inflamed than he ought to be, under the pretext of just punishment he is unbridled unto ferocity. This is frequently the case for this reason: the hearts of rulers are too little intent on the love of their Creator alone. For while they desire many things in this life, they are distracted by innumerable thoughts. And when they suddenly meet with faults of their subjects, they are unable to judge them rightly in God's name because they cannot at once rally their hearts dispersed in transitory cares to the summit of circumspection. Therefore when agitated, they discover less readily the balance of equity for the punishment of sins, the less tranquil are the circumstances under which they seek it.

We therefore—because we are weak men—when correcting those under our charge must first of all remember what we are so that from our infirmity we may decide in what due order of teaching we may encourage our weak brethren. Let us consider, then, that we are either now such as some of those whom we are correcting, or were such at one time, although by the working of divine

grace we are no longer thus, so that with humble heart we may the more temperately administer correction, the more truly we recognize ourselves in those
whom we correct. But if we neither are nor have been such as those still are for
whose improvement we are solicitous, lest our heart perhaps be proud and fall
the more wickedly by reason of that innocence, let us summon before our eyes
the other good qualities of those whose faults we are correcting. If there are
no such qualities, let us have recourse to the secret judgments of God, because
as we have received this good we possess by no merits of our own, so is he able
to infuse them with the grace of heavenly power, so that although spurred later
on, they may be able to overtake even those good qualities which we received
beforehand. For who would believe that Saul, who at his death watched over
the garments of those who were stoning him, would surpass Stephen, who had
been stoned, by the dignity of apostleship?[84] Therefore our heart must first be
humbled by these thoughts, and not till then should the sins of offenders be
reproved.

<h1 style="text-align:center">18</h1>

The pride of prelates who despise subjects and the pride of subjects who judge prelates

It should be known that pride attacks rectors in one way and subjects in
another. Thus it suggests to the thoughts of a rector that he has simply by the
quality of his life become greater than others, and what things he has done
well, it constantly brings to mind. When it suggests that he has been exception-
ally pleasing to God, in order to enforce its suggestion more easily, if offers as
evidence the award of power entrusted to him, saying in effect: Unless almighty God regarded you as better than those entrusted to you, he would not
have placed them under your governance. And soon pride exalts his mind,
pointing out that those under his power are mean and worthless, so that he no
longer regards anyone fit for him to speak to on equal terms. And hence his
peace of mind is soon replaced by wrath, because when he looks down on all,
when he rebukes without moderation the perceptiveness and conduct of all,
he billows the more unrestrainedly into anger, the more he considers that
those entrusted to him are his inferiors.

But on the other hand, when pride stirs up the heart of subjects, it particularly prevails upon them to neglect altogether consideration of their own
conduct and in their inmost thoughts to become constant judges of their ruler.
While they watch excessively for something to blame in him, they never see
anything to correct in themselves. And hence they come to more terrible grief,
the more they turn their eyes from themselves, because stumbling in the jour-

ney of this life, they fall prostrate while their attention is directed elsewhere. They admit that they are indeed sinners, but not to such an extent that they deserve to be consigned to the control of such a guilty person. And while they belittle his accomplishments, they scorn his precepts, they fall headlong into such madness that they think God has no concern for human circumstances because they feel anguish at having been placed under the charge of one who is as if canonically censured. And thus, while they show arrogance toward their rector, they also rise up against the judgments of their Creator. And while they pass sentence on the character of their bishop, they also cast aspersions upon the wisdom of him who governs all things. But they often impudently resist the commands of their rector and regard this haughtiness of language as the expression of freedom. For pride thus passes itself off as rightful liberty, just as fear is frequently identified as humility. For just as many remain silent through fear and yet consider that they are silent from humility, so do some speak from the impatience of pride, and yet think that they are speaking with the freedom of righteousness. But sometimes subjects do not voice their bold feelings, and they whose volubility is scarcely restrained are speechless on occasion solely from the bitterness of their inward animosity. They who withhold through distress of mind their expression of effrontery, although they are accustomed to speak wickedly, are more wickedly silent because when, having sinned, they hear any reproof, they keep back through indignation words of retaliation. When they are treated harshly, they often burst forth into words of complaint at this very harshness. But when their masters forestall them with gentleness, they are more highly indignant at this very humility by which they are outdone. And their mind is the more thoroughly inflamed, the more thoughtfully it is regarded as weak. Undoubtedly these persons—because they are ignorant of humility, the mother of virtues—lose the benefit of their labor even if there are any good things they seem to do since the lofty stability of the rising structure is not strongly assured when it lacks the strength of a foundation based on rock. Therefore what they build rises up only to fall because before erecting the superstructure, they do not provide the foundations of humility.

19

Subjects should not rashly judge the life of prelates

It is certain that the merits of rectors and people are so mutually connected that often the people's way of life is made worse from the fault of their pastors, and the pastors' way of life is changed according to the people's merits.

But because rulers have their own judge, subjects must be very careful not to judge rashly the conduct of their rulers. For the Lord himself did not without a reason pour out the money of the changers and overthrow the chairs of those who sold doves,[85] undoubtedly signifying that he judges the conduct of people by their rulers, but that he himself examines the deeds of rulers, although even those sins of subjects which are at present concealed from the masters or which cannot be judged by them are without doubt reserved for his judgment. Therefore while the matter is treated in good faith, it is the part of virtue if whatever pertains to a superior is tolerated; yet it ought to be humbly questioned whether anything that is displeasing can be amended. But great care must be taken lest an inordinate defense of justice degenerate into pride; lest humility, the teacher of what is right, be lost while righteousness is loved without due caution; lest anyone disrespect a superior whom he may perhaps happen to find blameworthy in some activity. But the mind of subjects is trained to guard its humility against this swelling of pride if its own weakness is constantly given attention. For we neglect to examine sincerely our own strength and because we believe ourselves stronger than we are, as a result we judge severely those who are placed over us. And the less heedful we are of ourselves, the more attention we give to those whom we endeavor to blame. These are the usual offenses that are often committed by subjects against their rulers, and by rulers against their subjects, because rulers consider all their subjects to be less wise than themselves, and again subjects judge the conduct of their rulers and if they happened to possess the power, think that they could do better. Hence it frequently comes to pass that rulers see less judiciously what is to be done because the blur of pride obscures their sight, and that a subject who becomes a prelate sometimes does what as a subject he used to maintain should not be done; and because of the fact that he does what he condemned, he is at least ashamed of his condemnation. Therefore as rulers must be on guard lest their higher position exalt their minds with a conviction of their singular wisdom, so must subjects take care not to be bent on finding fault with the conduct of their rulers.

20

Subjects fail exceedingly when they criticize good deeds or words of prelates when they do not understand them

Often the deeds or words of exemplary men displease those under their charge who fail to understand them, but they are not to be rashly criticized by their subjects insofar as what they do and say cannot be fully understood. Often something is prudently done by major superiors that is considered to be a mistake by others; often many things are said by the strong upon which the weak pass judgment without being properly informed. This is well represented by that ark of the testament being made to lean aside by oxen kicking: a Levite wishing to set it upright because he thought it would fall, immediately received sentence of death.[86] For what is the ark of the testament but the mind of the just man? As it is being carried, it is made to lean aside by the kicking of the oxen, since sometimes even he who rules well while he is shaken by the disorder of the people subject to him, is moved simply by love to a condescension in direction. But in this which is done prudently, that very leaning of firmness is considered a fall by the inexperienced. And hence some subjects put forth the hand of censure against it, but by that very rashness they at once pass from life. Thus the Levite stretched forth his hand in an attempt to be of help, but he lost his life in being guilty of offense, because while the weak censure deeds of the strong, they are themselves rejected from the lot of the living. Sometimes, too, holy men mention some things condescendingly on unimportant matters; some things they say while contemplating the most important, and foolish men, unaware of the meaning either of such condescension or loftiness, boldly censure them. And what is it to wish to correct a good man for his condescension but to support the ark that is leaning aside with the proud hand of rebuke? What is it to censure an upright man for misunderstood speech but to consider strong action a fall from grace? But he loses his life who haughtily lifts up the ark of God since no one would presume to correct the upright acts of the saints unless he first thought better of himself. And hence this Levite is rightly called Oza, which to be sure is interpreted the strong one of the Lord, since all the presumptuous, unless they boldly believed themselves strong in the Lord, would not condemn as weak the deeds and words of superiors.

But when any actions of meritorious men are displeasing to the undistinguished, the former are not to keep silent about their motives but should give expression to them with great humility, so that the purpose of one whose feelings are upright may truly follow the pattern of righteousness insofar as he proceeds along the path of lowliness of spirit. Therefore both all our thoughts are to be freely declared and all our disclosures are to be made most humbly lest even what we do with right intention we detract from by enunciating it in a spirit of pride. Paul had spoken many things to his hearers with humility, but it was about that humble exhortation itself he sought with still more humility to appease them, saying: *And I beseech you, brethren, that you suffer this word of consolation. For I have written to you in a few words.*[87] Likewise, bidding farewell to the Ephesians at Miletus who were grieved and lamenting, he recalls his humility to their remembrance, saying: *Watch, keeping in memory that for three years I ceased not with tears to admonish every one of you, night and day.*[88] Again he says to the same persons by letter: *I, therefore, a prisoner in the Lord, beseech you that you walk worthy of the vocation in which you are called.*[89] Therefore let whoever thinks at all rightly infer from what has been said, with what humility the disciple ought to address the teacher, if the apostle of the gentiles himself, in the things he preaches with authority, beseeches the disciples so submissively. Let everyone hereby conclude how humbly he should address those from whom he has received examples of good living, indeed whatever he rightly comprehends, if Paul restricted himself to humble speech addressing those whom he himself raised up to life.

21

A revered prelate is not always to be imitated / Why God places on the stern and industrious the burden of ruling

If the way of life of rulers is justly reprehensible, subjects must revere them even when they are disliked. But you must see to it that you do not seek to imitate a person whom it is necessary for you to revere and that you do not scorn revering him whom you refuse to imitate. For the narrow path of rectitude and humility must be followed so that the blameworthy conduct of rulers is disliked in such a way that the mind of subjects may not abstain from observing respect for their office. This is well portrayed in Noe when inebriated, whose exposed secret parts his good sons came and covered with averted gaze.[90] For we are said to be averse to that which we reject. What is signified then by the fact that his sons, coming with averted gaze, cover the shame of their father with a cloak thrown over their backs, except that the misdeeds of their rulers are to be offensive to their good subjects in such a way that they still conceal them from others? They bring a covering with averted gaze because judging the deed and revering the office, they do not wish to see what they conceal.

But there are some who, if they have made any small beginning in a spiritual mode of life, on considering that their rulers are engaged in worldly and temporal pursuits, soon find fault with the decree of heavenly disposition because they were improperly appointed to rule by whom examples of worldly ways are made manifest. But these persons, while they neglect to refrain from censure of their rulers, as their fault ostensibly demands, proceed to blame even the Creator. His dispensation is judged to be more correct by the humble for the very reason that it is not judged to be right by the proud. For because the power of office cannot be exercised without tending to worldly concerns, often almighty God in his wondrous dispensation of mercy, enjoins the burden of ruling on stern and industrious hearts in order that the sensitive minds of spiritual men may be disjoined from worldly care so that the latter may be more safely shielded from the world, the more willingly the former devote themselves to worldly anxieties. For harsh are the ways of earthly drudgery, even in the discharge of duty that has been undertaken for the needs of subjects.

And frequently, as has been said, as the merciful Lord tenderly loves his own, so in his concern does he shelter them from external occupations. For often the father of a family assigns his servants to that work from which he frees his frail sons, and the sons are of pleasing appearance and free from annoyance, from the fact that the servants are the ones begrimed with dust. How properly this is effected in the Church by divine appointment is signified by the construction of the tabernacle. For Moses is commanded by the voice of God to weave curtains of fine linen, scarlet and purple, for the covering of the Holy of Holies within. And he was ordered to spread, for the protection of the tabernacle, curtains of haircloth and hides, to withstand the rains, and winds and dust.[91] What then do we understand by the hides and haircloth but the stern minds of men who sometimes although they are harsh are by the secret judgment of God placed high in the Church? Because they do not fear being engaged in temporal concerns, they must bear the winds and rains arising from the hostile elements of this world. But what is signified by the purple, scarlet and fine linen if not the life of holy men, finely wrought but brilliant? While it is carefully hidden in the tabernacle under haircloth and hides, its beauty is preserved unimpaired. For in order that in the inner recesses of the tabernacle the fine linen may shine, the scarlet glitter, and the purple be resplendent with dark–colored brilliance, the hides and the haircloth ward off the rains, the winds, and the dust overhead. Therefore they who advance in great virtues within the bosom of holy Church must not belittle the activities of their rectors when they see that they apply themselves to external matters. For the fact that the former delve in safety into secret mysteries is attributable to the help of the latter who struggle exteriorly against the storms of this world. For how would the fine linen retain the attractiveness of its brilliance if it were in contact with the rains? Or what splendor and clarity would the scarlet or purple display if the dust were to penetrate and defile them? Therefore let the strong texture of the haircloth be placed above to resist dust, the brightness of the purple fit for adornment be placed beneath. Let those who are engaged in spiritual pursuits alone adorn the Church. Let the Church be protected by those who are not wearied even by the toil of temporal matters. But let not the one who now gleams spiritually murmur against his superior who performs external tasks.

For if you shine securely within, like scarlet, why do you inveigh against the haircloth that protects you?

22

Those who seek to govern lest they be subject to others, and those who fear to reprove the powerful

Certain people, thinking themselves persons of great merit, preferring themselves to others through pride of heart, believe all to be inferior to them. Of what other person are they members but of him of whom it is written: *He beholdeth every high thing. He is king over all the children of pride?*[92] Certain other people seek the power of this world, not that they may be of help to others but that they may not be subject to another. Of what other are they members than of the one concerning whom it is written: *Who said: I will sit in the mountain of the covenant, in the sides of the north. I will ascend above the height of the clouds. I will be like the most High?*[93] For the most High alone so rules over all things that he cannot be subject to another. The devil perversely wished to imitate him when seeking dominion of his own, he refused to be subject to the Lord. Whoever therefore seeks for power of his own, imitates the devil because he disdains to submit to him who is placed over him by heavenly decree.

There are in addition many things which proclaim certain persons, established in the peace of the Church, to be faithless. For I see that some so accept the rank of someone in power as not to hesitate when requested by him to deny in return for his good will the truth of a neighbor's cause. And who is truth but the one who said: *I am the way, and the truth, and the life?*[94] For John the Baptist did not die when questioned about his faith in Christ, but about the truth of justice,[95] but because Christ is the truth, he therefore went even to his death for Christ, that is, for the truth. Let us suppose that a person has, when questioned, accepted the rank of the powerful and has denied the truth that he might not suffer revenge for an affront. What, I ask, would he do in the pain of punishments, who was ashamed of Christ among the scourges of words? Observe that even after this he is still a Christian before the eyes of men, and yet if God is disposed to judge him strictly, he is one no longer.

But I see others to whom are assigned through their position as teachers, the duties of exhorting and reproving, who see something unlawful committed and yet, when they fear losing the good will of certain powerful persons, do not dare to reprove it. Whoever he is, what else does he do but see the wolf coming and flee?[96] He flees because he was silent; he was silent because, eternal grace having been disowned, he preferred temporal glory. Observe that faced with a powerful man, he hid himself in the recesses of his silence and gave way to secret fear just as to open persecution. It is well said of such: *They loved the glory of men more than the glory of God.*[97] If these things are strictly judged, whoever is such, even though public persecution was lacking, yet he denied Christ by his silence. Therefore the temptations of Antichrist are not lacking even in the peace of the Church. Let no one, then, shake with terror at those times of the last persecution as the only ones to fear. For the cause of Antichrist is daily promoted among the ungodly, because although hidden he is even now working his craft in their hearts. And if many, now apparently established within the Church, pretend to be what they are not, yet at the coming of the judge they will be revealed for what they are. Solomon well says of them: *I saw the wicked buried; who also when they were yet living were in the holy place, and were praised in the city as men of just works.*[98]

23

The task of preachers and mindfulness of the theme, the time, and the hearer in preaching

It is certainly not a common practice to consider what labor there is in the preachings of the Fathers, with what great pains and endeavors they, as it were, bring forth souls in faith and righteousness, with what attentive prudence they control themselves that they may be forthright in their commands, compassionate toward weakness, terrifying in threats, persuasive in exhortations, humble in exercising their authority, outstanding in their contempt for temporal goods, unyielding in the endurance of adversity, and yet weak, when they do not attribute their strength to themselves; how great is their grief for those who fall, how great their fear for those who stand firm, with what zeal they seek to gain some things, with what uneasiness they maintain others which they have achieved.

They first consider their inner selves and become cleansed of all stains of vices, taking great care to shine forth against anger with the light of patience, against the lust of the flesh to gleam with purity of heart, against sloth to be bright with zeal, against the confused emotions of rashness to be ardent with serene gravity, against pride to shine with true humility, against fear to be aflame with the rays of authority.

Especially must they beware, when they are endowed with gifts of teaching, lest they be proud on that account. How displeasing to almighty God it is to be exalted among one's neighbors because of divine gifts!

With whatever great learning the mind may be favored, it is a sign of great inexperience to wish to instruct someone who is further advanced. For words fail to convey conviction when they are not suited to the hearer, since even medicines lose their efficacy when they are applied to healthy parts of the body. Therefore in all that is said, it is necessary that the theme, the time, and the hearer be taken into consideration: whether the truth of the statement justifies the words employed, whether the time is suitable for the declaration, whether the character of the hearer renders the message both inapposite and untimely. For he lets loose his arrows in a creditable manner who first looks at the enemy that he is to strike; he ineffectively wields the horns of the strong bow who in propelling the arrow strikes a comrade.

Therefore it is carefully to be considered that the same exhortation is not suited to all, because equally strong habits do not influence all. For those things that help some, often hinder others. For often even herbs that refresh certain animals kill others; a gentle whistle pacifies horses, urges on dogs; medicine which eases one disease, aggravates another; bread which strengthens the life of the sturdy, destroys that of the young. Therefore the speech of teachers must be devised according to the condition of the hearers, in order to suit individuals and yet be of service in promoting general edification. For what are attentive minds but certain strings which are drawn taut in a harp? These the skillful master touches in different ways that they may not produce a discordant sound. And the strings render a melodious tone because they are struck with the same pick but not with identical force. Hence also each teacher, in order to edify all in one virtue of charity, must not touch the hearts of his hearers with one and the same exhortation.

All seasons are not adapted to teaching. For the force of observations is frequently lost if they are uttered out of season. And often even what is said gently is strengthened by the concurrence of a fitting season. Therefore he knows how to speak well who also knows how to remain silent at the proper times. For of what avail is it to rebuke an angry man at the time when with disturbed mind he is not only unable to listen to the words of others but is scarcely able to put up with himself? For he who reproves an angry man by attacking him is like someone inflicting blows on an inebriate who does not feel them. Therefore in order to be able to reach the heart of the hearer, teaching must be reserved for moments of time suitable to it.

Therefore if a fault has suddenly ambushed one who is mild and self-controlled, the preacher by rebuking the offense at once, follows up and corrects him, and by correcting frees him from guilt and directs him again in the way of righteousness. But on the other hand, when a powerful and impudent man is known to have been guilty of an offense, an opportunity is sought in order that he may be rebuked for the evil he has done. For unless the preacher waits until he may be able to bear correction appropriately, he increases in him the evil that is being attacked. For it often happens that he is such as to be unreceptive to any words of rebuke. What then is the preacher to do in the case of the sin of this person except that in the discourse of admonition, given for the common well–being of all his hearers, he brings up such faults as he sees that he has been guilty of who is present and cannot as yet be confronted on his own personal account lest he be made worse? And while general condemnation is directed against the fault, the word of rebuke readily penetrates the mind since the powerful offender does not know that it is specifically uttered against him. Hence it very often happens that he laments the sin committed the more bitterly even when he feels himself involved, the more he considers his guilt to be unknown.

Therefore it must be arranged with great skill in preaching that those who are made worse by open rebuke by a certain moderation of reproof regain health. Hence also Paul says: *And such as we think to be the less honorable members of the body, about these we put more abundant honor; and those that are our uncomely parts have more abundant comeliness. But our comely parts have no need.*[99] For as there are uncomely members in the body, so there are persons in holy Church, powerful and impudent, who while they cannot be attacked with open condemnation, are as it were veiled with the respectfulness of a covering. But we speak, as mentioned above, of the secret transgressions of the powerful, for when they sin and others know of it, they are also to be rebuked, and others should be aware of it, lest if the preacher be silent, he seem to have sanctioned the sin, and what the tongue of the pastor does not curtail, should come to be a precedent.

24

Holy preachers from outward signs examine secret faults

Holy teachers are often accustomed to exaggerate the vices of offenders, and from certain outward signs to examine secret faults, in order from the smallest of them to discover greater. Hence also it is said to Ezechiel: *Son of man, dig in the wall.* Next he says: *And when I had digged in the wall, behold, a door.*[100] To dig in the wall is to expose hardness of heart by sharp reproofs. When he digs in it, a door appears because when hardness of heart is revealed, a kind of opening is beheld through which all the secret thoughts of the person who is reproved are seen.

But when they proceed in this way, they are fired with the love of charity, and are not puffed up with the swelling of pride. For they greatly fear that if they should cease to reprove the wicked, they would be punished themselves for their damnation. And when they are stirred to words of reproof, they un-willingly have recourse to them, but yet prepare them as a defense for themselves before their strict judge.

Hence it is said to Ezechiel: *O son of man, take thee a tile and lay it before thee: and draw upon it the plan of the city of Jerusalem. And lay siege against it and build forts and cast up a mount and set a camp against it and place battering rams round about it. And take unto thee an iron pan and set it for a wall of iron between thee and the city.*[101] Ezechiel represents rulers, and to him it is said: *Take thee a tile and lay it before thee: and draw upon it the plan of the city of Jerusalem.* For holy teachers take to themselves a tile when they take hold of the earthly heart of hearers in order to instruct it. And they place this tile before them because they guard it with the full attention of their watchfulness. And they draw the city of Jerusalem upon it when in their preaching they earnestly show to earth-ly hearts how great is the vision of heavenly peace. All around, or against the tile on which Jerusalem is drawn, they lay siege when they make known to an earthly mind now seeking its heavenly country what an opposition of sins as-sails it during this life. For when it is pointed out how each separate sin plots against the mind, the siege of Jerusalem is, as it were, outlined by the voice of the preacher. For preachers build forts when they do not cease making known what virtues oppose what vices. They cast up a mount when they point out the mass of increasing temptation. And they set up camps against Jerusalem when they warn their rightly disposed hearers about the cautious and almost unbe-lievable snares of the crafty enemy. And they place battering rams round about when they make known the stings of temptations surrounding us on ev-ery side in this life and piercing through the wall of virtues.

An iron pan is taken up by them when zeal for the Lord tortures and tor-ments the minds of preachers. For by the pan is indicated torture, and by the iron, strength. Paul was burned by the torture of this pan when he said: *Who is weak, and I am not weak? Who is scandalized, and I am not on fire?*[102] They place an iron pan as a wall between them and the city because all who are inflamed against sinners by divine zeal make themselves secure with a neverfailing stronghold lest from neglected attention to preaching and governance they in-cur the misfortune of condemnation. For the iron pan is placed as an iron wall between the prophet and the city, because when teachers now display a deter-mined zeal, they afterwards maintain the same zeal as a strong rampart between themselves and their hearers, lest they then be given over to punish-ment if they have now been remiss in reproof.

25

Let preachers not set forth to the unlearned the mysteries of divinity but confine themselves to dealing with the Incarnation of the Lord

He who teaches must exercise diligent care to stay within the bounds of his hearers' capacity. For it is his duty to accommodate himself to their level lest while he speaks to the untutored on lofty matters that will not benefit them, he be more intent on self–aggrandizement than on instructing his hearers. But it is at the Lord's command that there are not only vessels but also cups prepared for the table of the tabernacle.[103] For what is denoted by vessels but expansive preaching, and what by cups but modest and restrained speaking about God? Therefore on the table of the Lord there are both vessels and cups made ready, so that in the teaching of the sacred word not only copious drafts but also more modest portions are offered to afford knowledge as in a tasting.

For what is too ample is not to be spoken to the weak, lest while they hear things beyond their comprehension, they be overtaxed by the words of preaching that should uplift them. For corporeal light that illumines sound eyes obscures weak ones, and while by dimmed eyes the gaze is directed to the brightness of the sun, frequently obscurity is generated by the light.

Therefore when holy preachers perceive that their hearers cannot grasp the import of divinity, their words are restricted to the Lord's Incarnation. Hence of the eagle, that is, of the understanding of the saints dwelling on the mysteries of divine nature and feeding on contemplation, it is said: *Her young ones shall suck up blood*.[104] As if it were plainly said: The eagle indeed feeds on the contemplation of divinity, but because the preacher's hearers cannot understand the mysteries of divinity, they are fed by hearing of the blood of the crucified Lord. For to suck up blood is to revere the weaknesses of the Lord's passion. Hence it is that the same Paul had already soared to the secrets of the third heaven,[105] and yet said to his disciples: *For I judged not myself to know anything among you but Jesus Christ, and him crucified*.[106] As if this eagle were plainly saying: I indeed behold afar off as my food the power of the divinity of Christ, but to you, still young, I give only the blood of his Incarnation to be absorbed. For he who, silent in his preaching as to the loftiness of divinity, teaches his weak hearers only of the blood of the cross, offers it, so to speak, to be assimilated by the young .

26

One ought not to preach for temporal gain; nevertheless preachers are to be supported so that they may homilize

When I washed my feet with butter.[107] The feet of the Lord we take to be holy preachers, of whom he says: *And I will walk in them.*[108] Accordingly, feet are washed with butter because holy preachers are filled with the richness of good works. For scarcely is preaching itself carried on without some shortcoming. For anyone preaching is either led to some slight indignation if he is not heeded or to some little pride if he is respected by those that hear him. Hence the Apostles also washed their feet so that from any slight contamination contracted in preaching they might be cleansed as from a type of dust picked up on a journey. And blessed James says: *Be ye not many masters, my brethren.*[109] And a little later: *For in many things we all offend.*[110] Therefore the feet are washed with butter because the dust gathered from the glory of preaching is wet and cleansed by the richness of good works. Or at least the feet are washed with butter when the wages due are paid to the holy preachers by those who hear, and those whom the enjoined labor of preaching wearies, the richness of good deeds exhibited by the disciples sustains, not that they preach that they may be fed, but that they are fed so that they may preach, that is, that they may have strength to preach; not so that the action of the preacher should be directed to getting nourishment, but so that the ministering of support should be of service to the usefulness of preaching. Hence by good preachers it is not for the sake of the means of subsistence that preaching is made available, but for the sake of preaching that nourishment is accepted. And as often as what is needed is bestowed on those who preach by those who hear them, preachers are not accustomed to rejoice in the gift of material things but in the reward granted to those who bestow them. Hence it is said by Paul: *Not that I seek the gift, but I seek the fruit.*[111] For the gift is the thing itself that is bestowed, but the fruit of the gift consists in bestowing it with a kindly disposition in view of the future reward. So we receive the gift in the object, the fruit in the heart. And because the Apostle was fed rather by the recompense of his disciples than by their giving, he indicates that he seeks not the gift, but the fruit.

Any preacher who teaches eternal truths that he may acquire temporal gains, is asssuredly brought to a foolish end,[112] since he is aiming to reach that point by effort from which he ought to have fled in uprightness of intention.

27

At times holy men refrain from preaching the word of God to unworthy hearers

When holy men cannot benefit those who hear them, they are even willing by keeping silence to be scorned lest they pride themselves on the display of their own wisdom. And when they say anything wise, they seek not their own glory but the life of their hearers. But when they see that they cannot by speaking win the life of their hearers, by keeping silence they hide their own knowledge. For we have recourse to imitating the life of the Lord as to a certain standard set before us. For he himself, since he saw that Herod did not seek improvement but wished to marvel at signs or knowledge, on being questioned by Herod gave no answer, and because he kept constantly silent, he departed amidst derision. For it is written: *And Herod, seeing Jesus, was very glad; for he was desirous of a long time to see him, because he had heard many things of him; and he hoped to see some sign wrought by him.*[113] Hence it is also added: *And he questioned him in many words. But he answered him nothing.*[114] But how greatly the Lord in remaining silent was despised is shown when it is promptly added: *And Herod with his army set him at nought and mocked him.*[115] On hearing this we must learn that as often as our hearers desire to learn from us noteworthy matters and not to change what is unworthy in themselves, we should say nothing, lest if we speak the word of God with display in mind, both the fault of those persons, which existed, would not cease and our own fault, which did not exist, would come about.

Someone may perhaps say: How do we know with what intent anyone hears? But there are many things that reveal the mind of him who hears, especially if our hearers both always praise what they hear, and never follow what they praise. This vainglory of speaking the great preacher Paul had shunned, when he said: *For we are not as many, adulterating the word of God; but with sincerity, but as from God, before God, in Christ we speak.*[116] For to adulterate the word of God is to think of him otherwise than he is, or to seek from it not spiritual fruits, but the corrupt offspring of human praise. But to speak with sincerity is not to seek for anything in God's word beyond what is requisite. But he speaks as from God who knows that he does not have from himself but that he has received from God what he says. But he speaks before God who in all that he says seeks not human applause but is mindful of the presence of almighty God, and who craves not his own glory, but the glory of his Creator. But he who indeed knows that he has received from God what he speaks, and yet in speaking seeks his own glory, speaks as from God but not before God, whom he considers as absent and does not set before his heart when he preaches him. But holy men speak both as from God and before God since they both know that they have from him what they say, and consider him to be as judge and hearer when they speak. Hence it happens that knowing themselves to be disregarded by their neighbors, and their words to be of no help to the life of the persons hearing them, they hide whatever goodness may be theirs lest if the speech uttered disclose the secret of the heart to no purpose, it should give way to vainglory.

BOOK 5

THE JUST

Prologue

The discussion of prelates, who are considered to be higher in the Church, is followed by the fifth book of Part 2 which treats of the just in general.

This book will make known to the reader the remedy for those things taken up in the fifth book of Part 1. For therein were discussed the reprobate, who giving free rein to their concupiscences, by impure pleasures and desires incur eternal punishments. But in the present book are discussed the just, who controlling the reins of carnal desires and remaining poor in spirit, through temporal troubles attain eternal inheritance.

1

Active and contemplative life

The two lives, active and contemplative, when they are preserved in the soul, may be likened to the eyes in our countenance: the right eye represents the contemplative, and the left the active life. But there are some who are by no means able to behold separately the highest and spiritual things, yet take to the heights of contemplation and by the error of distorted understanding fall into the pit of unbelief. Thus the contemplative life, taken up by them beyond their powers, compels them to fall, truth not having been examined: the active life alone might have kept them humbly safe in the state of righteousness. To them Truth rightly says: *And if thy right eye scandalize thee, pluck it out and cast it from thee. It is better for thee having one eye to enter into life than, having two eyes, to be cast into hell fire.*[1] As if he said in plain words: When you are not qualified for the contemplative life by suitable discretion, hold more safely to the active life alone, and when you fail in what you choose as great, be content with what you consider as very little, so that if by the contemplative life you are compelled to fall from the knowledge of the truth, you may by the active life alone be able to enter into the kingdom of heaven at least with one eye. Hence he says again: *He that shall scandalize one of these little ones that believe in me, it were better for him that a millstone should be hanged about his neck and that he should be drowned in the depth of the sea.*[2] What is signified by the sea but this present age, and what by the millstone but earthly activity? The latter, while it weighs down the neck of the mind by foolish desires, dispatches it to a continual round of labor. And then there are some who, while they abandon earthly activities and rise beyond the powers of their understanding in pursuit of contemplation, having put humility aside, not only hurl themselves into error but remove any that are weak from the lap of unity. Therefore it would be better for him that offends one of the least to be cast into the sea with a millstone fastened to his neck since indeed it would have been more advantageous for one of untrained mind that, attentive to the world, he were engaged in earthly matters, than for him in exercises of contemplation to contribute to the destruction of many. On the other hand, if the contemplative life were not better suited to some minds than the active life, the Lord would not say by the voice of the Psalmist: *Be still and see that I am God.*[3]

But in this matter it should be noted that often both love stimulates slothful souls to activity and fear holds back restless souls in contemplation. For a weight of fear is an anchor of the heart, and very often the heart is shaken by a flood of thoughts but is held fast by the chains of self–control, and the tempest of its disquietude does not make shipwreck of it since perfect charity holds it fast on the shore of divine love. Hence it is necessary that whoever is preparing for the exercises of contemplation first question himself precisely as to how much he loves, for the force of love is a motive power of the mind which while it withdraws it from the world, lifts it on high. Let him then first examine whether he loves in seeking the highest things, whether he fears in loving, whether he knows how either to comprehend unknown truths while he loves them, or to revere truths not comprehended while he fears them. For in contemplation if love does not stimulate the mind, the torpor of its lukewarmness makes things unintelligible. If fear does not oppress it, sense lifts it by vanities to the mist of error, and when the closed door of secret things is being opened to it rather slowly, by its own presumption it is driven farther away from that door for it strives to force a way to what it seeks without finding, and when the proud mind takes error for truth, by seeming to advance inwardly, it is moving outward. Hence it is that the Lord about to give the Law, came down in fire and smoke,[4] since he both enlightens the humble by the brightness of his manifestation and darkens the eyes of the proud by the cloud of error. Therefore the soul must first be cleansed from longing for temporal glory and from the pleasure of all carnal concupiscence and then be lifted up to the insight of contemplation. Hence also when the Law is received, the people are forbidden to go up the mount, obviously so that they who with frail minds still desire earthly objects, may not presume to consider sublime things. And hence it is rightly said: *And if so much as a beast shall touch the mount, it shall be stoned.*[5] For a beast touches the mount when the mind that is dominated by irrational desires lifts itself to the heights of contemplation. But it is stoned, since not being equal to the highest things, it is laid low by weighty blows from above.

Therefore let all who strive to possess the summit of perfection when they desire to attain the eminence of contemplation, first test themselves by exertion in the field of effort, so that they may carefully discover if they now no longer bring harm upon their neighbors, if—when troubles are brought upon them by their neighbors—they bear them with composure, if—when temporal advantages come their way—the mind is never wasted by self–indulgence, if—when they are withdrawn—it is not affected by excessive regret, and then let them weigh carefully if—when they return inwardly to themselves in this task of exploring spiritual things—they never bring along with them the shadows of corporeal objects, or when brought along, as they may be, if they drive them away with the hand of discretion; if—when they long to behold uncircumscribed light—they repress all images of their limitation, or in what they seek to attain above themselves, conquer what they are. Hence it is now rightly said: *Thou shalt enter into the grave in abundance.*[6] For the perfect man comes to the grave in abundance since he first collects the works of the active life and then by contemplation completely hides from the world his fleshly sense that is now dead. Hence also it is fittingly added: *As a heap of wheat is brought in its season.*[7]

Thus the season for action comes first, that for contemplation comes last. Hence it is necessary for every perfect man first to train his mind in virtues and afterwards store it in the granary of repose. For hence it is that he whom the legion of devils left at the command of the Lord, seats himself at his Savior's feet, receives words of instruction, and eagerly desires to leave his region in company with the author of his recovery. But Truth himself, who brought recovery to him, says: *Return to thy house and tell how great things God hath done to thee.*[8] For when we receive ever so little knowledge of God, we are indeed disinclined to return to human affairs, and we object to burdening ourselves with the needs of neighbors; we seek the peace of contemplation, and love only what refreshes us without exertion. But after we are healed, Truth sends us home, orders us to tell the things that have been done for us; so that manifestly the soul must first tax itself in labor and afterwards may be refreshed by contemplation.

Hence it is that Jacob served for Rachel and received Lia, and it is said to him: *It is not the custom in this place to give the younger in marriage first.*[9] For Rachel is interpreted the beginning seen, but Lia laborious. And what is designated by Rachel but the contemplative life, what by Lia but the active life? For in contemplation the beginning, which is God, is sought, but in action we labor under a weighty burden of needs. Whence Rachel is beautiful but sterile, Lia is dull-eyed but fruitful, since truly when the mind seeks the leisure of contemplation, it sees more, but it begets fewer children of God. But when it takes up the laborious work of preaching, it sees less, but it has more offspring. Accordingly, after the embrace of Lia, Jacob attains to Rachel since everyone that is perfect is first joined to an active life in productiveness and afterwards united to a contemplative life in rest. The fact that contemplation comes later in time but is greater in merit than the active life is shown by the words of the holy Gospel, in which two women are described as having made different choices. For Mary sat at our Redeemer's feet, hearing his words, but Martha was occupied with material services. And when Martha complained about Mary's inactivity, she heard these words: *Martha, Martha, thou art careful and art troubled about many things; but one thing is necessary. Mary hath chosen the best part which shall not be taken away from her.*[10] For what is typified by Mary, who sitting down heard the words of the Lord, but the life of contemplation, and what by Martha, taken up with outward services, but the active life? Yet Martha's occupation is not reprehended, but that of Mary is even praised. For the merits of the active life are great, but of the contemplative, greater. Hence Mary's part is declared not destined to be taken away from her, since the works of the active life pass away together with the body, but the joys of the contemplative life become stronger hereafter.

2

In the active life the just by alms and tears gain eternal life

There are some who, engaged in earthly activities, by the help of alms and tears attain to eternal life; concerning them it is said by the Psalmist when the Lord is announced as coming to judgment: *He shall call heaven from above; and the earth, to judge his people.*[11] For he calls heaven from above when they who leaving all their possessions maintain a heavenly mode of life, are called to sit with him in judgment and come with him as judges. The earth also is called from above when they who had been bound to earthly courses of action, nevertheless sought in them heavenly more than earthly gains; to these persons it is said: *I was a stranger, and you took me in; naked, and you covered me.*[12]

But there are others in the hardship of this pilgrimage who, because they are not yet permitted to contemplate that appearance of their Creator which they yearn for, regard all the fullness of the present life as indigence because nothing apart from God satisfies the mind that truly seeks him; and very often to such persons their abundance itself becomes extremely burdensome because this they bear oppressively: that in hastening to their country they carry many things on the journey. Hence it happens that these things they devotedly share with their neighbors who are in need, in order that while this one gets what he has not, the other puts aside what he had in excess, lest either the companion on the journey go empty-handed or an excessive burden weigh down the one whom it might delay on the way. Therefore the elect do not rejoice at their great abundance, which for love of their heavenly patrimony they either by giving distribute or by disdaining abandon.

3

In the active life some of the just use possessions lawfully and others through the contemplative life give up all things

There are some of the righteous who desire heavenly things in such a way that they are still not torn away from the hope of earthly things. The inheritance bestowed on them by God they keep for the relief of necessities, the honors awarded them on a temporal basis they retain; they do not seek to gain the things of others, they make lawful use of their possessions. Yet they are indifferent to those things they have, since they are not bound in affection to those goods which they keep in their possession. And there are some of the righteous who, fortifying themselves to attain the very height of perfection, while they aim at higher inward goals, abandon all external things, divest themselves of possessions, despoil themselves of the pride of honor, dispose themselves by persevering patronage of grief to long for the things of the interior, refuse to receive consolation from those that are exterior: while in spirit they draw near to inward joys, they fully dissociate themselves from the life of earthly enjoyment. For it is said by Paul to such as these: *For you are dead; and your life is hid with Christ in God.*[13] The Psalmist had spoken in their voice when he said: *My soul longeth and fainteth for the courts of the Lord.*[14] For they long but do not faint who already indeed seek heavenly things, but yet are still not tired of the enjoyments of earthly things. But he longs, even faints, for the courts of the Lord who while he desires eternal things, does not continue on in the love of the temporal. Hence the Psalmist says again: *My soul hath fainted after thy salvation.*[15] Hence Truth himself gives admonition, saying: *If any man will come after me, let him deny himself.*[16] And again: *Every one of you that doth not renounce all that he possesseth cannot be my disciple.*[17]

Hence Jacob, sleeping on his journey, saw angels ascending and descending.[18] To sleep on a journey is in this life to close to the desire of temporal objects the eyes of the mind which concupiscence opened for our first parents. Angels ascend and descend when they cling to their Creator above them and in

the compassion of charity come down to help us. He who sees the angels in his
sleep is he who lays his head upon a stone, that is, clings to Christ in his mind.

Hence Jacob, who took hold of an angel, immediately afterwards was
lame in one foot,[19] for he who looks upon sublime things with true love, already is unable to turn to this world with double–faced desires. For he rests
upon one foot who is strong in the love of God alone; and it is necessary that
the other should wither, for when the virtue of the soul gains increase, it follows that the strength of the flesh becomes inert.

4

The way the newly regenerate must look upon themselves

They who leave the world must not be promoted to external offices unless through humility they are long established in contempt of that world. For
good deeds soon perish when made known to men prematurely, for if the hand
touches and shakes newly–planted shrubs, it makes them wither. If a wall that
is being built is pushed, it is easily destroyed; if it is permitted to become dry,
often it is not crushed by the blows of the battering rams. Hence it is that
Moses forbade employment of what was starting life, saying: *Thou shalt not
work with the firstling of a bullock: and thou shalt not shear the firstlings of thy
sheep.*[20] For to work with the firstling of a bullock is to display the beginning of
a good career in the employment of public business; to shear the firstlings of
sheep is to deprive incipient good deeds of concealment from the eyes of men.
Both are forbidden, since if we begin anything notable, we must not be too
ready to perform it in public. And if we begin something simple and unobjectionable, it must not be shown divested before the eyes of men.

Therefore let the firstlings of the bullocks and the sheep serve for the
divine sacrifices alone, doubtless so that whatever we begin well, we may sacrifice to the honor of God on the altar of our heart. Often even the beginnings
of a new way of life are commingled with carnal life, and on that account must
not at once become known, lest while the good aspects that are pleasing receive praise, the evils that lie concealed cannot be discovered. Hence again
Moses says: *When you shall have planted fruit trees, you shall take away the first–
fruits of them. The fruit that comes forth shall be unclean to you: neither shall you
eat of them.*[21] Trees that bear fruit are works fruitful in virtue, and we take
away the first-fruits when we do not give our approval to the beginnings of our
good works. The fruit that comes forth, as unclean to us, we do not eat because
when the beginnings of good works are praised, it is fitting that the praise
should not gratify the mind of the one who is its object.

Hence the Psalmist says: *It is vain for you to rise before light: rise ye after you have sitten.*[22] To rise before light is to rejoice in the night of the present life before the brightness of eternal reward appears. Therefore first we are to be seated, that we may rightly rise hereafter, for whoever does not now humble himself of his own accord is not exalted by the glory to come.

5

The regenerate who fall short and those who advance

And as a palmtree I shall multiply my days.[23] The palm below is rough to the touch, above it is fair in appearance and fruitful; below it is compressed, above it is spread out in profusion of greenness. A property the palm tree has as opposed to other trees is that it starts out slender from the bottom, but grows huge at the top.

Hence properly it is also compared to the life of the righteous who, weak in earthly pursuits, in heavenly ones are strong. Other trees, however, are like those enamored of the world who are strong in earthly things, weak in those that are heavenly; who for things of earth submit to injuries, for those of heaven refuse to bear the insult of a single word. Again, like most trees are those who, when they are brought to conversion, do not persevere in what they have begun; who propose to themselves brave things, but achieve only lowly ones and imperceptibly while they progress by increase of age, suffer losses of virtue. To the palm, however, which is of vaster extent in the summit, is the conversion of the elect to be compared: it accomplishes more in finishing than it proposes on setting out; and if it begins the first things somewhat lukewarmly, it completes the last more fervently; that is, it considers itself to be always beginning, and therefore it lasts unwearied in vigor. The prophet, regarding this constancy of the righteous, said: *They that hope in the Lord shall renew their strength: they shall take wings as eagles; they shall run and not be weary; they shall walk and not faint.*[24] For they renew their strength because they desire to be vigorous in spiritual practice who were for long attached to the flesh. And they take wings as eagles because by practicing contemplation they soar; they run and are not weary because they preach to the swift with great adroitness; they walk and do not faint because they control the quickness of their understanding so that they may accommodate themselves to their slower hearers. But under all circumstances the good things they receive they more willingly adapt to others, the more they keep themselves unchangeable in eagerness; and they who issue slender from the root of the beginning flourish in attainment of the topmost summit.

6

How the regenerate must regard temporal things

It is written in the Gospel: *If a man will take away thy coat and will contend with thee in judgment, let go thy cloak also unto him.*[25] And again: *Of him that taketh away thy goods, ask them not again.*[26] The apostle Paul also, wishing the disciples to despise outward things in order to be able to retain those that are within, admonishes them, saying: *Already, indeed, there is plainly a fault among you, that you have lawsuits one with another. Why do you not rather take wrong? Why do you not rather suffer yourselves to be defrauded?*[27] Yet there are those, having taken on the appearance of a holy way of life, who abandon the charge of their spiritual children and seek to defend, even by legal processes, certain temporal goods. They are not afraid to ruin hearts by their example and are afraid of losing their earthly patrimony as if by negligence. And if they have felt any temporal loss slightly inflicted on them, they suddenly burst forth, from their inmost souls, into the anger of revenge. And while they bear with equanimity the loss of souls, they hasten, even with agitation of spirit, to repulse the loss of temporal goods. And the more they love earthly things, the more vehemently are they afraid of being deprived of them. For we learn not in what state of mind we possess anything in this world except when we lose it. For whatever is possessed without love is lost without pain. But those things which we ardently love when possessed, we sigh for heavily when taken away. But who can be unaware that the Lord created earthly things for our use, but the souls of men for his own? Therefore a person is convicted of loving himself more than God if he protects those things that are his own, having neglected those that belong to God. For hypocrites do not fear to lose those things that belong to God, that is, the souls of men, and as if about to render an account to a strict judge, are afraid of losing what are their own, things namely that are passing away with the world. It is as if they would find him appeased to whom they offer material and undesirable objects, having lost those which are desirable, that is, which are rational. We wish to possess something in this world, and behold Truth proclaims: *Unless a man hath renounced all that he possesseth, he cannot be my disciple.*[28]

How then may a model Christian defend by argument earthly goods that he is ordered not to possess? Surely, when we lose our own possessions, we are relieved of a great burden in the journey of this life if we perfectly follow God. But when the necessity of this same journey imposes on us the care of possessions, some persons are simply to be endured while they seize them, but others are to be prohibited without violation of charity, not however merely from anxiety lest they take away our possessions, but lest by taking another's possessions, they destroy themselves. For we must fear more for the robbers themselves than desire to defend material possessions. For these, even though not stolen, we lose at our death; but we are united with the other persons both now in the human condition we share, and should they strive to amend their lives, after their reception of grace. But who can be unaware that we must love less the goods we use and love more what we ourselves are? Therefore if we argue with thieves, even for their own benefit, we are not only claiming for ourselves those things that are temporal, but for them also those that are eternal.

But in this matter careful attention is called for lest through fear of need, covetousness overtake us and a prohibition, kindled by zeal, when stretched by rather intemperate force, be transformed into the baseness of hateful contention. And while peace with our neighbor is wrested from our hearts for the sake of something earthly, it is clearly apparent that our wealth is loved more than our neighbor. For if we have no deep feelings of charity even for our thieving neighbor, we do more harm to ourselves than the thief does, and despoil ourselves more thoroughly than he could because by renouncing, of our own accord, the blessing of love, we forfeit internal wealth whereas through him we lost only what is external.

Therefore the saints know that all human justice is censured as injustice if it is judged strictly by God. Hence what is rightfully theirs they rigidly refrain from exacting lest it come to pass that heavenly justice examines their actions with exactness. But that they may be found just in divine judgment, very often in human judgments they suffer themselves to be treated even unjustly.

7

Some have died to the world, but the world is still alive for them

In bitterness of soul are all the elect, because they either do not cease by weeping to punish the transgressions they have committed or they grieve that relegated here far from the face of their Creator, they are not yet admitted to the happiness of the eternal fatherland. Of their hearts it is well said by Solomon: *The heart that knoweth the bitterness of his own soul, in his joy the stranger shall not intermeddle.*[29]

But it very often happens that a person no longer holds the world in his mind, but the world still fetters that person by its affairs. And he indeed is already dead to the world, but the world is not yet dead to him. For in a certain sense the world, very much alive, still keeps him in view so long as it strives to bear him away by its activities when he is inclined another way. Hence, since

Paul himself utterly scorned the world and saw that he had become one whom this world could not at all desire, having burst the bonds of this life and become free, he rightly exclaims: *The world is crucified to me, and I to the world.*[30] For the world was crucified to him because dead to his affections, he no longer loved it. But he had also crucified himself to the world since he strove to show himself such to it that, as though dead, he could never be coveted by it. For if there should be in one place a dead person and a living one, although the dead does not see the living, yet the living person does see the dead; but if both are dead, neither by any means sees the other. Thus he who no longer loves the world, but yet even against his will is loved by it, although he himself being as if dead sees nothing of the world, yet the world still not dead sees him. But if neither he himself keeps the world in his affections, nor in return is kept in the affections of the world, both are mutually dead to each other, since insofar as neither seeks the other, it is as if the dead heeds not the dead. Many, however, do not altogether reach the peak of this extinction, for although they do not themselves clasp the world, yet they still fear being such as the world grips, since unless they were living to it in some slight degree, the world would surely never love them for their usefulness in its interests. For the sea keeps living bodies in it, but dead ones it at once thrusts away from itself.

8
Not suddenly but gradually are the heights reached

At every step of mine I would pronounce it.[31] Of these steps it is said by the Psalmist: *They shall go from virtue to virtue.*[32] Contemplating holy Church, again he says of them: *In her houses shall God be known, when he shall protect her.*[33] For there is no attaining suddenly to the highest things, but to the loftiness of virtues the soul is led through increments.

The prophet Daniel took care to tell us the posture of his body when the Lord was speaking to him, and indicated these stages of merit. For he says: *I heard the voice of his words: and when I heard, I lay in a consternation upon my face, and my face was close to the ground. And, behold, a hand touched me and lifted me upon my knees and upon the joints of my hands. And he said to me: Daniel, thou man of desires, understand the words that I speak to thee, and stand upright: for I am sent now to thee. And when he had said this word to me I stood trembling. And he said to me: Fear not.*[34] This same posture of his body while he heard the words of one speaking inwardly, he would not set forth for us with so much care, if he had thought it was without mysteries. For in sacred Scripture not only what righteous men say is prophecy, but also very often what they do. Thus the holy man, abounding in hidden mysteries, by the posture of his body replaces the faculty of speech and by the fact that he first lay prostrate on the earth, that he afterwards raised himself on the joints of his hands and on his knees, that finally he stood erect but trembling, makes known to us in his bodily form the whole succession of our progress. For the words of God we hear lying on the ground when, buried in sins and subject to earthly defilement, we are acquainted with spiritual precepts by the voice of the saints. After these precepts, we are as it were lifted up upon our knees and the joints of our hands when, withdrawing ourselves from earthly infection, we henceforth raise our mind from things below. For as he wholly clings to the ground who lies in consternation, so he who is bent over upon his knees and the joints of his hands, his progress beginning, is already to a great extent separated from earth. But at last by the voice of the Lord we stand erect yet trembling when, wholly detached from earthly desires, the more fully we hear and recognize the words of God, the more we are afraid. For he still lies as though prostrate on the ground who fails to be raised from earthly desires to heavenly interests. But, being lifted up, he still leans upon hands and knees who already abandons some defilements but does not yet forgo some earthly practices. But at the word of God he now stands upright who fully lifts up his mind to sublime things and disdains being bent down by impure desires.

But it is rightly indicated that he stood trembling because the analysis of interior exactness is the more feared, the closer at hand it is. Hence it is fittingly added by the voice of God: *Fear not*, because the more we ourselves learn what we should fear, the more we have infused in us from God by interior grace what we may love, so that both our disdain little by little may turn into fear, and fear turn into charity so that because, with God seeking us, we resist by disdain and flee by fear, both disdain and fear being in time set aside, we may be joined to him by love only. For gradually we forget that fear and we are attached to him only by the force of love. Therefore, certain steps of progress having been taken, through fear we set our mind down low and afterwards through charity raise it to the heights of love.

9

The steps by which the soldier of God reaches highest things

Let us make known how the soldier of God advances from his original way of life, how he progresses from the least to greater things, or by what steps he proceeds from the lowest to the highest.

Let it be said then: *Wilt thou give strength to the horse, or clothe his neck with neighing?*[35] To every soul over which the Lord mercifully rules, he offers above all things strength of faith, of which Peter says: *Your adversary the devil, as a roaring lion, goeth about seeking whom he may devour; whom resist ye, strong in faith.*[36] But neighing is joined to this strength when that occurs which is written: *For, with the heart, we believe unto justice; but, with the mouth, confession is made unto salvation* .[37]

There follows: *Wilt thou lift him up as the locusts?*[38] Every follower of God is lifted up as a locust, for although in some of his actions he clings to the earth like the locusts with bended knees, yet in some of them he raises himself into the air with wings spread. For the beginnings of conversions are intermingled with good and evil habits, while both the new life is carried on in intention and the old life is still retained from habit.

The glory of his nostrils is terror.[39] Because of the fact that a thing which is not seen is detected through its scent, by the word nostrils are expressed, not improperly, the thoughts of our hope; by them we already foresee in hope the coming judgment, although we do not as yet discern it with our eyes. But everyone who begins to live righteously, on hearing that the just are by the last judgment called to the kingdom, is joyful; but because he considers that some evils still remain within him, he fears the approach of this very judgment about which he is beginning to rejoice. For he perceives his life to be a mixture of good and evil and confuses his thoughts to some degree with hope and fear. For when he hears what are the joys of the kingdom, happiness immediately encourages his mind; and again when he considers what are the torments of hell, fear immediately disturbs his mind. The glory of his nostrils is therefore properly called terror because placed between hope and fear, while he views in his mind the future judgment, he is terrified by the very thing in which he exults. His own glory is itself his terror because, having begun good deeds, he rejoices with hope in the judgment, and not having yet ended all evils, he is not entirely untroubled. But meanwhile he anxiously returns to his own mind, and disapproving storms of such great fear and composing himself in the calmness of peace alone, he endeavors with all his strength to be found unshackled by the strict judge. For he considers it base to fear the presence of the Lord and that he may not be afraid of seeing his Father, he does those things by which he may be recognized as his son. Therefore he learns to love his judge with full anticipation and, so to speak, through fear he casts away fear. But he considers that fear arises in the heart because of carnal conduct, and therefore before all things he chastises his flesh with firm dominance.

Hence, after it has been said: *The glory of his nostrils is terror*, it is rightly added: *He breaketh up the earth with his hoof.*[40] For to break earth with the hoof is to master the flesh by strict abstinence. But the more the flesh is restrained, the more securely does the mind rejoice at the hope of heaven.

10

The two–fold solitude of the regenerate, namely, that of the body and of the heart

We must diligently consider that solitude of the body is one thing, solitude of the heart another. But of what avail is solitude of the body if solitude of the heart is lacking? For he who lives bodily isolated but yet meddles with the disturbances of human mode of life through thoughts of worldly desires, is not in solitude. But if anyone is bodily hemmed in by crowds of people and yet experiences no commotions of temporal cares in his heart, he is not in a metropolis. To those therefore of good conduct solitude of spirit is first granted in order that they may control inwardly the rising sound of worldly desires, so as to restrict by the grace of heavenly love the cares of the heart which boil up from the lowest depths, and drive away from the eyes of the mind with the hand of seriousness all the agitations of trifling thoughts which rudely present themselves as flies fluttering around them, and may seek for themselves with the Lord some inner refuge where they may speak with him silently by their inward longings as outward sound subsides.

Of this shelter of the heart it is said elsewhere: *There was silence in heaven, as it were for half an hour*.[41] For the church of the elect is called heaven: as it rises to eternal verities by the uplifting of contemplation, it alleviates the tumults of thoughts which are springing up from below and produces a kind of silence within itself for God. Because this silence of contemplation cannot be complete in this life, it is said to have come about for half an hour. For while the contentious upheavals of thoughts force themselves into the mind against its will, they violently draw the eye of the mind, even when intent on things above, to look again at those of earth. Hence it is written: *The corruptible body is a load upon the soul: and the earthly habitation presseth down the mind that museth upon many things*.[42] Therefore the silence is well described as having taken place not for a whole but for a half hour, because contemplation is never perfected here, however ardently it is begun.

Therefore the righteous long for their eternal country and since they love none of the things of this world, they enjoy great tranquility of mind; and hence it is said with justice: *They build themselves solitudes*.[43] For to build solitudes is to banish from the heart's interior the stirrings of earthly desires and with a clear perspective of their eternal home to yearn in love for inward peace. Hence the prophet said: *One thing I have asked of the Lord, this will I seek after: that I may dwell in the house of the Lord*.[44] For he had sought quietness of mind as a kind of retreat where he would see God the more clearly, the more he saw the Lord alone with himself also alone.

And again: *Lo, I have gone far off, flying away: and I abode in the wilderness.*[45] Flying away, he goes far off who raises himself from a host of earthly desires in high contemplation of God. But he abides in the wilderness because he perseveres in the solitary intent of his mind. Of this solitude Jeremias says to the Lord: *From the presence of thy hand I sat alone, because thou hast filled me with threats.*[46] For the presence of God's hand is the just blow of his judgment with which he drove man in his pride from paradise, and banished him to the darkness of his present exile. But his threat is the dread of punishment yet to come. Accordingly after the presence of his hand, his threats further terrify us because both the penalty of our present banishment has already been imposed upon us in the experiencing of his judgment, and if we do not refrain from sinning, he further condemns us to everlasting punishments.

11

Three times of change by which the elect are influenced, namely, conversion, temptation, death

All these things God worketh three times within every one.[47] We must carefully consider what are these times during which man is affected by the disturbance of grief and after sorrow is returned to the security of joy. Therefore if we examine them attentively, we find that these three alternations of sorrow and joy take place in the mind of each of the elect at these stages, that is, conversion, temptation, and death.

In the first instance, conversion, great is the sorrow for each one considering his own sins who wishes to cast aside the heavy burden of temporal desires and to bear the light yoke of the Lord in a servitude that is really freedom. For as he thinks on these things, there comes to mind the carnal pleasure which, having become inveterate, binds him more closely the longer it has held him. Making its presence felt is distress of heart, when the Spirit calls him on one side, the flesh calls him back on the other; love for his new change of heart attracts on the one hand, his habit of wickedness contends on the other. Thus it can be said of this man: *Bread becometh abominable to him in his life,*[48] bread being the delight of human pleasure. Hence Jeremias said: *All her people sigh, they seek bread; they have given all their precious things for food to relieve the soul.*[49] The people sigh for bread when the wicked are not satisfied at will with the pleasantness of the present life, and they give all their precious things for food when they turn the virtues of the mind to transitory praise and relieve the soul with wicked desires.

But because divine grace does not permit us to be long affected by these difficulties, when the chains of our sins have been broken asunder, it leads us quickly by its consolation to our new life, and the joy which follows alters the former sorrow. Thus the mind of one who is converted rejoices the more on attaining its wish, the more it remembers what it has endured in pursuit of it, because through its hope of security it now draws near to the one whom it desires; so that it can rightly be said of it: *He shall pray to God, and he will be gracious to him.*[50]

But lest one who is converted should believe himself to be already perfect and a sense of security should overthrow him whom the struggle with sorrow could not overcome, in the dispensation of God, after his conversion he is harried with the goads of temptations. In a way, the Red Sea was already crossed by his conversion, but enemies still oppose him while he is in the wilderness of this life. We already leave our past sins behind us as so many dead Egyptians, but harmful vices as new enemies still confront us to block the way to the land of promise to which we are proceeding. Therefore lest conversion beget security, and security beget negligence, it is written: *Son, when thou comest to the service of God, prepare thy soul for temptation.*[51] He says, not for rest, but temptation, because the more our enemy perceives we are rebelling, the more he strives to conquer, for he refrains from attacking those whom he holds in quiet possession. Those subject to attack, the Lord by divine dispensation typified in his own person: he did not permit the devil to tempt him until after his baptism, thereby indicating to us that his members, when they were making progress toward God, would endure more severe sufferings. Therefore after the first alternation of sorrow and joy, which everyone experiences in his conversion, the second one begins, because he is assailed by temptations lest he become unwary through neglect of precaution. And generally at the beginning of his conversion great kindliness of consolation is bestowed, but afterwards there follows the hardship of trial.

In fact those who experience moral change pass through three stages: the start, the midpoint, the completion. In the beginning they find exhilaration; midway, struggles; in the end, fulfillment. First they are granted amenities to encourage them; next, austerities to test them; finally, transcendencies to establish them firmly.

Hence they generally receive in the beginning tranquility in the flesh, or gifts of prophecy, or the preaching of doctrine, or signs and wonders, or the grace of healing. And later they are harassed by the severe trials of temptations. This comes about through divine dispensation, for if the harshness of temptation were to coincide with their beginnings, they would easily relapse into the sins they had abandoned, from which they were not yet long separated. Hence: *When Pharao had sent out the people, the Lord led them not by the way of the land of the Philistines which is near: thinking lest perhaps they would repent, if they should see wars arise against them, and would return into Egypt.*[52] Thus to those who leave the world behind there is presented at first a certain tranquility, lest being affrighted in their sensitivity, they should return to that world from which they have escaped. They first feel gentleness; afterwards they find temptations more bearable, as they have found in God what is more worthy of love. Hence Peter first beholds the brightness of the Lord's transfiguration,[53] and then later on is permitted to be tempted by a maid, in order that having by contemplation become conscious of his weakness, he might have recourse with tears and love to what he had beheld.[54]

But the struggles with temptations often last as long as the exhilaration of those starting out. Frequently there is more pleasure given at first, and less trial in distress. But a disproportionate achievement of plenitude never follows the toil of temptation, because everyone is rewarded according to the outcome of the contest. But a convert commonly errs insofar as he considers that he has received the fullness of achievement when he is welcomed with the exhilaration of the beginning. Hence he less resists ensuing offenses because he does not more keenly foresee them. Even though he foresees them, he does not entirely avoid them, for our journey is not brought to a close without the dust of temptation. Yet a convert is generally assailed with the thrusts of such temptations as he was not subjected to before conversion, not because this same root of temptation did not then exist, but because it did not show itself. For the mind distracted with many matters is diverted from knowledge of itself; if it desires to be devoted to God, it then beholds without restriction what springs forth from the root of the flesh.

But generally these assaults of temptations, when they are of longer duration, cause less pain but do more harm for they become less feared the more usual they are. Meanwhile the straitened mind of the convert is so hard pressed that it may rightly be said of him: *Bread becometh abominable to him in his life,* and so on.[55] But because God in his mercy permits us to be tried by temptations, not to be cast away, he speedily calms with inward peace the surging thoughts that rise up in opposition. And soon the mind derives so much joy from its heavenly hope that of this man, tempted and liberated, it can be justly said: *He shall see God's face with joy.*[56] Ineffable joy is called jubilation, a joy which can neither be concealed nor expressed in words. It shows itself by certain emotions although it defies definition by invoking any of its qualities. Hence David: *Blessed is the people that knoweth jubilation,*[57] because jubilation can be known in the intellect but cannot be expressed in words. When these two stages of conversion have been passed in sorrow and joy, there remains the third, that is, the severe condition of death, because no one can arrive at the joys of perfect liberty unless the debt of the human condition is first paid. When each convert sees the end of his life approaching, he awaits the strictness of judgment, and although he has avoided all evil deeds that he could identify, yet he is more fearful on account of faults of which he is unaware. For it is easy to avoid wicked deeds but extremely difficult to cleanse the heart from unlawful thoughts.

But fear becomes more acute as, at the approach of death, eternal retribution comes closer. Hence our Lord, as death drew near, being for our sake in agony, prayed the longer,[58] indicating that the soul is then justly alarmed when it finds at hand the state of being that can never change. For then we carefully consider that we could not go through this life without guilt, because even what we have creditably done is not guiltless if we are judged without mercy. Hence David: *For in thy sight no man living shall be justified.*[59] And Paul: *I am not conscious to myself of anything. Yet am I not hereby justified.*[60] Likewise James: *In many things we all offend.*[61] And John: *If we say that we have no sin, we deceive ourselves and the truth is not in us.*[62] What then will the flooring do, when the columns tremble? Therefore, with death at hand, sometimes the just are stricken with the dread of punishment, so that it must be said: *Bread becometh abominable to him in this life,* and so on.

But because often there is cleansing of slight defilements through the very fear of death, by a sort of contemplation of eternal reward, there is rejoicing even before the dissolution of the flesh. There is already such enjoyment of gladness at the new gift that it is rightly said: *He shall see God's face with joy,* and so on. Therefore as the mind of each of the elect is three times—namely, in the distress of conversion, the temptation of trial, the dread of dissolution—first afflicted by sharp pangs of sorrow, so afterwards it is comforted by serenity of security: through his suffering he is purified and set free.

12

The peace of mind of the just who spurn earthly things

It insures great freedom from care to have no worldly covetousness. For if the heart longs to attain earthly things, it can not be secure and tranquil because either it desires to have things not possessed or it is afraid lest it lose things obtained, and while in adversity it hopes for prosperity, in prosperity it fears adversity, and it is tumbled about, hither and thither, by certain waves and is shifted about in various ways by the changeability of vacillating affairs.

But once the mind is settled with unwavering firmness in longing for its heavenly home, it is less troubled by the disorder of earthly things. Amidst all outward tumult it pursues its aim as a kind of most hidden refuge, and there clinging to the immutable and rising above all changeable things, by the very calmness of its repose, while it is in the world, it is not of the world. It truly goes beyond all things below by its striving for the highest, and it feels itself by a certain freedom to be superior to all the things that it does not seek, and inwardly it is not exposed to the tempest of temporal things it views outside, for all earthly things which, being longed for, could oppress the mind, being looked down upon, lie below. Hence it is rightly said to the prophet: *Set thee up a watchtower for thyself,*[63] so that anyone who observes things above, may surmount the bottommost things. Hence likewise Habacuc says: *I will stand upon my watch.*[64] For he stands upon his watch who by shrewdness of discipline does not succumb to earthly desires but rises above them, so that while he seeks ever stable eternity, everything transitory is beneath him.

Yet because with whatever virtue a holy man has advanced, the infirmity of the flesh still outwardly oppresses him while placed in this life, as it is written: *Although man walks in the image of God, yet he is disquieted in vain,*[65] it very often happens that he is at the same time disquieted externally and remains impervious to disquietude inwardly, and that he is liable to be disquieted in vain comes from the infirmity of the flesh, and the fact that he walks in the image of God comes from the power of the mind, in order that he should both be inwardly strengthened by divine assistance, and yet be still externally oppressed by the human burden. Hence Habacuc again has well put forth a single statement applicable to both instances. For he says: *And trembling entered into my bones, and my power was disquieted under me.*[66] As though he said: It is not my power, insofar as being transported above, I remain free from liability to disquietude, and it is my power insofar as I am disquieted under me. The same person is imperturbable above himself and perturbable below himself, because he had risen above himself insofar as he was transported to things on high, and he was below himself insofar as he trailed a remainder amid things beneath. The same person above himself was imperturbable because he had already entered into the contemplation of God; perturbable, because underneath he still remained a frail human being. The prophet David, agreeing with this opinion, says: *I said in the excess of my mind: Every man is a liar.*[67] To him it may be said in reply: If every man, then you too; and your statement will be false which you, being a liar, have uttered. But if you are not a liar, then the statement will not be true because while you are telling the truth, every man is not a liar. But observe the prefatory: *I said in the excess of my mind.* And so by

excess of the mind he even went beyond himself when he made a pronouncement about the character of man. As though he said in plain speech: I thence
delivered a true statement concerning the falseness of all men, whence I was
myself above man. He was thus himself a liar insofar as he was a man; but not
at all a liar insofar as by excess of the mind, he was above man.

In just this way all the perfect, although they are still subject to something
disquieting from the infirmity of the flesh, yet they already enjoy inwardly the
calmest retirement by the contemplation of the mind, so that whatever happens outwardly, it in no way disquiets them within.

13

The freedom of the just who stifle earthly desires

Great is the bondage of worldly pursuits by which the mind is grievously
worn down although such exertion is carried on of its own accord. To be free
from this state of slavery is no longer to desire anything in this world. For when
prosperity is sought and adversity feared, a typical yoke of servitude is imposed. But if anyone has once freed his mind from the bond of temporal
desires, he enjoys already a kind of liberty even in this life while he is affected
by no yearning for happiness here below and is confined by no dread of adversity. The Lord had in view this heavy yoke of slavery laid on the necks of worldly
men when he said: *Come to me, all you that labor and are burdened; and I will
refresh you. Take up my yoke upon you and learn of me, because I am meek, and
humble of heart; and you shall find rest to your souls. For my yoke is sweet and my
burden light.*[68] For it is, as we have said, a rough yoke and a weight of harsh
bondage to be subject to temporal concerns, to strive for things of earth, to
grasp things which are slipping away, to wish to stand on unstable things, to
seek transitory objects but yet to be unwilling to pass away with them. For while
all things, contrary to our wish, are fleeting, those things which had previously
distressed the mind with longing to acquire them oppress it afterwards with the
fear of loss. Hence it is asked by the Lord: *Who hath sent out the wild ass free,
and who hath loosed his bonds?*[69] Understand: except myself. For the wild ass,
which dwells in solitude, aptly signifies the life of those who dwell far removed
from crowds of people. That person is set free who, having despised earthly
desires, is released in security of mind from seeking temporal things. And his
bonds are loosed when with divine assistance the ties of carnal desires are broken asunder.

14

One must not rejoice because of his good deeds in such a way that there is no fear concerning similar acts which are neglected

There are many persons who when they do any good deeds, at once forget their misdeeds, and they fix their attention on consideration of the good works they perform; they deem themselves holy to such an extent that they shun, amidst the good things they do, the memory of their evil deeds, in which perhaps they are still entangled. If these same persons gave watchful heed to the strictness of the judge, they would fear more for their evil deeds than exult for their imperfect good ones; they would look more into the fact that for things that are still to be done they are held debtors, than the fact that by practicing some things they are already paying part of the debt. For he is a foolish debtor who with joy receives borrowed funds and does not direct his attention to the time when he must repay them. For neither is the debtor released who pays back much, but who pays back all; nor does he attain the prize of victory who during a great part of the contest runs with speed if, on nearing the goal, during what is left he falls behind. Nor to persons going to any determined places is it helpful, when setting out, to cover a long distance if they are not also able to go the whole way. What else are we doing who are seeking eternal life but making a kind of journey by which we are hastening to our home? But what gain is it that we go a great distance if we neglect the travel that remains before our arrival?

Thus after the manner of travelers we must consider not how much ground we have already traversed but how much there remains for us to cross so that by degrees the distance may be completed that is constantly and fearfully projected. Therefore we must have much more regard for the things we have not yet done than for those good things which we delight in having already done. But human weakness has this characteristic: to find it more inviting to look at what is pleasing in oneself than at what is displeasing. For the sick eye of the heart, while it fears being troubled in its observation, searches as it were for a comfortable couch in the mind on which it may lie at ease; and for this reason it descries what benefits it has acquired by the good things it has done, but it takes no notice of the losses it sustains from those which it has left undone. For very often even the elect are tempted by this vice. Very often their heart suggests they should recall to mind the good deeds they have done and rejoice now in the comfort of security. But if they are really elect persons, they turn away the eyes of the mind from that in which they are pleasing to themselves and repress any joyfulness for the good things they have done, and for those good things which they perceive that they have done in an inferior way, they seek sorrowfulness, they consider themselves unworthy and are almost the only ones not to see the good things which they demonstrate in themselves for the edification of all.

15

We must fear having sloth and deceit associated with good works

There are two things to be genuinely feared in our good deeds, namely, sloth and deceit. And hence in the old translation it is said by the prophet: *Cursed be he that doth the work of the Lord deceitfully and negligently*.[70] But it to be earnestly noted that idleness arises from insensibility, deceit from self-love. Inferior love of God accentuates the former while self-love, wretchedly possessing the mind, engenders the latter. For he practices deceit in the work of the Lord who, loving himself to excess, by what he may have done well is eager for the benefits of transitory reward. It is also to be noted that there are three ways in which deceit itself is committed when undoubtedly what is desired is either the secret regard of a human heart, or the breath of favor, or some outward gain, contrary to what is aptly said by the prophet of the righteous man: *Blessed is he that shaketh his hands from all bribes*.[71] For as deceit does not reside only in the receiving of money, a bribe is not confined to one thing, but there are three types of receiving which deceit is quick to pursue. A favor from the heart is regard elicited from esteem, a favor from the mouth is glory from approval, a favor from the hand a reward by gift. But every righteous person shakes his hands from all bribes since in whatever good he does he neither seeks vainglory from the heart of humans, nor approval from their lips, nor a gift from their hands. Therefore he alone does not practice deceit in doing God's work who while he is intent on right conduct, neither longs for material rewards, nor for words of praise, nor regard in man's judgment. Therefore because our good actions themselves are vulnerable to the sword of deceitful sin unless they are daily fortified by heedful fear, it is rightly said by holy Job: *I feared all my works*.[72] As if he said in humble confession: I see what I have openly done, but I am unaware what I may have thereby secretly carried out. For often our good qualities are utterly ruined by the piracy of deceit since earthly desires ally themselves with our upright actions. Often they are eclipsed by the interposition of sloth since by the cooling of love they are detached from the fervor in which they began. Therefore because blame slips into the very act of virtue and is eliminated with difficulty, no safeguard remains for our security if even in our virtue we are not inclined to quake with fear.

16

The desire of the saints, who delight in the remembrance of God

Whoever is still nourished by the pleasures of this life is cut off from the perception of eternal wisdom. For if he were truly wise, being banished from interior delights, he would mourn that blindness of exile into which he has fallen. For hence it is said by Solomon: *He that addeth knowledge addeth pain.*[73] For the more a man begins to know what he has lost, the more he begins to mourn the sentence of his corruption that he has incurred. For he sees whence and where he has fallen, that from the joys of paradise he has come to the tribulations of the present life; from relationships with the angels to troubles of exigencies. He considers in how many perils he now lies, who before disdained to stand without peril; he laments the exile that he undergoes in his condemnation and longs for the state of heavenly glory that he might be enjoying in security if he had refused to commit sin. Considering this fact the Psalmist rightly says: *I said in my fear: I am cast away from before thy eyes.*[74] For having contemplated the interior joys of the vision of God and the constant association with the faithful angels, he turned his gaze to things beneath and saw where he had fallen who was created that he might stand in heavenly realms; he considered where he was and lamented what he was, he mourned for himself as cast away from before the eyes of God because through the exemplification of the interior light he had felt the darkness of his exile that he was undergoing to be more pronounced. Hence it is that he does not admit to his soul the benefaction of any solace from the present life, saying: *My soul refused to be comforted.*[75] As though he said plainly: I who do not grieve for the loss of temporal things, can in no way be comforted by the abundance of them. And as though we ourselves, hearing these things, said to him: What then do you seek, who refuse to find comfort in those things that are of the world? Directly he added: *I remembered God, and was delighted.*[76] As if he said plainly: Nor does the abundance of earthly things refresh me, but even the simple remembrance of my Creator, whom as yet I am not able to see, gives me delight. Therefore this is the bitterness of the wise, that while they are raised on high in hope, they do not lower the mind to any delight here below. For hence it is written: *The heart of the wise is where there is mourning: and the heart of fools where there is mirth.*[77] Hence James says: *Be afflicted and mourn and weep; let your laughter be turned into mourning, and your joy into sorrow.*[78] Hence Truth himself bears witness, saying: *Blessed are they that mourn; for they shall be comforted.*[79] But the foolish, parting with greater things, delight in the least. Peter blames their folly, saying: *Counting for a pleasure the delights of a day of defile-*

ment and stain.[80] Hence Solomon says: *Laughter I counted error: and to mirth I said: Why art thou vainly deceived?*[81]

17

Those who think they are wise cannot contemplate the wisdom of God

They who seem to themselves to be wise are unable to contemplate God's wisdom since they are the more distant from his light, the less humble they are. And while the swelling of pride increases in their minds, it blocks the insight of contemplation: by reason of their belief that they outshine others, they thence deprive themselves of the light of truth. Therefore if we seek to be truly wise and to contemplate wisdom itself, let us humbly acknowledge ourselves to be dullards. Let us renounce harmful wisdom, let us learn praiseworthy folly. For hence it is written: *The foolish things of this world hath God chosen, that he may confound the wise.*[82] Hence again it is said: *If any man among you seem to be wise in this world, let him become a fool, that he may be wise.*[83] Hence the words of the Gospel narrative attest that when Zachaeus could see nothing because of the crowd, he ascended a sycamore tree in order to see the Lord as he passed by.[84] For the sterile fig tree is called a sycamore. Therefore Zachaeus, being low of stature, ascended a sycamore and saw the Lord because they who humbly choose the foolishness of the world contemplate to a certain degree the wisdom of God. For the crowd prevents those small in stature from beholding the Lord because the tumult of worldly cares restrains the infirmity of the human mind from looking at the light of truth. But we prudently ascend a sycamore if we carefully preserve in our mind that foolishness which is divinely commanded. For what is more foolish in this world than not to seek for what has been lost; to give up our possessions to robbers; to requite no wrong for the wrongs we have received, indeed, to show patience when other wrongs have been added? For the Lord commands us, as it were, to ascend a sycamore when he says: *Of him that taketh away thy goods, ask them not again.*[85] And again: *If one strike thee on thy right cheek, turn to him also the other.*[86] By means of the sycamore the Lord is seen as he passes by: although the wisdom of God is not yet firmly beheld as it really is by this wise folly, yet it is already seen by the light of contemplation as though passing by. They who seem to themselves to be wise can not see it, for caught up in the proud confusion of their thoughts, they have not yet found a sycamore in order to behold the Lord.

18

The divine majesty is not to be analyzed nor his secrets rashly examined

And if indeed I have been ignorant, my ignorance shall be with me.[87] Holy Church in all that she truly discerns, humbly depreciates her perception lest she be puffed up by knowledge, lest she show pride is seeking out hidden things and presume to examine some matters that are beyond her powers. For with more profit she is careful not to search things she is unable to examine rather than boldly define things she does not know. It is written: *As it is not good for a man to eat much honey, so he that is a searcher of majesty shall be overwhelmed by glory.*[88] For if the sweetness of honey is consumed in greater measure than is necessary, from the same source whence the palate is gratified, the life of the eater is impaired. Searching into majesty is also sweet, but he who seeks to examine more than human understanding permits is overwhelmed by its glory, since like honey consumed to excess, when it is not comprehended, it rends the perception of the searcher.

Hence it is written: *Barren with want and hunger.*[89] All who in sacred revelation strive to search into secrets of God beyond their capability, by their hunger become barren. For they do not seek those things by which they may educate themselves in humility, patience, forbearance, but those alone which may prove them copious in speech and eminently learned. For they very often treat with daring of the nature of divinity while they do not know their pitiable selves. Therefore they are barren with want and hunger who desire to search into those things by which they do not nurture the germinations of a good life. For the things that they scrutinize are beyond them, and while they direct their attention to what they are unable to comprehend, they neglect to acquaint themselves with those things by which they might have been instructed. This boldness of theirs the distinguished preacher rightly restrains, admonishing: *Not to be more wise than it behoveth to be wise, but to be wise unto sobriety.*[90] Hence Solomon says: *Set bounds to thy prudence.*[91] Hence again he says: *Thou hast found honey; eat what is sufficient for thee, lest being glutted thou vomit it up.*[92] For he who seeks to partake of the sweetness of spiritual understanding beyond his capacity, vomits up even what he had eaten, because while he seeks beyond his powers to understand the highest things, he loses even the things that he had well understood.

When Moses invites us to eat of the lamb, he commands those who partake of it: *If there be any thing left, we are to burn it with fire.*[93] For we eat the lamb when in understanding many particulars of the Lord's humanity, we mentally ingest them. Over and above, for us there are some things left that cannot be eaten because many particulars still remain concerning him that cannot be understood. Nevertheless, they are to be burned with fire because the things that we are unable to understand concerning him, we reserve with humility for the Holy Spirit. This humility very often reveals to the perceptions of the elect even those things that seemed impossible to understand.

19

No one can plumb the marvels of God who created all things from nothing

Who doth great things and unsearchable and wonderful things without number.[94] Who is able to plumb the marvelous works of almighty God: that he made all things from nothing; that the very structure of the world is arranged with wonderful might of power, and the vault of heaven hung above the atmosphere, and the earth balanced above the abyss; that this whole visible universe emerges from invisible things; that he created man, gathering together, so to say, in a small compass another world, a world of reason; that constituting this world of soul and flesh, he mixed the breath and the clay by an inscrutable ordering of his might? And so of these wonders, a part we know; a part we even are, but yet we fail to admire them, because those things that are marvels for investigation beyond comprehension have from habit become common in the eyes of men. Hence it happens that if a dead man is raised to life, all are startled with astonishment; yet every day a man who once was not is born, and no one marvels, while it is no doubt plain to all that it is a greater thing for that to be created which was without being, than for that which had being to be revived. Because the dry rod of Aaron blossomed,[95] all were in astonishment; every day a tree is produced from the dry earth, and the potency inhering in dust is turned into wood, and no one is amazed. Because five thousand men were filled with five loaves, all were astonished that the food had multiplied in their mouths; every day the grains of seed that are sown are multiplied in abundant ears of corn, and no one is surprised. All the guests were fascinated to see water once turned into wine;[96] every day the earth's moisture, being drawn into the root of the vine, is converted by way of the grape into wine, and no one is in awe. Full of wonder then are all the things that men fail to wonder at, because as we have said above, they have by habit become unresponsive to a consideration of them.

20

A person must not presume to investigate the secrets of divinity

Even if a man shall speak, he shall be swallowed up.[97] Everything that devours anything draws it inwards, conceals it from the eyes of onlookers, and bolts down something that could be seen in the light of day. Therefore when a man is silent about God, he seems to be important because of the reason with which he has been endowed. But if he begins to speak about God, it is at once shown how negligible man is because he is devoured by the immensity of God's greatness, and is borne below, as it were, and is concealed, since wishing to speak of the ineffable, he is swallowed up by the confines of his own ignorance. For flesh speaks of the Spirit, the circumscribed spirit of the uncircumscribed, the creature of the Creator, the temporal of the eternal, the mutable of the immutable, the mortal of the giver of life. And since, being placed in darkness, he does not know the inward light as it really is, a man who desires to discuss eternity speaks as a blind man does of the light. *If then a man shall speak, he shall be swallowed up*, because if a man wishes to speak of eternity as it is, he removes from himself even the perception he has of it when silent.

But in these circumstances it is to be noted that divine miracles must both be always under consideration with earnestness of mind and never be examined with inquisitiveness. For often the mind of man when it seeks and fails to find the reason of certain things, sinks into an abyss of doubt. Hence it happens that some men reflect that the bodies of the dead are reduced to dust, and while they are unable to deduce the power of resurrection from reasoning, they lose hope that bodies can be brought back to their former condition. Therefore wondrous things are to be believed through faith, not examined by reason, for if reason were to explain them to our satisfaction, they would no longer be marvelous. But when the mind wavers in these matters, those things it knows habitually, yet does not infer by reason, must be brought to mind so that by the reality of a similar occurrence it may strengthen faith that is found to be shaken by one's own cleverness.

21

Lightly esteeming temporal things, in temporal troubles the just seek eternal rest

The just neither take the benefits offered them here as anything great nor fear unduly misfortunes that are inflicted on them. But they both fear inconveniences to come while they use present advantages and are comforted by love of the good things to come when they lament present hardships. And thus they are aided by temporal assistance, just as a traveler uses a bed in an inn; he pauses and is eager to take his leave: his body is at rest, but his mind looks ahead elsewhere. But sometimes the just even long to suffer afflictions, they prefer not having all go well in transitory matters, lest by the delight of the journey they be delayed in arriving at their home, lest they hamper the progress of the heart on the path of their pilgrimage, and one day they get sight of the heavenly land with no reward. They delight to be looked down upon, nor do they grieve to be in affliction and necessity, and considering themselves pilgrims and strangers because they desire to delight in their own country, they refuse to be happy in a foreign land.

Hence it is written: *As a servant longeth for the shade, and the hireling looketh for the end of his work; so I also have had empty months, and have numbered to myself wearisome nights.*[98] To long for the shade is after the heat of trial and the sweat of labor to seek the rest of eternal revitalization. Moreover, he that longs for the shade is properly called a servant because as long as he endures temptations, he bears the yoke of lowly status.

He rightly also, *as the hireling, looks for the end of his work,*[99] for what the hireling considers heavy with regard to the work, he esteems light in view of the reward. Thus does each of the elect, when he suffers worldly adversities—when he endures insults concerning his character, losses in his possessions, bodily torments—the things which he regards as onerous he discovers are light, considering the reward. He also spends months empty of worldly profits when he does not seek present recompense through his actions; he also numbers wearisome nights because he bears the darkness of adversity not only to the point of indigence but often of bodily torment. For in this life there are some things that are hard, not empty, as from love of God to be disciplined by tribulations; some things are empty, not hard, as from love of the world to perish in pleasures; some things are empty and hard, as from love of the world to suffer adversity.

22

Eternal delights are gained only through temporal afflictions

Who hath given songs in the night?[100] A song in the night is joy in tribulation because, although afflicted with the distress of our temporal state, we already rejoice in the hope of eternity. Paul proclaimed songs in the night, saying: *Rejoicing in hope. Patient in tribulation.*[101] David had taken up his songs in the night when he said: *Thou art my refuge from the trouble which hath encompassed me: my joy, deliver me from them that surround me.*[102] Observe that his word for night is trouble, and yet in his distress he calls his deliverer his joy. There was indeed night externally in the encompassing trouble, but songs were resounding inwardly from the consolation of joy. For because we cannot come to eternal joys except through temporal afflictions, it is the whole purpose of sacred Scripture that hope of abiding joy should strengthen us amid these passing adversities. Hence also the prophet Ezechiel attests that he had received a book in which were written lamentations, a song, and woe.[103] For what are symbolized by this book except the words of God? For since they prescribe mourning for us, lamentations are said to be written in the book. The divine words contain also a song and woe, for they so proclaim joy from hope that they still announce present troubles and difficulties; they contain a song and woe, because although we seek for what is sweet hereafter, it is first necessary for us to endure bitterness. The Lord was proclaiming a song and woe to his disciples when he said: *These things I have spoken to you, that in me you may have peace. In the world you shall have distress.*[104] As though he said plainly. May you have from me what may fortify you inwardly by encouragement, because by the outside world you will be furiously hard pressed.

BOOK 6

THE GLORY OF THE JUST
Prologue

After the course of the present life and the happy completion of labors, the just receive the eternal prize. Hence the discussion of the life of the just having been completed, there suitably follows the book that is entitled The Glory of the Just. This, the sixth and last book of Part 2, treats of the remedy for what is discussed in the sixth book in succession of Part 1: The Punishment of the Reprobate. For there can be no more fitting remedy imagined for the torments of the unrighteous than the eternal blessedness of the saints, in which with Christ they reign for ever and ever. Amen.

1

How the resurrection of the body differs from the Resurrection of Christ

The mediator of God and men, Jesus Christ, was not born as other men, and he was not like them in his death, or in his resurrection. For he was conceived not by natural intercourse but by the Holy Spirit coming upon his mother, as it is said to Mary: *The power of the Most High shall overshadow thee.*[1] For a shadow is formed by light and body. But the Lord is light with respect to divinity, who—a soul being present—deigned in Mary's womb to become a body with respect to humanity. Therefore because the incorporeal light was in her womb to be made corporeal, to her who conceived the incorporeal with respect to a body, it is said: *The power of the Most High shall overshadow thee*; that is, the incorporeal light of divinity shall in thee take a human body.

Moreover, when born he showed the fruitfulness of his mother's womb and preserved her virginity. But again, when we do not wish it, we all die; it was not so in his case; he says: *I have power to lay down my life, and I have power to take it up again.* He also first said: *No one taketh it away from me; but I lay it down of myself.*[2] Again, our resurrection is deferred to the end of the world, but his gloriously took place on the third day. And we rise by him, he rises by himself. For as God he maintained with the Father and the Holy Spirit the power of resurrection, yet he alone in his human nature experienced it. Therefore because the Lord, truly born, truly dead, truly risen, still differs from us in all things by the greatness of his power, but conforms with us only in the authenticity of our nature, it is well said that, sent from heaven, he speaks for us as one *become like unto us.*[3]

2

Before Christ's death, saintly souls after death went to the netherworld

Before our Redeemer by his own death suffered the punishment of the human race, the gates of hell held fast after their release from the flesh even those who followed the paths leading to the heavenly country, not so that pain should punish them as sinners, but that while abiding in rather remote regions they would be barred by the guilt of the first sin from entrance into the kingdom since the intercession of the mediator had not yet been offered. Hence, according to the word of our Redeemer himself, the rich man who is tormented in hell beholds Lazarus in the bosom of Abraham.[4] Surely if the latter two were not still in the lower regions, the one in the place of torment would not have seen them. And hence our Redeemer, dying to pay the debt of our sin, descends into hell that he may bring to the realms of heaven all his followers who had been attached to him. But if man had refused to sin, he surely would attain even without redemption the state to which redeemed man ascends.

And yet we do not say that the souls of the righteous did thus go down into hell that they might be held in places of punishment, but it is to be believed that there are higher regions in hell and that there are other lower regions, so that both the righteous might be at rest in the upper regions and the unrighteous be tormented in the lower ones. Hence also the Psalmist says: *Thou hast delivered my soul out of the lower hell.*[5]

For the saints of old, when brought out of the body, could still not be at once freed from the regions of hell since he had not yet come who would descend there without sin that he might liberate those who were held there because of sin. In those very regions of hell the souls of the righteous were kept without torment, so that both on account of original sin they should still go there, and yet because of their own deeds not undergo punishment.

But there is no doubt that man, who fell in person, was unable in person to enter into the rest of paradise unless the one came who by the mystery of his Incarnation were to open the way for us to that same paradise. Hence also after the sin of the first man it is mentioned that a flaming sword was placed at the entrance of paradise; the sword is also said to be turning every way,[6] since the time would come one day that it could also be removed.

But when the Lord returned from hell, he did not carry off the elect and the lost together, but he took away from there all that he knew beforehand would have been attached to him.

3

How angels and saints desire to see God whereas they do see him

There are some who suppose that the angels do not see God because it is said by the first preacher of the Church: *On whom the angels desire to look,*[7] and yet we know that it is said in a statement by Truth himself: *Their angels in heaven always see the face of my Father, who is in heaven.*[8] Does, then, Truth voice one thing and the preacher of truth another? But if both statements are compared, it is determined that they are not at variance with each other. For the angels at once see and desire to see God; and thirst to behold, and do behold. For if they so desire to see that they do not enjoy the fulfillment of their desire, fruitlessly does desire have anxiety, and anxiety has punishment. But the blessed angels are far removed from all punishment of anxiety because never can punishment and blessedness come together. Again when we say that the angels are satisfied with the vision of God, because the Psalmist says: *I shall be satisfied when thy glory shall appear,*[9] we must keep in mind that aversion usually follows satiety. Therefore, so that the two may rightly agree, let Truth say: *They always see,* and let the eminent preacher say: *They always desire to see.* For that there may not be anxiety in desire, in desiring they are satisfied, and that there may not be aversion in their satiety, while being satisfied, they desire. And therefore they desire without distress, because desire is accompanied by satiety. And they are satisfied without aversion, because the very satiety itself is ever being inflamed by desire. So also shall we too one day be, when we shall come to the fountain of life. There shall be enjoyably ingrained in us at one and the same time a thirsting and a satiety. But from the thirsting, necessity is far removed, and aversion far from satiety, because both in thirsting we shall be satisfied, and in being satisfied we shall thirst. Therefore we shall see God himself, the reward of our labor, so that after the darkness of our mortality we may be made happy by the illumination of his light.

4

In eternal light we shall see God as he is

Thou shalt call me, and I will answer thee.[10] We are said to answer anyone when we requite his deeds with corresponding actions in return. Consequently, in that sort of exchange the Lord calls and man answers to the extent that in the brightness of the incorruptible, man is revealed as incorrupt after corruption. For now, as long as we are subject to corruption, we do not in any way answer our Creator, inasmuch as corruption being far from incorruption, there is no similarity suited to our answering. But of a change in that regard it is written: *When he shall appear we shall be like to him; because we shall see him as he is.*[11] Then therefore we shall truly answer God who calls when at the command of the supreme incorrupt being we shall arise incorruptible. And because the creature is not able to achieve this by itself, it is brought about by the gift of almighty God alone that a created being should be changed to that exalted glory of incorruption.

5

Full peace of the saints and what their souls know

In sacred Scripture full peace is described in one way, and incipient peace in another. For Truth had given to his disciples peace in its beginning when he said: *Peace I leave with you; my peace I give unto you,*[12] and Simeon had desired to have full peace when he had prayed, saying: *Now thou dost dismiss thy servant, O Lord, according to thy word in peace.*[13] For our peace begins in longing for the Creator, but it is perfected by a clear vision. For it will then be perfect when our mind will neither be blinded by ignorance nor weakened by an attack of the flesh.

Hence it is written: *The rest of thy table shall be full of fatness.*[14] The rest of the table is the restoring of inward satiety, which is said to be full of fatness because it is provided by the delight of internal pleasure. The prophet desired to eat the food of this table when he said: *I shall be satisfied when thy glory shall appear.*[15] He was thirsty for the drink of this table when he said: *My soul hath thirsted after the strong living God: when shall I come and appear before the face of God?*[16]

But it should be observed that just as they who are still living do not know in what place the souls of the dead are held, so the dead are unaware how the life of those living after them in the flesh is being carried on, since the life of the spirit is far from the life of the flesh, and as the corporeal and incorporeal are different in kind, so are they distinct in knowledge. This, however, is not to be understood concerning the souls of the saints, since we cannot in any way suppose that there is anything external that they do not know who inwardly behold the brightness of almighty God. Outwardly there is nothing that they do not know who know him to whom all things are known.

6

The saints remember past faults without any diminution of glory for them

The servant will be *free from his master.*[17] In heaven the servant will be free from his master on this account: he will be where there shall no longer be doubt about the pardon of sin, the memory no longer condemns the untroubled soul for its guilt, the conscience does not tremble under a sense of guilt but rejoices at forgiveness in a state of freedom.

But if man is affected there by no remembrance of his sin, how does he congratulate himself that he has been saved from it? Or how does he give thanks to his benefactor for the pardon that he has received if, owing to forgetfulness of his past wickedness, he does not know that he is indebted in regard to punishment? For we should not pass over negligently what the Psalmist says: *The mercies of the Lord I will sing for ever.*[18] For how does he sing the mercies of the Lord forever if he does not know that he has been delinquent, and if he does not remember past delinquency, why does he give praise to the bestower of mercy? But again it should be asked how will the mind of the elect be in perfect blessedness if in the midst of its joys the memory of its guilt affects it? Or how does the glory of unfailing light shine forth when it is overshadowed by sin that is recalled? But it should be observed that just as we now, when joyful, frequently remember sad events, so then we will recall past sin without detracting from our blessedness. For very often, when healthy, we bring to mind past illnesses without feeling pain, and the more we remember having been sick, the more we cherish our health. And so in that blessedness there will be remembrance, not that which disturbs the mind but binds us more closely to our joy, so that the mind without pain reminds itself to be indebted to the physician, and appreciates all the more the health it has received, the more it remembers the trouble it has avoided. Therefore in that state of happiness we will thus without aversion look upon our misdeeds as we now, when placed in light, without any blindness of heart see the darkness of mind; for although that is obscure which we perceive with the mind, this comes from the foreshortening of light, not from the suffering of blindness. And forever we render to our benefactor praise of his mercy, and we are not weighed down with the consciousness of delinquency; for while we look back on our misdeeds without ill effects on the mind, on the one hand there will never be anything from past iniquities to defile the hearts of those giving praise, and there will always be something to inflame them to praise their liberator.

7

Perfect happiness of the saints in eternal beatitude

God will not cast away the simple, nor reach out his hand to the evildoer: until thy mouth be filled with laughter, and thy lips with rejoicing.[19] The mouth of the righteous will then be filled with laughter when, the tears of their pilgrimage being ended, their hearts are filled with the exultation of eternal joy. Concerning this laughter Truth himself says to his disciples: *The world shall rejoice: and you shall be made sorrowful, but your sorrow shall be turned into joy.*[20] And again: *But I will see you again and your heart shall rejoice. And your joy no man shall take from you.*[21] Concerning this laughter of holy Church, Solomon says: *And she shall laugh in the latter day.*[22] On this subject he again says: *With him that feareth the Lord, it shall go well in the latter end.*[23] But there shall not then be laughter of the body but laughter of the heart. For now from jollity in lack of restraint there springs laughter of the body, but then from joy in security there will arise laughter of the heart. Therefore when all the elect are filled with the joy of clear contemplation, they spring forth as it were into the joyousness of laughter in the mind. But we call it shouting when we conceive such joy in the heart that we cannot give vent to it by way of speech, and yet the exultation of the heart voices what it cannot express in speech. Moreover, the mouth is rightly said to be filled with laughter, the lips with shouting, since in that eternal country, when the mind of the righteous is carried away in exultation, the tongue is lifted up in the song of praise. Because they see so much that they cannot express, they shout in laughter since, without accomplishing it, they seek to vocalize their love.

Now it is said "until," not that almighty God refrains for that length of time from raising up evildoers until he takes his elect to the joys of their jubilation, as if afterwards he saved from punishment those whom he first left in sin and condemned, but that he does not save them even before the judgment when it may seem doubtful to men whether it is to be done. For the fact that after the jubilee of his elect he does not reach out his hand to the evildoer is already clear from the very strictness of the final judgment. For thus it is said by the Psalmist: *The Lord said to my Lord: Sit thou at my right hand: until I make thy enemies thy footstool.*[24] Not that the Lord does not sit at the Lord's right hand after by striking his enemies he makes them subject to his power, but that he is placed over all things in eternal blessedness even before he treads underfoot the hearts of those rebelling against him. In this instance it is clear that his enemies being brought into subjection, even afterwards he still rules without end. In the same way, it is said through the Gospel of the spouse of Mary: *And he knew her not till she brought forth her firstborn son.*[25] Not that he did know her after the birth of the Lord, but that he did not touch her even when he did not know her to be the mother of his Creator. For because it could not be that he touched her after he knew that the mystery of our Redemption was to be proclaimed from her womb, it was clearly necessary that the evangelist should bear witness of that time for which there might be some doubt by reason of Joseph's lack of information. Therefore it is said here in like manner: *God will not cast away the simple, nor reach out his hand to the evildoer: until thy mouth be filled with laughter, and thy lips with shouting.* As though he said plainly: Neither before the judgment does he abandon the life of the faithful, nor before he appears does he refrain from affecting the minds of the evildoers by abandoning them. Assuredly there is no doubt that he torments without end the reprobate and that after he shall have appeared, his elect reign forever.

8
Saints will be judges with Christ

As the entrance of a city is called the gate, so is the day of judgment the gate of the kingdom, since by all the elect through it entrance is gained to the glory of their heavenly country. And hence when Solomon saw this day approaching for the recompense of holy Church, he said: *Her husband is honorable in the gates, when he sitteth among the senators of the land.*[26] For the Redeemer of the human race is the husband of holy Church who shows himself honorable in the gates who first was seen despised in insults but shall appear exalted on entering into his kingdom. He sits among the senators of the land, for he decrees sentence of judgment with the holy preachers of that same Church. Of these gates Solomon says again: *Give her of the fruit of her hands: and let her works praise her in the gates.*[27] For holy Church then receives of the fruit of her hands when the recompense of her labors lifts her up to heavenly comprehension, Her works then praise her in the gates when the words are spoken to her members at the very entrance to his kingdom: *For I was hungry, and you gave me to eat; I was thirsty,* and so on.[28]

But it is to be noted carefully that some of the elect are judged and reign: those who wipe away sins with tears and atoning for their former misdeeds by their subsequent actions, conceal by the erasure of almsgiving whatever unlawfulness they committed. To them, as has been said, the words will be addressed: *I was hungry, and you gave me to eat*, and so on. But others are not judged and reign: those who surpass even the precepts of the Law by the virtue of perfection, because they are not content with fulfilling what the divine Law enjoins on all, but with surpassing desire seek to accomplish more than they could perceive from general precepts. To them it is said by the voice of the Lord: *You who have left all things and have followed me, when the Son of Man shall sit on the seat of his majesty, you also shall sit on twelve seats judging the twelve tribes of Israel.*[29] And of them the prophet says: *The Lord will enter into judgment with the ancients of his people.*[30] Therefore these are not judged in the final judgment and reign because they also come as judges with their Creator. For leaving all things they carried out, from ready devotion, more than they heard ordered in general. For what the rich young man heard, is said by a special command to the more perfect few and not generally to all: *Go sell what thou hast and give to the poor and thou shalt have treasure in heaven. And come follow me.*[31] For if a general command bound all under this precept, it would surely be a fault for us to possess anything of this world. But what is generally prescribed in sacred Scripture for all persons is one thing; what is ordered specially to the more perfect is another. Therefore these are rightly not bound by the general judgment since in their way of life they have surpassed even general precepts. For as they are not judged and perish who, from the persuasion of faithlessness, scorn to be bound by the Law, so they are not judged and reign who, from the persuasion of devotion, advance even beyond the general precepts of divine Law. Hence it is that Paul, transcending even special precepts given him, performed more in his work than he took upon himself by the instruction of permissibility. For when, preaching the Gospel, he had been allowed to have his living from the Gospel, he both brought the Gospel to his hearers, and yet refused to be maintained at the expense of the Gospel.[32]

9

The saints will not commiserate the condemned

In destruction and famine thou shalt laugh.[33] The just man in the strictness of the final judgment is comforted by the voice of the judge when it is said: *I was hungry, and you gave me to eat; I was thirsty, and you gave me to drink; I was a stranger, and you took me in; naked, and you covered me; sick, and you visited me; I was in prison, and you came to me.*[34] This declaration is introduced by the words: *Come, ye blessed of my Father, possess you the kingdom prepared for you from the foundation of the world.*[35] Therefore in destruction and famine the just man shall laugh, for when the final judgment strikes all the wicked, he himself rejoices in the glory of a worthy reward. And he does not then any longer through kindness commiserate the condemned, for adhering to divine justice by specific effect, he is made firm by the unshaken force of interior strictness. For the souls of the elect, being raised up in the clear light of heavenly uprightness, are affected by no sense of compassion since the loftiness of their bliss makes them strangers to tribulations. Hence also it is well said by the Psalmist: *The just shall see and fear, and shall laugh at him, and say: Behold the man that made not God his helper.*[36] For now the just see the wicked and fear; then they shall see and laugh. For because they can now fall in imitation of them, here they are fearful, but because they cannot then be of help to the condemned, there they do not have compassion. Therefore they read in that very justice of the judge by which they are blessed that they should not commiserate those that are doomed to eternal punishment. For—an outcome that it is not right to suppose in their regard—they slight the character of the happiness granted to them if when placed in the kingdom, they wish for something that they cannot accomplish.

10

The glorification of the flesh and the distinction of honors in eternal blessedness

There are some persons who—considering that the spirit is separated from the flesh, that the flesh is turned into corruption, that corruption is reduced to dust, that this dust is broken up into simple substances so that it is incapable of being seen by human eyes—lose hope that resurrection can take place, and while they look upon dry bones, they lack faith that these bones can be clothed with flesh and again restored to life. If these persons do not have faith in the resurrection on the principle of obedience, they should have it on the principle of reason. For in the progress of the seasons we see trees lose the greenness of their foliage and cease from putting forth fruit; and suddenly as if from dry wood by a kind of imminent resurrection, we see the leaves burst forth, the fruit grow large, and the whole tree clothed with renewed beauty. We constantly see small seeds of trees consigned to the moistness of the earth, from which long afterwards we see large trees arise and put forth leaves and fruit. Let us then consider the seed of a given tree such as was cast into the earth so that a tree might be produced from it, and let us grasp, if we can, where in that utter minuteness of seed was buried the immense tree which developed from it; where was the wood; where the bark; where the verdure of the foliage; where the abundance of fruit. Was there perchance anything of the kind perceived in the seed when it was cast into the ground? And yet by the hidden framer of all things, ordering all in a wonderful way, both in the softness of the seed there lay buried the roughness of the bark, and in its tenderness there was hidden the strength of the wood, and in its dryness, richness of fruitfulness. What wonder, then, if that finest dust, which to our eyes is reduced to its elements, is at will formed again into a human being by him who from the tiniest seeds makes whole the largest trees? Therefore because we have been created rational beings, we must bolster the hope of our own resurrection from the sight and contemplation of natural objects.

However, our body will not, as Eutychius, bishop of Constantinople, wrote, in that glory of the resurrection be impalpable, and more subtle than the wind and the air: for in that glory our body will be subtle indeed by the effect of a spiritual power, but palpable by the reality of its nature. Hence also our Redeemer, when the disciples doubted his resurrection, showed them his hands and side, and offered his bones and flesh to be touched, saying: *Handle, and see, for a spirit hath not flesh and bones, as you see me to have.*[37]

Now we, truly believing our Redeemer's body to have been palpable after his Resurrection, acknowledge that our flesh after resurrection will be at once both the same and different: the same with respect to nature, different with respect to glory; the same in its reality, different in its virtuality. Thus it will be spiritual, since it will be incorruptible. It will be palpable, since it will not lose the essence of its true nature.

Hence it is rightly said by Paul: *For the creature was made subject to vanity; not willingly, but by reason of him that made it subject in hope, because the creature also itself shall be delivered from the servitude of corruption, into the liberty of the glory of the children of God.*[38] For the creature, made subject to vanity and corruption, not willingly, is then rescued from the wretchedness of corruption when in rising again, it is raised incorrupt to the glory of the children of God. Therefore the just, bound in this life with the chains of corruption, are released from these bonds when they are stripped of their corruptible flesh. Paul, being bound in these chains, cries out: *I desire to be dissolved and to be with Christ.*[39] For he would not seek to be dissolved unless he saw himself to be bound. Now the prophet, because he had seen that these bonds were most certainly to be burst, rejoiced as if they were already broken when he said: *Thou hast broken my bonds: I will sacrifice to thee the sacrifice of praise.*[40]

However, since there is for us in this life a difference in works, there will be in the life that is eternal a difference in degrees of dignity, so that as here one surpasses another in merit, there one may transcend another in recompense. Hence Truth himself says in the Gospel: *In my Father's house there are many mansions.*[41] But in those many mansions the very diversity of rewards will somehow be in harmony, for so mighty a force joins us together in such peace that whatever anyone has not received in himself, he rejoices that he received it in another. Hence they that did not labor equally in the vineyard, equally received every man a penny.[42] And indeed with the Father are many mansions, and yet all those who labored in different degrees receive the same

pay since the blessedness of joy will be one and the same for all, although sublimity of life will not be one and the same for all. Hence it is written: *The small
and great are there.*[43] He had seen the small and great in this light who said in
the voice of each individual: *Thy eyes did see my imperfect being, and in thy book
all shall be written.*[44] And again: *He hath blessed all that fear the Lord, both little
and great.*[45]

EPILOGUE

And now, this work being completed, I see that I must go back to myself, returning from the outward utterance of words to the council chamber of the heart. I ask therefore that anyone who reads these words may confer on me before the strict judge the solace of his prayers and with charitable insight may by his supplications commend the soul of Peter to our Lord and God, Jesus Christ, to whom with the Father and the Holy Spirit be honor and dominion for ever and ever. Amen.

ERRATA
(Latin Text)
[Correction in **_bold–italics_** except word division]

Page	Line	Read
38	91	occid*i*t
41	1	su*r*repit (12 su*r*rep*u*nt, 14 su*r*repit)
43	16	vid*i*t
56	33	ips*e*
62	31	quant*a*
70	4	desidera*n*t
73	43	ei*u*s
80	19	***omit***
82	46	sub ministri
85	7₂	us*u*
120	10	u*l*tricibus
121	6	disciplina*m*
126	2	rel*inquit*
160	76	di*i*udicat
163	10	qu*e*m
163	15	grati*a*
169	25	lenticul*a*m
192	21	coll*e*git
225	3	a*b*
258	2	mandatum
267	45	*p*aulo
286	20	pr*o*fecto
296	65	**XX*X***
297	25	exut*a*m
301	29	mult*a*
320	67	no*s*
392	83	me*r*uit
415	30	rectorem
436	48	venerari
457	86	qui*a*
460	26	qui*a*
486	7₂	vita*m*
487	28	Qui*a*
491	5	Ies*u* (***bis***)

NOTE: The sentence on p. 463, 12/14 (*Stultus ... attendit*)—omitted by MSS A G P₁—occurs in the *Moralia* at an earlier point: CC XXII, v, 72/74, μ 702.

LIST OF TOPICS
[Indicating page numbers]

Part 1, Book 1

THE SUGGESTIONS OF THE DEVIL

Part 1, Book 2

SIN

Part 1, Book 3

VICES

Part 1, Book 4

THE RICH

Part 1, Book 5

THE REPROBATE

Part 1, Book 6

PUNISHMENT OF THE REPROBATE

Part 2, Book 1

THE GRACE OF GOD

Part 2, Book 2

PENITENCE

Part 2, Book 3

VIRTUES

Part 2, Book 4

PRELATES

Part 2, Book 5

THE JUST

Part 2, Book 6

THE GLORY OF THE JUST

END NOTES

Prologue

1. Cf. 1 Cor 9, 24. **2.** Cf. Mt 13, 4/8. **3.** Cf. Ps 1, 3. **4.** Cf. Gregory's *Moralia* Dedicatory Letter to Leander: *Corpus Christianorum* 143, p. 6, 177/178; *Editio Maurinorum*, 6; *Patrologia Latina*, ed. J.P. Migne, 75, 515. **5.** Cf. Mt 25, 14/23.

Part 1, Book 1

1. Cf. Gen 2, 17; 3, 6. **2.** Cf. Ecclus 25, 33. **3.** 1 Kg 16, 23; 18, 10. **4.** Job 41, 11. **5.** Ps 6, 8. **6.** Ps 37, 11. **7.** Ps 45, 11. **8.** Job 41, 11. **9.** Jer 1, 13. **10.** Is 14, 13. **11.** Is 14, 13/14. **12.** Job 19, 12. **13.** Ibid. **14.** Lam 1, 5. **15.** Ps 141, 4. **16.** Jer 41, 5/7. **17.** Jer 41, 8. **18.** Ps 55, 7. **19.** Gen 3, 15 (cf. LXX). **20.** Job 40, 12. **21.** Ibid. **22.** Mk 9, 24/25. **23.** Job 20, 16. **24.** Is 59, 5. **25.** Job 40, 12. **26.** Ez 14, 14 & 20. **27.** Lk 17, 34/36. **28.** 1 Cor 7, 2. **29.** 1 Cor 7, 6. **30.** Job 40, 13. **31.** Job 18, 10. **32.** Job 2, 12. **33.** Job 40, 13. **34.** Job 6, 18. **35.** Is 34, 13/14. **36.** Ez 23, 20. **37.** Ps 21, 13. **38.** Is 34, 14. **39.** Job 30, 3. **40.** Ps 24, 17. **41.** Job 33, 26. **42.** Mt 6, 11; Lk 11, 3. **43.** Cf. Gen 3, 5. **44.** Gen 3, 1. **45.** Job 7, 14. **46.** Cf. Ecclus 34, 7. **47.** Lev 19, 26. **48.** Eccl 5, 2. **49.** Cf. Gen 37, 7. **50.** Cf. Mt 2, 13/14. **51.** Dan 2, 29. **52.** Dan 2, 31. **53.** Job 7, 13/14. **54.** Job 38, 24. **55.** Is 9, 2; Mt 4, 16. **56.** Cf. Gal 2, 11 ff., but see Ac 15, 5 ff. **57.** Jn 3, 8. **58.** Ex 5, 21. **59.** 1 Cor 10, 13. **60.** Job 21, 33. **61.** Ps 30, 25. **62.** Job 2, 9. **63.** Ecclus 32, 26. **64.** Jer 9, 4. **65.** Mt 10, 36. **66.** Mt 16, 22. **67.** 2 Kg 19, 21. **68.** Mt 16, 23. **69.** 2 Kg 19, 22. **70.** Job 16, 14. **71.** 1 Pet 1, 13. **72.** Job 41, 4. **73.** 2 Cor 11, 14/15. **74.** Jos 5, 13. **75.** Job 40, 18. **76.** Mt 7, 21. **77.** Lk 6, 46. **78.** Tit 1, 16. **79.** 1 Jn 2, 4. **80.** Mk 7, 6. **81.** Ps 77, 36. **82.** Cf. Jas 2, 20. **83.** Lk 9, 23. **84.** Ps 41, 7. **85.** Cf. Hab 1, 16. **86.** Mt 7, 22/23; cf. Lk 13, 27. **87.** Cf. Am 7, 4. **88.** Job 3, 8. **89.** Ps 118, 115. **90.** Cf. Gen 26, 15. **91.** Ecclus 2, 1. **92.** Job 39, 21. **93.** Job 2, 6. **94.** Job 2, 8. **95.** Mt 5, 28. **96.** Jg 6, 11/12, 19/21. **97.** Job 2, 9. **98.** Lam 1, 20. **99.** Ps 34, 5. **100.** Job 2, 10. **101.** Job 41, 12. **102.** Cf. Gen 3, 6. **103.** Cf. Gen 4, 5/8. **104.** Cf. 3 Kg 11, 4. **105.** Cf. 3 Kg 21, 1/19. **106.** Job 41, 12. **107.** Cf. 1 Cor 3, 12. **108.** Hab 2, 1. **109.** Cf. Jer 31, 21; Is 40, 9. **110.** Prov 28, 14. **111.** Cant 3, 8. **112.** Ps 2, 11. **113.** Ps 85, 11. **114.** Cf. Job 7, 1. **115.** Wis 9, 15. **116.** Is 27, 1. **117.** Is 14, 13. **118.** Gen 3, 1. **119.** Mt 8, 20. **120.** Apoc 6, 8. **121.** Jn 12, 31. **122.** Ps 103, 20/21. **123.** Ps 103, 22. **124.** Ps 80, 3. **125.** Mt 17, 20. [What follows, *with the help* etc., is not in the *Moralia.*]

Part 1, Book 2

1. 1 Jn 3, 4; 5, 17. **2.** Ps 18, 13. **3.** Tit 1, 6. **4.** 1 Jn 1, 8. **5.** Job 31, 12. **6.** 1 Tim 1, 13. **7.** Cf. Mt 26, 69/75; Mk 14, 66/72; Lk 22, 56/62; Jn 18, 17. **8.** Jn 15, 22. **9.** Jn 15, 24. **10.** Job 34, 27. **11.** Ibid. **12.** Lk 12, 47/48. **13.** Is 3, 9. **14.** Prov 1, 10. **15.**

Ps 10, 3 (according to the Hebrews). **16.** Lk 9, 60. **17.** Rom 1, 21. **18.** Rom 1, 24. **19.** 1 Thess 2, 16. **20.** Apoc 22, 11. **21.** Ps 68, 28. **22.** Ps 77, 49/50. **23.** Gen 15, 16. **24.** Job 16, 15. **25.** Os 4, 2. **26.** Ps 50, 16. **27.** Job 34, 21. **28.** Prov 11, 21. **29.** Is 1, 16. **30.** Heb 4, 13. **31.** Job 10, 14. **32.** Ps 37, 6. **33.** Deut 23, 10/11. **34.** Eccl 10, 1. **35.** Mt 9, 25. **36.** Cf. Job 31, 7: *And if my heart hath followed my eyes.* **37.** Cf. 2 Kg 11, 2. **38.** Lam 3, 51. **39.** Job 31, 1. **40.** Mt 5, 27/28. **41.** 1 Pet 1, 13. **42.** Cf. Apoc 1, 13. **43.** 1 Cor 10, 13. **44.** Rom 6, 12. **45.** Lev 1, 6/13. **46.** Job 18, 12. **47.** Am 8, 11. **48.** Lk 12, 19. **49.** Job 18, 14. **50.** Is 47, 1. **51.** Job 18, 15. **52.** Ibid. **53.** Cf. Gen 19, 24. **54.** Job 18, 16. **55.** Mic 2, 1. **56.** Rom 2, 16. **57.** Rom 2, 15. **58.** Ps 11, 3. **59.** Ps 57, 3. **60.** Heb 4, 13. **61.** Ez 1, 18; 10, 12; Apoc 4, 8. **62.** Ps 44, 14. **63.** Ps 44, 14/15. **64.** Job 11, 14/15. **65.** Prov 24, 27. **66.** 1 Jn 3, 21/22. **67.** Prov 28, 9. **68.** Job 11, 2. **69.** Is 32, 17. **70.** Prov 25, 28. **71.** Prov 10, 19. **72.** Ps 139, 12. **73.** Prov 9, 9. **74.** Prov 9, 7. **75.** Job 2, 9. **76.** Mt 3, 2. **77.** Rom 1, 26. **78.** Rom 1, 27. **79.** Jn 9, 28. **80.** Jn 11, 50. **81.** Rom 12, 14. **82.** 1 Pet 3, 9. **83.** Eccl 7, 22/23. **84.** Gen 3, 17. **85.** Gen 12, 3. **86.** Rom 12, 14. **87.** 1 Cor 6, 10. **88.** Ac 8, 20. **89.** 4 Kg 1, 10/12. **90.** 2 Kg 1, 21. **91.** Jer 20, 15. **92.** Job 6, 26. **93.** Ibid. **94.** Prov 17, 14. **95.** Prov 18, 4. **96.** Prov 26, 10. **97.** Ps 139, 12. **98.** Prov 10, 19. **99.** Is 32, 17. **100.** Jas 1, 26. **101.** Jas 1, 19. **102.** Jas 3, 8. **103.** Mt 12, 36. **104.** Job 39, 34. **105.** Jas 3, 1/2. **106.** Jas 3, 8. **107.** Mt 12, 36. **108.** Ps 31, 1. **109.** Heb 4, 13. **110.** Cf. Job 27, 4. **111.** Wis 1, 11. **112.** Ps 5, 7. **113.** Ex 1, 21. **114.** Job 15, 24. **115.** Jer 9, 5. **116.** Job 27, 5. **117.** Prov 17, 15. **118.** Ez 13, 18. **119.** Ez 13, 10. **120.** Job 39, 20. **121.** Mk 1, 6. **122.** Eccl 12, 5. **123.** Ps 108, 23. **124.** Ex 10, 13/15. **125.** Job 20, 14. **126.** Job 19, 22. **127.** Ps 100, 5. **128.** Prov 23, 20. **129.** Prov 23, 21. **130.** Cf. Prov 15, 5. **131.** Job 5, 21. **132.** Ps 90, 3. **133.** Job 30, 4. **134.** 3 Kg 18, 27. **135.** Job 20, 12. **136.** Ps 11, 3. **137.** Cant 4, 11. **138.** Cf. 2 Kg 20, 9/10. **139.** Ps 9, 28. **140.** Job 30, 3. **141.** Lam 1, 1. **142.** Ps 71, 9. **143.** Job 31, 4. **144.** Jer 7, 3. **145.** Mt 11, 28. **146.** Jn 4, 21. **147.** Jn 4, 23. **148.** Mt 5, 22. **149.** Jer 32, 18/19. **150.** Apoc 2, 13. **151.** Apoc 2, 14. **152.** Apoc 2, 19/20. **153.** Job 4, 2. **154.** Prov 17, 14. **155.** Ps 72, 9. **156.** Cf. Lk 16, 24. **157.** Num 19, 15. **158.** Jer 20, 9/10. **159.** Ps 38, 2/3. **160.** Ps 38, 3/4. **161.** Job 6, 26. **162.** Is 6, 5. **163.** Ecclus 20, 7. **164.** Eccl 3, 7. **165.** Ps 140, 3. **166.** Job 21, 5. **167.** Ps 143, 1. **168.** Job 20, 25. **169.** Lk 16, 19. **170.** Cf. Lk 12, 47. **171.** Jas 4, 17. **172.** Ps 54, 16. **173.** Job 15, 25. **174.** Job 15, 26. **175.** Ibid. **176.** Eccl 11, 8. **177.** Ecclus 7, 40. **178.** Job 4, 8/9. **179.** Ps 9, 26. **180.** Ps 9, 28. **181.** Ps 72, 5. **182.** Jer 12, 1. **183.** Ecclus 5, 4. **184.** Cf. Lk 13, 6/9.

Part 1, Book 3

1. Job 39, 25. **2.** Ecclus 10, 15. **3.** Cf. Gen 1, 27. **4.** Job 41, 25. **5.** Ecclus 10, 15. **6.** Prov 16, 18. **7.** Dan 4, 26/27. **8.** Dan 4, 28/29. **9.** Is 40, 6. **10.** Cf. Lk 13, 27.

11. Ps 61, 11. **12.** Cf. Mt 25, 11/12. **13.** Jas 4, 6. **14.** Prov 16, 5. **15.** Ecclus 10, 9. **16.** Mt 11. 29. **17.** Is 14, 13. **18.** Ps 87, 4. **19.** Is 14, 13. **20.** Zach 2, 10. **21.** Is 14, 13. **22.** Ps 21, 7. **23.** Is 14, 14. **24.** Phil 2, 6/7. **25.** Wis 2, 8/9. **26.** Jn 16, 20. **27.** Ps 72, 7/8. **28.** Jn 12, 26. **29.** Mt 7, 16. **30.** Mt 6, 2. **31.** Job 8, 14. **32.** Os 8, 7. **33.** Job 8, 14. **34.** 1 Cor 8, 1. **35.** Mt 6, 16. **36.** Mt 27, 32. **37.** Gal 5, 24. 38. Job 8, 15. **39.** Mt 25, 8. **40.** Job 8, 15. **41.** Mt 7, 22. **42.** Mt 7, 23. **43.** 4 Kg 20, 17. **44.** Ps 77, 61. **45.** Jl 1, 7. **46.** Mt 6, 3/4. **47.** Ps 44, 14. **48.** 2 Cor 1, 12. **49.** Mt 5, 16. **50.** Mt 6, 1. **51.** Mt 25, 12. **52.** Job 5, 2. **53.** Cf. Gen 4, 5/8. **54.** Cf. Gen 25, 34; 27, 41. **55.** Cf. Gen 37, 19/20; 27/28. **56.** Cf. 1 Kg 18, 8/11. **57.** Wis 2, 24. **58.** Prov 14, 30. **59.** Job 5, 2. **60.** Ibid. **61.** Wis 12, 18. **62.** Eccl 7, 10. **63.** Prov 15, 1 (cf. LXX). **64.** Jas 1, 20. **65.** Prov 22, 24/25. **66.** Prov 29, 22 (cf. LXX). **67.** Eph 4, 26. **68.** Is 66, 2. **69.** Cf. Mt 7, 3. **70.** Prov 11, 23. **71.** Cf. Prudentius, *Amartigenia*, vv. 582/583, 608/620. **72.** Cf. Num 25, 11. **73.** Cf. 1 Kg 3, 13. **74.** Ps 4, 5. **75.** Eccl 7, 4. **76.** Ps 6, 8. **77.** Job 5, 2. **78.** Cf. Job 24, 16. **79.** Job 24, 17. **80.** Cant 6, 9. **81.** Ps 143, 2. **82.** Deut 24, 6. **83.** 2 Cor 11, 20. **84.** 1 Tim 6, 10. **85.** Job 20, 19/20. **86.** Mt 25, 42/43. **87.** Mt 25, 41. **88.** Job 20, 20. **89.** Ps 77, 30/31. **90.** Job 20, 22. **91.** Lk 12, 17/18. **92.** Job 20, 22. **93.** Job 31, 23. **94.** Heb 12, 26; Agg 2, 7. **95.** Job 39, 7. **96.** Cf. 1 Kg 14, 27. **97.** Cf. Num 21, 5. **98.** Cf. 1 Kg 2, 12/17. **99.** Ez 16, 49. **100.** Cf. Gen 25, 29/34. **101.** Cf. 3 Kg 17, 6. **102.** Cf. Gen 3, 6. **103.** Cf. Mt 4, 3. **104.** 4 Kg 25, 8/10; Jer 52, 12/14. **105.** 1 Cor 9, 27. **106.** 1 Cor 9, 26. **107.** Dan 3, 46. **108.** Job 39, 7. **109.** Rom 13, 14. **110.** Mt 6, 34. **111.** Rom 13, 14. **112.** Cf. Gen 18, 2. **113.** Job 31, 12. **114.** Ibid. **115.** Deut 32, 22. **116.** Gen 3, 14; cf. 3, 15 (LXX). **117.** Job 40, 11. **118.** Lk 12, 35. **119.** 1 Pet 1, 13. **120.** Heb 7, 10. **121.** Ez 16, 4. **122.** Cf. Gen 3, 7. **123.** Mt 5, 28. **124.** 1 Cor 6, 9/10. **125.** Job 31, 9. **126.** Ibid. **127.** 1 Cor 3, 3/4. **128.** Ez 34, 31. **129.** Jl 1, 17. **130.** Jer 5, 8. **131.** Ez 23, 20. **132.** Ps 48, 13. **133.** Job 25, 6. **134.** Cf. Job 24, 20. **135.** Job 35, 11. **136.** Ps 31, 9. **137.** Ecclus 3, 22. **138.** Col 3, 5. **139.** Col 2, 8. **140.** Ps 48, 13. **141.** Rom 1, 21. **142.** Rom 1, 24. **143.** Os 5, 4. **144.** Os 5, 5. **145.** Cf. Gen 3, 7. **146.** The Latin text attributes this figurative interpretation to Job instead of Gregory. Cf. Job 19, 24. **147.** Ps 4, 3. **148.** Zach 5, 5/8. **149.** Zach 5, 9/11. **150.** Zach 5, 6. **151.** Jer 4, 22. **152.** 2 Cor 2, 14/15. **153.** 1 Tim 6, 10. **154.** Cf. Gen 11, 4/8. **155.** Job 6, 18. **156.** Job 20, 25. **157.** Jl 1, 4/5. **158.** Jl 1, 5. **159.** Job 29, 14. **160.** Eccl 9, 18. **161.** Jas 2, 10. **162.** Jas 2, 11. **163.** Prov 4, 23. **164.** Lk 18, 12. **165.** Lk 18, 11. **166.** Cf. 1 Mac 6, 46. The two books of Machabees were declared canonical at the Councils of Florence (1438 – 1445) and Trent (1545 – 1563). **167.** Gen 2, 15.

Part 1, Book 4

1. Cf. Mt 25, 14. **2.** 1 Jn 2, 15. **3.** Ibid. **4.** 1 Jn 2, 16/17. **5.** Os 7, 8. **6.** Job 30. 7. **7.** Lam 3, 15. **8.** Os 10, 11. **9.** Lk 21, 34. **10.** Mt 11, 28/29. **11.** Cf. Ex 16, 3; Num 11, 4/6. **12.** Wis 6, 6. **13.** Lk 12, 48. **14.** Lk 18, 24; cf. Mt 19, 23. **15.** Mt 19, 26; cf. Lk 18, 27. **16.** Cf. Lk 16, 23. **17.** Gen 18, 27. **18.** Job 24, 24. **19.** Mt 3, 12. **20.** Lk 12, 19. **21.** Lk 12, 20. **22.** Job 27, 19. **23.** Ps 75, 6. **24.** Lk 16, 9. **25.** Job 27, 19. **26.** Wis 5, 8/9. **27.** Cf. Lk 16, 23. **28.** Job 13, 12. **29.** Ps 1, 4. **30.** Ps 111, 7. **31.** Job 13, 12. **32.** Job 8, 22. **33.** Cf. Gen 5, 3/18. **34.** Cf. Gen 4, 17. **35.** Cf. Heb 11, 9/10. **36.** Cf. Gen 32, 13 ff.; 33, 4 ff. **37.** Cf. Deut 17, 15/16. **38.** Cf. 1 Kg 13, 2. **39.** Lk 12, 19. **40.** Lk 12, 20. **41.** Job 6, 16. **42.** Ps 13, 5. **43.** Job 6, 17. **44.** Ibid. **45.** Is 28, 19. **46.** Job 11, 20. **47.** Ps 145, 4. **48.** This is based on the reading *tristia* [for *tristitia*] in 11 of 17 MSS. **49.** Lk 6, 24. **50.** Job 21, 10. **51.** Job 21, 11. **52.** Job 21, 11/12. **53.** Job 21, 13. **54.** Job 34, 20. **55.** Lk 12, 20. **56.** 1 Thess 5, 4/5. **57.** Job 27, 20. **58.** Lk 16, 24. **59.** Lam 3, 53. **60.** Ps 29, 3/4. **61.** Job 27, 20. **62.** Ps 49, 3. **63.** Prov 1, 26/27. **64.** Lk 12, 39/40. **65.** Mt 24, 48/50. **66.** Job 40, 15. **67.** Ps 96, 5. **68.** Ps 103, 8. **69.** 2 Tim 3, 2. **70.** 2 Tim 3, 4. **71.** Job 40, 15. **72.** Os 13, 8. **73.** Is 35, 9. **74.** Mt. 13, 38. **75.** Ps 24, 2/3. **76.** Job 21, 25. **77.** Job 21, 26. **78.** Eph 5, 14. **79.** Job 15, 27. **80.** Ibid. **81.** Job 6, 19. **82.** Mt 8, 21. **83.** Lk 9, 60. **84.** Lk 14, 26. **85.** Deut 33, 9/10. **86.** 1 Kg 6, 10/12. **87.** Ex 32, 6; 1 Cor 10, 7. **88.** Lk 16, 24. **89.** Cf. Job 4, 19. **90.** Job 4, 20. **91.** Ps 54, 24. **92.** Eph 5, 16. **93.** Jer 31, 30.

Part 1, Book 5

1. Is 5, 22. **2.** Ps 58, 4. **3.** Apoc 3, 17. **4.** Job 41, 13. **5.** Os 7, 9. **6.** Job 18, 8. **7.** Job 18, 9. **8.** Ibid. **9.** Cf. Lk 14, 1/4. **10.** Lk 16, 14. **11.** Jg 16, 21. **12.** Jer 39, 6/7. **13.** Job 6, 18. **14.** Ecclus 35, 6; cf. Ex 23, 15; Deut 16, 16. **15.** Ps 125, 6. **16.** Ps 23, 4. **17.** Ps 68, 16. **18.** Lam 3, 53. **19.** Job 36, 16. **20.** Ps 30, 8/9. **21.** Ps 30, 9. **22.** Job 36, 16. **23.** Prov 18, 3. **24.** Job 12, 14. **25.** Ps 126, 1. **26.** Eccl 7, 14. **27.** Job 12, 14. **28.** Cf. Mt 27, 5; Ac 1, 18. **29.** Ex 4, 21; 7, 3. **30.** Heb 12, 17. **31.** Cf. Gen 27, 1/40. **32.** Job 21, 21. **33.** Cf. Lk 16, 28. **34.** Lk 18, 2. **35.** Is 3, 9. **36.** Job 19, 3. **37.** Job 36, 11/12. **38.** Jer 5, 3. **39.** Jer 51, 9. **40.** Jer 15, 7. **41.** Job 21, 14. **42.** Ibid. **43.** Job 21, 15. **44.** Ps 13, 1. **45.** Job 20, 18. **46.** Prov 2, 14. **47.** Eccl 8, 14. **48.** Job 36, 13. **49.** Mt 23, 27/28. **50.** Deut 22, 11. **51.** Job 15, 21. **52.** Prov 14, 26. **53.** Prov 15, 15. **54.** Prov 18, 3. **55.** Job 35, 9. **56.** Mt 23, 27/28. **57.** Job 8, 11. **58.** Mt 7, 22/23. **59.** Job 8, 12. **60.** Prov 9, 8. **61.** Is 40, 6. **62.** Ps 128, 6. **63.** Job 8, 13. **64.** Ibid. **65.** Job 3, 7. **66.** Ecclus 21, 1. **67.** Gen 3, 12. **68.** Job 41, 6. **69.** Is 34, 14/15. **70.** Job 40, 17. **71.** Is 34, 13. **72.** Job 41, 7. **73.** Job 41, 8. **74.** Ecclus 21, 10. **75.** Nah 1, 10. **76.** 1 Cor 4, 7. **77.** Eph 2, 8/9. **78.** 1 Tim 1, 13. **79.** Cf. Jer 48, 29/30. **80.** Apoc 3, 17. **81.** Cf. Lk 18, 10/14. **82.** Lk 10, 17. **83.** Lk 10, ı8. **84.** Is 14, 13/14. **85.** Job 24, 24. **86.** Ps 72, 18. **87.** Ps 36, 35/36. **88.** Ps 36, 10. **89.** Jas 4, 15. **90.** 1 Pet 1, 24; cf. Is 40, 6. **91.** Job 31, 3. **92.** The Latin word in question is *alienatio*. For the Greek *anathema*, the Hebrew counterpart, sometimes transliterated *cherem*, is not attested for Job 31, 3. The first four verses of the chapter are omittted in the Septuagint; editors supply the equivalent of *alienatio* in verse 3.

Part 1, Book 6

1. Rom 6, 23. **2.** Job 26, 14. **3.** Ps 49, 3. **4.** Is 13, 9. **5.** Soph 1, 14/16. **6.** Jl 2, 1/2, 11. **7.** Jn 18, 4/6. **8.** Job 26, 14. **9.** Job 31, 35. **10.** Cf. Jn 1, 17. **11.** Jn 5, 22. **12.** Job 19, 29. **13.** Mt 25, 42/43. **14.** Mt 25, 41. **15.** Ps 1, 5. **16.** Jn 3, 18. **17.** Rom 2, 12. **18.** Mt 25, 34/35. **19.** Mt 25, 34. **20.** Cf. Mt 19, 28. **21.** Job 10, 21. **22.** Eccl 1, 4. **23.** Ez 32, 24. **24.** Job 10, 20. **25.** Job 10, 22. **26.** Jn 12, 35. **27.** Job 10, 22. **28.** Mt 25, 41. **29.** Mt 22, 13. **30.** Ps 57, 9. **31.** Ez 32, 27. **32.** Rom 6, 13. **33.** Wis 6, 7 & 9. **34.** Apoc 18, 7. **35.** Mt 13, 30. **36.** Jn 14, 2. **37.** Job 10, 22. **38.** Is 66, 24; Mk 9, 45. **39.** Cf. Lk 16, 23/28. **40.** Cf. Dan 3, 92. **41.** Ez 32, 22. **42.** Eccl 9, 10. **43.** Is 55, 6. **44.** 2 Cor 6, 2. **45.** Gal 6, 10. **46.** Job 20, 18. **47.** Is 26, 10 (cf. LXX). **48.** Jn 6, 41 & 51. **49.** Ps 20, 10. **50.** Job 20, 26. **51.** Job 27, 22. **52.** Apoc 3, 19. **53.** Heb 12, 6. **54.** Ps 9, 17. **55.** Jer 30, 14. **56.** Jer 30, 15. **57.** Ps 93, 20. **58.** Jer 5, 3. **59.** Deut 32, 22. **60.** Cf. Nah 1, 9. **61.** Jer 17, 18. **62.** Jude 5. **63.** Job 21, 17. **64.** Ps 10, 7. **65.** Job 9, 17. **66.** Cf. Job 15, 14. **67.** Jn 3, 5. **68.** Eph 2, 3. **69.** Mt 25, 46. **70.** Cf. Mt 5, 44. **71.** 2 Tim 2, 25/26. **72.** Job 40, 28. **73.** Mt 25, 41. **74.** 2 Pet 2, 4.

Part 2, Book 1

1. Job 9, 34. **2.** Ps 44, 5. **3.** Rom 8, 15. **4.** Job 9, 35. **5.** 1 Jn 4, 18. **6.** Lk 1, 74. **7.** Cf. 4 Kg 4, 30/35. **8.** Heb 7, 19. **9.** Phil 2, 6/7. **10.** Job 22, 30. **11.** Rom 2, 6. **12.** Ex 34, 7. **13.** 1 Cor 15, 10. **14.** Job 5, 17. **15.** Eph 5, 13. **16.** Eccl 10, 4. **17.** Heb 12, 6; cf. Prov 3, 12. **18.** Apoc 3, 19. **19.** Heb 12, 11. **20.** Job 5, 18. **21.** Deut 32, 39. **22.** Cant 2, 5 (LXX). **23.** Jer 30, 15. **24.** Jn 5, 14. **25.** 2 Cor 12, 7. **26.** Jn 9, 3. **27.** Is 23, 4. **28.** Os 2, 6/7. **29.** Job 27, 9. **30.** Prov 28, 9. **31.** Mt 25, 11/12. **32.** Is 55, 6. **33.** Prov 1, 20. **34.** Prov 1, 22/23. **35.** Prov 1, 24/25. **36.** Prov 1, 26/28. **37.** 1 Kg 2, 10. **38.** Jer 29, 23. **39.** Is 42, 14. **40.** Cf. 4 Kg 20, 6; Is 38, 5. **41.** Rom 2, 4/5. **42.** Is 65, 20. **43.** Job 24, 23. **44.** Phil 2, 21. **45.** Prov 17, 24. **46.** Eccl 2, 14. **47.** Cf. 1 Cor 12, 12/27. **48.** Job 34, 21; cf. Prov 5, 21. **49.** Ecclus 5, 4. **50.** Job 24, 23. **51.** Job 40, 21. **52.** Cf. Mt 26, 70. **53.** Cf. 2 Kg 11, 4. **54.** Ecclus 5, 6. **55.** Ecclus 5, 7. **56.** Job 13, 11. **57.** Is 28, 19. **58.** Ps 77, 34. **59.** Cf. Job 10, 20. **60.** Ps 37, 18/19. **61.** Ps 115, 16/17. **62.** Prov 15, 19. **63.** Ibid. **64.** Job 7, 7. **65.** Lk 16, 27/28. **66.** Eccl 9, 10. **67.** Job 7, 8. **68.** Lk 22, 61/62. **69.** 2 Cor 6, 2. **70.** Ps 117, 1.

71. Eccl 11, 3. **72.** Wis 11, 24. **73.** Job 7, 8. **74.** Job 25, 5. **75.** Job 16, 23. **76.** Job 17, 1. **77.** Ibid. **78.** Ecclus 7, 40. **79.** Job 14, 1. **80.** Gal 4, 4. **81.** Ecclus 42, 14. **82.** Job 14, 2. **83.** Ps 102, 15. **84.** Is 40, 6; cf. 1 Pet 1, 24. **85.** Job 7, 20. **86.** Ecclus 40, 1. **87.** Ecclus 2, 16. **88.** Mt 25, 13. **89.** 1 Thess 5, 2. **90.** Ps 36, 10. **91.** Ps 102, 15. **92.** Is 40, 6; cf. 1 Pet 1, 24. **93.** Jas 4, 15. **94.** Job 6, 19. **95.** Job 14, 5. **96.** Cf. 4 Kg 20, 6. **97.** 4 Kg 20, 1. **98.** Prov 24, 9 (LXX); cf. Ecclus 20, 9. **99.** Cf. Job 15, 32. **100.** Job 15, 20.

Part 2, Book 2

1. Job 16, 15. **2.** Job 16, 16. **3.** Job 16, 17. **4.** Mt 11, 21. **5.** Job 3, 3. **6.** Gen 1, 26. **7.** Ps 81, 6/7. **8.** 1 Cor 3, 3. **9.** Jer 17, 5. **10.** Job 3, 4. **11.** Rom 2, 15. **12.** Job 3, 4. **13.** 1 Cor 11, 31. **14.** Job 3, 4. **15.** Eph 5, 13. **16.** Ps 31, 1. **17.** Jn 8, 34. **18.** Job 24, 19. **19.** 1 Jn 5, 16. **20.** Job 24, 20. **21.** Job 34, 23. **22.** 1 Cor 11, 31. **23.** Is 59, 8. **24.** Ps 98, 4. **25.** Job 35, 14. **26.** Is 43, 26. **27.** Prov 12, 5. **28.** Jer 8, 6. **29.** 3 Kg 21, 29. **29a.** Job 34, 23. **30.** Job 37, 4. **31.** Ibid. **32.** Job 34, 23. **33.** Lev 6, 12. **34.** 1 Pet 2, 9. **35.** Apoc 5, 10. **36.** Cf. Jer 38, 11/13. **37.** Ps 47, 8. **38.** Cf. Job 3, 6. **39.** Gen 4, 7. **40.** Job 9, 28. **41.** Lk 22, 61/62; Mt 26, 75. **42.** Ac 9, 16. **43.** 2 Kg 12, 13. **44.** Job 9, 30/31. **45.** Cf. Ps 50, 19. **46.** Job 10, 1. **47.** Jude 5 **48.** Ps 108, 29. **49.** 1 Cor 11, 32. **50.** Apoc 3, 19. **51.** Heb 12, 6. **52.** Job 14, 16. **53.** 1 Cor 11, 31. **54.** Job 14, 17. **55.** Deut 32, 34/35, 41. **56.** Ac 9, 15/16. **57.** Ps 50, 5. **58.** Cf. Gen 26, 14 ff. **59.** Ez 8, 8. **60.** Is 2, 10. **61.** Cf. Deut 23, 12/13. **62.** Lev 5, 6/7. **63.** Job 33, 16. **64.** Prov 20, 30. **65.** Job 10, 16. **66.** Job 10, 17. **67.** Ibid. **68.** 1 Pet 4, 17. **69.** Job 10, 17. **70.** Job 7, 11. **71.** Ps 94, 2. **72.** Prov 28, 13. **73.** Prov 18, 17. **74.** Job 7, 11. **75.** Ps 37, 19. **76.** Job 31, 33. **77.** Cf. Gen 3, 8. **78.** Gen 3, 12. **79.** Gen 3, 13. **80.** Gen 3, 5. **81.** Jn 11, 43. **82.** Cf. 2 Kg 12, 13. **83.** Job 31, 33. **84.** Ps 78, 12. **85.** Jas 5, 16. **86.** Prov 28, 13. **87.** Prov 18, 17. **88.** Job 31, 19/20. **89.** Ecclus 18, 15. **90.** Ecclus 18, 17. **91.** Jas 2, 15/16. **92.** 1 Jn 3, 18. **93.** Lk 16, 9. **94.** 2 Cor 8, 14. **95.** Job 31, 16. **96.** Jas 4, 3. **97.** Mt 5, 3. **98.** Prov 3, 28. **99.** Job 31, 17. **100.** Cf. Job 31, 18: *For from my infancy mercy grew up with me: and it came out with me from my mother's womb.* **101.** Ps 48, 8/9. **102.** Job 15, 31. **103.** Ecclus 30, 24. **104.** Mt 19, 19. **105.** Ecclus 14, 5. **106.** Job 31, 32. **107.** 1 Cor 13, 4. **108.** Lk 6, 37/38. **109.** Gen 4, 4/5. **110.** Job 22, 6. **111.** 2 Cor 1, 22. **112.** Cf. Ex 22, 26. **113.** Mt 18, 32. **114.** Mt 6, 12.

Part 2, Book 3

1. Jer 1, 10. **2.** Cf. *Moralia in Iob*, XVIII, x, 7/14; 564. **3.** Cf. 1 Cor 12, 7/11. **4.** Cf. 1 Kg 17, 36; 18, 25. **5.** Cf. 2 Kg 3, 18. **6.** Cf. 2 Kg 6, 14. **7.** Cf. 2 Kg 6, 20/22. **8.** Job 12, 4. **9.** Ex 8, 26. **10.** Ecclus 2, 14. **11.** Rom 16, 19. **12.** 1 Cor 14, 20. **13.** Mt 10, 16. **14.** Cf. Mt 3, 16; Ac 2, 3. **15.** Prov 30, 28. **16.** Job 11, 6. **17.** Jn 15, 12. **18.**

Rom 13, 10. **19.** Gal 6, 2. **20.** Cf. Deut 6, 5. **21.** Tob 4, 16. **22.** Mt 7, 12; Lk 6, 31. **23.** 1 Cor 13, 4/6. **24.** Ps 57, 11. **25.** Gal 6, 2. **26.** Lk 21, 19. **27.** Cf. Gen 4, 3/8. **28.** Cf. Gen 4, 1/8. **29.** Cf. Gen 9, 18/25; 16, 15; 21, 2/3; 21, 12; 25, 23/25. **30.** Cf. Gen 37, 28. **31.** Cf. Jn 6, 71/72. **32.** Cant 2, 2. **33.** Ez 2, 6. **34.** 2 Pet 2, 7/8. **35.** Phil 2, 15/16. **36.** Apoc 2, 13. **37.** Job 5, 16. **38.** Cf. Rom 8, 24. **39.** Lk 12, 32. **40.** Lk 10, 20. The sequence of this and the 14 following citations does not correspond with that found in the *Moralia*. **41.** Jn 10, 27/28. **42.** Mt 10, 22; 24, 13. **43.** Lk 23, 43. **44.** Jer 3, 1. **45.** Jer 3, 4. **46.** Jer 3, 12. **47.** Mt 26, 41; Mk 14, 38. **48.** Lk 10, 18. **49.** Mt 24, 24. **50.** Lk 18, 8. **51.** Jn 6, 71. **52.** Jer 30, 15. **53.** Ez 16, 3. **54.** Jer 11, 14; 15, 1. **55.** Job 29, 16. **56.** 2 Cor 8, 9. **57.** 2 Cor 8, 13. **58.** 2 Cor 9, 6. **59.** 2 Cor 8, 10. **60.** Job 30, 25. **61.** Job 30, 31. **62.** Cf. 1 Cor 9, 27. **63.** Rom 13, 13. **64.** Col 3, 5. **65.** 1 Tim 5, 23. **66.** Job 38, 3. **67.** Ps 30, 25. **68.** Heb 12, 12. **69.** Prov 8, 4. **70.** Lk 12, 35. **71.** Deut 10, 16. **72.** Cf. Is 7, 9. **73.** Heb 11, 6. **74.** Ps 1, 5. **75.** Is 56, 10. **76.** Num 24, 16. **77.** Eccl 8, 10. **78.** Ps 136, 7. **79.** 1 Cor 3, 11. **80.** Jer 2, 16. **81.** Job 1, 1. **82.** Eccl 7, 19. **83.** Ps 36, 27. **84.** Eccl 9, 18. **85.** 1 Cor 5, 6. **86.** Job 28, 28. **87.** Ps 110, 10. **88.** Job 42, 11. **89.** Cf. Gen 2, 17. **90.** 1 Kg 15, 22/23. **91.** Prov 21, 28. **92.** Jn 6, 37/38. **93.** Cf. Gen 3, 23/24. **94.** Jn 5, 30. **95.** Gen 2, 16/17. **96.** Cf. Ex 3, 1 ff. **97.** Ex 4, 10. **98.** Ex 4, 13. **99.** Gal 2, 1/2. **100.** Ac 21, 11. **101.** Ac 21, 13. **102.** Ac 20, 24. **103.** Ecclus 2, 16. **104.** Lk 22, 28. **105.** Cf. Gen 37, 23. **106.** Cf. Lev 3, 9. **107.** Job 1, 5. **108.** Cf. 2 Kg 4, 5/6. **109.** Prov 4, 23. **110.** Ecclus 7, 15. **111.** Mt 6, 15. **112.** Mk 11, 25. **113.** Lk 6, 37/38. **114.** Mt 6, 12. **115.** Mt 6, 33; Lk 12, 31. **116.** Ex 14, 15. **117.** Cf. 1 Kg 1, 13. **118.** Mt 6, 6. **119.** Ps 10, 17 (according to the Hebrews). **120.** Cf. Gen 15, 11. **121.** Num 23, 10. **122.** Cf. Num 24, 14; 31, 16. **123.** 1 Kg 1, 18. **124.** Mk 12, 40. **125.** Mt 5, 44. **126.** Mk 11, 25. **127.** Ps 118, 6. **128.** 1 Jn 3, 21/22. **129.** Lam 3, 40/41.

Part 2, Book 4

1. Cf. Mt 25, 14/23. **2.** Cf. Job 31, 38. **3.** Job 31, 39. **4.** Mt 25, 27. **5.** Jas 3, 14/15. **6.** Job 31, 39. **7.** Num 11, 29. **8.** Cf. Num 8, 24/26. **9.** Rom 7, 23. **10.** Wis 6, 6. **11.** Job 34, 18. **12.** Ecclus 32, 1. **13.** Ez 34, 4. **14.** Job 34, 18. **15.** Is 14, 14. **16.** Job 34, 18. **17.** 1 Thess 2, 6/7. **18.** Job 36, 5. **19.** 1 Cor 7, 33. **20.** 1 Cor 7, 35. **21.** Job 41, 25. **22.** Prov 30, 13. **23.** Is 14, 14. **24.** 1 Kg 15, 17. **25.** Is 5, 21. **26.** Rom 12, 16. **27.** Rom 13, 4. **28.** Ac 10, 26. **29.** Cf. Ac 5, 1/10. **30.** 2 Cor 1, 23. **31.** 1 Thess 2, 7. **32.** 2 Cor 4, 5. **33.** 1 Cor 4, 21. **34.** Ps 130, 1. **35.** Ps 130, 2. **36.** Gen 9, 1/2. **37.** Apoc 19, 10; 22, 9. **38.** Job 29, 25. **39.** Cf. Lk 10, 34. **40.** Cf. Heb 9, 4. **41.** Ps 22, 4. **42.** Ex 32, 7. **43.** Ex 32, 10. **44.** Ex 32, 31/32. **45.** Ex 32, 27/28. **46.** Job 3, 26. **47.** Dan 4, 27/30. **48.** Cf. Mt 5, 22. **49.** 1 Cor 6, 12. **50.** Ibid. **51.** Ps 45, 11. **52.** Cf. Lev 11, 12. **53.** Gen 25, 27. **54.** Gen 18, 20. **55.** Job 1, 17. **56.** Cf.

Lev 11, 4; Deut 14, 7. **57.** Eccl 7, 19. **58.** 2 Tim 2, 21. **59.** Lk 9, 60. **60.** Is 1, 17. **61.** 1 Cor 6, 4. **62.** 1 Cor 14, 1. **63.** 1 Cor 6, 4. **64.** 1 Cor 6, 5. **65.** Cf. Heb 2, 9. **66.** Ecclus 38, 25. **67.** Ps 45, 11. **68.** Cf. Gen 42/43. **69.** Cf. Dan 2, 48. **70.** Ps 68, 24. **71.** Os 8, 4. **72.** Lk 13, 27. **73.** Cf. Ex 4, 21; 7, 3; 14, 4 & 17; 10, 1. **74.** Deut 16, 20. **75.** Job 29, 16. **76.** Cf. Heb 4, 13. **77.** Gen 18, 20/21. **78.** Wis 12, 18. **79.** Ecclus 5, 4. **80.** Ps 50, 19. **81.** Job 30, 28. **82.** Ibid. **83.** Job 36, 18. **84.** Cf. Ac 7, 57/59; 22, 20. **85.** Cf. Mt 21, 12; Mk 11, 15; Jn 2, 15. **86.** 2 Kg 6, 6/7. **87.** Heb 13, 22. **88.** Ac 20, 31. **89.** Eph 4, 1. **90.** Cf. Gen 9, 23. **91.** Cf. Ex 26, 1/31. **92.** Job 41, 25. **93.** Is 14, 13/14. **94.** Jn 14, 6. **95.** Cf. Mk 6, 27; Mt 14, 10. **96.** Cf. Jn 10, 12. **97.** Jn 12, 43. **98.** Eccl 8, 10. **99.** 1 Cor 12, 23/24. **100.** Ez 8, 8. **101.** Ez 4, 1/3. **102.** 2 Cor 11, 29. **103.** Cf. Ex. 37, 16; 25, 29. **104.** Job 39, 30. **105.** 2 Cor 12, 2. **106.** 1 Cor 2, 2. **107.** Job 29, 6. **108.** Cf. Lev 26, 12; 2 Cor 6, 16. **109.** Jas 3. 1. **110.** Jas 3, 2. **111.** Phil 4, 17. **112.** Cf. Job 12, 17. **113.** Lk 23, 8. **114.** Lk 23, 9. **115.** Lk 23, 11. **116.** 2 Cor 2, 17.

Part 2, Book 5

1. Mt 18, 9. **2.** Mt 18, 6. **3.** Ps 45, 11. **4.** Cf. Ex 19, 18. **5.** Hcb 12, 20; cf. Ex 19, 12/13. **6.** Job 5, 26. **7.** Ibid. **8.** Lk 8, 39. **9.** Gen 29, 26. **10.** Lk 10, 41/42. **11.** Ps 49, 4. **12.** Mt 25, 35/36. **13.** Col 3, 3. **14.** Ps 83, 3. **15.** Ps 118, 81. **16.** Lk 9, 23. **17.** Lk 14, 33. **18.** Cf. Gen 28, 11/12. **19.** Cf. Gen 32, 31. **20.** Deut 15, 19. **21.** Lev 19, 23. **22.** Ps 126, 2. **23.** Job 29, 18. **24.** Is 40, 31. **25.** Mt 5, 40. **26.** Lk 6, 30. **27.** 1 Cor 6, 7. **28.** Lk 14, 33. **29.** Prov 14, 10. **30.** Gal 6, 14. **31.** Job 31, 37. **32.** Ps 83, 8. **33.** Ps 47, 4. **34.** Dan 10, 9/12. **35.** Job 39, 19. **36.** 1 Pet 5, 8/9. **37.** Rom 10, 10. **38.** Job 39, 20. **39.** Ibid. **40.** Job 39, 21. **41.** Apoc 8, 1. **42.** Wis 9, 15. **43.** Job 3, 14. **44.** Ps 26, 4. **45.** Ps 54, 8. **46.** Jer 15, 17. **47.** Job 33, 29. **48.** Job 33, 20. **49.** Lam 1, 11. **50.** Job 33, 26. **51.** Cf. Ecclus 2, 1. **52.** Ex 13, 17. **53.** Cf. Mt 17, 1; Mk 9, 1; Lk 9, 28. **54.** Cf. Mt 26, 69/72; Mk 14, 66/69; Lk 22, 56/57; Jn 18, 17. **55.** Job 33, 20. **56.** Job 33, 26. **57.** Ps 88, 16. **58.** Cf. Lk 22, 43. **59.** Ps 142, 2. **60.** 1 Cor 4, 4. **61.** Jas 3, 2. **62.** 1 Jn 1, 8. **63.** Jer 31, 21. **64.** Hab 2, 1. **65.** Cf. Ps 38, 7. **66.** Cf. Hab 3, 16. **67.** Cf. Ps 115. 11. **68.** Mt 11, 28/30. **69.** Job 39, 5. **70.** Jer 48, 10. **71.** Is 33, 15. **72.** Job 9, 28. **73.** Eccl 1, 18. **74.** Ps 30, 23. **75.** Ps 76, 3. **76.** Ps 76, 4. **77.** Eccl 7, 5. **78.** Jas 4, 9. **79.** Mt 5, 5. **80.** 2 Pet 2, 13. **81.** Eccl 2, 2. **82.** 1 Cor 1, 27. **83.** 1 Cor 3, 18. **84.** Cf. Lk 19, 1/5. **85.** Lk 6, 30. **86.** Mt 5, 39. **87.** Job 9, 14. **88.** Prov 25, 27. **89.** Job 30, 3. **90.** Rom 12, 3. **91.** Prov 23, 4. **92.** Prov 25, 16. **93.** Ex 12, 10. **94.** Job 5, 9. **95.** Cf. Num 17, 8; Heb 9, 4. **96.** Jn 2, 9. **97.** Job 37, 20. **98.** Job 7, 2/3. **99.** Cf. Job 7, 2. **100.** Job 35, 10. **101.** Rom 12, 12. **102.** Ps 31, 7. **103.** Cf. Ez 2, 9. **104.** Jn 16, 33.

Part 2, Book 6

1. Lk 1, 35. **2.** Jn 10, 18. **3.** Cf. Is 14, 10; Heb 2, 17. **4.** Cf. Lk 16, 23. **5.** Ps 85, 13.
6. Cf. Gen 3, 24. **7.** 1 Pet 1, 12. **8.** Mt 18, 10. **9.** Ps 16, 15. **10.** Job 14, 15. **11.** 1
Jn 3, 2. **12.** Jn 14, 27. **13.** Lk 2, 29. **14.** Job 36, 16. **15.** Ps 16, 15. **16.** Ps 41, 3. **17.**
Job 3, 19. **18.** Ps 88, 2. **19.** Job 8, 20/21. **20.** Jn 16, 20. **21.** Jn 16, 22. **22.** Prov 31,
25. **23.** Ecclus 1, 13. **24.** Ps 109, 1. **25.** Mt 1, 25. **26.** Prov 31, 23. **27.** Prov 31,
31. **28.** Mt 25, 35. **29.** Cf. Mk 10, 28; Mt 19, 28. **30.** Is 3, 14. **31.** Mt 19, 21. **32.**
Cf. 1 Thess 2, 7/9. **33.** Job 5, 22. **34.** Mt 25, 35/36. **35.** Mt 25, 34. **36.** Ps 51, 8/9.
37. Lk 24, 39. **38.** Rom 8, 20/21. **39.** Phil 1, 23. **40.** Ps 115, 16/17. **41.** Jn 14, 2.
42. Cf. Mt 20, 10. **43.** Job 3, 19. **44.** Ps 138, 16. **45.** Ps 113 B, 13.

BIBLICAL ABBREVIATIONS

[Biblical translations are from the Douay version
except when Gregory departs from the Vulgate]

The Old Testament

Genesis .... Gen
Exodus .... Ex
Leviticus .... Lev
Numbers .... Num
Deuteronomy .... Deut
Josue .... Jos
Judges .... Jg
1 Kings .... 1 Kg
2 Kings .... 2 Kg
3 Kings .... 3 Kg
4 Kings .... 4 Kg
Job .... Job
Psalms .... Ps
Proverbs .... Prov
Ecclesiastes .... Eccl
Canticle of Canticles ..... Cant
Wisdom .... Wis
Ecclesiasticus .... Ecclus
Isaias .... Is
Jeremias .... Jer
Lamentations .... Lam
Ezechiel .... Ez
Daniel .... Dan
Osee .... Os
Joel .... Jl
Amos .... Am
Micheas .... Mic
Nahum .... Nah
Habacuc .... Hab
Sophonias .... Soph
Aggeus .... Agg
Zacharias .... Zach

1 Machabees .... 1 Mac
2 Machabees .... 2 Mac
[Septuagint .... LXX]

Gospel according to:

Matthew .... Mt
Mark .... Mk
Luke .... Lk
John .... Jn
Acts of the Apostles .... Ac

Epistles of Paul to:

Romans .... Rom
1 Corinthians .... 1 Cor
2 Corinthians .... 2 Cor
Galatians .... Gal
Ephesians .... Eph
Philippians .... Phil
Colossians .... Col
1 Thessalonians .... 1 Thess
1 Timothy .... 1 Tim
2 Timothy .... 2 Tim
Titus .... Tit
Hebrews .... Heb

Epistles of:

James .... Jas
1 Peter .... 1 Pet
2 Peter .... 2 Pet
1 John .... 1 Jn
Jude .... Jude
The Apocalypse .... Apoc